Changing European Employment and Welfare Regimes

This book examines how and to what extent the European Employment Strategy and the Open Method of Coordination (OMC) on Social Protection and Social Inclusion have influenced national labour market and social welfare policies.

Focusing on the implementation of the OMC in different national environments, this book examines how the proposals and targets of the OMC are interpreted and implemented within the context of existing national employment and welfare regimes. At a theoretical level and on the basis of national case studies, the book considers how OMC objectives, guidelines, targets, and recommendations may reshape the domestic institutional framework, how learning and participation of governmental bodies are organized across different hierarchical levels, and how non-state actors may be involved in the formulation and implementation of national reform plans. The authors conclude that the OMC has contributed significantly to both substantive and procedural reforms, in spite of the many institutional barriers to Europeanization in this policy area.

Featuring comparative case studies across a number of European states, this book will be of interest to students and scholars of sociology, political science, public policy, and international relations.

Martin Heidenreich is Founding Director of the Jean-Monnet Centre of Europeanization and Transnational Regulations and Jean-Monnet-Professor of European Studies in Social Sciences at the University of Oldenburg, Germany.

Jonathan Zeitlin is Founding Director of the European Union Center of Excellence and Professor of Sociology, Public Affairs, Political Science, and History at the University of Wisconsin-Madison, USA.

Routledge/EUI Studies in the Political Economy of Welfare

Series editors: Martin Rhodes & Maurizio Ferrera,
The European University Institute, Florence, Italy

This series presents leading edge research on the recasting of European welfare states. The series is interdisciplinary, featuring contributions from experts in economics, political science and social policy. The books provide a comparative analysis of topical issues, including;

- reforms of the major social programmes – pensions, health, social security
- the changing political cleavages in welfare politics
- policy convergence and social policy innovation
- the impact of globalisation

1 **Immigration and Welfare**
Challenging the Borders of the Welfare State
Edited by Michael Bommes & Andrew Geddes

2 **Renegotiating the Welfare State**
Flexible Adjustment through Corporatist Concertation
Edited by Frans van Waarden & Gerhard Lehmbruch

3 **Comparing Welfare Capitalism**
Social Policy and Political Economy in Europe, Japan and the USA
Edited by Bernhard Ebbinghaus & Philip Manow

4 **Controlling a New Migration World**
Edited by Virginie Giraudon and Christian Joppke

5 **The Moral Economy of Welfare States**
Britain and Germany Compared
Steffen Mau

6 **Welfare State Reform in Southern Europe**
Fighting Poverty and Social Exclusion in Italy, Spain, Portugal and Greece
Edited by Maurizio Ferrera

7 **Normative Foundations of the Welfare State**
The Nordic Experience
Edited by Nanna Kildal and Stein Kuhnle

8 **Regulating New Forms of Employment**
Local Experiments and Social Innovation in Europe
Edited by Ida Regalia

9 The Politics of Post-Industrial Welfare States
Adapting post-war social policies to new social risks
Edited by Klaus Armingeon and Giuliano Bonoli

10 Pension Reform in Europe
Politics, policies and outcomes
Edited by Camila Arza and Martin Kohli

11 Pension Politics
Consensus and social conflict in ageing societies
Patrik Marier

12 Changing European Employment and Welfare Regimes
The influence of the open method of coordination on national reforms
Edited by Martin Heidenreich and Jonathan Zeitlin

Changing European Employment and Welfare Regimes

The influence of the open method of coordination on national reforms

Edited by
Martin Heidenreich
and Jonathan Zeitlin

Routledge
Taylor & Francis Group
LONDON AND NEW YORK

First published 2009
by Routledge
2 Park Square Milton Park, Abingdon, Oxon OX14 4RN

Simultaneously published in the USA and Canada
by Routledge
270 Madison Avenue, New York, NY 10016

Routledge is an imprint of the Taylor & Francis Group, an informa business

Typeset in Times New Roman
by Taylor & Francis Books
Printed and bound in Great Britain
by TJ International Ltd, Padstow, Cornwall

British Library Cataloguing in Publication Data
A catalogue record for this book is available from the British Library

Library of Congress Cataloging in Publication Data
Changing European employment and welfare regimes : the influence of the open method of coordination on national reforms / edited by Martin Heidenreich and Jonathan Zeitlin.
p. cm. – (Routledge/EUI studies in the political economy of welfare ; 12)
Includes bibliographical references and index.
1. Manpower policy–European Union countries. 2. European Union countries–Economic policy. I. Heidenreich, Martin. II. Zeitlin, Jonathan.
HD5713.6.E85C43 2009
331.1094–dc22

2008047311

ISBN 978-0-415-48278-3 (hbk)
ISBN 978-0-203-87887-3 (ebk)

Contents

Illustrations

Figures

Tables

Acknowledgements

This book originated in a conference held at the University of Bamberg in February 2007, with financial support from the Jean Monnet Chair programme of the European Union. From that conference, the editors selected the most promising papers and then recruited additional contributions from other authors in order to secure a broad coverage of countries, policy issues, and theoretical approaches. All of the chapters have been extensively revised in response to comments from the editors and the other contributors. The result, we believe, is much more than a conventional conference volume, though it is deliberately designed as a conversation among authors with distinct but intersecting perspectives rather than as the product of a unified research project based on a common theoretical framework.

Both editors contributed equally to the book and are listed in alphabetical order. We are grateful to Martin Rhodes and Maurizio Ferrera for agreeing to publish this volume in their series, and for providing us with valuable suggestions for improving its quality and coherence. We would also like to acknowledge the valuable contributions to the project made by the other participants in the Bamberg conference, especially those whose papers could not be included in this volume: Gabriele Bischoff, Bernhard Ebbinghaus, Colin Lindsay, Philippe Pochet, Martin Potůček, and Stefano Sacchi. Martin Heidenreich would like to thank Benjamin Brake, Andreas Huber, Jenny Preunkert, and Sascha Zirra for their help, and the German Research Foundation for their financial support of the research for this book. Jonathan Zeitlin would like to thank the Center for World Affairs and the Global Economy (WAGE) and the European Union Center of Excellence at the University of Wisconsin-Madison, together with the 'Governance as Learning' project of the Netherlands Scientific Research Council (NWO), for their support of his research on the Open Method of Coordination.

Contributors

Mieke Beckers, PhD candidate, Flemish Research Foundation and Centre for Sociological Research, Catholic University of Leuven, Belgium.

Minna van Gerven, Post-doctoral Researcher, Amsterdam Institute for Advanced Labour Studies (AIAS), University of Amsterdam, The Netherlands.

Marie-Pierre Hamel, PhD candidate at the Centre de Recherches Politiques (CEVIPOF), Institut d'études politiques de Paris (Sciences Po Paris), France.

Martin Heidenreich, Professor of Sociology and Jean-Monnet Chair of European Studies in Social Sciences, University of Oldenburg, Germany.

Kerstin Jacobsson, Associate Professor of Sociology and Senior Lecturer at Södertörn University, Sweden.

Håkan Johansson, Associate Professor of Social Work, Växjö University, Sweden.

Mariely López-Santana, Assistant Professor of Political Science, George Mason University, USA.

Mikkel Mailand, Associate Professor, Employment Relations Research Centre, Department of Sociology, University of Copenhagen.

Jenny Preunkert, Research Associate, Jean-Monnet Chair for European Studies in Social Sciences, University of Oldenburg, Germany.

Bart Vanhercke, PhD Candidate at the University of Amsterdam, The Netherlands; Policy Analyst, European Social Observatory (OSE), Brussels; and Associate Academic Staff , Centre for Sociological Research, Catholic University of Leuven, Belgium.

Jelle Visser, Professor of Sociology of Labour and Organization, University of Amsterdam, and Scientific Director of the Amsterdam Institute for Advanced Labour Studies (AIAS), The Netherlands.

Charlotte West, Writer and Editor, Battison & Partners AB, Stockholm, Sweden; previously Research Associate, Södertörn University, Sweden.

Jonathan Zeitlin, Professor of Sociology, Public Affairs, Political Science, and History; Director of the Center for World Affairs and the Global Economy (WAGE) and Founding Director of the European Union Center of Excellence, University of Wisconsin-Madison, USA.

Sascha Zirra, Research Associate, Jean-Monnet Chair for European Studies in Social Sciences, University of Oldenburg, Germany.

Abbreviations

AGE	European Older People's Platform
ALMP	active labour market policy
CDSEI	Comité du dialogue pour les questions européennes et internationales
CEC	Commission of the European Communities
CEEC	Countries of Central and Eastern Europe
CILE	Comité interministériel de lutte contre l'exclusion sociale (Inter-Ministerial Committee to Combat Social Exclusion)
CNLE	Conseil national des politiques de lutte contre la pauvreté et l'exclusion sociale (National Council for the Fight Against Poverty and Social Exclusion)
CNE	contrat nouvelles embauches (new hires contract)
CPE	contrat première embauche (first-time job contract)
DGAS	Direction générale de l'action sociale (General Directorate for Social Action)
DIIS	Direction interdépartementale de l'intégration sociale (Interdepartmental Directorate for Social Integration)
DPT	Document de politique transversale (cross-cutting policy document)
DREES	Direction de la recherche, des etudes, de l'evaluation et des statistiques (Division of Research, Studies, Assessment and Statistics)
EAPN	European Anti-Poverty Network
EAPSI	European Association of Public Sector Pension Institutions
ECHP	European Community Household Panel Study
EES	European Employment Strategy
EMCO	Employment Committee
ESF	European Social Fund
EU	European Union
FEANTSA	European Federation of National Organizations Working with the Homeless
GRAPA	Garantie de revenu aux personnes agées (Minimum income for elderly people)

Hartz IV	Viertes Gesetz für moderne Dienstleistungen am Arbeitsmarkt (Fourth Law on the Modernization of Labour Market Services)
IGAS	Inspection Générale des Affaires Sociales (Inspectorate-General for Social Affairs)
IMC	Inter-Ministerial Conference
IMF	International Monetary Fund
INSEE	l'Institut national de la statistique et des etudes economiques (National Institute for Statistics and Economic Studies)
JAP	Joint Assessment Paper
JobAQTIV	'Aktivieren, Qualifizieren, Trainieren, Investieren, Vermitteln' (German law on reforming labour market policy schemes)
JS	Jobs Strategy
LMP	Labour Market Policy
LOLF	Loi organique relative aux lois de finances (Constitutional Bylaw on Budget Acts)
MS	Member State
NAP	National Action Plan
NAP/ Inclusion	National Action Plan on Social Inclusion
NGO	Non-Governmental Organization
NIS	National Statistical Institute
NRP	National Reform Programme
NSR	National Strategic Report
OECD	Organisation for Economic Cooperation and Development
OMC	Open Method of Coordination
OMC/SPSI	OMC on Social Protection and Social Inclusion
ONPES	Observatoire national de la pauvreté et de l'exclusion sociale (National Monitoring Centre for Poverty and Social Exclusion)
PES	public employment service
PHARE	The PHARE programme was one of the three pre-accession instruments financed by the European Union to assist the applicant countries of Central and Eastern Europe in their preparations for joining the European Union.
PROGRESS	Programme for Employment and Social Solidarity
PSBH	Panel Studie van Belgische Huishoudens (Panel Survey on Belgian Households)
RMA	Revenue minimum d'activité
RMI	Revenu minimum d'insertion (Guaranteed Minimum Income)
RSA	Revenu de solidarité active (Active Solidarity Income)
SGAE	Secrétariat général des affaires européenes
SILC	Survey of Income and Living Conditions
SPC	Social Protection Committee
VAP	Vlaams Actieplan Armoedebestrijding (Flemish Action Plan for Poverty Reduction)

Introduction

Martin Heidenreich and Jonathan Zeitlin

Economic globalization, demographic ageing, and changing household/family structures confront European employment and welfare regimes with new challenges. Hence national governments find themselves under pressure to reform their social and labour-market policies. These are common challenges for the Member States of the European Union, as well as for the EU itself, due to the linkages between the increasingly Europeanized regulation of markets for capital, goods, and services, together with monetary and (to a lesser extent) fiscal policies, on the one hand, and the still predominantly national regulation of labour markets and social protection systems on the other. Hence in March 2000, the European Council decided at Lisbon to strengthen national economic, employment, and social policy reforms in order '*to make the EU the most competitive and dynamic knowledge-based economy in the world, capable of sustainable economic growth with full employment and greater social cohesion*' by 2010. The principal device for attaining these goals was the Open Method of Coordination (OMC), annunciated in Lisbon as a broadly applicable new governance instrument, and building on innovative approaches to the coordination of Member State policies that had been developed over the preceding decade, most notably the European Employment Strategy (EES) inaugurated in 1997.[1]

The core features of the OMC are iterative benchmarking of national progress towards common European objectives and organized mutual learning. Despite procedural variations across different policy domains, most developed OMC processes comprise four central elements:

1 joint definition by Member State governments and the European Commission of initial objectives, indicators, and often but not always guidelines and targets;
2 national action plans or strategy reports, which assess performance in light of the objectives and metrics, and propose corrective reforms adapted to domestic institutions and circumstances;
3 peer review of these national plans, including mutual criticism and exchange of good practices, backed up in some cases by recommendations from the Commission and the Council;

4 re-elaboration of the national plans and, at less frequent intervals, of the broader European objectives and metrics in light of the experience gained in their implementation.[2]

The most advanced such coordination processes are the EES and the OMC on Social Protection and Social Inclusion (OMC/SPSI),[3] which also form the main focus of this volume. The EES and the OMC/SPSI have been developed at the European level, but the crucial question is whether they are an effective means of reforming national employment and social welfare systems. This question arises not only because their commonly agreed objectives – such as raising the employment rate or reducing the at-risk-of-poverty rate – are not legally binding obligations backed up by the threat of judicial sanctions, but also because of the wide variations in levels of economic development, institutional structures, and domestic political alignments across the 27 Member States of the enlarged EU.

The crucial challenge for these OMC processes is thus whether they can effectively influence the ongoing reforms of national employment and social protection systems. This is first of all a methodological problem because the impact of European coordination processes on national policies cannot be measured directly (Zeitlin and Pochet 2005; Zeitlin, this volume). But it is also a theoretical challenge, which is discussed in the flourishing literature on Europeanization and the influence of the EU on domestic policies (for an overview, see Graziano and Vink 2007).

In the Europeanization literature and in the related debate on the effectiveness of the OMC, three different ways of dealing with this theoretical challenge have been proposed.

1 Some authors have analysed the OMC as a means of facilitating transnational learning and discursive diffusion processes connecting European and national arenas (e.g. Begg and Berghman 2002; Radaelli 2003; Cohen and Sabel 2003; Eberlein and Kerwer 2004, Jacobsson 2004a, 2004b; Zeitlin 2003, 2005c).
2 Others have stressed instead the inertia and path-dependent dynamics of national institutions on the one hand and the adaptational pressure of the EU on the other, analysing the limitations and possibilities of the OMC in reshaping the pre-existing trajectories of national regimes (e.g. Scharpf 2002, 2003; Héritier 2003; Idema and Kelemen 2006; Citi and Rhodes 2007, Linsenmann et al. 2007).
3 A third strand of research has focused on the domestic constellation of actors, their strategies, and the resulting political dynamics that generate reforms. The OMC has been analysed in this vein as a process which shapes national reforms by stimulating procedural shifts in domestic policy-making structures and/or by involving new actors in the formulation of employment and social policies (e.g. Zeitlin and Pochet 2005; Jacobsson and Vifell 2007, Heidenreich and Bischoff 2008).[4]

The chapters in this volume shed new theoretical and empirical light on how and to what extent the OMC has influenced the reform of national employment and welfare regimes in EU Member States. The authors differ among themselves in their analytical approaches, research strategies, and substantive focus, as well as in some of their interpretative conclusions. Such perspectival diversity, we believe, is not only unavoidable but also productive at this stage in studying a complex, multiform phenomenon like the OMC, which cuts across policy domains and levels of governance in a union of 27 Member States. Despite variations among the individual authors and countries, however, the cumulative evidence presented in this book shows, in our view, that the OMC has systematically (though neither deterministically nor uniformly) stimulated substantive changes in national policy agendas, cognitive paradigms, and (in some cases) programmes, as well as procedural shifts in governance and policy-making processes, through a series of direct and indirect mechanisms, including but not confined to transnational learning and creative appropriation by domestic actors. The chapters in this volume trace these influences and mechanisms, using a variety of theoretical lenses, across a broad range of policy issues and country cases, including both old and new Member States.

The remainder of this introduction briefly presents the individual chapters and draws out their contributions to understanding the national influence of the OMC, in relation to the three main approaches to the relationship between European coordination processes and national reforms identified above, which are by no means mutually exclusive. These focus respectively on transnational learning and discursive diffusion, supranational adaptational pressures and national institutional trajectories, and domestic actor constellations and political dynamics.

A number of chapters shed particular light on the OMC's influence in promoting transnational learning and discursive diffusion. *Jelle Visser* analyses policy learning as the capacity for innovation and reform, which does not necessarily lead to cross-national convergence. Policy learning, in his view, is typically bounded within a historically and socially determined problem space. But even if specific solutions can rarely be transposed directly from one institutional setting to another, transnational benchmarking and information exchange processes may nonetheless 'help to identify promising examples for better policies', and 'can play a key role in making policy failure more visible and politicians less complacent', provided that they are carefully contextualized and contestable by alternative views. In the specific case of European labour-market reforms, Visser argues that the EES (and to a lesser extent the OECD Jobs Strategy) made a crucial contribution to changing policy makers' 'mental map' away from management of unemployment through restriction of labour supply, towards new approaches based on activation, prevention, and employment promotion, which in turn prepared EU Member States 'to move in the same direction, with different degrees of intensity and varying success'.

Taking the example of unemployment protection reforms in Belgium, Finland, the Netherlands, and the UK, *Minna van Gerven* and *Mieke Beckers* likewise discuss the role of the EES and the OECD Jobs Strategy in national reform projects. They show that these reforms follow common patterns and agendas (increased work-relatedness, activation, and targeting), but use very different policy instruments. Member States therefore use transnational benchmarking processes mostly to determine the goals and priorities, but not the concrete implementation of reforms. Finally, they compare the EES and the Jobs Strategy and conclude that the former has been more successful than the latter in influencing national agendas because it focuses on goal attainment rather than means prescription, and is based on ongoing cooperation and self-reflection among practical decision makers within and between EU Member States, thereby facilitating policy learning.

Marie-Pierre Hamel and *Bart Vanhercke* analyse learning as one mechanism through which the OMC/Inclusion influences domestic policies in France and Belgium. Domestic actors 'discover' new institutional issues (e.g. the need for better coordination among regions) and previously neglected problems (e.g. child poverty), as well as new policy solutions, both home-grown and imported (such as the creation of new federal coordination bodies and regional action plans, or an 'opposable right to housing'). But the authors underline that learning is only one mechanism alongside the creative appropriation of OMC targets, the legitimation of actors' own preferences, and the strategic use of external pressures such as recommendations and rankings.

Reviewing the experience of the EES in the Baltics, *Kerstin Jacobsson and Charlotte West* similarly assess the relative weight of five Europeanization mechanisms: gate-keeping, models, money, monitoring, and mutual learning (through peer review, provision of advice, and 'twinning' of European and domestic officials). They find that various dimensions of learning, especially the transfer of models, provision of advice, twinning, monitoring, and peer review associated with the EES played an important part in creating a coherent labour-market field and reshaping domestic employment policies during the turbulent post-communist transition and EU accession. But given the weakness of both the state administration and the social partners in these countries, the effectiveness of such governance mechanisms was crucially reinforced by EU membership conditionality and financial support from the European Social Fund, which 'provided the Baltic states with the motivation to build up the institutional capacity necessary to implement the EES'.

A second set of chapters focuses particularly on the interplay between supranational and domestic factors shaping the implementation of the OMC, notably the adaptational pressures arising from the degree of 'fit' or 'misfit' between European objectives, targets, and guidelines on the one hand, and national institutions and policies on the other.

Martin Heidenreich argues that analysis of the OMC's domestic impact requires a theory of institutional change that neither assumes quasi-automatic mechanisms of isomorphism and direct learning between nation-states and the EU nor treats the former as closed institutional spheres. Gradual but transformative processes of institutional change can be analysed following the conceptual framework proposed by Streeck and Thelen (2005), who identify a number of such mechanisms such as the displacement, layering, and conversion of institutions. Such an analysis of gradual change may help us to understand the influence of the OMC on national reform projects, which result mainly from the strategic use of European commitments by domestic actors. Even if the direct influence of the OMC may be limited to a small group of European and national officials, these processes have contributed to the transformation of domestic discourses and institutions through the adoption of new employment and social welfare concepts, the involvement of new actors, and changes in policy-making structures.

Mariely López-Santana distinguishes ideational and institutional dimensions of fit and misfit between European policies and domestic policy making. On the basis of empirical analysis of Spain, Belgium, and Sweden, she shows that the national influence of the EES depends on the degree of ideational and institutional compatibility between European policy prescriptions and domestic settings. In the case of Spain for example, the ideational fit was high (as a result of the prior transfer of European concepts through the Structural Funds), while the institutional fit between European and national employment policy approaches was low. Belgium, which had a medium level of institutional and ideational misfit, has politically internalized the EES, and especially its activation policy, more than Spain and Sweden. Despite low levels of misfit, Sweden selectively used the EES to reform its tax, gender, and immigration policies. She concludes that misfit is neither a necessary nor a sufficient conclusion for the internalization of European 'soft law' commitments.

Mikkel Mailand demonstrates that the influence of the EES on national labour-market reforms has been greater in Poland and Spain than in Denmark and the United Kingdom – even if the EES has supported a shift to activation policies and a preventive approach in all four countries. One factor which explains the greater impact of the EES in Spain, and especially in Poland, is the low prior conformity with the EES of national employment policy and performance. Hence 'misfit' might seem to explain the higher substantial and procedural impact in Poland and Spain, but this would underplay the autonomous role of domestic politics. He therefore proposes a strategic explanation of the differential national impact of the EES, emphasizing the greater economic and political dependence on the EU of Poland and Spain, and the lower level of domestic political consensus on the main lines of employment policy.

Most of the chapters in this book also illuminate the third main approach to the relationship between the OMC and national reform processes: its influence on domestic actor constellations and political dynamics. Thus, many of the authors examine the organizational dimension of European coordination processes, analysing both procedural shifts in policy making and the participation of social partners, NGOs, and local/regional authorities. As we have already noted, for example, *Marie-Pierre Hamel* and *Bart Vanhercke* demonstrate that one of the most important and unexpected results of the OMC/ Inclusion in Belgium was enhanced interregional cooperation and federal coordination.

Kerstin Jacobsson and *Håkan Johansson* similarly show that the OMC/ Inclusion in Sweden influenced the relationship between national ministries and social NGOs, as well as among the latter themselves. It has contributed to new forms of consultation between ministries and social NGOs and the institutionalization of an inter-organisational network against social exclusion which became an important new pressure group and a partner in the formulation of the National Action Plan. The OMC therefore played a decisive role in the emergence and structuring of a domestic field of social inclusion policies by providing new opportunities for the development of national organizations and networks.

Jenny Preunkert and *Sascha Zirra* analyse the domestic impact of the EES and OMC/Inclusion on three Bismarckian countries, Germany, Italy, and France. Despite commonalities among these countries, both OMC processes in Germany influenced mostly beliefs and mindsets, in Italy mostly the highly fragmented and polarized governance structures, and in France mostly policy measures. In Germany, the EES has been used as a new frame of reference for fundamental policy reforms – thus strengthening especially the Federal Ministry of Labour as the crucial actor in employment policy. In the field of social inclusion, the NGOs used the OMC to build up new contacts among themselves and with local administrations. In Italy, the power and the political will for fundamental reforms did not exist under the 2001–6 Berlusconi government. Therefore, both OMCs as well as the European Social Fund were used predominantly to improve the organizational capabilities of the ministries, regions, and the non-governmental sector. In France, the domestic and the European employment policies were organizationally separated between the Ministry of Labour and the Prime Minister's Office, which hindered the deeper use of the EES. By contrast, the civil servants responsible for the OMC/ Inclusion were among the main actors in the domestic fight against social exclusion. The authors conclude that the influence of both OMC processes depends on a responsive domestic institutional setting in cognitive, legal, and above all strategic terms, i.e. a dominant organization such as the Labour Ministry or Prime Minister's Office which could improve its position by using the prescriptions and possibilities offered by the OMC.

The final chapter, by *Jonathan Zeitlin*, draws together the findings of the volume and synthesizes them with the broader empirical literature on the national influence of the OMC. He distinguishes two main types of OMC influence on the basis of the case-study evidence. The first comprises various forms of substantive policy change, including cognitive shifts in national policy thinking, political shifts in national policy agendas, and programmatic shifts in specific national policies. The second type of influence involves procedural changes in governance and policy-making arrangements, including reinforced horizontal coordination and cross-sectoral integration between interdependent policy fields, improvements in national steering capacity, enhanced vertical coordination between levels of governance, increased involvement of non-state actors, and development of new horizontal and diagonal networks for participation of non-state and subnational actors in EU policy making. He then goes on to examine and assess the respective contribution to these different types of national influence of a series of distinct mechanisms and effects associated with the OMC, including external pressure from EU institutions and other Member States; financial support from the structural funds; socialization and discursive diffusion, mutual learning (through both direct/first-order and indirect/higher-order effects), and creative appropriation by domestic actors (via leverage and democratizing destabilization effects). While finding supporting evidence for each of these mechanisms, the author determines that the OMC's strongest influence on national policies has come through their creative appropriation by domestic actors within and beyond government. The chapter concludes by considering the implications of these findings for wider debates about changing national welfare and employment regimes, arguing that OMC processes tend to encourage hybridization and path-shifting adjustment of national social and employment policies, rather than merely reproducing pre-existing institutional constellations and regime pathways.

Hence, despite the many structural barriers to the Europeanization of national social and employment policies, the chapters in this volume demonstrate that the OMC has contributed significantly to domestic reforms in EU Member States. As detailed above, they analyse the influence of the OMC across multiple policy fields and country cases from several distinct but overlapping perspectives. Some chapters focus primarily on the OMC's impact on transnational learning processes, examining the different instruments of mutual learning and the interaction of these cognitive mechanisms with other governance instruments such as financial incentives and EU membership conditionality. Others concentrate instead on the logics and inertia of national institutions, on institutional path-dependencies and complementarities as barriers to learning, but also on the possibilities of incremental innovation. Many of the chapters focus on the political and organizational dynamics of domestic reform processes, and the OMC's role in expanding involvement by weaker or more marginal actors such as NGOs, social partners, and local/regional governments. Through these innovative approaches and state-of-the art analyses of the OMC's influence on changing national welfare and employment regimes, the volume as a whole thus also contributes to more general debates on Europeanization and institutional change.

Notes

1 For fuller accounts of the emergence of the OMC, see Zeitlin (2005a, 2008b).
2 The OMC, as defined by the Portuguese Presidency at Lisbon, consisted of four interdependent elements closely modelled on the EES:

- 'Fixing guidelines for the Union combined with specific timetables for achieving the goals which they set in the short, medium and long term;
- establishing, where appropriate, quantitative and qualitative indicators and benchmarks against the best in the world and tailored to the needs of different Member States and sectors as a means of comparing best practices;
- translating these European guidelines into national and regional policies by setting specific targets and adopting measures, taking into account national and regional differences;
- periodic monitoring, evaluation and peer review organized as mutual learning processes' (European Council 2000: §37).

For analysis of procedural variations among actually existing OMC processes and their divergence from the original Lisbon template, see Zeitlin (2005a: 20–2; 2008a); Sabel and Zeitlin (2008: 289–92).

3 The OMC/SPSI comprises three 'strands', covering social inclusion, pensions, and health and elder care respectively, which were organized as separate OMCs before their 'streamlining' into a single process in 2006. Where appropriate, we will refer to these distinct processes as 'OMC/Inclusion', 'OMC/Pensions', etc.

4 For overviews of the linkages between the Europeanization and OMC debates, together with fuller references to the literature, see the chapters by Heidenreich and Zeitlin in this volume.

References

Begg, I. and Berghman, J. (2002) 'Introduction: EU Social (Exclusion) Policy Revisited?', *Journal of European Social Policy*, 12: 179–94.

Citi, M. and Rhodes, M. (2007) 'New Modes of Governance in the EU: Common Objectives versus National Preferences', *EUROGOV Working Papers* No. N-07-01. Available HTTP: www.connex-network.org/eurogov/pdf/egp-newgov-N-07-01.pdf (accessed 8 September 2008).

Cohen, J. and Sabel, C.F. (2003) 'Sovereignty and Solidarity: EU and US', in J. Zeitlin and D. Trubek (eds) *Governing Work and Welfare in a New Economy: European and American Experiments*, Oxford: Oxford University Press, pp. 345–75.

Eberlein, B. and Kerwer, D. (2004) 'New Governance in the European Union: A Theoretical Perspective', *Journal of Common Market Studies*, 42: 121–42.

European Council (2000) *Presidency Conclusions of the Lisbon European Council*, SN 100/00, 23–24 March.

Graziano, P. and Vink, M.P. (eds) (2007) *Europeanization: New Research Agendas*, Houndmills: Palgrave Macmillan.

Heidenreich, M. and Bischoff, G. (2008) 'The Open Method of Coordination. A Way to the Europeanization of Social and Employment Policies?', *Journal of Common Market Studies*, 46: 497–532.

Héritier, A. (2003) 'New Modes of Governance in Europe: Increasing Political Capacity and Policy Effectiveness?', in Börzel and Cichowski (eds) *State of the European Union VI: Law, Politics and Society*, Oxford: Oxford University Press, pp. 105–26.

Idema, T. and Kelemen, R.D. (2006) 'New Modes of Governance, the Open Method of Co-ordination and Other Fashionable Red Herring', *Perspectives on European Politics and Society*, 7: 108–23.

Jacobsson, K. (2004a) 'Soft Regulation and the Subtle Transformation of States: The Case of EU Employment Policy', *Journal of European Social Policy*, 14: 355–70.

—— (2004b) 'Between Deliberation and Discipline', in U. Mörth (ed.) *Soft Law in Governance and Regulation*, Cheltenham: Edward Elgar, pp. 81–101.

—— and Vifell, Å. (2007) 'New Governance Structures in Employment Policy-Making', in I. Linsenmann, C.O. Meyer and W.T. Wessels (eds) *Economic Government of the EU: A Balance Sheet of New Modes of Policy Coordination*, Houndmills: Palgrave Macmillan, pp. 51–71.

Linsenmann, I., Meyer, C.O. and Wessels, W.T. (eds) (2007) *Economic Government of the EU: A Balance Sheet of New Modes of Policy Coordination*, Houndmills: Palgrave Macmillan.

Radaelli, C. (2003) *The Open Method of Coordination: A New Governance Architecture for the European Union?* Sieps Report no. 1, Stockholm: Swedish Institute for European Policy Studies.

Sabel, C.F. and Zeitlin, J. (2008) 'Learning from Difference: The New Architecture of Experimentalist Governance in the EU', *European Law Journal*, 14: 271–327.

Scharpf, F. (2002) 'The European Social Model: Coping with the Challenge of Diversity', *Journal of Common Market Studies*, 40: 645–70.

—— (2003) 'Legitimate Diversity: The New Challenge of European Integration', in T. Börzel and R. Cichowski (eds) *The State of the European Union VI: Law, Politics, and Society*, Oxford: Oxford University Press, pp. 179–204.

Streeck, W. and Thelen, K. (2005) 'Introduction: Institutional Change in Advanced Political Economies', in W. Streeck and K. Thelen (eds) *Beyond Continuity: Institutional Change in Advanced Political Economies*, Oxford: Oxford University Press, pp. 1–40.

Zeitlin, J. (2003) 'Introduction: Governing Work and Welfare in a New Economy: European and American Experiments', in J. Zeitlin and D. Trubek (eds) *Governing Work and Welfare in a New Economy: European and American Experiments*, Oxford: Oxford University Press, pp. 1–30.

—— (2005a) 'Introduction: The Open Method of Co-ordination in Question', in J. Zeitlin and P. Pochet with L. Magnusson (eds) *The Open Method of Co-ordination in Action: The European Employment and Social Inclusion Strategies*, Brussels: Peter Lang, pp. 19–33.

—— (2005b) 'Conclusion: The Open Method of Co-ordination in Action: Theoretical Promise, Empirical Realities, Reform Strategy', in J. Zeitlin and P. Pochet with L. Magnusson (eds) *The Open Method of Co-ordination in Action: The European Employment and Social Inclusion Strategies*, Brussels: Peter Lang, pp. 447–503.

—— (2005c) 'Social Europe and Experimental Governance: Towards a New Constitutional Compromise?', in G. de Búrca (ed.) *EU Law and the Welfare State: In Search of Solidarity*, Oxford: Oxford University Press, pp. 213–41.

—— (2008a) 'A Decade of Innovation in EU Governance: The European Employment Strategy, the Open Method of Co-ordination, and the Lisbon Strategy', in Portuguese Presidency of the EU, *Perspectives on Employment and Social Policy Coordination in the European Union*, Lisbon: Ministry of Labour and Social Solidarity, pp. 129–44.

—— (2008b) 'The Open Method of Co-ordination and the Governance of the Lisbon Strategy', *Journal of Common Market Studies*, 46: 436–46.

Zeitlin, J. and Pochet, P. with Magnusson, L. (eds) (2005) *The Open Method of Co-ordination in Action: The European Employment and Social Inclusion Strategies*, Brussels: Peter-Lang.

Zeitlin, J., and Trubek, D.M. (eds) (2003) *Governing Work and Welfare in a New Economy: European and American Experiments*, Oxford: Oxford University Press.

1 The Open Method of Coordination

A pathway to the gradual transformation of national employment and welfare regimes?[1]

Martin Heidenreich

1 The debate on the effectiveness of the Open Method of Coordination

The Open Method of Coordination (OMC) is an attempt to reach common European goals, without uniform, legally binding rules or targets, through cross-national benchmarking and exchange of experiences, especially in the field of social and employment policies. It is based on a cyclical process of developing common objectives and indicators; national reform programmes, action plans, or strategy reports in which EU Member States explain how they will reach these objectives; peer reviews; annual progress reports evaluating national performance; and in some processes recommendations. OMC processes are generally treaty based (Heidenreich and Bischoff 2008: 509–10): the European Employment Strategy (EES) even in a separate title (articles 125–30 Treaty establishing the European Community). In the first years of its existence, the OMC was either hailed enthusiastically for its possibilities of mutual learning or criticized for its soft, neo-voluntarist approach. On the basis of more concrete empirical evidence, the limitations and possibilities of the OMC became clearer: it is neither the silver bullet for achieving a social Europe nor just a new label for day-to-day exchanges between high-ranking national labour market officials. At a European level, it is a highly professionalized, bureaucratic process with a limited involvement of social partner organizations and NGO networks, in which common goals for national employment and social policies are formulated. In the long run, this may result in more binding European regulations, but there is no concrete evidence of this up to now.

But the essential question remains whether and how these European coordination processes can effectively influence ongoing national reforms. At a general level, this question has been discussed in the debates on policy diffusion, policy transfer, convergence, and compliance. Knill and Lenschow (2005), for example, distinguish three different patterns of adaptation to EU policy (compliance, competition, and communication). Holzinger and Knill (2005) differentiate the third category – to which the OMC belongs – into lesson drawing, transnational problem solving, policy emulation and international policy promotion, which refer to different dimensions of learning processes within the OMC.

In the more specific literature about the OMC's influence on domestic processes, at least three different approaches can be distinguished (Citi and Rhodes 2007). A first critical one focuses on the differential institutionalization of 'Economic' and 'Social' Europe, contrasting analytically the advanced state of economic or 'negative' integration with the systematic barriers to political regulation of European markets ('positive integration'), which is based mainly on soft rather than hard law (Scharpf 1999, 2002). A second, more conceptual approach focuses on the possibilities of communication, learning, and deliberation (Sabel and Zeitlin 2008; Mosher and Trubek 2003; Eberlein and Kerwer 2004), while the third approach assesses these possibilities empirically, thus specifying and also challenging both optimistic visions of transnational learning and sceptical ones of the OMC's limited legitimacy and effectiveness (Zeitlin and Pochet 2005; Sacchi 2004; Armstrong 2006; Zeitlin, this volume).

The first approach starts from the distinction between hard and soft law (Héritier 2001) and the supposed shortcoming of the latter in comparison with binding rules. The crucial question is whether 'non-legislative modes of policy-making and modes of governance' (Héritier 2001: 2) are effective ways of modernizing national employment and social welfare systems. This question arises because the commonly agreed objectives of OMC processes – for example employability, activation, life-long learning, active ageing, or flexicurity – are not concrete, justiciable legal obligations. No sanctions enhance the credibility of national commitments. In contrast to other soft regulations, not even the threat of legal sanctions, the 'shadow of the law', supports the domestic implementation of the OMC objectives. Schäfer (2006: 70) therefore suspects 'that governments select voluntarist procedures mainly to secure their own competencies rather than to realize common goals'. For Scharpf (2002: 665), the absence of sanctions and enforcement procedures reflects the 'fundamental asymmetry between policies promoting market efficiencies and those promoting social protection and equality'. In order to counterbalance the legally enforceable liberalization of markets, he therefore demands a greater legal enforceability of OMC objectives. Otherwise the logic of the EES, which has been characterized as 'intergovernmentalism plus deregulation' instead of 'supranationalism plus regulation' (Ashiagbor 2005: 306), would be dominated by neoliberal concepts of employability and flexibility. The OMC might be a 'red herring that distract[s] attention from the more important and pervasive increase in the formality and judicialisation of EU policy-making' (Idema and Kelemen 2006: 108).

But the absence of sanctions is not necessarily a disadvantage: other authors even see the lack of legally binding commitments as a prerequisite for 'experimentation, learning and the development of new procedures' (Begg and Berghman 2002: 192). In this second perspective, the OMC is a prototype of a soft, 'post-regulatory regulation' (cf. Eberlein and Grande 2005). It is not a second-class alternative to 'hard' legal guidelines but is, rather, superior to them, 'because it fosters learning and provides flexibility to the policy process'

(Radaelli 2003a: 22). Soft coordination can even be seen as the crucial advantage of the OMC, since national experts exchange views and thus develop a common language relatively independently from the political constraints of their respective national frameworks. In this context, the OMC is understood as a deliberative form of governance (Jacobsson and Vifell 2007). It is expected that, instead of legal enforcement, systematic benchmarking, public 'naming and shaming' and 'peer pressure' could promote learning processes (Trubek and Trubek 2005).

A third, more empirically based approach underlines the limits of the OMC, and especially the difficulties of attaining the commonly agreed objectives (cf. Barbier 2004 for France, Büchs and Friedrich 2005 for Germany, Sacchi 2004 for Italy, and Armstrong 2006 for the UK). Casey and Gold (2005: 37) focus especially on peer reviews and stress that this procedure 'was, at best, a learning process for a limited community of labour market technicians and experts ... but it hardly acted as a catalyst for policy transfer' (cf. also Hartlapp 2006). The limits of the OMC and the difficulty of implementing the commonly agreed objectives have become clear: 'There is a long and vulnerable implementation chain before the common objectives have been translated into practice within the Member States.' (Jacobsson 2004b: 99–100). In a comprehensive review of the literature Zeitlin (2005: 472) concludes that 'there are relatively few concrete cases at national level of direct or first-order policy learning [which] is a natural consequence of the OMC's "contextualised benchmarking" approach' (cf. also Zeitlin, this volume). The 'limited evidence of direct policy transfer' and 'limited evidence of reflexive learning from the results of OMC processes at EU level' (Zeitlin 2005: 473) are explained by institutional inertia, by the procedural shortcomings of OMC processes (for example the insufficient opportunities for exchange of experiences and limited participation of regional and non-governmental actors), and by the fact that the implementation of policy reforms is dependent not only on new insights (cf. López-Santana 2006), but also on a firm political commitment, i.e. on power. Nevertheless, Zeitlin (this volume) demonstrates that indirect or second-order learning is real and significant when foreign practices are adapted and modified in order to fit new host environments.

Each of the three theoretical perspectives raises considerable questions. The OMC-sceptical literature rightly refers to the limited impact of 'soft law'. These implementation difficulties of the OMC, however, are unilaterally explained by the interest of the Member States in preserving their prerogatives ('subsidiarity') and by the institutional heterogeneity of European employment and welfare regimes. In view of the massive protests and opposition encountered by the German, French and Italian governments to labour market reforms inspired in part by the EES (Hartz IV, Contrat première embauche, Legge Biagi), the implementation barriers to the OMC cannot be explained only by Member States' resistance to EU interventions or a lack of political will. In fact, conflicting political interests, the inertia of welfare and employment regimes, and, most of all, the difficulties of inventing new, historically unprecedented forms of transnational social protection have also to be taken into account. The second perspective emphasises the learning opportunities of the OMC, without analysing how learning processes at the European level may lead to new regulatory structures at the national level. The third perspective raises the questions of how and through which concrete instruments and mechanisms the OMC influences national reform processes (Zeitlin, this volume).

These three questions are addressed in the body of this chapter. In the following section, employment and welfare regimes will be analysed as social fields characterized by pre-existing rules, within which skilled strategic actors and organizations seek to regulate labour market processes and social policies according to their interests and conceptions of control (Fligstein 2001a, 2001b). New challenges and external stimuli like the OMC are seized upon by domestic actors in order either to defend and reproduce their dominant positions or to challenge incumbent organizations (2). Secondly, the possibilities and limitations of the OMC to induce changes in domestic employment and social fields are discussed along three dimensions (3). The chapter concludes by summarizing existing evidence on the specific contribution of the OMC to changing national employment and social regimes (4).

2 Employment and welfare regimes as social fields

New internal and external challenges to domestic welfare and employment policies and the necessity for their 'recalibration' form the background to the development of a European social and employment policy (Ferrera et al. 2000; Hemerijck 2007). The question of how European-level coordination processes can influence national institutions and reforms is the central question in the debate on Europeanization:

> the concept of Europeanization refers to: Processes of (a) construction, (b) diffusion, and (c) institutionalization of formal and informal rules, procedures, policy paradigms, styles, 'ways of doing things', and shared beliefs and norms which are first defined and consolidated in the making of EU public policy and politics and then incorporated in the logic of domestic discourse, identities, political structures, and public policies.
>
> (Radaelli 2003b: 30)

In this debate, the fit or misfit between European and domestic policies, the importance of veto points, and different logics of adaptational pressures, especially the logic of anticipated consequences and logic appropriateness have often been analysed (Börzel and Risse 2000). But the questions remain open of how institutional changes in domestic welfare and employment regimes may be possible and what role the OMC might play in these adaptation processes. At a general level, three approaches can be identified which 1) focus on learning and isomorphic pressures, 2) stress the relative closedness and stability of institutional regimes, or 3) analyse the dynamics of challengers' struggles to invent new concepts of control, thereby redefining the domestic field of internal power and exchange relations (Table 1.1). These three approaches provide a theoretical basis for the previously described sceptical, deliberative, and empirical strands of the OMC debate.

First: neo-institutional approaches analyse organizations as open systems which, by force, imitation or normative pressure, adjust their structures to the demands and challenges of their institutional, non-technical environments. John Meyer analyses these isomorphic pressures, taking the example of nation-states. He observes 'the rise of global models of nationally organized progress and justice' (Meyer et al., 1997: 174) and analyses their spread as the result of pressures from transnational organizations, professions, and social movements: 'globalized models are produced by the sciences and professions ...

Table 1.1 Conceptualising supranational influence on national policies: three theoretical perspectives

	Nation-states as open systems	*Nation-states as relatively closed and stable institutional orders*	*Nation-states as institutionalised social fields*
Crucial assumption	Domestic policies and governance structures may be reshaped by external demands, challenges, and opportunities	Relative closure and stability of national regimes. Crucial role of institutional complementarities and path dependencies	Domestic orders as provisional compromises between heterogeneous interests, perceptions, and logics of regulation
Institutional change	Learning or isomorphic pressures from transnational professions, organizations and civil society	Only at 'critical junctures' in which institutional trajectories are created	Gradual transformation through hybridization of conflicting institutional logics
European coordination processes	Crucial role of dialogue, learning, local experimentation	External interventions are generally ineffective	External challenges, concepts, agenda, resources and rules are appropriated through organized domestic bargaining and sense-making processes
Limitations of OMC	Power, enforceability (mainly at the European level)	No efficient coordination. OMC may even undercut legitimacy of EU legislation	Implementation problems mainly at the national level due to different institutional logics in national and European fields

by rapidly expanding, international associations that rest on scientized and universalized pretenses, by social movements on a global scale and by actors themselves who present their forms as universal models' (Meyer 2000: 246). These global models reveal themselves especially in 'common models of national state identity and purpose', 'common models of socio-economic development', 'common models of human rights', and in the expansion of national education systems 'linking both ideologies of human rights and of social progress' (Meyer 2000: 234). The OMC might be analysed as a specific institutionalisation of these isomorphic pressures based either on copying widely used models or on the adoption of a model recommended by the EU (Holzinger and Knill 2005: 780).

At first sight, theories of organizational, political or institutional learning argue in a completely different way (cf. Visser in this volume). They usually understand learning as a 'process whereby actors, through interaction with broader institutional contexts (norms or discursive structures) acquire new interests and preferences' (Checkel 1999: 548). The effectiveness of the OMC is attributed to a transnational learning process 'that engages multiple levels, promotes dialogue, cuts across traditional boundaries, and fosters local experimentation' (Mosher and Trubek 2003: 84). The inclusion of national officials in the European arena may induce supranational learning processes, and these learning processes may then influence domestic policies: 'Contextual, fuzzy and "bottom-up" benchmarking, as in the European Employment Strategy, is more effective in influencing the operating conditions of policies, especially when combined with measurable indicators and quantitative targets, and efficient monitoring agencies' (Hemerijck and Visser 2003: 48). A basic similarity of the learning and the neo-institutional approaches to institutional change is that they analyse nation-states as open systems. The focus either on isomorphic pressures or on policy learning does not take sufficient account of the role of domestic organizations, governance structures, interests, and agendas. Ministries, regions, municipalities, social partners, and other domestic organizations do not react directly to external influences. Proposals of international organizations, challenges, and opportunities are perceived and filtered by national administrations within the framework of domestic policies and institutions. In order to analyse the impact of the OMC, it is therefore necessary to take account of the relative autonomy, inertia, and path-dependent trajectories of national institutions and constellations of actors, power relationships, and interests.

Second: the influence of the OMC on domestic policies depends on its capacity to intervene in domestic employment and welfare regimes. These are specific types of institutional orders: employment regimes regulate the type, the level of qualifications, and wages on the one hand, and the relationship between the labour market and other social systems – especially families and welfare regimes – which provide alternative means of subsistence, on the other (Schmid and Gazier 2002). A welfare regime is 'the combined, interdependent way in which welfare is produced and allocated between state, market and family' (Esping-Andersen 1999: 34–5). Both regimes regulate conflicts about the role of market mechanisms as a source of subsistence, the possibility of different groups to participate in working life, and the role of family-based and public forms of social security, thus shaping the degree to which the working-age population is included in or excluded from the labour market. Exclusionary employment regimes, particularly those of continental and southern Europe, reflect preferences for stable, socially secured employment relations, especially for skilled male, core workers, at the expense of women, youth, older people, and other peripheral groups. On the other hand, in Anglo-Saxon and Scandinavian countries the far greater inclusion of the population in gainful employment is achieved in different ways. While individualistic, market-based relationships and unequal income structures facilitate the expansion of personal and social services in the Anglo-Saxon countries, the state and stronger unions in Scandinavian countries form the basis for more egalitarian work and income conditions and a larger segment of educational, family, and care services (Iversen and Wren 1998). From a sociological perspective, the employment rate is thus the institutional result of conflicts over the form and extent of wage labour and the inclusion of female, older, younger, migrant and handicapped persons in the workforce, while social protection expenditure is the result of conflicts over the relative weight of public, family, and market-based forms of welfare provision.

A possible conclusion which could be drawn from such an institutional perspective is that the possibilities of institutional change are rather limited. Organized interests are the basis of high inertia and resistance to change. Path dependence and complementarities explain the relative stability of institutions (Höpner 2005: 333). New challenges are dealt within the framework and on the basis of previous patterns. Change is therefore reduced to the continuation of established trajectories (Crouch and Farrell 2004: 12). New equilibria are an exceptional, rare event. The impact of external interventions such as the OMC might therefore be assumed to be minimal. But this view does not take account of the dynamics and conflicts even within apparently stable regimes. While the first perspective conceives national institutions as wind tunnels permeable to every external intervention and pressure, the second perspective tends to conceive domestic regimes as closed arenas impermeable to any external intervention.

A third perspective, which focuses on social fields (Fligstein 2001a, 2001b; Fligstein and Stone Sweet 2002) tries to walk the tightrope between the indisputable stability and relative closure of institutions on the one hand, and their dynamics and responsiveness to external influences on the other, by combining the insights of the two previous perspectives. The conception of institutional regimes, which encompasses the structural dimension of national policies, is combined with the analysis of skilled actors and organizations, thus adding the agency dimension to the analysis of domestic regimes. In this perspective, change is analysed not as a direct result of learning processes or as a reaction to exogenous shocks destroying the previous domestic equilibrium, but as the result of regulated, institutionally shaped processes of negotiation and compromise between incumbent actors and others who use European proposals and models to challenge the existing employment and welfare regimes.

Social fields are local social orders 'composed of (1) organizations seeking to structure their environments, (2) pre-existing rules (i.e., existing institutions) that operate to constrain and enable actors in the arena, and (3) skilled strategic actors who work within organizations to help attain cooperation among disparate groups and interests' (Fligstein and Stone Sweet 2002: 1211). By analogy to the sociology of markets proposed by Fligstein (2001b: 69), employment and welfare regimes can be analysed as systems of power whereby incumbent (dominant) organizations and actors use various strategies to stabilize and reproduce their positions in relation to challengers (dominated actors and organizations). The cognitive dimension of the field-specific governance structures is designated as 'conceptions of control', which Fligstein (2001b: 70) defines as 'understandings that structure perceptions of how a market works and allow actors to interpret their world, and as the real social relations that produce that world'. National employment and welfare regimes thus are the stable results of previous institutionalization projects in which the future incumbents have succeeded in establishing their 'conceptions of control' as the generally accepted rules of appropriateness and interpretation.

This implies that institutional orders are contested terrains, not consistent, coherent, consensual regulatory systems. As a result of historical compromises between divergent, potentially conflicting interests and perceptions, they integrate heterogeneous logics of action and shape the ways in which social actors deal with the conflicts between different social spheres. These latent, provisionally regulated conflicts leading to the internal heterogeneity of institutions become important when an institutional order is faced with new challenges and opportunities – as in the case of national employment and welfare regimes in Europe today (Hemerijck 2007). Challengers within established social fields can develop new conceptions of control. The transformation of domestic fields may be facilitated first of all by establishing new frames of interpretation or creating new agendas – especially if, for example, new, professionally designed labour market concepts are propagated by prestigious institutions like the OECD or the EU which can easily be used within the political or administrative arena. Especially useful for domestic professionals are popular buzzwords with an immediate 'sex appeal'. Conceptions such as employability, active and preventive labour market policy ('activation'), stronger incentives for the non-employed ('make work pay'), gender mainstreaming, active ageing, life-long learning and 'flexicurity' may be convincing trumps in domestic ideational struggles for new labour market policies. Hence the concepts of the EES may be highly interesting for domestic actors, who can create new systems of meaning as 'institutional entrepreneurs' (Fligstein 2001a: 106). Second, the OMC may provide new opportunities and constraints for domestic bargaining and negotiation processes: financial support from the

European Social Fund, required participation of social partners, regions, and NGOs, or the political support of the heads of Member State governments for the targets and guidelines of OMC processes may serve as important trumps in domestic arenas. Third, the new EU targets typically require new forms of communication and cooperation between previously separated domestic policy arenas. New forms of policy making and participation involving social partners, NGOs, regions, and municipalities may facilitate the emergence of new governance structures (Zeitlin, this volume). The OMC thus may contribute to the restructuring of national political and administrative fields by defining new frames and agendas, by providing new resources, and by facilitating the emergence of new patterns of administration and cooperation (Heidenreich and Bischoff 2008).

The analysis of such a threefold domestic use of the OMC must take account of sense-making and power struggles between challengers and incumbent actors. The OMC on Social Protection and Social Inclusion (OMC/SPSI), for example, is often used by NGOs, regions or ministries to redefine the field of anti-poverty policy (Jacobsson, Johansson, Hamel and Vanhercke, this volume), while the German Federal Ministry of Labour has also used the EES to strengthen its position in relation to the unions, thereby breaking at least partially and temporarily the consensual, neo-corporatist governance structure of national labour market policies (Preunkert and Zirra, this volume).

Institutional orders are thus not shelters of stability but fields for social action, for patterns of bargaining and negotiation. They are structured games or local orders (Friedberg 1997) whose regulatory structures can, in principle, be transformed by domestic actors who may also use external instruments, opportunities and concepts as resources in internal bargaining and reform processes: 'Political institutions … are the object of ongoing skirmishing as actors try to achieve advantage by interpreting or redirecting institutions in pursuit of their goals, or by subverting or circumventing rules that clash with their interests … the aim must be to understand … the way actors cultivate change from within the context of existing opportunities and constraint' (Streeck and Thelen 2005: 19).

The result of these field-specific processes of negotiation and bargaining is generally incremental institutional transformations. New opportunities, instruments, and challenges may facilitate the shift of hitherto peripheral or marginal interests, actors, and rules into a central position, previous patterns may be reinterpreted and used in a different manner, or peripheral rules and old institutions may be neglected, suppressed, or overlaid by new ones (for these five patterns of institutional change, see Streeck and Thelen 2005). National institutional orders are not completely open and permeable to their environments, reacting directly to isomorphic pressures and exploiting all the learning opportunities on offer, but are instead created, sustained, and transformed by domestic actors who use new opportunities, instruments, and challenges for their own purposes, and whose strategies are shaped by field-specific regulations, perceptions, theories of action, and interest constellations.

In conclusion: in order to answer the question of how European coordination processes can shape national discourses, identities and policies, the principal limitations of external intervention must first be emphasized. Domestic social and employment regimes cannot be directly changed from the outside by external discourses, guidelines, and learning opportunities – a fact that is neglected by most of the literature on policy diffusion, policy transfer, and policy convergence. National policies and European coordination processes are two relatively autonomous social fields. Domestic ministries in which reforms of national employment and social welfare systems are conceived cannot directly be influenced from the outside, because they operate according to their own rules, legal responsibilities, and administrative traditions. A basic feature of domestic institutional orders (for example national employment and welfare regimes) is their relative autonomy, which prevents direct learning and response to isomorphic pressures.

The OMC's influence on national institutions thus depends on the structure of domestic fields which shape the strategies and learning processes of domestic actors and organizations. European actors, guidelines, and recommendations, as well as the experiences of other countries within the framework of mutual learning processes, will have an influence on domestic politics and institutions only if external opportunities, concepts, instruments, and challenges are used within the domestic field to change previous positions, problem definitions, interests, and patterns of cooperation. European proposals must have some sort of resonance within the national political field. Domestic actors and organizations must be able to use European rules, requirements, suggestions, and opportunities within national discourses, power structures, organizational reforms, or political reforms. Such 'connectability' or 'creative appropriation' (Zeitlin, this volume) is therefore crucial for the impact of European coordination processes on national discourses, action constellations, and regulatory structures. Domestic fields are both 'filters' and targets of European interventions.

The effective implementation of European recommendations and guidelines at the national level – the Achilles heel of the OMC – can thus be reformulated as the question how European coordination processes can effectively shape domestic processes of bargaining, negotiation, and cooperation. 'European' opportunities are thus exploited by domestic actors and organizations in redefining the national 'rules of the game'. Financial incentives and requirements for the participation of hitherto under-represented actors and interests may create new strategic opportunities at the national level. In the regulatory or procedural dimension, the guidelines, progress reports, and joint evaluation reports are expectations to national policies which may change prior domestic patterns of bargaining and cooperation. The European Council is also concerned with the implementation of the Lisbon strategy on a regular basis and formulates conclusions, which also develop a self-binding normative effect. Last but not least, the implementation processes also have a cognitive dimension because 'learning' is the principal objective of the OMC. In the following, we will discuss how the OMC intervenes in these three dimensions in the governance of national employment and welfare regimes.

3 The impact of the OMC on domestic reform policies

A result of the earlier analysis is that European targets, recommendations and learning processes can influence national policies if they 'irritate' the domestic discourses, models, political structures, and power constellations in their procedural, cognitive and strategic dimension, i.e. if some sort of 'resonance' (resistance, compliance, lesson drawing, agenda setting, demands for participation, suggestions ...) can be generated in the domestic field. The interventions on the European level must be able to initiate, accompany, facilitate, and legitimize political processes of self-transformation at the domestic level. It is crucial that the European coordination processes generate some sort of 'resonance' at the domestic level, i.e. that they influence in some way the national discourses and models, the national power and exchange processes and incentive structures, and the national norms and routines. However, the impact of the OMC cannot be evaluated on the basis of the successful implementation of European proposals into national rules and laws, since such a direct transfer is difficult, given the operational closure of the national political and administrative arenas. In the next section, the cognitive, strategic, and procedural dimensions of the OMC's influence on domestic employment and social orders are reconstructed on the basis of the other articles in this volume and the current literature on the OMC.

3.1 Learning with the OMC

European coordination processes aim at a fundamental reorientation and modernization of national employment and social policies (Table 1.2). The direction of the intended transformation processes can be indicated by some catchphrases: from job protection to employability (guidelines 23 and 24), from income compensation to active labour market policies and local partnerships and inter-agency cooperation in the field of employment services, from labour market exclusion of women, youth, and older people to gender mainstreaming and active ageing (guidelines 17 and 19), from status protection to flexicurity (guideline 21). European proposals may be exploited by domestic actors as opportunities for legitimizing domestic change. Especially in the case of 'soft' governance mechanisms like the OMC, their influence on national discourses, orientations, and frames of reference may be crucial for understanding the European impact on the national level (Zeitlin 2005; Heidenreich and Bischoff 2008).

The OMC is an arena for mutual learning processes between Member States. It may facilitate the emergence of a common language and a common knowledge base and the 'discovery' of new actors and problems (Hamel and Vanhercke, this volume). The debates in the European committees are regarded

Table 1.2 Objectives of the Employment and Social OMCs

The Employment Guidelines (2005 to 2008 and proposal for 2008–10) (Integrated Guidelines 17 to 24)
(17) Implement employment policies aiming at achieving full employment, improving quality and productivity at work, and strengthening social and territorial cohesion
(18) Promote a lifecycle approach to work
(19) Ensure inclusive labour markets, enhance work attractiveness, and make work pay for job-seekers, including disadvantaged people, and the inactive
(20) Improve matching of labour market needs
(21) Promote flexibility combined with employment security and reduce labour market segmentation, having due regard to the role of the social partners
(22) Ensure employment-friendly labour cost developments and wage-setting mechanisms
(23) Expand and improve investment in human capital
(24) Adapt education and training systems in response to new competence requirements
Overarching objectives of the OMC for social protection and social inclusion from 2006 (a) social cohesion, equality between men and women and equal opportunities for all through adequate, accessible, financially sustainable, adaptable and efficient social protection systems and social inclusion policies
(b) effective and mutual interaction between the Lisbon objectives of greater economic growth, more and better jobs and greater social cohesion, and with the EU's Sustainable Development Strategy
(c) good governance, transparency and the involvement of stakeholders in the design, implementation and monitoring of policy
Sector-specific objectives (2006) A decisive impact on the eradication of poverty and social exclusion Adequate and sustainable pensions Accessible, high-quality and sustainable healthcare and long-term care

Source: *Official Journal of the European Union* L 205/2; 16.8.2005 and COM (2007) 803 final.

'as a promising instrument for addressing common European concern while respecting national diversity' (Zeitlin 2005: 448). Jacobsson (2004a: 360) points out that '[t]he establishment of a common interpretative framework for analysing the labour market has ... been key to the joint employment strategy'. The OMC/SPSI and the EES are regarded as two processes which can enhance 'mutual awareness of policies, practices and problems in other Member States' (Zeitlin 2005: 470). The peer reviews and the discussion in the European committees have strengthened and institutionalized transnational exchange processes (Jacobsson 2004a). The OMC is considered as creating the possibility to question one's own national approach and to develop new ways of problem solving within domestic fields.

But at the same time, empirical analyses of the national implementation of the EES and the OMC/SPSI indicate that the results of the learning processes are not used directly and fully by the Member States. Radaelli points out that the 'convergence in "talk" may not produce convergence in decisions' (2003a: 24). The targets of the OMC and the results of the mutual learning exchange are implemented in a special national way (Zeitlin 2005). In the case of the EES in Germany, for example, Büchs and Friedrich (2005) observe a national adoption of the comprehensive employment policy approach, which is limited to the traditional confines of labour market policy and therefore intertwined with its particular shortcomings. Casey and Gold (2005: 36) assessed the operation of the first years of the EES peer review procedures as 'at best, a learning process for a limited community of labour market technicians and experts' (for an empirical critique, see Zeitlin, this volume).

Despite this sceptical evaluation of the direct effects of OMC processes, the reframing and opening of national discourses that they produce seems to be considerable (see van Gerven and Beckers, this volume, who observe a convergence of objectives but not of instruments). The labour market policies of the OECD and the EU have contributed to a slow shift of national discourses, for example in Germany and France. Huber (2006) analyses this impact in four selected policy fields: gender mainstreaming, flexicurity, an active and preventive approach to labour market policies, and a shift from early retirement programmes to active ageing. He concludes 'that there has been a considerable, mostly cognitive influence on the labour market policies of Germany and France [even if] employment policies in both countries are still basically nationally determined' (Huber 2006: 45).

Even if the cognitive impact on the supranational discourses is indirect and generally limited to specific scientific and professional communities, the frame of reference of labour market and social policies, especially in continental and southern European countries, has fundamentally changed in recent years: While the 1980s were still dominated by attempts to reduce working time, the underlying 'lump of labour' thesis, which demanded a more egalitarian distribution of existing employment among the available workforce and thus a reduction of weekly working time, early retirement schemes, and lower labour market participation of women, are no longer considered to be a legitimate option. Even the targets of labour market policies have changed: higher employment rates have been added to lower unemployment rates. Strong employment protection is increasingly considered as a mechanism which divides the labour force into insiders and outsiders, which should be combated through 'flexicurity'. Previous discourses about the fair division of work, job protection, and the gender division of labour have gradually been replaced by other discourses on employability, active labour market policies and stronger incentives to work ('make work pay').

In conclusion: the development of common targets and supranational discourses are ways of effectively influencing domestic reform processes. Common guidelines and objectives are interpreted and framed in each domestic field according to its own traditions and power structures: '[D]ifferent national systems will interpret and select the signals and steers from OMC in different ways, albeit within the context of an EU governance framework' (Armstrong 2006: 97). Especially the EES, but also the labour market policies of other international organizations seem to have contributed to a fundamental reorientation of national discourses (van Gerven and Beckers). The concepts of employability, active labour market policies, and flexicurity have become legitimizing devices for successful labour market and social reforms in recent years.

3.2 Financial incentives and participation: the strategic dimension of policy implementation

In the strategic dimension, the EU tries to shape the implementation of the EES and the OMC/Inclusion in two different ways – through financial incentives and through increased participation of currently under-represented interests.

The use of the EU budget as a lever for national reform, e.g. the improvement of 'employment opportunities through financial support from the European Social Fund and the other Structural Funds' was already a proposal of the Kok Employment Task Force (Kok 2004: 58). From 2005, the Barroso Commission fully integrated the Lisbon priorities into the cohesion policy for the period 2007–13: 'For the convergence objective, the earmarked resources should represent a minimum of 60% of the total funding, whereas for the regional competitiveness objective it should be 75%' (European Commission 2005, 2006). Structural funds (€347 billion from 2007 to 2013) therefore will be concentrated on the Lisbon objectives, as defined by the Integrated Guidelines for Growth and Jobs in order to increase the added value of the structural policy of the EU (Mairate 2006). In this context, the EES guides the European Social Fund (ESF), which will spend €75 billion over the period 2007–13 on the attainment of its objectives. López-Santana, Mailand, Jacobsson and West, and Preunkert and Zirra show in their contributions to this volume that the ESF has been particularly important in less wealthy countries, such as Italy, Spain, Poland, and the Baltic states. But van Gerven and Beckers (this volume) observe that ESF support was also crucial in Belgium for activation policies, for example the introduction of 'guidance trajectories' for the unemployed.

In addition to these financial incentives, the OMC also creates opportunities for the involvement of regional, municipal, and non-governmental actors (especially social partners, welfare associations, companies, non-governmental organizations), which 'might constitute strong pressure groups as well as a solid democratic platform for decision-making and implementation' (Borràs and Jacobsson 2004: 200). The OMC should 'enhance the legitimacy of EU decision-making, allowing more decentralized participation by stakeholders' (cf. Eberlein and Kerwer 2004: 133). This participation may also increase the effectiveness of the OMC, because it can integrate multiple perspectives

(Trubek and Trubek 2005), thus increasing the capability to develop adequate solutions to complex problems (Héritier 2001; Mosher and Trubek 2003).

The participation of non-governmental organizations, social partners, municipalities, and regions can be interpreted as a deliberate European strategy aimed at introducing and strengthening new perspectives within the political system of Member States. National policies may be changed indirectly, through stronger consideration of previously under-represented and hardly articulated interests. The transformation 'from a "male breadwinner" industrial to a "dual earner" post-industrial society' (Hemerijck 2007: 31) also increases the role of social groups which are under-represented in the existing bargaining arenas (for example women, employees with temporary, part-time, precarious, or otherwise atypical employment relationships). If the OMC therefore contributes to a stronger representation of the interests of youth or older employees, women, precarious workers, or the socially excluded, then this could also contribute to the transformation of domestic social and employment regimes in Europe. Stronger participation therefore not only benefits the reputation of the EU in the Member States and contributes to better, more experimental, and more deliberative governance, but may also improve the capability to implement alternative policy designs.

Empirically, this can be observed above all in the field of social inclusion policies (for Sweden and Denmark see Jacobsson 2005): 'The anti-poverty associations are not as well anchored into the national contexts as the social partners … They therefore have a more genuine motivation to take advantage of the window of opportunity offered by the Social Inclusion OMC' (de la Porte and Pochet 2005: 383). Armstrong (2006: 89) confirms that for the UK: '[W]ithout "the driving force from Europe" to work with civil society and other actors, it was unlikely that the DWP (Department of Work and Pensions) would have developed a willingness to engage with social NGOs … The NAPincl [usion] has redistributed the opportunities both for civil servants and for civil society to engage in dialogue on issues of poverty and social exclusion.' Zeitlin (2005: 469) therefore concludes that 'national Social Affairs ministries appear more interested than their Labour or Employment counterparts in mobilising external support for their policies from NGOs and civil society groups.'

On the other hand, the EES might be used also to strengthen the position of incumbent organizations in domestic fields – as seems to be the case for the German Ministry of Economics and Labour, which has used the EES to reshape the national agenda.

In conclusion: OMC processes were hailed as a new road towards more participative governance involving local, regional, and non-governmental actors. The possibility of increased participation by these groups has been described as a major advantage of the OMC, because it could contribute to the legitimacy of reform outcomes and involve potential veto players, but also organizations representing hitherto subordinate interests. In a strategic perspective, the EU induced a stronger representation of new actors and interests. This opportunity was used mainly in the field of social exclusion and to a much lesser degree by the interest representations of younger, older, female or precarious employees in the field of employment policies.

3.3 The OMC as a challenge to existing administrative procedures and rules

The OMC aims at a fundamental transformation of national welfare and employment policies. These policies, which have been developed in a transnational, highly professionalized and bureaucratized bargaining arena, require new domestic forms of administration and policy making. The organizational separation of employment, social security, family, and educational policies has to be critically re-examined. For example, a better compatibility of work and family life is a crucial prerequisite for greater participation by women in employment. A higher female employment rate cannot be achieved through labour market policies alone, but also involves parental benefits, the provision of childcare, the working-time models of businesses, and even the tax laws (for example, the separate taxation of spouses). This engages not only ministries of labour, but also numerous other ministries, actors at other political levels (countries, regions, communities), and private organizations and businesses. Similarly, this applies to youth employment policies, which must also be linked with the education system, in order to reduce the number of early school leavers and to improve skills. New policies therefore depend on new modes of linking different political arenas, levels, and organizations.

A central goal of the OMC is thus to stimulate new modes of governance and policy making. This was achieved, in particular, due to the necessity of cooperation in drafting national action or reform plans. Numerous studies emphasize that the OMC has 'stimulated improvements in horizontal or cross-sectoral integration across formally separated but practically interdependent policy fields' (Zeitlin 2005: 457). Coordination was improved, in particular, within and between different ministries – for example, through working groups and ad hoc meetings:

> Given that responsibilities for employment and labour market policies are divided between different ministries in most Member States (for example Austria, Belgium, France, Germany and the UK), ministries such as those of finance, economic affairs, education or public health are also involved. Hence, in most cases the central co-ordinating departments are located at the ministries of labour, while other ministries contribute to parts of the NAP falling under their specific areas of competencies … The EES supported the creation of horizontal inter-ministerial working groups and ad hoc co-ordination meetings … Even though the central co-ordination mechanisms under the EES follow the domestic decision-making logic of the individual Member States, the co-ordination strategy offered a window of opportunity to actors formerly not directly involved in national employment policy-making.'
>
> (Meyer and Umbach 2007: 103)

There was also an improvement in the national statistical, evaluation, and monitoring capacities as well as an improved concert between national, regional, and local policy levels (Zeitlin 2005: 458). Meyer and Umbach (2007: 103) report that the EES led to considerable procedural innovations, especially in Belgium, Portugal, Sweden, Austria, Ireland, and to a lesser extent in France and Italy. This also applies to the Scandinavian countries, whose policies already correspond, to a large extent, to the objectives of the European employment and inclusion strategies (Jacobsson 2005: 133). In many countries the EES therefore led to a stronger coordination of measures at the national level – for example, through the creation of formal interministerial coordination structures (see Tholoniat 2001 for the French case).

In some countries, however, experimentation with new forms of policy making has not yet led to convincing new solutions. In Germany, for example, the failure to develop an encompassing employment policy has also been explained by the discrepancy between new challenges and the existing administrative structures:

> The demand to actively seek a job is closely aligned with the necessity to train young people and prevent early school leaving. Conceptually, these two aspects are inextricably intertwined; however, the competences of the federal states and municipalities in Germany prevent the federal ministry from exerting influence on this policy field … the reforms of recent years have predominantly concerned the narrower sphere of labour market policy and have hardly affected the complementary, supportive areas that are crucial to an inclusive employment strategy … Neither child-care, nor job rotation nor the PSAs are properly placed within the given institutional framework … Best-Practice-Concepts in the sense of 'taking the pick of the bunch' must be regarded as having failed.
>
> (Zirra and Buchkremer 2007: 75, 77)

The regular reporting obligations also transform policy evaluation and monitoring. The permanent benchmarking processes increase the sensitivity to one's own weaknesses and strengths. The increased statistical requirements and the continuous evaluation create a higher sensitivity to hitherto ignored social problems and thus facilitate the emergence of a transnational consensus on the shortcomings, achievements, and reform needs in the different fields in which the OMC is applied.

In conclusion: new policies, and thus the implementation of the OMC targets, require new forms of regulation and policy making, as well as a different style of policy evaluation. A stronger inclusion of women, younger, and older persons into the labour market is only possible through the concerted cooperation of labour, finance, social, and education ministries, together with regions, municipalities, businesses, welfare associations, and social partners. This often requires a transformation of domestic political and administrative fields: new, closely interconnected project-team types of cooperation may gradually overlay and supplement the previous, functional, and hierarchically specialized forms of politics and administration. The procedural influence of the OMC described in the following chapters and summarized by Zeitlin (this volume) demonstrates that it facilitates the emergence of new horizontal, vertical, and networked patterns of governance and policy coordination which are a necessary prerequisite for these new policies.

3.4 Five worlds of domestic influence?

European coordination procedures have initiated processes of domestic institutional change in the cognitive, strategic, and procedural dimensions. First, the OMC supports the development of new models and agendas; this is indicated by catchphrases such as active ageing, flexicurity, activation, and preventative labour market policies and gender mainstreaming, which nonetheless have different meanings in each country. Second, financial incentives and requirements for the inclusion of social partners, non-governmental organizations, regions, and municipalities may involve new interests and actors in national policy making. This possibility was particularly important in the OMC/SPSI. Third, the changed goals of social and employment policy can only be implemented if adequate forms of interministerial and multilevel policy coordination as well as policy evaluation can be developed. In this respect, the obligation to prepare national reform plans can function as an incentive for strengthening inter-ministerial coordination. The OMC thus initiated the development of new models and concepts, the inclusion of previously peripheral interests and actors, as well as the development of new divisions of labour and forms of cooperation.

On the one hand, the new European coordination processes have comparable effects on the participating countries, as Zeitlin (this volume) rightly stresses. But on the other hand, as always in comparative research, there are also national and field-specific differences on the impact of the OMC. Given the crucial role of domestic discourses, political structures, and power constellations in the fields of social protection and employment, it can be hypothesized that the OMC's influence is also shaped by existing national employment and welfare regimes, traditions, and the organizational structure of domestic fields. Discussion of possible regime-specific patterns of influence can start from the inertia and path dependence of national employment and welfare regimes. On the basis of the analyses by Scharpf and Schmidt (2000) and Esping-Andersen (1999), it may be useful to look for social-democratic (Scandinavian), liberal (Anglo-Saxon), conservative (continental European), familialistic (southern European), and post-socialist (central and eastern European) patterns of influence of the OMC on domestic employment and welfare regimes. The hypothesis of regime-specific patterns of influence therefore does not exclude the existence both of general effects and of effects specific to particular policy domains, countries, or historical periods. This hypothesis is only intended as a focusing device which draws attention to the possibility of regime-specific effects of the OMC.

On the basis of the chapters of Mailand, López-Santana, Jacobsson and Johansson (this volume), one might expect that the impact of the EES in social-democratic and liberal regimes would be mostly limited to cognitive and incremental improvements. This may be due to the fact that the employment policies of these countries already largely coincided with its prescriptions. Especially in countries with inclusive employment regimes, previous paths and logics of development are reinforced and legitimated (for the Danish and Swedish examples, see also Jacobsson 2005; for the example of the UK cf. Armstrong 2006). Only in some cases (for example in the case of the stronger involvement of municipalities in Sweden or active ageing in Denmark; cf. López-Santana and Mailand, this volume) an influence on national patterns of bargaining and interest formation can be observed. Among the crucial foci of the EES are a higher employment rate ('employability') and inclusive access to the labour market – goals which are primarily shaped by the experiences of the Anglo-Saxon and Scandinavian countries (Barbier 2005). Mailand (this volume), for example, finds more evidence for the influence of the EES 'in Spain and, especially, Poland than in Denmark and the UK'. Jacobsson (2005: 130–1) also reports that in Sweden and Denmark 'the EES has not led to any major policy shift'. But this does not mean that the EES had no impact in the Scandinavian and Anglo-Saxon countries. The recommendations of the EES clearly show that there are a lot of possibilities for improvement – in the case of the UK, for example, improvement of skill levels and the development of an integrated approach to employment and training. In the case of Sweden, the recent country-specific recommendations under the Integrated Guidelines for Growth and Jobs (4/3/08) focus on the need to 'increase work incentives, to tackle youth unemployment, to raise the employment rate of immigrants and to reintegrate people on sickness-related schemes'. Hence even the 'best pupils in the class' can and sometimes do use the EES to improve their performance, as Jacobsson (2005) and O'Donnell and Moss (2005) show for the Swedish and Irish cases. Thus the discrepancy (or 'goodness of fit') between national regimes and the EES guidelines is an important, but not a determining factor. Even if the perceived 'adaptational pressures' are lower in the Scandinavian and Anglo-Saxon countries, the latter may use the OMC as a tool for identifying possibilities to improve their policies.

Adaptational pressures are higher in the continental, southern, and eastern European member states. Preunkert, Zirra, López-Santana, Jacobsson and West (this volume) observe the emergence of new approaches to activation, prevention, gender issues, the inclusion of older workers, and life-long learning and the modernization of the public employment services in Germany, France, Belgium, Italy, Spain, Poland, and the Baltic countries (cognitive dimension). Especially in the post-socialist countries, the EES served as a role model for new employment policies (activation and public employment services). In the strategic dimension, Preunkert and Zirra (this volume) observe in Germany a stronger role of the Federal Ministry of Labour and a weaker role of social partners and municipalities. López-Santana, Preunkert and Zirra (this volume) observe in Italy and Spain a stronger involvement of regions (also due to the ESF) and a strategic use of the EES in domestic arenas. The pressures and incentives of the EES and the ESF are especially strong in the post-socialist countries, as Mailand, Jacobsson and West (this volume) report for Poland and the Baltic countries. In the procedural dimension, Preunkert, Zirra, López-Santana, Jacobsson and West (this volume) observe an improved inter-ministerial coordination for the continental, southern, and eastern European member states analysed in this volume.

A second factor which might explain regime-specific patterns of influence is the capacity of national ministerial bureaucracies to implement political reforms. Preunkert, Zirra, Jacobsson and West (this volume) observe limited administrative capacities and serious implementation difficulties in Italy and the Baltic states. The EES is a highly bureaucratized and professionalized bargaining process between the national and the European level, in which national ministries are the crucial link. Schnapp (2004) has analysed the influence of ministerial bureaucracies on three different dimensions of political decision making (agenda setting, strategic action, exploitation of the room for manoeuvre) and has shown that this influence is consistently higher in most of the continental European countries, such as France, Belgium, Austria, and Germany – but also in Ireland. In Germany, for example, the strong professional basis of the administration is crucial for their impact on political reforms – and in France the high hierarchical rank of the office which is responsible for the NAP/NRP, is part of the Prime Minister's Office (Preunkert and Zirra, this volume). But in the southern European countries, the agenda-setting capacity of the ministerial bureaucracies and their control of the implementation of political reforms is much weaker – in the Italian case, for example, due to a fragmented political system and unstable forms of policy coordination between different ministries and territorial levels (cf. López-Santana, Preunkert and Zirra, this volume). In the post-socialist countries, too, the gap between adopted legislation and its implementation often is considerable (Mailand, Jacobsson and West, this volume). For the Czech and Slovak Republics, Sirovátka (2008: 25–7) also observes on the one hand a 'broadly recognized legitimacy of activation', but on the other hand a weak implementation due to limited personnel and financial capacities. The impact of the EES in the familialistic and post-socialist countries of southern and eastern Europe therefore may be limited, due to weak administrative capabilities which are not sufficient for a fundamental transformation of strongly segmented labour market structures. The limited organizational capacities of the ministerial bureaucracies, however, may partially be overcome, due to financial incentives or by mutual learning processes. Lopez-Santana, Mailand, Preunkert and Zirra, for example, observe procedural and substantial effects of the EES in Poland, Spain and Italy, due to financial support from the ESF.

The strongest influence of the EES on national employment policies thus can be expected in the conservative 'Bismarckian' countries of continental Europe, where the significant discrepancies between national employment patterns and the EES (due to the relatively high level of public welfare and status-based, exclusionary employment relations), but also the administrative capabilities to face new challenges and use new policy concepts, were both relatively high. These countries try to transform their policies: activation, preventive approach, benchmarking, gender equality, life-long learning, active ageing, and flexicurity are some of the most important aspects of this transformation.

In the case of the OMC/SPSI, the common aspects seem to be more important than the regime-specific features. The legitimation of own reform plans and the strengthening of NGOs in the domestic fields are a major result of the OMC/SPSI in most countries (cf. the chapters of Jacobsson, Johansson, Preunkert, Zirra, Vanhercke and Hamel). In many countries, the national affiliate of the European Anti-Poverty Network has become an important actor, thereby strengthening the link between national and European inclusion policy. This is especially true for social-democratic and liberal countries (Armstrong 2006), but also for Germany, where NGOs could successfully challenge the official view that exclusion is mostly the result of financial poverty – and that social assistance is dealing effectively with this problem (Preunkert and Zirra, this volume). The rather broad objectives of the OMC/SPSI have often inhibited a larger cognitive and substantive impact on domestic inclusion policies. In the continental European countries, however, new topics (child poverty, exclusion of immigrants) were brought to the agenda. Procedural changes have been more important – for example in France and Belgium: Hamel and Vanhercke (this volume) show that the OMC has initiated a culture of monitoring and evaluation in these countries, which is already largely diffused in the Anglo-Saxon countries. Jacobsson and Johansson (this volume) observe in Sweden the strengthening of cooperation between ministries and between social NGOs.

4 Conclusion

The OMC should contribute to mastering one of the central challenges facing EU Member States – the adaptation of national welfare and employment regimes to the conditions of demographic ageing, greater individualization, and deeper economic as well as political integration. Hence, the OMC is located in the tradition of regulatory European social policies: it takes account of Member States' sovereignty and the complexity of national institutional regimes that have evolved largely independently of each other over decades, if not centuries, and thus have developed a considerable momentum.

Each attempt at a supranationally coordinated modernization of domestic welfare and employment regimes must therefore start from the assumption of the operational closure of these national regimes. This does not necessarily mean inertia and immobility: '[M]any European welfare states have ... taken measures in order to redirect economic restructuring and structural [change] by pushing through adjustments in macroeconomic policy, industrial relations, taxation, social security, labour market policy, employment protection legislation, pensions and social services, and welfare financing' (Hemerijck 2007: 24–5). Operational closure signifies, rather, that national employment and welfare regimes change only according to their internal criteria and logics. Consequently, the OMC is an external intervention that is only able to irritate national regimes and domestic fields, but cannot steer them intentionally in the planned direction. We cannot expect a direct implementation of European objectives at national level.

Hence a theory of institutional change is required that neither assumes quasi-automatic mechanisms of institutional isomorphism or direct learning processes between nation-states and their supranational environments, nor perceives the nation-states as institutional regimes that are closed, incapable of change, and determined only by their own history. In order to develop such a perspective, we have sought to combine the concept of social fields (Fligstein 2001a, 2001b) with the analysis of gradual processes of institutional change (Streeck and Thelen 2005). Actors in domestic bargaining arenas may use European coordination processes and objectives as a resource in order to represent their own suggestions and interests more effectively in the domestic arena. Since national institutional regimes are always composed of heterogeneous, inconsistent, and latently controversial logics whose transformation occurs through internal negotiations, the strategic use of external challenges and opportunities may result in a gradual transformation. According to Streeck and Thelen (2005), this can lead to a 'slowly rising salience of subordinate relative to dominant institutions' (displacement), as well as to an overlapping of old by new elements (layering), a disregard or a break-up of outdated regulatory structures (drift or exhaustion), or a new use of pre-existing institutions (conversion).

Analytically, three different types of supranational intervention in domestic arenas can be distinguished: cognitive interventions aim at the establishment and strengthening of new (or existing) orientations and guidelines within the framework of national discursive arenas; strategic interventions aim at the strengthening of 'new' interests, actors, and organizations within the framework of the national action constellations; procedural interventions aim at the transformation of legal, professional, or organizational rules within the framework of the national governance structures.

Through European coordination processes, national employment and welfare regimes have been 'irritated' along these three dimensions. Even if the direct influence of the OMC processes is limited to a small group of European and national top officials and scientists, the EU has succeeded in changing national discourses through new concepts of employment and social welfare. Here key phrases such as flexicurity, active ageing, employability, active labour market policies, and gender mainstreaming have to be mentioned. On the strategic dimension, the EU has succeeded in increasing incentives for the pursuit of the EES through financial support from the European Social Fund. Furthermore, the national arenas have been enlarged by the participation of social partners, non-governmental organizations, regions, and municipalities in the development and implementation of national action and reform plans, thus facilitating the articulation of 'new' interests and perceptions. Empirically, this opportunity has been exploited above all in the field of social inclusion policies. Third, the administrative structures of policy making are also changing. While labour market policies until now have been largely conceived by national labour ministries, numerous ministries (labour, social, education, economy, finance ...) are increasingly being involved in the formulation of more inclusive employment policies.

The question of whether the OMC can effectively shape domestic policies thus cannot be answered by the enumeration of laws that have been legitimized in the domestic arena with reference to European objectives. Labour market and welfare reforms always have several fathers and mothers, above all, if they are successful: national politicians, who sometimes even link their political fate to a project, from which typically only future governments will benefit; national civil servants, who transform the general visions of academics and politicians into administratively feasible legislative proposals; a national–European fusion bureaucracy, which elaborates new options for employment and welfare politics in open, internationally integrated societies, producing attractive visions and conceptual frames, and legitimizes them with reference to actual or alleged foreign success stories; and new European and domestic networks, especially in the field of social protection and social inclusion, which may open up traditional fields of policy making. This is a lot less than the advocates of a 'social Europe' might aspire to – but also much more than the critics of a neoliberal Europe might expect. Either way, the OMC may contribute to the modernization of national welfare and employment regimes in Europe, thereby facilitating the precarious tightrope walk between economic integration and social security which is a basic feature of the European Union.

Note

1 I am grateful to Jenny Preunkert, Jonathan Zeitlin and Sascha Zirra for their suggestions. The usual disclaimers apply. This article has been translated by Marc Rohr.

References

Armstrong, K.A. (2006) 'The "Europeanisation" of Social Exclusion: British Adaptation to EU Coordination', *The British Journal of Politics and International Relations*, 8: 79–100.

Ashiagbor, D. (2005) *The European Employment Strategy: Labour Market Regulation and New Governance*, Oxford: Oxford University Press.

Barbier, J.-C. (2004) *Les méthodes ouvertes de coordination dans le social et l'emploi européennes: comment les aborder?* Online. Available HTTP: www.cee-recherche.fr/fr/fiches_chercheurs/texte_pdf/barbier/BarbierMatisse2004.pdf (accessed 22 July 2008).

—— (2005) 'The European Employment Strategy, a Channel for Activating Social Protection?', in J. Zeitlin and P. Pochet with L. Magnusson (eds) *The Open Method of Coordination in Action: The European Employment and Social Inclusion Strategies*, Brussels: Peter Lang, 417–46.

Begg, I. and Berghman, J. (2002) 'Introduction: EU Social (Exclusion) Policy Revisited?', *Journal of European Social Policy*, 12: 179–94.

Borràs, S. and Jacobsson, K. (2004) 'The Open Method of Co-ordination and New Governance Patterns in the EU', *Journal of European Public Policy*, 11: 185–208.

Börzel, T.A. and Risse, T. (2000) *When Europe Hits Home: Europeanization and Domestic Change.* Online. Available HTTP: http://eiop.or.at/eiop/texte/2000–2015a.htm (accessed 20 June 2008).

Büchs, M. and Friedrich, D. (2005) 'Surface Integration: The National Action Plans for Employment and Social Inclusion in Germany', in J. Zeitlin and P. Pochet with L. Magnusson (eds) *The Open Method of Coordination in Action: The European Employment and Social Inclusion Strategies*, Brussels: Peter Lang, 249–85.

Casey, B.H. and Gold, M. (2005) 'Peer Review of Labour Market Programmes in the European Union: What Can Countries Really Learn from One Another?', *Journal of European Public Policy*, 12: 23–43.

Checkel, J.T. (1999) 'Social Construction and Integration', *Journal of European Public Policy*, 6: 545–60.

Citi, M. and Rhodes, M. (2007) *New Modes of Governance in the EU: Common Objectives versus National Preferences.* Online. Available HTTP: www.connex-network.org/eurogov/pdf/egp-newgov-N-07-01.pdf (accessed 22 June 2008).

Crouch, C. and Farrell, H. (2004) 'Breaking the Path of Institutional Development? Alternatives to the New Determinism', *Rationality and Society*, 16: 5–43.

De la Porte, C. and Pochet, P. (2005) 'Participation in the Open Method of Co-ordination. The Cases of Employment and Social Inclusion', in J. Zeitlin and P. Pochet with L. Magnusson (eds) *The Open Method of Coordination in Action: The European Employment and Social Inclusion Strategies*, Brussels: Peter Lang, 353–90.

Eberlein, B. and Grande, E. (2005) 'Beyond Delegation: Transnational Regulatory Regimes and the EU Regulatory State', *Journal of European Public Policy*, 12: 89–112.

Eberlein, B. and Kerwer, D. (2004) 'New Governance in the European Union: A Theoretical Perspective', *Journal of Common Market Studies*, 42: 121–42.

Esping-Andersen, G. (1999) *Social Foundations of Postindustrial Economies*, Oxford: Oxford University Press.

European Commission (2005) *Cohesion Policy in Support of Growth and Jobs, Community Strategic Guidelines 2007–2013*, Brussels: Commission of the European Communities.

—— (2006) *Time to Move up a Gear, Annual Progress Report on Growth and Jobs*, Brussels: Commission of the European Communities.

Ferrera, M. and Sacchi, S. (2005) 'The Open Method of Co-ordination and National Institutional Capabilities: The Italian Case', in J. Zeitlin and P. Pochet with L. Magnusson (eds) *The Open Method of Coordination in Action: The European Employment and Social Inclusion Strategies*, Brussels: Peter Lang, 137–72.

Ferrera, M., Hemerijck, A. and Rhodes, M. (2000) *The Future of Social Europe. Recasting Work and Welfare in the New Economy*, Oeiras: Celta Editora.

Fligstein, N. (2001a) 'Social Skill and the Theory of Fields', *Sociological Theory*, 19: 105–25.
—— (2001b) *The Architecture of Markets. An Economic Sociology of Twenty-First-Century Capitalist Societies*, Princeton, NJ: Princeton University Press.
Fligstein, N. and Stone Sweet, A. (2002) 'Constructing Polities and Markets: An Institutionalist Account of European Integration', *American Journal of Sociology*, 107: 1206–43.
Friedberg, E. (1997) *Local Orders: Dynamics of Organized Action*, Greenwich: JAI Press.
Hartlapp, M. (2006) *Über Politiklernen lernen. Überlegungen zur Europäischen Beschäftigungsstrategie*. Online. Available HTTP: http://skylla.wzb.eu/pdf/2006/i06–114.pdf (accessed 22 June 2008).
Heidenreich, M. and Bischoff, G. (2008) 'The Open Method of Coordination. A Way to the Europeanization of Social and Employment Policies?', *Journal of Common Market Studies*, 46: 497–532.
Hemerijck, A. (2007) 'Reinventing the Lisbon Imperative of "Double Engagement"', Presentation on the conference on the European Social Model 'Joining forces for a social Europe', Nuremberg, February.
Hemerijck, A. and Visser, J. (2003) 'Policy Learning in European Welfare States', unpublished manuscript, University of Amsterdam.
Héritier, A. (2001) '*New Modes of Governance in Europe: Policy-Making without Legislating?*', Bonn: MPI Collective Goods Preprint No. 2001/14. Online. Available HTTP: http://ssrn.com/abstract = 299431 (accessed 11 September 2008).
Holzinger, K. and Knill, C. (2005) 'Causes and Conditions of Cross-national Policy Convergence', *Journal of European Public Policy*, 12: 775–96.
Höpner, M. (2005) 'What Connects Industrial Relations and Corporate Governance? Explaining Institutional Complementarity', *Socio-Economic Review*, 3: 331–58.
Huber, A. (2006) 'The Impact of the European Employment Strategy on the Labour Market Policies of Germany and France', *Bamberger Beiträge zur Europaforschung und zur internationalen Politik*, 13. Online. Available HTTP: www.uni-oldenburg.de/sozialstruktur/dokumente/beip13.pdf (accessed 22 July 2008).
Idema, T. and Kelemen, D.R. (2006) 'New Modes of Governance, the Open Method of Coordination and other Fashionable Red Herring', *Perspectives on European Politics and Society*, 7: 108–23.
Iversen, T. and Wren, A. (1998) 'Equality, Employment, and Budgetary Restraint: The Trilemma of the Service Economy', *World Politics*, 50: 507–46.
Jacobsson, K. (2004a) 'Soft Regulation and Subtle Transformation of states: The Case of EU Employment Policy', *Journal of European Social Policy*, 14: 355–70.
—— (2004b) 'Between Deliberation and Discipline', in U. Mörth (ed.) *Soft law in Governance and Regulation*, Cheltenham: Edward Elgar.
—— (2005) 'Trying to Reform the "Best Pupils in Class"? – The Open Method of Co-ordination in Sweden and Denmark', in J. Zeitlin and P. Pochet with L. Magnusson (eds) *The Open Method of Coordination in Action: The European Employment and Social Inclusion Strategies*, Brussels: Peter Lang, 107–136.
Jacobsson, K. and Vifell, A. (2007) 'Deliberative Transnationalism? Analysing the Role of Committee Interaction in Soft Co-ordination', in I. Linsenmann, C.O. Meyer and W. Wessels (eds) *Economic Government of the EU. A Balance Sheet of New Modes of Policy Coordination*, Houndmills: Palgrave Macmillan, 163–86.
Knill, C. and Lenschow, A. (2005) 'Compliance, Competition and Communication: Different Approaches of European Governance and their Impact on National Institutions', *Journal of Common Market Studies*, 43: 583–606.

Kok, W. (2004) *Facing the challen£ge*, Luxembourg: Office for Official Publications.
López-Santana, M. (2006) 'The Domestic Implications of European Soft Law: Framing and Transmitting Change in Employment Policy', *Journal of European Public Policy*, 13: 481–99.
Mairate, A. (2006) 'The "Added Value" of European Union Cohesion Policy', *Regional Studies*, 40: 167–77.
Meyer, C. and Umbach, G. (2007) 'Europeanisation of National Economic Governance Through Policy Co-ordination? Gains and Pains of a New Policy Instrument', in I. Linsenmann, C.O. Meyer and W. Wessels (eds) *Economic Government of the EU. A Balance Sheet of New Modes of Policy Coordination*, Houndmills: Palgrave Macmillan, 91–118.
Meyer, J.W. (2000) 'Globalization. Sources and Effects on National States and Societies', *International Sociology*, 15: 233–48.
Meyer, J.W., Boli, J., Thomas, G.M. and Ramirez, F.O. (1997) 'World Society and the Nation-state', *American Journal of Sociology*, 103: 144–81.
Mosher, J.S. and Trubek, D.M. (2003) 'Alternative Approaches to Governance in the EU: EU Social Policy and the European Employment Strategy', *Journal of Common Market Studies*, 41: 63–88.
O'Donnell, R. and Moss, B. (2005) 'Ireland: The Very Idea of an Open Method of Co-ordination', in J. Zeitlin and P. Pochet with L. Magnusson (eds) *The Open Method of Coordination in Action: The European Employment and Social Inclusion Strategies*, Brussels: Peter Lang, 311–52.
Radaelli, C. (2003a) *The Open Method of Coordination: A New Governance Architecture for the European Union?*, Swedish Institute for European Policy Studies. Online. Available HTTP: www.epin.org/pdf/RadaelliSIEPS. pdf (accessed 22 July 2008).
—— (2003b) 'The Europeanization of Public Policy', in K. Featherstone and C. Radaelli (eds) *The Politics of Europeanization*, Oxford: Oxford University Press.
Sabel, C.F. and Zeitlin, J. (2008): 'Learning from Difference: The New Architecture of Experimentalist Governance in the European Union', *European Law Journal*, 14: 271–327.
Sacchi, S. (2004) 'New Modes of Governance in the EU and Italy's Institutional Capability. A Comparison of Employment and Social Inclusion Policies', *Rivista Italiana di Politiche Pubbliche*, 3: 5–35.
Schäfer, A. (2006) 'A New Form of Governance? Comparing the Open Method of Co-ordination to Multilateral Surveillance by the IMF and the OECD', *Journal of European Public Policy*, 13: 70–88.
Scharpf, F. and Schmidt, V.A. (eds) (2000) *Welfare and Work in the Open Economy*, Vol. I: *From Vulnerability to Competitiveness*, Oxford: Oxford University Press.
Scharpf, F.W. (1999): *Governing in Europe. Effective and Democratic*, Oxford: Oxford University Press.
—— (2002) 'The European Social Model: Coping with the Challenges of Diversity', *Journal of Common Market Studies*, 40: 645–70.
Schmid, G. and Gazier, B. (2002) *The Dynamics of Full Employment: Social Integration through Transitional Labour Markets*, Cheltenham: Edward Elgar.
Schnapp, Kai-Uwe, (2004) *Ministerialbürokratien in westlichen Demokratien*. Opladen: Leske + Budrich.
Sirovátka, T. (2008) 'Activation Policies Under Conditions of Weak Governance: Czech and Slovak Cases Compared', *Central European Journal of Public Policy*, 2: 4–29.

Streeck, W. and Thelen, K. (2005) 'Introduction: Institutional Change in Advanced Political Economies', in W. Streeck and K. Thelen (eds) *Beyond Continuity*, Oxford, New York: Oxford University Press, 1–40.

Tholoniat, L. (2001) 'L'administration française et la stratégie européenne pour l'emploi: Jeux de légitimité et enjeux de gouvernance', unpublished paper. Online. Available HTTP: http://eucenter.wisc.edu/OMC/open12.html (accessed 22 July 2008).

Trubek, D.M. and Trubek, L.G. (2005) 'The Open Method of Coordination and the Debate over "Hard" and "Soft" Law', in J. Zeitlin and P. Pochet with L. Magnusson (eds) *The Open Method of Coordination in Action: The European Employment and Social Inclusion Strategies*, Brussels: Peter Lang, 83–106.

Zeitlin, J. (2005) 'Conclusion: The Open Method of Coordination in Action: Theoretical Promise, Empirical Realities, Reform Strategy', in J. Zeitlin and P. Pochet with L. Magnusson (eds) *The Open Method of Coordination in Action: The European Employment and Social Inclusion Strategies*, Brussels: Peter Lang, 447–503.

Zeitlin, J. Pochet, P. with Magnusson, L. (eds) (2005) *The Open Method of Coordination in Action: The European Employment and Social Inclusion Strategies*, Brussels: Peter-Lang.

Zirra, S. and Buchkremer, J. (2007) 'Learning within Fields: The Limited Success of the European Employment Strategy in Germany', *European Spatial Research and Policy*, 14: 63–84.

2 Neither convergence nor frozen paths

Bounded learning, international diffusion of reforms, and the Open Method of Coordination[1]

Jelle Visser

> The bad news is that the labour market does not function as we might wish it did … The good news is that today we have a better idea than we did not so long ago of what the best practices are in order to fight unemployment and create jobs. These best practices are not easy to apply, for they do not yield spectacular results in the short term, and inevitably arouse opposition, sometimes legitimate opposition from vested interests … The role of the politician is to overcome these difficulties …
>
> (Cahuc and Zylberberg 2006: 125)

Introduction: the double shift in employment policy

In November 1997, Europe's leaders launched the European Employment Strategy (EES). Based on the new employment title of the Amsterdam Treaty, they hoped to emulate the success of the Maastricht convergence criteria, using similar methods of putting pressure on Member States to improve employment performance, albeit without the possibility of formal sanctions. The EES marked a *double shift* in employment policy: it strove *to end two decades of restrictive supply policies* with which European politicians had responded to the job crisis; and it was the first attempt to engage EU Member States in an *internationally coordinated policy.*

Allan Larsson, then Director-General of Employment and Social Affairs at the Commission, described the new European approach to unemployment as a 'radical policy reorientation … replacing the old "wait and see" attitude – the politics of passivity – with a new active, preventive policy' (Larsson 1998: 402). The new policy engaged European politicians in a *common effort* to combat long-term unemployment *and* increase labour market participation, reversing the many policies (more and longer benefits for older, disabled, and long-term unemployed workers; delaying the entry into the labour force or bringing forward retirement; general rounds of working-time reduction) with which many people in working age had been eased out of the labour market. In the 1990s these policies became widely seen as *policy failure* and, if continued, a *threat* to the survival of the European welfare state.

This chapter analyses the multiple policy and learning effects of the new approach. It starts, in the next section, with a brief presentation of the background and operation of the EES and its older sister, the OECD Job Strategy. In the absence of binding sanctions, and with weak financial incentives, mutual learning and discursive diffusion, together with peer pressure, are the most plausible among the mechanisms of influence on Member States (Knill and Lehmkuhl 2002). The comparative case studies of Sweden, Denmark, the UK, the Netherlands, Germany, Italy, and France in Zeitlin and Pochet (2005) revealed four mechanisms for domestic influence: *peer pressure*, i.e. reputation loss through naming and shaming; socialization and *discursive diffusion* of the new 'activation' and 'flexicurity' discourses; *mutual learning* of 'best' or 'good' practices; and the *strategic use* of European policies as a 'lever' by domestic actors, for instance as a means to gain more financial resources for public employment services (Zeitlin 2005: 476–7). My focus, in this chapter is on the role of discursive diffusion and mutual learning. Section 2 outlines the theory of policy learning, diffusion and convergence, and offers three key hypotheses on the dynamics of learning and diffusion applied to employment policy. Sections 3–5 review the evidence for these hypotheses. Section 6 summarizes the chapter and draws conclusions.

1 The EES: the best of both worlds?

Between the mid-1970s and mid-1990s employment ratios and unemployment rates in the OECD, in particular between its European and non-European members, diverged (Saint-Paul 2004). This is an indication of *different* policy choices and the *absence* of international policy coordination. As has been shown by Scharpf (1991, 2000), confronted with similar economic difficulties, policy responses to the jobs crisis were predominantly shaped by *national* vulnerabilities and *domestic* capabilities for policy coordination between governments, monetary authorities, trade unions, and employers (Scharpf 1991, 2000). Many European countries conducted a policy of job sharing and limiting labour supply, and there were no EU-coordinated policies on employment.[2]

The first attempt at intergovernmental coordination came from the OECD Job Study, which was mostly directed at its European members. Alarmed by the relative falling behind of Europe's economies, Jean-Claude Paye, OECD General Secretary, had already in 1988 sought a mandate to review Member policies and offer prescriptions for change. This mandate was given in 1992 and two years later, in 1994, the OECD issued its nine commandments for policy reform, all but three targeted at the labour market: increase working time flexibility; make wage and labour costs more flexible; reform employment security provisions; strengthen active labour market policies; improve labour market skills; and reform unemployment and related benefit systems (OECD 1994: 43).

Meanwhile, the European Commission, alarmed by rising joblessness in the 1992–93 recession and popular anxiety in the aftermath of Maastricht (1992), had produced its own analysis of Europe's faltering economy (EC 1993). In Essen in 1994, Europe's leaders for the first time ever devoted a summit meeting to unemployment. The break-through came in the Amsterdam Intergovernmental Conference of June 1997, when a new Employment Chapter was added to the Treaty and Commission and Council were charged with the task of promoting a coordinated strategy for employment. Preparing the special Employment Summit in Luxembourg later that year, the Commission had wanted to establish specific unemployment targets, similar to the EMU convergence criteria decided in Maastricht, but this was rejected by a majority of leaders. Instead they settled for a 'mutual surveillance procedure', combined with peer reviews but without specific targets or legal sanctions. The result was a compromise between pressure for increased EU action and opposition against expanding EU competence (Trubek and Mosher 2003: 38).

Since its inception the EES has been changed twice. The first time was in 2000, when the EES became tied to the Lisbon Agenda and a set of quantitative targets and timetables concerning employment levels was added, together with statistical indicators for the purpose of benchmarking. Prompted by critical reviews of EU employment policy and the entire Lisbon process,[3] the EES was again revised in 2004–5. The employment guidelines became part of a package of 24 guidelines for structural reform, to be presented and evaluated in conjunction with the macro- and microeconomic guidelines as part of the Lisbon Strategy for Growth and Jobs.

Despite differences (Casey 2002; Noaksson and Jacobsson 2003; Sapir 2005), the OECD Job Strategy and the EES pull in the same direction. The main social policy objective is to engineer a shift from income protection to participation in the labour market. The discourse of activation, aimed at changing the behaviour of the unemployed and increasing their individual responsibility for job search while reducing dependency on public support, is a key feature of both campaigns. They also share the analysis that Europe's product and labour markets were too protected, hampering growth, innovation and employment; that unemployment was, by a large measure, structural; and that over-protective employment legislation worked to the detriment of employment chances of women, the young, the old, the unskilled, and ethnic minorities. The differences are that the EES softened its reform proposals with language that emphasizes the need for social cohesion, while the OECD, until 2004 when it revised its position (OECD, 2006), had been more outspoken in its judgement that wage bargaining should decentralize in order to reflect local conditions, skill levels and productivity. Overall, however, the similarities are greater than the differences.

The governance methods of the two campaigns share many similarities. Both rely on persuasion, recommendations, and policy review procedures. In the case of the OECD this involves direct contacts between the organization and Member States via so-called 'country desks'. The EES involves to a greater extent horizontal processes of mutual influence and learning, for instance through participation in the Employment Committee (EMCO), the mutual learning process, and the involvement of social partners at European and national level (EC 2006). Top civil servants and advisers of ministers of EU

Member States meet six times per year in EMCO, which is charged with responsibility for advising the Council and the Commission on the Joint Employment Report and organizes a special (Cambridge) review of Member States' reforms. The Mutual Learning Programme has its legal basis in Article 129 EC Treaty, according to which the Council 'may adopt incentive measures designed to encourage cooperation among Member States and to support their action in the field of employment through initiatives aimed at developing exchanges of information and best practices, providing comparative analysis and advice as well as promoting innovative approaches and evaluating experiences, in particular by recourse to pilot projects'. Peer review workshops for the purpose of exchanging 'best practice' information started in 1999. The Mutual Learning Programme was revised in 2004 into a rotating half-yearly schedule divided between one broadly attended seminar and three peer review workshops. On the invitation of the Commission and recommendation of EMCO, one Member State hosts the peer review and others join on a voluntary basis.[4]

The Employment Chapter in the Amsterdam Treaty is based on the idea that national governments and the EU *share responsibility* for achieving particular outcomes, and has for this purpose expanded the EU employment policy toolkit (EU law; social dialogue and the European Social Fund) with common guidelines, targets, common indicators, benchmarking, peer reviews, recommendations, and best practice learning (Kilpatrick 2006). Responsibility for employment policy remains in the hands of national policy makers, their only obligation being to participate in the EES review procedure. They cannot be forced, however, to follow the Council's advice. The success of such an approach is predicated on the assumption that Member States will be *motivated* to learn about more effective policies because they jointly and individually *benefit* from the adoption of better policies; or, failing that, they will jointly and individually *suffer*. This assumption is implicit in the Commission's admonition that 'Member States which are moving forward more slowly with reform need to close the gap with those setting the pace, for the benefit of all'[5] and echoes the claim in the second Kok Report that EU Member States are in the same boat and that reforms in one will raise the level for all. The OECD is more cautious in claiming reform spillover. Its approach is that countries should reform for self-interested reasons and that the failure to implement reform is irrational or, in the words of its chief economist, 'paradoxical because the effectiveness of good labour market policies is there for all to see and emulate'.[6]

These claims overstate their case. Alesina and Perotti (2004) suggest that the European Commission, wanting to expand its role, tends to exaggerate policy interdependence for self-serving reasons. In some studies the economic effects of reforms are found to be negligible, even between neighbouring countries, like Germany and the Netherlands, that trade heavily with one another (Ederveen et al. 2005). It may be irrelevant for Sweden or Ireland whether Italy or Spain do or do not reform their labour market. The effects may be so small that they do not justify the costs of engaging in a cumbersome process of policy coordination. In a recent assessment, the European Commission admits that Common Policy Frameworks like the EES may be more useful for propagating *common thinking* than *common action*: they are 'successful in allowing Member States and the Community to define common goals; but less so in stimulating the necessary degree of ambition and policy efforts to reach these goals'.[7]

Hodson and Maher (2001) emphasize the merits of decentralization and soft policy coordination based on learning and persuasion in policy domains where there is considerable *uncertainty* about what the best policy is. The danger of imposing the wrong, one-size-fits-all solution on diverse national economies is thus kept at a minimum, at the price of a certain degree of indecisiveness. Their position resembles the theory of *laboratory federalism*, advanced by William Oates. That theory turns on two propositions that are crucial for international learning. First, '[i]n a setting of imperfect information with learning-by-doing, there are potential gains from experimentation with a variety of policies for addressing social and economic problems' (Oates 1999: 1132). Second, according to Oates, there are considerable merits in a system that allows conducting policy experiments at a lower level and contains the risks of failure to a smaller part of the polity, while the central level can perform the public good of disseminating the lessons from these experiments. Both elements are most prominently present in the Mutual Learning Programme.

Decentralized approaches operating through horizontal peer networks without central authority have the advantage that ideas and technologies can be 'modified by users as they fit their particular conditions' (Rogers 1983 [1962]: 334). The downside is that 'bad innovations can spread due to lack of quality control' and the 'big picture' gets lost 'due to the absence of a coordinator'. Moreover, local decision makers will not innovate because others tell them, but only when they see the need for it (ibid.: 338). Local environments, in our case Member States, may get stuck with substandard solutions. A combined approach with targets, a high level of professionalism, and local knowledge forced to talk in a convergent model of communication, based on shared problem definitions and transparent performance indicators, may produce the best of both worlds.

Surely, such *hybrids* create tensions. Common problem definitions and targets give focus and ambition to the search process, but they may also limit the range of search and unduly discard information (Eckard 2005). For instance, by focusing on a quantitative target of more jobs, the search for policies generating better, more productive or more satisfying jobs may be reduced. Benchmarking techniques can help to identify promising examples for better policies, but if solutions are interpreted out of context they may encourage uncritical and counterproductive following of trends, or 'mimicking' (Hemerijck and Visser 2001). Ambitious targets, comparative statistics, and international benchmarking can play a key role in making policy failure more visible and politicians less complacent, and they can inform both politicians and voters about opportunities for greater social welfare and improved performance. However, procedures that help participants to keep their data honest by allowing for second opinions and contested claims are crucial (Campbell 1977).

2 Learning, diffusion, and convergence

Policy learning happens, according to Peter Hall (1993: 278), when political decision makers 'assimilate new information, including that on past performance' and 'apply it to their subsequent actions', evidenced in a revision of policy goals or instruments, or, more fundamentally, the 'paradigms or frameworks that defines the very nature of the problems they are meant to be addressing' (Hall 1993: 279). Policy learning need not be based on systematic evaluation of rival policies, but usually happens unplanned, operating through day-to-day policies and triggered by events, failures, deadlines, shining successes of others, and international pressure. Learning processes in politics are difficult, since they involve a change of norms and practices that were successful in the past and attracted often 'unthinking' loyalty and support – in short, involved problem descriptions, norms and practices that were institutionalized. Institutional change brings uncertainty and anxiety. This is why failure of the 'status quo', dissociating powerful interests from extant institutions, is crucial for learning and reform.

The orientation of actors is critical to learning; they must be receptive to new information and open to modifying prior beliefs. Learning is indicated when some actors give a *different* response to problems than they did in the past. Following Heclo's powerful metaphor, reform is the outcome of *puzzling* – diagnosing the nature and magnitude of the problems, setting priorities, and identifying potentially effective policy solutions – and of *powering* – organizing the political and societal support for the selection of particular solutions (Heclo 1974: 305). These are not separate or parallel activities, but constantly interrupt each other, and reformers must puzzle a good deal about powering, i.e. how to gain the support for their preferred policy choices (Ferrera and Gualmini 2004). Vivien Schmidt (2000) has extended this argument and argued that reform in an area crowded with vested interests and norms of moral appropriateness, as in the domain we are dealing with here, is unlikely unless reformers succeed in disseminating a policy discourse justifying the reform on intellectual *and* moral grounds, and persuade others to see problems in a new light.

The learning effect of the OECD Job Strategy and the EES is based on exposing national policy makers to a *new definition of the problem*, thus allowing them to learn something new. Figure 2.1 visualizes the influence chain from international agency to problem definition, policies and outcomes. The greatest effect of participation in the EES or OECD Job Strategy is on what I call, following North (2005), the collectively *shared mental map* with which national policy makers define the problem. Generally, the EES engages

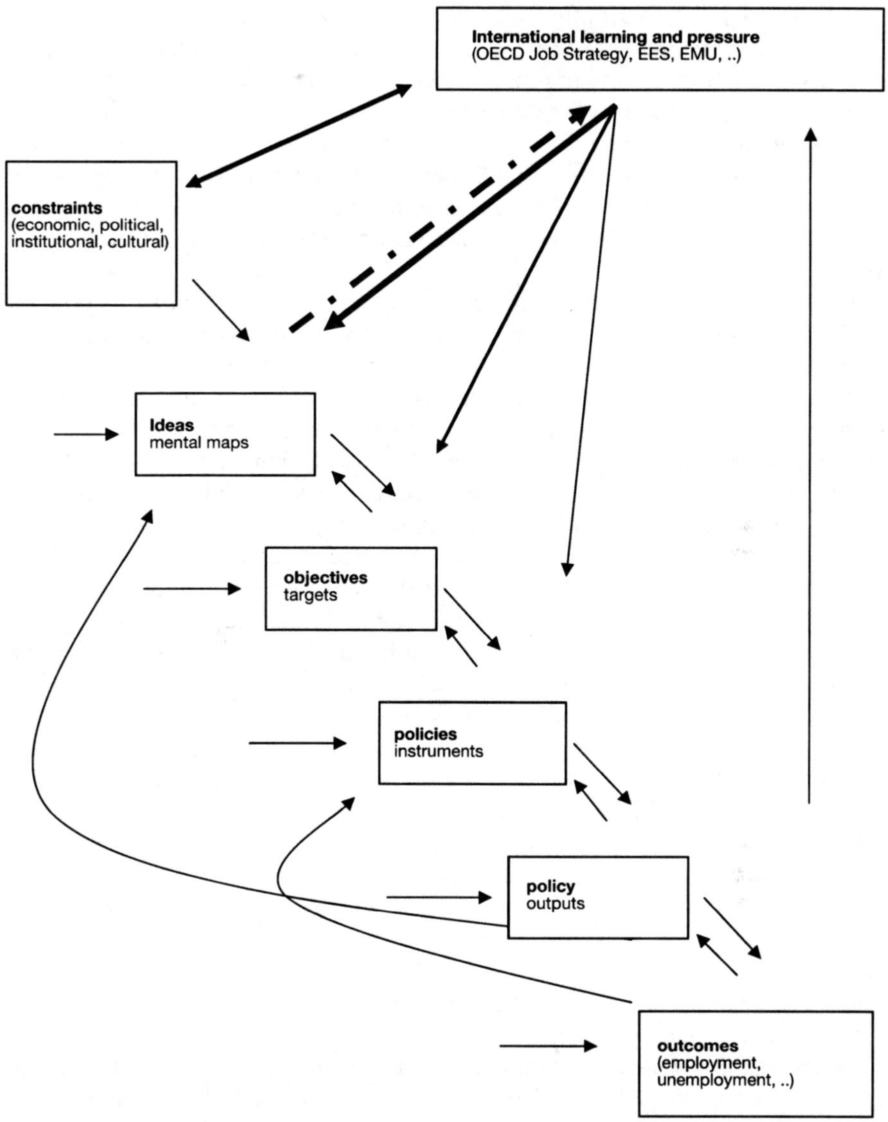

Figure 2.1 International learning, policy chains and convergence

in 'management by objective' rather than 'management by regulation'. We should therefore expect the EES to influence objectives, targets, and ambitions rather that actual policies, outputs, or outcomes. However, through the Mutual Learning Programme and on a voluntary basis, the EES also stimulates *cross-national* learning about the nature and value of policies and reforms.

I do not expect that all influence travels exclusively through the EES or that its influence is distinct from that of the OECD. Moreover, other EU policies and decisions (market integration, EMU, labour law, migration) change the context and opportunities for domestic policy choice. Finally, learning in the EES or OECD is not a one-way street, nor are Member States passive receptors. Member States often try to 'upload' their views and policies to the European level in order to gain advantage and minimize adjustment costs (Börzel and Risse 2003), though such attempts may backfire (Hamel and Vanhercke, this volume).

In her stimulating overview of the role of ideas and discourse in politics, Vivien Schmidt advocates research on how ideas travel 'from thought to word to deed' (Schmidt 2008). The first part ('from thought to word') is the main business of the interaction in committees like EMCO as the intermediary between national and European policies. As an instance of policy learning, we should find growing convergence in the concepts and language used in describing and justifying policy problems and solutions. The second part ('from word to deed') is a long channel of transmissions, each subject to external pressures and with feedback learning that is easily distorted or disturbed (Pierson 2004). Even if it is true that the EES narrowed the range of permissible policies, as Ashiagbor (2004) claims, and EU leaders can no longer freely choose the policies they favour, convergence of outcomes is probably 'contingent', reflecting and even fostering 'regime-specific' policies that take into account entrenched national capacities and sensitivities (Hemerijck 2007).

International reform campaigns like the OECD Job Strategy and the EES are based on the simple truth that, just as policy failures provide information about *what not to do*, policy successes elsewhere provide information about *what might have been done instead*. In a world of open borders and pervasive information flows, full of international organizations and rating agencies, it would be exceptional if reform, and learning associated with reform, were solely motivated and informed by domestic problems and knowledge. Jagdish Baghwati (cited in Meseguer 2005: 41) claims that 'learning by others' doing and one's own undoing' is probably the most common form of education in international politics.

Observing *convergence* in outcomes and *similar* policy responses is not proof that domestic policy makers learned or borrowed policy solutions from each other. 'Situations where actors are acting independently of one another, but where their decision-making environments share important components, can often be difficult to distinguish from genuine imitation', writes Hedström (1998: 309–10), citing Weber's example that people putting up their umbrella at the start of a rain shower do not respond to each other but react similarly to the same need for protection. Genuine diffusion differs from such contingent actions in that one actor's behaviour is the impetus for another's. This may be understood in the direct sense of a policy successfully tried in one country and subsequently imported by another, or more indirectly as a process of discursive diffusion based on posing new questions to old problems, which subsequently encourages the search for new solutions. A better weather forecast – to stay with Weber's metaphor – tells more people when they should bring their umbrella. Diffusion may thus spark learning, even *learning ahead of failure*.

Diffusion is a social process in which the 'prior adoption of a trait or practice in a population alters the probability of adoption for remaining non-adopters' (Strang 1991: 325). The typical S-curve, identified by Everett Rogers, tells us that the rate of adoption of new technologies increases with the number that have already adopted those technologies, until a levelling off when more resistant or far-away participants must be reached. Such dynamics obviously depend on the 'openness' or lack of segregation in the system. In our case, we may think of production or welfare-state regimes, or even language, as barriers to diffusion. Moreover, in international politics, we can think of two ways in which a new policy can change the probability of adoption. First, the new policy may change the *value* of that policy for others, provoking a policy adjustment by neighbours, partners or competitors. Second, the new policy may impart *information* about its problem-solving qualities and thus provoke learning (Elkins and Simmons (2005: 39). The EES or OECD Job Strategy, I believe, is closer to the second type – diffusion through learning.

Diffusion and learning produce convergence through feedback from one's own or others' experience. Convergence has been understood as an indicator of *rational* or unbounded policy learning in which political decision makers weigh all information on better policies through feedback and best-practice learning (Meseguer 2005).[8] But this assumes that problems are the same, conditions similar, and solutions fungible. Learning from neighbours must produce convergence only on the condition that all neighbourhoods from which information is drawn are connected (Bala and Goshal 1998). EU Member States face both common and differing problems, and the economic and political contexts in which these problems must be solved are only partly connected and comparable across countries. National capabilities for effective policies,and vulnerabilities, differ, meaning that similar problems often require different solutions in order to attain the same outcome (Scharpf 2000).

The next three sections discuss the EES and mutual learning in relation to three specific hypotheses: learning is mainly failure driven, occurs when and where problems are most pressing, and results in convergence; cognitive diffusion and the construction of a new collective mental map rather than cumulating errors constitute the switchboard for 'path-breaking' learning and reform; and cross-national learning triggers learning and reform in most-similar clusters of countries.

3 Reform and learning are driven by policy failure

In politics, crisis situations function as catalysts for non-routine policy learning. They tend to focus the mind and allow the mobilization of extraordinary resources. In Hall's scheme, repeated failure will eventually move political decision makers from first-order learning (i.e. attempts to improve the working of existing policy instruments) through second-order learning (the introduction of new policy instruments) to third-order learning, involving a radical reorientation in 'the hierarchy of goals and set of instruments employed to guide policy' (Hall 1993: 284). Third-order learning tends to be accompanied by a 'shift in the locus of authority over policy' (ibid.). Hall's example was the shift from Keynesian to monetarist macroeconomic management in the UK during the 1970s and 1980s. I contend that the decision to reorient policies from 'management of unemployment' to 'activation' and 'participation' is of similar magnitude – involving a new way of thinking about employment and social policy, and leading to a rearrangement of power between the agencies responsible for job placement, social insurance, and assistance, along with an increased role of market provision and less trade union influence.

When the EES was launched, unemployment averaged 10% of the labour force. The employment–working population ratio had fallen below 60%.[9] With an employment ratio 12 points below the USA and an unemployment rate twice as high, Europe compared very unfavourably. Four specific European ailments were: long-term unemployment (nearly 9 million of the 19 million unemployed were out of a job for more than a year); high levels of youth unemployment (22.1%); the low employment rates of women (51.5%) and of people aged between 55 and 64 (35.5%).

From the outset, it was decided that the new employment strategy should produce results in five years. National evaluations for the EU15 were finished in 2002. In its synthesis report the European Commission cited statistics on employment growth since 1998 and on falling levels of unemployment as proof of the policy's success, and claimed that the EES had led to a higher priority for employment among national policy makers and produced convergence towards successful policies.[10] The strongest argument in favour of a positive EES effect, combined with the stability created by the EMU, was that the employment losses during the 2002–3 downturn were much smaller than they had been in 1992–93. However, the downward turn of the economy and rising unemployment after 2001 showed that outcomes depended strongly on the general state of the economy.

The Commission's evaluation had little impact on what happened next (Zeitlin 2005). In 2003, the Council did not buy the Commission's judgement that the strategy was working – Europe was still far off the Lisbon targets and many Member States were moving very slowly or not at all in the right direction. Some Member States – a coalition including most of the time the UK, the Netherlands, Denmark, Sweden, and Ireland – expressed fears that the strategy had become fudged, with too many objectives (Mailand 2006). The Council decided to commission its own evaluation, prepared by a special Task Force on Employment. In its report the Task Force endorsed the strategy, advocating more urgency and focus on the main message: increase adaptability (read: flexibility) of firms and workers; attract more people to the labour market (read: decrease disincentives to participation, based on high labour taxes, benefits, easy exits or failing services); invest more in people and training (read: stop talking about job quality, focus on the quality of people instead); and ensure effective implementation (read: reform the public employment service and commit trade unions, employers, and local government to reform). Wim Kok, the Task Force's chair, saw his mission as bolstering the 'will to reform', in particular in Germany, which at the time was seen as critical to the whole European reform enterprise.[11] In order to succeed, he had to preset the Lisbon objectives as credible and the EES as failing its objectives, thus imparting a sense of crisis and urgency.

The year 2003 represented a difficult moment, and developments have since turned out more positively. Unemployment has dropped to 7.4% in 2007 and the employment ratio has climbed to 65.5%. Long-term unemployment is now averaging 3.5%, down from 4.8% in 1997. Youth unemployment has decreased but still affects one in six under the age of 25. Employment of older workers and women has risen, but is still off target. In its assessment over the past three years, EMCO has been very optimistic: 'With employment growth seeing its steepest improvement since 2000 combined with the increase in labour productivity growth, the Lisbon strategy is delivering results … With ten years of experience of employment policy coordination through the EES and three years along the cycle of the revised Lisbon strategy, the empirical evidence shows that the instruments are adequate to work towards more and better jobs.'[12] The Commission, too, is positive, albeit with reservations: 'Three years after it was relaunched in 2005, the Lisbon Growth and Job Strategy is working … , though some Member States have responded more robustly than others and some signs of "reform fatigue" have become apparent over the last twelve months.'[13] These conclusions need some qualification in view of the limited convergence, shown in Figure 2.2, the still very high youth unemployment rate, and the stagnation in productivity and real wage growth, which undermines support for reform.

Clearly, the performance of the northern group (Finland, Sweden, Denmark, the Netherlands) was different at the start of the EES. While this group, together with Ireland and the UK, has lowered long-term unemployment rates to 1–1.5%, the gap with the continental group (France, Germany, Belgium, Austria) has widened. There was a spectacular improvement in long-term unemployment rates in the south, especially in Spain and Italy (Greece and Portugal are the other countries in this group), but the gap is far from closed. The difference is further accentuated by the much higher employment ratios for older workers in the north-west – averaging near 60%, with the two laggards in this group, Ireland and the Netherlands, rapidly catching up. Low employment rates for older workers – the effect of restrictive supply-side policies in the past – have remained a problem in continental and southern Europe and have, together with long-term unemployment, *become* a problem in east-central Europe (here: Poland, Hungary, Czech Republic, Slovakia).

How much of what countries might have learned from their participation in the OECD Job Strategy and EES was translated into policy reforms?

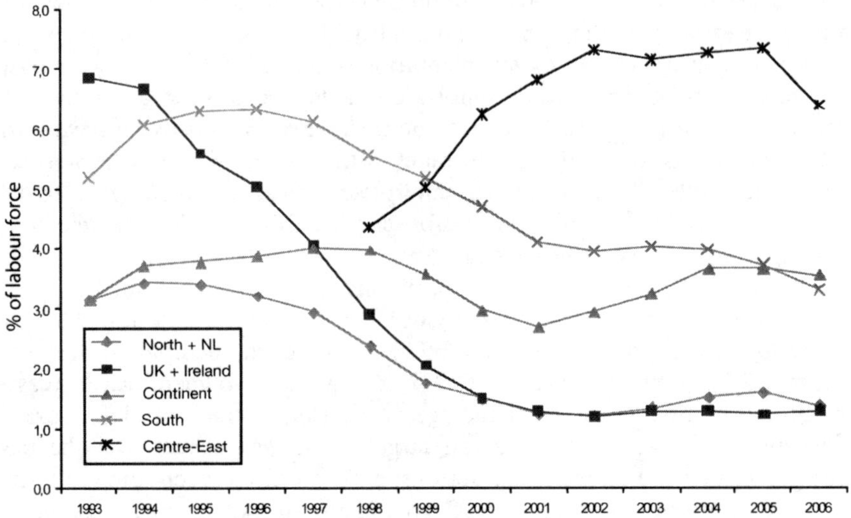

Figure 2.2 Long-term unemployment rates

Armingeon and Beyeler (2004) edited a collection of case studies investigating the OECD's influence on national policies and could find few direct effects. As part of the assessment of Ten Years OECD Job Strategy, Brandt et al. (2005) constructed a composite indicator of policy reforms. This 'broad brush picture' puts Denmark and the Netherlands at the top, followed by Finland, Germany, and Italy. During these 10 years Denmark introduced twice as many reforms as did France and Greece, and almost three times as many as Spain. Brandt et al. also observed higher average reform intensity in EU Member States as compared to the non-EU members of the OECD. This may reflect the additional effect of the EES, but also the Job Strategy's focus on reform in Europe.

The Social Policy Reform Inventory, maintained by Tito Boeri at the Rodolfo Debenedetti Foundation, distinguishes between 'marginal' and 'radical' reforms. Radical reforms must pass the double test of 1) changing replacement rates by more than 10%, affecting existing rather than future entitlements, and 2) changing actual behaviour of the actors or population most affected by the reform, observed in time series research (Boeri et al. 2005). This distinction may be less clear cut than it seems, because many small reforms, when going in the same direction and changing the parameters for adjacent policy fields, may add up to radical departures from the past (Visser and Hemerijck 1997; Hinrichs and Kangas 2003). On Boeri's criterion, 95% of all reforms between 1985 and 2002 were 'marginal'. From this inventory we can learn that the reform intensity increased after 1997 and that the ratio of reforms offering less employment protection and benefit generosity, as compared to those offering more, rose from 0.93 in 1985–90 to 1.25 in 1990–96 and 1.63 in 1997–2002. This might be seen as evidence that, on average, Member States followed the new policy orientation embodied in the EES and OECD Job Strategy, and that reforms were more focused on the flexibility than the security side of the new 'flexicurity' approach.[14]

The idea that Member States with the highest 'problem intensity' (i.e., those with the highest level of structural unemployment) demonstrate the highest 'reform intensity' is not borne out by the facts. The countries that managed more reforms between 1994 and 2004 were not those that suffered from the highest levels of structural unemployment. 'Overall, there is little evidence of a link between initial conditions and subsequent reform efforts, with some countries taking only modes measures despite a poor starting point, while others carrying out ambitious programmes even though their initial conditions were already favourable' (Brandt et al. 2005: 2). On this count, we must reject the hypothesis that failure drives reform. The opposite hypothesis, maintained by Hemerijck and Visser (1999), that initial policy success, breaking the pessimism of failure and offering prospects of job growth, create the political and intellectual precondition for further reforms, appears closer to the facts.

Quantitative data on reforms and outcomes miss a great deal of what happens in between. Qualitative case studies are better placed to trace the process from problems to learning to policies to outcomes, but have the disadvantage of selection bias and limited comparability. With regard to the EES and other OMC processes, de la Porte and Pochet (2002) and Zeitlin and Pochet (2005) offer two collections of case studies. The first authors followed the 'failure produces learning' hypothesis that the strongest (learning and reform) response to the EES was likely to come from Member States which, in their performance, were most distant from the EES policy goals. They predicted that the EES would receive strong responses from continental and southern Member States, a marginal response from the UK and Ireland, and no response in the north (recall Figure 2.2). Their study covered only the first few years and may have come too early for testing the hypothesis.

The case studies in Zeitlin and Pochet (2005) cover the period up to 2004. It turned out that the EES hardly played a role in labour market reforms in Sweden and Denmark. These countries were, rather, the source of inspiration for the EES. The Netherlands, too, saw its own policies more as an export product, though on one or two occasions it did change its policies in response to the EES. In Britain, the New Deal for the Unemployed, started under the Conservatives and developed when New Labour gained power, preceded the EES, while elements that did not fit New Labour's agenda were ignored. The case studies of Germany, Italy, and France showed a mixed response, varying from initial resistance (Germany) to marginal adjustment or formal adherence (France), and a political and variable use of the EES in Italy. Heidenreich and Bischoff (2008) showed that after 2002, with Agenda 2010, German policy makers bought into the EES diagnosis, whereas the French, under similar pressure of high structural and much higher youth unemployment, did not.

The reluctance of France to adopt the new message of the OECD or EES was manifested in the unease over the 'activation' agenda (Barbier 2005). Summing up the evidence, we cannot affirm the hypothesis that failure, learning, reform, and convergence are directly and positively related. It is plausible that learning and failure are related, but to travel 'from thought to words to deeds' is a political enterprise in which each Member State faces different conditions and difficulties for coalition building and normative consensus. There appears to be more support for the idea that early reformers gained an advantage all along, in part by uploading their ideas and policies to the EU level.

4 Cognitive diffusion as a switchboard for 'path-breaking' learning

Limited convergence in reform activity or outcomes does not rule out discursive diffusion and mutual learning. Though there is not much evidence of direct policy transfer based on 'best practice' identification (Zeitlin 2005), the EES is believed to have produced collective learning by engaging Member States in joint problem identification and inviting politicians to revise their past policy choices 'in the light of others as well as in the light of the common framework' (Jacobsson 2005: 108). Processes of cognitive diffusion through participation in a joint policy programme can act as switchboards for 'path breaking' learning and overcome some of the known difficulties of experience-based learning in politics.

There are also *cognitive* grounds for expecting bounded or path-dependent learning. We learn in relation to problems we recognize as *ours.* Confronted with problems and things we don't know or understand, we form expectations based on what we do know or believe. These priors are based on expectations and solutions that have stood their test in the past; they become the mental maps with which we confront the world (Holland et al. 1986). In society and in politics, change of mental maps involves not only a process of 'unlearning' or tearing down past mental maps, but also sharing a new one – in politics and social life many actors must have understood and learned the new rules before they can be played and operate as a new cognitive structure (Denzau and North 1994).

The shift from 'managing unemployment' to 'mobilizing for growth and jobs' was a major policy reorientation, which required new thinking. This took a protracted fight over words like 'activation', 'inclusion', 'employability', and 'flexicurity' in EMCO. For many Member States and politicians this equalled path-breaking cognitive and normative change, not as the last phase in a process of increased policy failure, as proposed by Hall, but determined by continued participation in an international structure for policy learning and information exchange, with clear 'leaders' in the struggle for ideas, in part based on the acclaimed successes of the policies they had enacted. Based on his survey of committee members, Nedergaard (2006) has shown that these leaders came overwhelmingly from Denmark, Sweden, Finland, the UK, and the Netherlands.[15] Adoption of the new problem description and of the policies based on that description increased over time, with more countries introducing reforms – as, for instance, in the cases of activation and reforms of the public employment service (PES). In the next section session we will see that this produced a great deal of *hybridization*.

5 Cross-national learning triggers learning and reform in most-similar clusters of countries

Discursive diffusion is of great importance for seeing policy challenges, deficits and solutions in a new light and preparing politicians for a fresh understanding of problems. But shared mental maps may also be constraining, and limit learning from others to a programme for mimicking preconceived policy solutions. There is always the risk that new ideas and approaches coming from abroad are copied out of context (Dolowitz and March 2000). Like all humans, political decision makers may want to keep it simple, save search costs, and follow the crowd. Inferential strategies and heuristics based on analogy and imitation often 'make us smart' (Gigerenzer et al. 1999) even if they sometimes fool us (March 1999). In many uncertain situations, the 'heuristic of social proof' (Cialdini 1984, cited in Hedström 1998) offers a powerful cognitive strategy: when in doubt what to do, do what others do. There are many well-studied examples of this, varying from the choice of restaurants (Granovetter 1978) and the adoption of new drugs by physicians (Coleman et al. 1966) to the classic run on the bank (Merton 1957). The last example shows that cognitively efficient *individual* answers to problematic situations can trap us into *socially perverse* outcomes. If national economies copy each other's apparently successful policies of financial deregulation and tax cutting, attracting ever more volatile and unpredictable capital, they may breed a financial monster or start a 'race to the bottom'. Something similar may happen when creating ever more legal titles for flexible employment with potentially negative consequences for trust, cooperative behaviour, human capital building, and productivity.

Tversky and Kahneman (1981) have analysed how much human judgement is influenced by the way in which problems are presented and information is framed. It turns out that humans, when making cognitive choices, are strongly guided by what is made *available* to them; that they tend to generalize from very small samples based on the *representation* of prominent examples or events; and *anchor* their choices early on and stick to them even in the face of contrary evidence. Meseguer (2005), analysing the reform pattern in trade policies in developing countries, concludes that saving on information costs was the main cause of *bounded* learning, i.e. decisions based on closely aligned information from model countries while disregarding alternative information. It is, however, equally plausible that the 'Washington consensus' of trade liberalization had made alternative solutions mentally and politically unavailable. In his study of pension reform in Latin America, Weyland (2007) finds evidence for all three 'cognitive' biases: reformers favoured solutions close to them, practised by neighbours; tended to overrate apparently successful cases (the Chilean pension reform in particular); and stuck to choices even if they were let down in their expectations.

These cognitive biases are also present in the OECD Job Strategy and the EES (Barbier 2005; OECD 2006).[16] The Mutual Learning Programme of the EES offers a potentially strong instrument against such biases, since it deliberately directs participants towards reflections about the transferability of reforms and introduces a light version of second opinion when requiring the presentation of a government and independent expert paper by the country hosting the peer review. The self-selection of participants into the peer workshops does, however, mirror, and possibly strengthen, pre-conceived clusters of like-minded Member States. Examining the three peer reviews that were devoted to reform of the public employment service (PES) in relation to the new activation policies reveals both tendencies.

Modernization of the PES is a key reform in both the Job Strategy and the EES, taken up in specific guidelines and recommendations. The OECD has since long advocated decentralization, bringing in private providers, integrating benefit and job placement administration in integrated one-stop offices, and experimenting with ‘contractual’ and ‘work first’ approaches to the unemployed. The US (Wisconsin), Australia, the UK, and the Netherlands have been promoted as models (OECD 2001, 2006).[17] Following a communication from the Commission in 1998, the first peer review on the issue within the EES took place in 1999, hosted by Finland, with participation from Denmark, the Netherlands, Germany, and Norway; representatives from France and Italy had announced their participation but did not attend. Under pressure of high and rising long-term unemployment, Finland had made reform of the PES into a priority, drawing inspiration from reforms in Denmark and Sweden (Räisänen et al. 1999).

As in the Danish, Dutch, and British cases, Finnish reform clearly predated the EES, but the EES became a conduit for learning from such experiences. The Dutch and German delegates came home with some ideas about experiment-based evaluation, entirely lacking in their own countries. All participants bought into the idea that a more individualized approach to reintegrating the unemployed was desirable but very costly and that internet and self-service activities for the higher end of the placement market should be used to relieve the pressure on highly strained PES resources. The synthesis report, however, considered that the Finnish reforms were of limited relevance to Denmark and the Netherlands, as the latter are ‘frontrunners in the reform of active labour market policies’, and that the peer review would have been more useful for Member States that did not participate. Being half-way in the reform process and receiving feedback from countries ahead of them, the Finns drew probably the greatest benefits from the review.

The second peer review, in May 2004, was also organized by Finland, which at that time was moving to the ‘second stage’ of PES reform.[18] The first stage (1997–2000) had focused on individualized services, IT, job interviews, and a more contractual approach to the rights and duties of benefit recipients. The second stage (2004–6) was about creating an integrated service for benefit management and job placement. The government's paper claimed that this move was directly related to the EES guideline on modernizing and strengthening the PES. The independent expert presented the reform as drawing on ideas and reforms in Sweden and the Netherlands, with additional input from Denmark and Austria. From Sweden, the Finns adopted the so-called 'two pronged' approach, offering self-service job brokering services to the easy-to-place unemployed and an 'individualized joint-service', together with local employers and job agencies, to the hard-to-place jobless. From the Dutch they borrowed some ideas about how to organize the placement market, allowing the use subcontracting and even some outsourcing to private firms, an element that was alien to the Swedish (or Danish) tripartite partnership approach.[19] Austrian and Danish influences were visible in the involvement of local social partners and the 'third' or voluntary sector. What the Finnish example really showed was how far 'hybridization' in this area has progressed. (Norwegian and Swedish reforms in 2006 and 2007 seem to be 'borrowing back' some of the Finnish reform experience.)

But there are limits to such promiscuities, clearly spelled out by the French contribution to the programme. In France, the Swedish approach based on making a distinction between different categories of unemployed was considered 'off limits'. An agreement between the main employers' associations and two of the five union federations in 2000, which was seen as distinguishing between insured and uninsured job seekers, was for this reason rejected by the then Socialist minister. The representative of Spain felt attracted to the Finnish system, but feared that such a reform would meet similar opposition as in France unless the social partners would jointly give their blessing, which was believed highly unlikely. Like participants from the new Member States, the Spanish representative also stressed that a more differentiated approach would require a highly professional service with far more resources than currently available. In the 2006 seminar on the issue of reform governance and delivery, the Italian delegate made the same point.

That such cross-national learning is not inimical to financial constraints and ideological divisions was also demonstrated in the third review, hosted by France in the fall of 2004 and devoted to the Return to Work Plan (*Plan d'Assistance de Retour a l'Emploi* [PARE]).[20] PARE had been rolled out between 2001 and 2004 as the government's alternative to the botched central agreement of 2000. It required all job seekers to develop a Personalized Action Plan for a new start and no fewer than 8.8 million plans had been drawn up. Little is known or was told about what happened next. During the peer workshop, the other participants were awed by the size and uniformity of the French approach, but it attracted followers among southern and new Member States for two reasons: as an example of successful mobilization of attention and resources, and as compatible with a rather bureaucratic style of doing things, where alternative solutions would require an unrealistically high degree of professionalism. The British participant observed curtly that, if nothing else, the workshop had been useful in showing him how 'different we do things back home'.

My conclusion is that cross-national learning about policy solutions tends to be most successful between welfare states with similar institutional set-ups, including the soft or normative side of these institutions. That is no indictment of the EES or the Mutual Learning Programme, but something to reflect upon in relation to convergence-enhancing policy ambitions for Europe. It is a conclusion that is probably most relevant for the *application* or new policy ideas, their translation into concrete programmes and organizational routines. The policy ideas themselves do travel across boundaries, inspired by success as much as by failure (hypothesis 1) and as the outcome of a protracted process of cognitive diffusion (hypothesis 2). Surely, more and better tests, beyond the limited experience of the Mutual Learning Programme in one policy area, are needed to disconfirm my third hypothesis. Nedergaard's survey, cited above, does not disconfirm that most learning happens within the northern (and western) group, but added that this has inspired policy makers in the south and east, and that 'there is no internal transnational learning within these [southern and eastern] groups, while almost none of these countries have acted as tutors' (Nedergaard 2006: 433). He concludes that there is most support for the 'best practice' hypothesis (close to my hypothesis 1), 'whereas the most similar hypothesis is also supported to some extent' (ibid.). Unfortunately, the survey draws no distinction between ideas and concrete policies based on ideas. It is quite likely that regime clusters and even national boundaries create different obstacles in translating 'ideas into words' compared to translating 'words into deeds'.

6 Conclusions

At the end of his famous essay on the 'self-fulfilling prophecy', Robert Merton wrote: 'In the world laboratory of the sociologist, as in the more secluded laboratories of the physicist and chemist, it is the successful experiment which is decisive and not the thousand-and-one-failures which preceded it. More is learned from the single case success than from the multiple failures. A single success proves it can be done. Thereafter it is necessary only to learn what made it work' (Merton 1957 [1949]: 436). Unfortunately, the conclusion of this optimistic quote is hard to share. In politics, learning and reform is never only about problems and solutions, but 'people fight over institutions and policy outcomes' (Thelen and Steinmo 1992: 22). Even if believed to be Pareto-optimal, reforms may not be undertaken if the transaction costs involved in making the change are considered by some powerful actors to be greater than the benefits. Political decision makers may prefer not to act or to be prevented from acting on what they have learned. Politics is not about learning or problem solving, but about power, and the two may sharply diverge. There is a very fundamental element of truth in Karl Deutsch's famous definition of power as 'the ability to afford not to learn' ('die Fähigkeit nicht lernen zu müssen') (Deutsch 1966: 111).

In this chapter I have discussed the problematic connection between international agency, cross-national learning, and policy convergence, using the example of the European Employment Strategy and the OECD Job Strategy. The 'double shift' of a *coordinated* European policy approach *reversing* the restrictive supply policies of past decades required a deep change in the collectively shared mental map defining the European (un)employment problem. The new approach can be described as a qualified success, though many difficulties remain and convergence in actual reforms and outcomes is limited. The key question of the chapter is how much of what happened is explained by cross-national learning and discursive diffusion. Its conclusions are that reform intensity appears unrelated to problem pressure, that learning is driven by success, elsewhere and at home, as much as by failure. However, discursive diffusion and the acceptance of a new language in which Europe's (un) employment problem was described have prepared Member States to move in the same direction, at different intensity, and with varying success. Finally, cross-national learning about concrete policy and organizational reforms is taking place within clusters of countries that, beyond having similar problems, appear to share similar normative concerns and financial conditions.

Notes

1 This chapter was written within the 'Governance as Learning' research programme and supported with grant no. 450-02-170 of the Netherlands Organization for Scientific Research. The author wishes to thank Birgit Bentzen, Maurizio Ferrera, Anton Hemerijck, Monika Ewa Kaminska, Marc van der Meer, Vivien Smith, and the two editors of this volume for their many useful suggestions, comments and editorial improvements. The responsibility for the present texts rests solely with the author.

2 In 1979 the European Trade Union Conferedation began a European action for working hours reduction and job redistribution, but its campaign to reach 35 hours by 1984 stalled, due to internal opposition, employer resistance, and a decreased appetite for leisure, following the stagnation of real wages growth.

3 See the two reports prepared under the chairmanship of Wim Kok: *Jobs, Jobs, Jobs: Report of the Employment Task Force*, Brussels, 2003; and *Facing the Challenge: The Lisbon Strategy for Growth and Employment*, Brussels, 2004.

4 Information on the Programme can be found on www.mutual-learning-employment.net. The author has actively participated in the 2006 edition of the Programme.

5 European Commission, 'More and Better Jobs: Delivering the Priorities of the EES', Joint Employment Report 2005/6, Brussels, 7347/06 Annex.

6 Jean-Philippe Cot, presentation of OECD, *Going for Growth*, 2007 edition, London and Paris, 13 February 2007.

7 European Commission, *Opportunities, Access and Solidarity: Towards a New Social Vision for 21st Century Europe*, Brussels, 20 November 2007, COM (2007) 726, p. 10.

8 'At the end of the day, being unable to converge is nothing other than losing the capacity to learn from others and their successes', J.-Ph. Cot, presentation of the first edition of OECD, *Going for Growth,* London: 1 March 2005.

9 These figures are based on the OECD Labour Force Statistics and Eurostat data, as published in the European Commission's annual publication *Employment in Europe*. The weighted averages are calculated for the 19 EU Member States which are members of both the EU and the OECD.

10 European Commission, *Taking Stock of Five Years of the EES*, Brussels, COM (2002) 416.
11 This assessment is based on two personal communications with Mr Kok, in the summer of 2003 and during the presentation of the Task Force report in a joint conference with the German government in November 2003.
12 EMCO, *Report on the 2007 Cambridge Review of the National Reform Programmes*, Brussels, 28 November 2007, p. 2.
13 European Commission, *Keeping the Pace of Change. Strategic Report on the Renewed Lisbon Strategy for Growth and Jobs: Launching the New Cycle (2008–2010)*, Brussels, COM (803), p.1.
14 Note that the New Member States are not part of the RDF Inventory.
15 The 402 members and their substitutes of four committees involved in the EES, including EMCO, were asked to identify the countries they had learned from. There were 101 valid responses (25.1%), each listing on average three countries. The five aforementioned countries collected 69.2% of the total tally.
16 Initially, the OECD held up the USA, New Zealand, and the UK as the model for overcoming Euro-sclerosis; much later, in its 10-year evaluation of the Job Strategy, it admitted that welfare states in northern Europe offered an equally valid and less unequal alternative (OECD, 2006).
17 The Netherlands – together with Australia – is the only country that has created a 'reintegration market' based on a 'purchaser/provider' split, where private sector and non-profit organizations compete for the acquisition of publicly funded tenders to supply re-employment services to the unemployed. Some experiments in the same direction are currently taking place in the so-called Employment Zones in the UK, while there is some limited contracting out occurring in Germany, Finland and, with many protests, in France.
18 In addition to Denmark, Norway, Germany, and the Netherlands, there were participants from Belgium, France, the UK, Bulgaria, Cyprus, the Czech Republic, Estonia, Hungary, and Slovakia.
19 In the Netherlands, tripartism in this domain had been tried but was gradually abandoned after the mid-1990s.
20 This peer review was attended by Cyprus, the Czech Republic, Denmark, Finland, Hungary, Ireland, Malta, Portugal, Slovenia, and the UK.

References

Alesina, A. and Perotti, R. (2004) 'The European Union: A Politically Incorrect View', *Journal of Economic Perspectives* (Fall): 27–48.

Armingeon, K. and Beyeler, M. (eds) (2004) *The OECD and the European Welfare States*, Cheltenham: Edward Elgar.

Ashiagbor, D. (2004) 'The European Employment Strategy and the Regulation of Part-time Work', in S. Sciarra, P. Davies and M. Freedland (eds) *Employment Policy and the Regulation of Part-time Work in the European Union. A Comparative Analysis*, Cambridge: Cambridge University Press.

Bala, V. and Goshal, S. (1998) 'Learning from Neighbours', *Review of Economic Studies*, 65: 595–621.

Barbier, J.-C. (2005) 'The European Employment Strategy, a Chance for Activating Social Protection', in J. Zeitlin and P. Pochet with L. Magnusson (eds) *The Open Method of Coordination in Action*, Brussels: Peter Lang.

Boeri, T., Castanheira, M., Faini, R. and Galasso, V. (eds) (2005) *Structural Reform without Prejudice*, Oxford: Oxford University Press.

Börzel, T. and Risse, Th. (2003) 'Conceptualizing the Domestic Impact of Europe', in K. Featherstone, and C. Radaelli, (eds) *Politics of Europeanization*, Oxford: Oxford University Press.

Brandt, N., Burniaux, J.-M. and Duval, R. (2005) 'Assessing the OECD Jobs Strategy: Past Development and Reforms', *OECD Economics Department Working Paper*, Paris, Organisation for Economic Cooperation and Development.

Cahuc, P. and Zylberberg, A. (2006) *The Natural Survival of Work. Job Creation and Job Destruction in a Growing Economy*, Cambridge, MA: MIT Press.

Campbell, D.T. (1977) 'Keeping the Data Honest in the Experimenting Society', in H.W. Melton, and J.H. David (eds) *Interdisciplinary Dimensions of Accounting for Social Goals and Social Organizations*, Columbus, OH: Grid Inc.

Casey, B. (2002) 'The OECD Jobs Strategy and the European Employment Strategy. Two Views of the Labour Market and of the Welfare State', organized by CEPII, together with FEDEA and DIW, Berlin.

Coleman, J.S., Katz, E. and Menzel, H. (1966) *Medical Innovations*, Indianapolis, IN: Bobbs-Merrill.

de la Porte, C. and Pochet, P. (eds) (2002) *Building Social Europe through the Open Method of Coordination*, Brussels: Lang.

Denzau, A.T. and North, D.C (1994) 'Shared Mental Methods: Ideologies and Institutions', *Kyklos*, 47: 3–32.

Deutsch, K.W. (1966) *The Nerves of Government. Models of Political Communication and Control*, New York: The Free Press.

Dolowitz, D.P. and March, D. (2000) 'Learning from Abroad. The Role of Policy Transfer in Contemporary Policy-making', *Governance. An International Journal of Policy and Administration*, 13: 5–24.

EC (1993) 'Growth, Competitiveness and Employment', *Bulletin of the European Commission*, supplement 6/93(Brussels, Commission of the European Communities).

—— (2004) 'Industrial Relations in Europe 2004': European Commission, Directorate-General for Employment, Social Affairs and Equal Opportunities.

—— (2006) 'Industrial Relations in Europe 2006', European Commission, Directorate-General for Employment, Social Affairs and Equal Opportunities.

Eckard, M. (2005) 'The Open Method of Coordination on Pensions: An Economic Analysis of its Effects on Pension Reform', *Journal of European Social Policy*, 5: 247–67.

Ederveen, S., van der Horst, A. and Tang, P. (2005) 'Is the European Economy a Patient and the Union its Doctor? On Jobs and Growth in Europe.' ENEPRI Working Paper No. 35: European Network of Economic Policy Research Institutes.

Elkins, Z. and Simmons, B. (2005) 'On Waves, Clusters and Diffusion: A Conceptual Framework.' *The Annals of the American Academy of Political and Social Science*, 598: 33–51.

Ferrera, M. and Gualmini, E. (2004) *Rescued by Europe? Social and Labour Market Reforms in Italy from Maastricht to Berlusconi*, Amsterdam: Amsterdam University Press.

Gigerenzer, G., Todd, P.M. and the ABC Research Group (1999) *Simple Heuristics That Make Us Smart*, New York: Oxford University Press.

Granovetter, M. (1978) 'Threshold Models of Collective Behaviour', *American Journal of Sociology*, 83: 1420–43.

Greer, A.L. (1988) 'The State of Art versus the State of Science', *International Journal of Technology Assessment and Health Care*, 4: 5–26.

Hall, P.A. (1993) 'Policy Paradigms, Social Learning and the State: The Case of Economic Policy-Making in Britain', *Comparative Politics* (April): 275.

Heclo, H. (1974) *Modern Social Politics in Britain and in Sweden*, New Haven, CT: Yale University Press.

Hedström, P. (1998) 'Rational imitation', in P. Hedström and R. Swedberg (eds) *Social Mechanisms. An Analytical Approach to Social Theory*, Cambridge: Cambridge University Press.

Heidenreich, M. and Bischoff, G. (2008) 'The Open Method of Coordination. A Way to the Europeanization of Social and Employment Policies', *Journal of Common Market Studies*, 46: 497–531.

Hemerijck, A.C. (2007) 'Contingente Convergentie. De doorontwikkeling van de Europese verzorgingsstaat', in E. Engelen, A.C. Hemerijck and W. Trommel (eds) *Van Sociale Bescherming naar Sociale Investering; zoektocht naar een andere verzorgingsstaat*, Special Issue Beleid en Maatschappij – Tijdschrift voor beleid, politiek & maatschappij, Amsterdam: Boom.

—— and Visser, J. (1999) 'The Dutch Model – An Obvious Candidate for the "Third Way"?' *Archives européennes du sociologie/European Journal of Sociology*, 40(1): 103–21.

—— and — (2001) *Learning and Mimicking. How European Welfare States Reform*, Amsterdam: Amsterdam School for Social Science Research, manuscript.

Hinrichs, K. and Kangas, O. (2003) 'When is a Change Big Enough to Be a System Shift? Small System-shifting Changes in German and Finnish Pension Politics', *Social Policy & Administration*, 37: 573–91.

Hodson, D. and Maher, I. (2001) 'The Open Method of Coordination as a New Method of Governance: The Case of Soft Economic Policy Coordination', *Journal of Common Market Studies*, 39: 719–46.

Holland, J.H., Holyoak, K.J., Nisbert, R. and Thagard, P.R. (1986) *Induction: Processes of Inference, Learning and Discovery*, Cambridge: MA: MIT Press.

Jacobsson, K. (2005) 'Trying to Reform the "Best Pupils in the Class"? The Open Method of Co-ordination in Sweden and Denmark', in J. Zeitlin, and P. Pochet with L. Magnussen (eds) *The Open Method of Coordination in Action*, Brussels: Peter Lang.

Kilpatrick, C. (2006) 'New EU Employment Governance and Constitutionalism', in G. de Búrca and J. Scott (eds) *Law and Governance in the EU and the US*, Oxford: Hart Publishing.

Knill, C. and Lehmkuhl, D. (2002) 'The National Impact of European Union Regulatory Policy: Three Europeanization Mechanisms', *European Journal of Political Research*, 41: 225–80.

Larsson, A. (1998) 'The European Employment Strategy – A New Approach' *Europe's approach to employment and social policy*, Luxembourg.

—— (2000) 'The European Employment Strategy and EMU. You Must Invest to Save', the 1998 Meidner lecture, *Economic and Industrial Democracy*, 19: 391–415.

Mailand, M. (2006) *Coalitions and Policy Coordination – Revision and Impact of the European Employment Strategy*, Copenhagen: DJØF Publishing.

March, J. (1999) *The Pursuit of Organizational Intelligence*, Oxford: Blackwell.

Merton, R.K. (1957) *Social Theory and Social Structure*, revised and enlarged edition, New York: The Free Press.

Meseguer, C. (2005) 'Policy Learning, Policy Diffusion, and the Making of a New Order', *The Annals of the American Academy of Political and Social Science*, 598: 67–82.

Nedergaard, P. (2006) 'Which Countries Learn From Which? A Comparative Analysis of the Direction of the Mutual Learning Process with Open Method of Coordination

Committees of the European Union and among the Nordic Countries', *Cooperation and Conflict*, 41: 422–42.

Noaksson, N. and Jacobsson, K. (2003) *The Production of Ideas and Expert Knowledge in the OECD: the OECD Jobs Strategy in Contrast with the EU Employment Strategy*, Stockholm: SCORE, report 7.

North, D.C. (2005) *Understanding the Process of Economic Change*, Princeton, NJ: Princeton University Press.

Oates, W.E. (1999) 'An Essay on Fiscal Federalism', *Journal of Economic Literature*, 37: 1120–49.

OECD (1994) *The OECD Job Study: Facts, Analysis, Strategy*, Paris: Organisation for Economic Cooperation and Development.

—— (2001) 'Regulatory Review', *OECD Economic Studies, Special Issue*, 32.

—— (2006) *OECD Jobs Strategy: Lessons from a Decade's Experience. Main report*, Paris: Organisation for Economic Cooperation and Development.

Pierson, P. (2004) *Politics in Time: History, Institutions, and Social Analysis*, Princeton, NJ: Princeton University Press.

Räisänen, H., Nio, I., Heinonen, E. and Tuomaala, M. (1999) 'Comprehensive Labour Market Reform: Presentation of Good Practice', paper prepared for the EU-Peer Review process on Activation and Individual Employment Service, Helsinki: Ministry of Labour.

Rogers, E. (1983) *Diffusion of Innovations*, 3rd edn, New York: The Free Press.

Saint-Paul, G. (2004) 'Why Are European Countries Diverging in their Unemployment Experience', *The Journal of Economic Perspectives* 18(4): 49–68.

Sapir, A. (2005) *Globalization and the Reform of the European Social Models*, Brussels: Bruegel Policy Brief.

Scharpf, F.W. (1991) *Crisis and Choice in European Social Democracy*, Ithaca, NY: Cornell University Press.

—— (2000) 'Economic Changes, Vulnerabilities, and Institutional Capabilities', in F.W. Scharpf and V.A. Schmidt (eds) *Welfare and Work in the Open Economy*, 1st edn, Oxford: Oxford University Press.

Schmidt, V.A. (2000) 'Values and Discourse in the Politics of Adjustment', in F.W. Scharpf and V.A. Schmidt (eds) *Welfare and Work in the Open Economy*, 1st edn, Oxford: Oxford University Press.

——(2008) 'Discursive Institutionalism: The Explanatory Power of Ideas and Discourse', *Annual Review of Political Science*, forthcoming.

Strang, D. (1991) 'Adding Social Structure to Diffusion Models: An Event-History Framework', *Sociological Methods and Research*, 19: 324–53.

Thelen, K. and Steinmo, S. (1992) 'Historical Institutionalism in Comparative Politics', in S. Steinmo, K. Thelen and F. Longstreth (eds) *Structuring Politics*, Cambridge, MA: Cambridge University Press.

Trubek, D. and Mosher, J. (2003) 'New Governance, Employment Policy, and the European Social Model', in J. Zeitlin and D. Trubek (eds) *Governing Work and Welfare in a New Economy: European and American Perspectives*, Oxford: Oxford University Press.

Tversky, A. and Kahneman, D. (1981) 'The Framing of Decisions and the Psychology of Choice', *Science*, 211: 453–58.

Visser, J. and Hemerijck, A.C. (1997) *'A Dutch Miracle'. Job Growth, Welfare Reform and Corporatism in the Netherlands*, Amsterdam: Amsterdam University Press.

Weyland, K. (2007) *Bounded Rationality an Policy Diffusion. Social Sector Reform in Latin America*, Princeton, NJ: Princeton University Press.

Zeitlin, J. (2005) 'The Open Method of Coordination in Action. Theoretical Promise, Empirical Realities, Reform Strategy', in J. Zeitlin and P. Pochet with L. Magnusson (eds) *The Open Method of Coordination in Action. The European Employment and Social Inclusion Strategies*, Brussels: Peter Lang.

Zeitlin, J. and Pochet, P. with Magnusson, L. (eds) (2005) *The Open Method of Coordination in Action. The European Employment and Social Inclusion Strategies*, Brussels: Peter Lang.

3 Unemployment protection reform in Belgium, Finland, the Netherlands, and the UK

Policy learning through open coordination?

Minna van Gerven and Mieke Beckers

Introduction[1]

Although the main driving forces behind welfare reform in today's European welfare states remain predominantly national, such processes of reform no longer take place in 'splendid isolation'. Not only have economic internationalization and European integration constrained national governments, but contemporary welfare states are also increasingly embedded in supranational efforts to coordinate their employment and social policies. During the 1990s, the seeds for such strategies grew out of the perception that structural problems of unemployment are shared concerns, and therefore call for supranational agenda setting. In the field of labour market policies, the OECD Jobs Strategy (1994) and the European Employment Strategy (1997) are among the most important procedures of benchmarking, systematic comparison, and recommendations. In short, this process of opening up to cross-national agenda setting has created a more complex setting in which policy learning comes not only from inside (in the form of 'trial-and-error lesson drawing'), but also from outward-looking international benchmarking (Hemerijck 2005: 47).

But to what extent does welfare reform in Europe reflect learning through such external channels? Both in academic and political circles, high hopes were raised about European-level coordination efforts. Great emphasis was put on the potential of the European Employment Strategy (EES) to elicit experimental learning, as well as on its ability to function as a cognitive and normative tool to build consensus around common objectives (Zeitlin 2005: 22). Indeed, after 10 years in operation, academic analyses of the functioning and effectiveness of policy coordination, including the Open Method of Coordination (OMC), of which the EES is the prototypical example, are abundant. Although the effectiveness of this governance tool in pushing forward convergence and adaptation of Member State policies has been the subject of fierce academic debate from its inception, more critical stances now seem to play the first fiddle. Opponents of this 'new' mode of governance claim that the OMC, due to its voluntarism, has proved 'weak' and 'ineffective', leading some to predict its imminent demise (Rhodes 2006, 31–2). One source of scepticism is the lack of convincing empirical evidence of clear effects on Member States' labour market policies, due to 'the lack of a solid experimental background, against which to test its actual effectiveness' (Hatzopoulos 2007: 309). Opponents therefore stress that conclusions always remain of a tentative nature.

Aiming to transcend the 'believer–non-believer' debate, this chapter will therefore take a different approach. Based on detailed qualitative data derived from primary sources (i.e. national legislation), we investigate the incidence, extent and nature of reforms in unemployment benefit provisions in four EU Member States (Belgium, Finland, the Netherlands, and the UK). Based on this analysis, we argue that the role of international benchmarking procedures cannot be discarded so easily and has been misjudged until now. We observe that convergence is occurring, but mainly in relation to policy *objectives*, much less so with regard to the *instruments* and *extent* of reform. This observation leads us to examine more closely the role of international benchmarking procedures. We argue that the EES has created a supranational forum of coordination of employment policies, precisely because of its deliberative character. The OECD Jobs Strategy (JS), by contrast, does not involve such deliberative fora but rather seeks to prescribe instruments and methods in a largely unilateral way. We will therefore argue that the EES has been more effective in influencing national reform agendas in the field of labour market policy.

Our findings call into question conventional theories of policy learning. On the one hand, Peter Hall's much-cited theory of social learning posits that a change in the hierarchy of goals (third-order learning) is necessarily preceded by minor adjustments in instruments (first-order learning) as well as by reconfigurations of policy techniques (second-order learning). Our observation of convergence of objectives but not of instruments challenges this premise. Our hypothesis is that Member States use international benchmarking procedures to determine the policy priorities and goals, rather than their detailed implementation. We argue further that the impact of these procedures occurs not only through a direct transfer of concepts, but also through cognitive influence and strategic usage. These claims are substantiated using information drawn from interviews with key policy makers at national (in Belgium and the Netherlands) and EU level.

The chapter proceeds as follows. First, we identify three common trends in unemployment protection reforms in the four countries under study and examine variations in the instruments used to attain these goals and the extent of reform. Second, by presenting the results of our interviews, we will elaborate on our claim that the EES works precisely through the prescription of goals and objectives, rather than of instruments. The third and final section will investigate to what extent our findings confirm or contradict conventional theories of policy learning.

1 Comparing benefit reform across countries: common trends in Belgium, Finland, the Netherlands, and the UK

To investigate welfare reform in Europe, we analysed changes in British, Belgian, Dutch, and Finnish unemployment insurance schemes since the early 1990s.[2] Based on these data, it will be argued that similar trends prevail. More precisely, in all four countries, we observed that: 1) reforms have increased the work-relatedness of the schemes, 2) the number (and intensity) of activation measures for those receiving unemployment benefits has grown, and 3) benefits have become increasingly targeted. Together, these trends reveal a visible shift from passive policies guaranteeing income replacement during unemployment and towards more active policies that aim at preventing unemployment and bringing people back to the labour market as promptly as possible. Each of these common trends will be discussed in turn.

1.1 Increased work-relatedness

A first trend emerging from our analysis is the strengthened link between work and welfare. Our analysis shows that, during the last few decades, eligibility for insurance benefits has been more tightly linked to past work records: tighter requirements have been set for work history, previous wages, and paid contributions. For instance, between 1980 and 2006 the work record requirement for unemployment insurance has been extended from one year in any year to one year in the last two years in the UK; from 30 days to at least 26 weeks in the Netherlands; from 300 days to 312 days (in the last 18 months) in Belgium, and from 6 to 10 months in Finland. Moreover, work records have become increasingly important in determining the level and duration of benefit payments. Generally, the longer the work history of the claimants, or the higher their previous wage income, the higher the benefits levels they could receive under an insurance benefit scheme. In the Netherlands and Finland, the benefit rate still remains directly linked to the past earnings of the unemployed. In the UK, this was removed in the early 1980s and the rate of unemployment benefits is now linked to the claimant's age. Linking the benefit rate to age means that 'older' workers (who also generally have a longer work record) are granted higher benefits. In Belgium, too, the older the unemployed person, the higher the benefits s/he receives, since the insurance payment is determined by the benefit duration (before and after the first 12 months, but only affecting those who have no family dependents) and the age of the claimant.

In all countries, benefit claimants must also satisfy more stringent work-related conditions. Such conditions require claimants to prove their willingness to work: for instance, they are required to be available for work, they must be registered at the employment office, they must attend some sort of take-up interview, they must demonstrably seek employment, and so forth. Perhaps the best-known example of such conditionality is the Jobseeker's Agreement which was introduced in the UK in 1995, setting many stringent requirements for people claiming benefits; but similar measures were also introduced in the other three countries. Exceptions to these conditions were rare, and a failure to satisfy them resulted in benefit being withdrawn, reduced, or not granted at all.

1.2 Increased activation

The link between work and social security benefits has also been reinforced through changes encouraging people *on benefit* to work rather than to remain dependent on welfare. We observed a clear trend towards increased activation in all countries investigated.[3] We noted changes that encourage recipients to work (by offering financial incentives, 'carrots') or that obligate claimants to participate in a work-experience scheme, training, or other activity in order to keep their benefit entitlement ('sticks'). Financial incentives to encourage claimants to work were commonly either earnings-disregards, allowing recipients to keep (some) work income without affecting their benefit rights, lump-sum bonuses to ease the transition to work, or regulations that protect recipients against loss of income in case of renewed unemployment. In the UK, for instance, the Back-to-Work Bonus was introduced in the 1990s. In the same period, daily allowance and accommodation allowance were introduced in Finland, complemented by travelling allowance and other increases for people participating in activation measures during the 2000s. Belgium increased subsidies to employers throughout the 1990s in order to get more people to work, whereas in the Netherlands, the Wet Inschakeling werkzoekenden (Re-employment Promotion) Act of 1997 also included financial incentives for people deciding to return to work. Claimants were also expected to satisfy additional requirements in order to legitimate receipt of benefits. For instance, recipients had to attend a greater number of mandatory interviews, where their situation was charted and plans were made for their (re-)entry to the labour market. Furthermore, recipients were obliged to accept work or training faster, and/or to participate in activation measures assigned to them.[4] In all countries, we see a tendency towards more stringent sanctions to enforce these obligations. Particularly in the UK, a much more stringent sanction policy was adopted alongside the new Jobseekers' Benefit scheme. The Wet boeten, maatregelen en terug- en invordering sociale zekerheid (Social Security Benefits (Fines and Recovery)) Act of 1996 in the Netherlands also maximized the sanctions embedded in the insurance schemes and made it compulsory for benefit administrators to use them. In Finland and Belgium, sanctions have also been gradually tightened throughout the years, yet governments efforts in these countries have been aimed at boosting work willingness through 'carrots' more than through 'sticks'.

1.3 Increased targeting

The third trend visible in benefit reforms in Belgium, Finland, the Netherlands, and the UK is increased targeting of benefits.[5] Similar in all countries is that the young (based on age, or status as students or labour market entrants) faced greater difficulties in accessing the insurance scheme during the 16 years of reform we scrutinized. In all countries under investigation, full-time students can no longer claim unemployment benefits. Instead, their income maintenance is now provided through study allowance schemes. School leavers also face a much longer waiting period to qualify for unemployment benefits and many of the harshest activation measures have been specifically targeted at young jobseekers. Furthermore, cuts in access to and duration of insurance benefits between 1980 and 2006 often mean that people fell faster from insurance benefits to their means-tested counterpart.

Signs of more stringent targeting are also visible in measures that tied benefit rights to 'genuine need', for instance to household size or the number of underage children. Schemes (particularly means-tested benefits) often granted certain increases to specific claimant groups (e.g. families with children). Since the late 1980s, however, few such improvements were implemented: tax credits in the UK for families with children and the disabled, reintroduction of child allowances to means-tested unemployment benefit in Finland, and the subdivision of categories in Belgium where a closer relation between the benefit rate and family situation is favourable for families with children and married/cohabiting couples.

To sum up, clear trends stand out from our analysis of the reforms to unemployment insurance benefit rules, which are summarized in Table 3.1.

Despite the similarity of the goals which these countries aimed to achieve while reforming their benefit systems, the discussion above also clearly highlights high levels of variation both in the ways these goals were pursued and in their intensity. Remarkably, most of the instruments used to alter national unemployment insurance schemes followed very much the national 'ways of doing things'. In that sense, our observations fit very well with claims about 'path-dependent' welfare-state reform (e.g. Pierson 1994; Esping-Andersen 1990, 1999).

To give a first example, the exclusion of the young shows how the trend towards increasing *work-relatedness* can be translated into very different practices. In Finland and Belgium, a much longer waiting period was set for the young, based on their status as labour market entrants (FI) or age (BE). In the Netherlands, the young, based on their status as labour market entrants and school leavers, were instead obliged to accept almost any job offered to them, with small exemptions for university graduates. In the UK, receipt of unemployment insurance benefit for the young was hampered by making the benefit levels less generous and subjecting them to more work-related conditions, and thus making benefits less attractive to claim.

Second, *activation* measures often take very different forms in the four countries. Whereas general activation measures in Finland and Belgium first and foremost included changes (financial incentives) that encouraged claimants to work (FI) or provided incentives for employers to hire the unemployed (BE), the activation measures in the UK and the Netherlands have

Table 3.1 Unemployment benefit reforms in Belgium, Finland, the Netherlands, and the UK, 1990–2006

Trend	*Operationalization*	*Variation in instruments by country*	*Extent of reform*
Increased work-relatedness	More stringent access requirements	NL: tighter work record requirement BE and FI: longer waiting period UK: more stringent job search conditions	NL: stricter insurance scheme UK: shift from earnings-related to minimum provision
Increased activation	More stringent conditions while receiving benefits	UK and NL: more sanctions FI and BE: more incentives	FI: polarization of provision for workers and means-tested schemes
Increased targeting	More stringent access benefit conditions	UK: targeting for needy workers FI: targeting for needy workers NL: targeting for key workers BE: targeting for minimum provision for a wide group of claimants	BE: comprehensive, but much less generous insurance scheme

Note: A certain shift towards activation is visible through more work-related conditions, both prior to and during benefit receipt. Furthermore, attempts have been made to modernize the unemployment benefit scheme so that it no longer merely guarantees a sufficient income, but rather aims at preventing people from staying on benefits too long, as well as at targeting the insurance benefit on those who already have a certain tie to the labour market (and the means-tested assistance on others).

appeared under the form of obligations and more stringent sanctions. Activation as a goal can thus be reached either by ‘sticks’ or by ‘carrots’.

Third, countries also varied considerably in how they *targeted* the benefits. The main trend was that the benefits were directed more carefully to the workers, yet again instruments used to achieve these goals varied. In the Netherlands and the UK, the benefits were primarily targeted through stricter work conditions, whereas in Finland the weakening of the basic provision led to a polarization of unemployment benefits: on the one hand, benefits were directed to workers (through the earnings-related insurance benefit schemes), and on the other hand to the needy (through the means-tested unemployment benefit). In all countries except Belgium, reforms were implemented to prevent early retirement, by foreclosing the possibility of exit through the unemployment scheme. Again, different instruments were used. In Finland, a separate unemployment pension was abolished and access to early retirement schemes functioning outside unemployment benefits has been tightened, whereas in the Netherlands and the UK elderly workers were obliged to seek work again and the benefit duration was cut. The Belgian unemployment insurance scheme remains the exception in that it continues to offer a strong pre-pension route for older workers (Hemerijck and Marx 2006: 24), apart from some recent steps taken in the so-called 'Generation Pact'.

In conclusion, even a brief glimpse at benefit reform reveals that very different mechanisms have been introduced in the countries under scrutiny to achieve the same policy goals. Countries also vary greatly with respect to how much they have been able or willing to reform. Perhaps the most drastic changes have been implemented in the UK, where the role of unemployment insurance has shifted from replacing lost income to merely a minimum provision, with strict conditions for its claimants. In the Netherlands, changes shifted the Dutch insurance scheme towards a more activating (and conditional) scheme, but they have not yet affected its earnings-replacement dimension (although this is now available to a much smaller group of core workers than before). Finnish social policy traditionally aimed at active labour market policies, and the years have reinforced this element. Although the basic security element of the scheme has been diluted, unemployment insurance has experienced rather little alteration in Finland (with the exception for the young). The Belgian example, like the UK case, shows signs of the blurring of insurance and assistance schemes. However, in contrast to the UK, the Belgian scheme remains at the same time rather easy to access. The rigid nature of Belgian unemployment insurance (embedding easy access and unlimited duration for at least some groups) hinders the complete success of the implemented activation measures (which also mainly take the form of 'carrots'). Countries thus vary considerably in the extent to which benefit reforms have affected entitlements and conditions.

2 Understanding the role of external learning channels as ideational resources for welfare state reform

The picture arising from our analysis of unemployment protection reform in four countries is a twofold one: one of both variety and similarity. On the one hand, these countries have used a wide diversity of policy instruments to reform their systems of unemployment protection. Variety is equally visible in the extent of reforms undertaken: interventions have not been equally far-reaching in each country under scrutiny. On the other hand, however, our most remarkable finding is that reform agendas have grown more similar. All four countries aimed to make their benefit systems more work related, activating, and targeted.

Arguably, these findings can be characterized as policy convergence. Following Knill (2005: 768), we understand policy convergence as 'any increase in the similarity between one or more characteristics of a certain policy across a given set of political jurisdictions over a given period of time'. In this study, we have considered three such characteristics, namely policy objectives, policy instruments, and policy scope. In other words, a process where (any of) these characteristics have become more similar over time can be labelled as convergence. The 'convergence' we aim to explain thus refers to the similarity we have observed at the analytical level of policy *objectives*.

A further question is which factors explain this cross-national convergence of policy goals. One plausible assumption would be that these countries' exposure to similar changes in their socio-economic environments accounts for convergence in their reform agendas. Hay (2004: 245) labels this *input convergence*. However, as comparative evidence abundantly demonstrates, this is hardly a sufficient explanation. To give just one example, two seemingly look-alike countries, Belgium and the Netherlands, which both struggled with a legacy of welfare without work, dealt with their crises in totally different ways – with the latter pursuing much more structural reform than the former (Kuipers, 2006: 16; Hemerijck and Marx 2006). Another explanatory factor further down the line in the policy-making process is 'a growing similarity in the cognitive filters in and through which pressures and challenges are identified and understood', which Hay (2004: 245) refers to as *paradigm convergence*. This explanation provides a better basis for understanding our findings, as it refers to one of the alleged core merits which have been attributed to international benchmarking procedures such as the OECD JS and the OMC processes (of which the EES is the most developed example), namely, to build a (European-)wide consensus around common objectives. However, the assumption of paradigm convergence also lacks explanatory power because, as will be explained below, both strategies promulgate analogous views of the labour market in European countries. Instead, it will be argued below that the causal *mechanisms* driving the effectiveness of the EES and the OECD JS account for their differential impact on national agenda setting.

This argument can be substantiated in three different steps (Figure 3.1). First, scrutiny of the JS and EES broad recommendations shows that there is a substantive match between the trends (described in the previous section), on the one hand, and the goals favoured by the EES and the OECD JS, on the other hand. Both strategies are committed to activation of labour market policies. While the JS stresses the need for modernized and effective active labour market policies (ALMPs), the EES instead urges a clear shift from a curative to a preventive approach to long-term unemployment. The revision of both strategies reinforced their emphasis on activation. The revised JS (of 2006) recommends that 'unemployment benefits … be made conditional on strictly enforceable work-availability criteria [1st trend] … and ALMPs … become compulsory after a certain length of joblessness that may differ across groups [2nd and 3rd trend]'. Within the integrated economic and employment guidelines, the promotion of active and preventive labour market measures are also at the forefront (Guideline 19, referring to early identification of needs, job search assistance, guidance and training as part of personalized action plans). Moreover, the current debate on flexicurity orchestrated by the

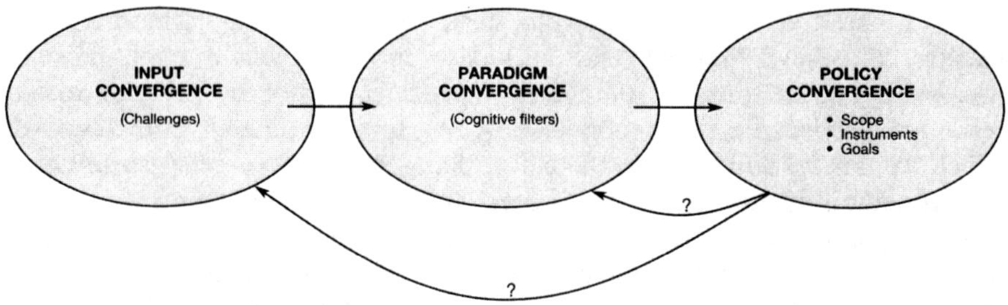

Figure 3.1 Convergence in different steps of the policy-making process
Source: based on Hay 2004: 245.

European Commission points to a likely continued interest in balancing rights and duties in unemployment benefit systems (European Commission 2007).

Second, explaining the differential impact of the EES and the JS requires a deeper look into differences and similarities between them in substantial as well as procedural terms. Casey's (2004) well-documented examination of the two strategies concludes that both are similar in procedural terms: guidelines, recommendations, and peer reviews are key elements of both. Moreover, it can be argued that both strategies are also quite similar as regards their policy diagnoses. Their recommendations to the countries investigated in this chapter show that, in the course of the 1990s, both strategies have signalled similar weak points in all four cases. Belgium, for instance, has been urged to tackle its problems of long-term unemployment and a persistently low employment rate. Both Finland and the Netherlands are recommended to tackle problems of an ageing working population. The effectiveness of active labour market programmes, as well as widening poverty, are concerns addressed to the United Kingdom. Given these parallels, one could hypothesize that *both* the EES and the OECD JS provide very similar learning tools and opportunities. However, there are some points of difference which make us expect quite the contrary. According to Visser (2005: 182) and Hemerijck and Visser (2001: 38–9), the OECD can be said to take a more centralized approach, presenting itself as a producer of 'expert knowledge'. This is very much in contrast with the EES's negotiated character, where national delegates are themselves part of the strategy's definition and design. Moreover, following Visser (2005: 181–3), the JS and EES can be contrasted as examples of 'de-contextualized' and 'contextualized mimicking' respectively. The former is based on 'pre-defined excellence without much attention to local conditions or scope for local interpretation', whereas the latter refers to the involvement of multiple interested partners and ample room for negotiability and feedback on implementation (Visser 2005: 180). In sum, as Visser (ibid.) argues, the OECD seems to prioritize validity (i.e. aiming at 'clean measurement and clear objectives'), whereas the EES prioritizes reliability (i.e. emphasizing 'shared understandings and consensus').

Third, based on these two previous steps, we can now argue that there are reasons to believe that the EES has been more successful in influencing national agenda setting. This claim may be substantiated by referring to the results of a series of interviews. Below, we will formulate two hypotheses, with which we aim to substantiate the claim that – regardless of the existence of similar commitments – the EES has been *more* effective in influencing national reform agendas in the field of employment policy. Our empirical analysis of unemployment protection reforms, which revealed similar goals in national reforms but not so much in their instruments and extent, leads to a first hypothesis: the EES can be expected to be more effective in that the latter capitalizes on goal attainment rather than the prescription of means to achieve these objectives (which more closely fits the OECD's profile). A second hypothesis builds on the differences between the EES and the JS. As the former's mechanisms rely more on political appropriateness than on scientific validity (Armingeon 2007: 909), we expect the EES to be better able to infiltrate national policy arenas. Rather than relying on country experts as does the OECD, the EES explicitly works through cooperation both within and between EU Member States. This element of learning 'with' others (Hemerijck and Visser 2001: 39) can be expected to open a window of opportunity to cultivate ideas (from EU to Member States and vice versa). The OECD, by contrast, does not utilize such forums, rather, it seeks to prescribe instruments and ways of doing in a quite unilateral way (learning 'from' others).

An empirical test of these hypotheses requires a deeper look into the active input of national officials in such international benchmarking efforts and the way they take 'external' ideas home. This is true because under so-called 'soft' procedures such as the EES and JS, the measurement of domestic outcomes is not limited to legislative change (López-Santana 2006: 486). Moreover, the parallels discussed above do not provide evidence as such of a *causal* impact of the two strategies. In what follows, we will examine the validity of these, using the results of a series of interviews with key EU and national employment policy experts in Belgium and the Netherlands.[6]

2.1 Hypothesis 1: the EES vs the Jobs Strategy: capitalising on goal attainment vs means prescription

Without exception, our respondents perceived clear differences in impact between the EES and the OECD JS. All interviewees among national officials and social partners in charge of following up international affairs claimed to invest much more time in the EES (or European affairs as a whole) as compared to the OECD. Beyond this unanimous view, it is thus most compelling to elaborate on how respondents explain these differences in priorities. In general, two major arguments emerge from our interviews.

A first, often-cited line of argument concerns the *political salience* the EU enjoys as compared to other international organizations. The EU is far more visible in public opinion and the political world; it is a structure consisting *of* the Member States (Interview BE1). In other words, whereas the OECD JS is generally described as a scientific and intellectual exercise, the EES is regarded as a political instrument *par excellence* (Interviews NL1; NL2; NL3; NL4; NL5; NL6). Nevertheless, respondents acknowledged the OECD's pioneering role in promoting policy comparisons (Interviews NL6; NL7; BE2; BE3; BE4). However, respondents indicated that the OECD's capacity to compare policies across national settings is doubly restricted. On the one hand, comparison between countries is not truly stimulated, since the OECD produces individual country examinations which do not encourage national policy makers to compare their setting with one another. On the other hand, when such cross-national comparisons are made, they also concern countries outside Europe with social protection systems perceived as too unfamiliar for comparisons to be useful (Interviews BE5; NL5). Policy comparison within the EES, in contrast, builds on national yet intra-European experiences. For instance, in the framework of mutual learning programmes, national policies are discussed at the level of their implementation. This makes the comparison more contextualized and perhaps also more politically legitimate.

Second, respondents without exception refer to the fact that the EES activities are far more *demanding*, as they represent an 'ongoing business', sometimes at a pace which is hard to keep up with. To begin with, the treaty status gives the EES a more 'compulsory' character through the drafting of an annual National Action Plan (NAP) (or the current National Reform Programme, NRP) (Interview NL13), in which a Member State is required to screen its national policies through the lenses of the EU employment guidelines. In the same vein, the Employment Committee (EMCO) is seen as one of the important engines keeping the EES 'fire' running at the domestic level. New issues for debate continuously demand renewed input from all stakeholders involved. In sum, although neither strategy has any binding power, the pressure coming from the European level is perceived to entail greater commitment than that coming from the OECD, as the latter is not 'institutionalized' to the same extent. In other words, it is precisely the EES's more short-term, political, and particularly cyclical character which boosts domestic actors' continued investment in the follow-up of its activities.

Nevertheless, respondents widely acknowledge and appreciate the OECD's far more extensive and sophisticated analysis of labour market problems in contemporary European welfare states (Interview BE1; BE6). Several interviewees, including those at the European level, referred to the sound basis the JS laid for the creation of the EES, first and foremost by de-ideologizing employment policies, and its mind-broadening effect in the field of the labour market (Interview NL3). The EES, however, is considered to have taken this process a step further by providing concrete examples of how to put it into practice (through peer reviews, exchange of best practices, and recommendations). If the EES is seen to have been effective in procedural terms (e.g. in stimulating policy evaluation, monitoring, target setting etc.), the JS is regarded as equally important in this respect (Interview BE4), since the OECD's comparative advantage is considered to be the intellectual input it can provide for policy making.

In conclusion, one could posit that the OECD seeks effectiveness through providing an 'independent', *reliable* sketch of labour market problems to be addressed, whereas the EES creates a consensus instrument seeking *feasibility* (cf. Noaksson and Jacobsson 2003 for rather similar findings). In that sense, our initial hypothesis about the EES vs the JS representing goal attainment and means prescription respectively is being confirmed. The EES can be characterized as a *political* process in which the Member States themselves are in the driver's seat, and which therefore is necessarily constrained to setting forward objectives rather than instruments; or, in the words of one of our interviewees: 'the EU convinces more with less' (Interview BE6).

2.2 Hypothesis 2: the EES vs the Jobs Strategy: infiltration in domestic arenas vs top-down expert-driven knowledge transfer

Direct effects

As we have now demonstrated the reasons underlying the highly differential infiltration of the EES and JS at national level, a second hypothesis will now elaborate on the way in which the EES exerts this impact (the actual *mechanism*). Below, we will show that such impact can, but rarely does, manifest itself in a direct or 'automatic' way, but can be better understood as a cognitive and leverage effect.

Our interviews revealed few examples of the EES serving as a direct benchmark for policy development. One notable exception is the case of the preventive approach to unemployment, which has been a key part of the EES from the outset. In the Netherlands as well as in Belgium, interviewees pointed to the EES's role in mobilizing additional (financial) resources for the development of active labour market policies. In the Netherlands, it has been claimed that the EES consolidated and expanded the government's version of the activation approach (see also Zijl et al. 2002), which already covered the young and long-term unemployed. According to our interviewees, the external pressures through the EES were decisive for extending the comprehensive approach to all adult unemployed (after 12 months of unemployment) by placing the issue higher on the political agenda, and subsequently generating more financial resources to implement it (Interview NL3; NL4; NL6). In Belgium, notably the Flemish region has made use of the guidelines in order to define its framework for the guidance offered to the (young) unemployed. The former 1st and 2nd guideline inspired the timing and phasing of counselling and training offered to job seekers (Interview BE7). Such direct impact appears to have been totally absent in the case of the JS. Moreover, another difference between the JS and the EES lies in the EU's provision of financial support for the implementation of the latter (particularly activating social policies) through the European Social Fund (ESF) (Interview NL3; NL6).

The effect of an external stimulus is understandably larger when there is a considerable amount of money put on the table to support its goals. Already at the end of the 1980s, the ESF had led to the obligatory introduction of so-called 'guidance trajectories' for the unemployed, whereby the start-up of guidance for jobseekers is not postponed until they become long-term unemployed, but is offered instead at an early stage. According to one high-level civil servant, the method would otherwise not have been introduced at this early point in time in the Belgian setting, and would still be under pressure should ESF funding disappear.

Indirect 'cognitive' effects

However, as argued above, such direct impact is but one of the many forms through which such a soft government tool can be effective. Beyond direct impact, we can discern indirect cognitive effects of the EES, notably its influence on agenda setting, problem definition, and conceptual vocabulary in labour market policies (for similar findings, see also López-Santana and Preunkert and Zirra, this volume). Respondents aptly described EU influence as 'a compass', 'infusion' or 'scenery', referring to the European identity many labour market issues acquired. One of our Dutch interviewees described this as follows:

> Concepts such as the comprehensive approach, making work pay, sustainability of social protection, flexicurity etc. have been coined within the EU context ... Member states have jointly discussed these issues, and now everybody knows what these concepts mean. The framework for thinking about policies has thus been harmonized. You can only exchange ideas if you share a common conceptual framework.
>
> (Interview NL8)

Belgian interviewees confirm this cognitive infiltration, and further elaborated on the driving force behind it:

> The impact of the EES exists particularly at the level of agenda setting, although it's very difficult to show how exactly that happens. I think that, over time, many themes acquired a European identity, like flexibility for instance, or part-time work. Gradually, these terms serve as a stepping stone for telling the 'stories' surrounding them. In that way, the EU and the EES have succeeded in showing the way forward to labour market reform, and preparing and adjusting Belgium to changed realities. Europe can thus be seen as an assimilation mechanism to adjust national systems to a new environment.
>
> (Interview BE8)

Another concrete example of such cognitive impact can be found in the debate on active ageing in Belgium. In 2005, the federal government announced a series of measures (under the umbrella of the so-called 'Generation Pact') to encourage older workers to continue at work, mainly in the form of 'carrots' rather than 'sticks'. According to this interviewee, the agenda-setting role of the EES should not be overlooked:

> Despite the limited impact on policies themselves, it's my strong impression that, at the level of conceptualization of labour market policies, the EES has indeed played an important role … The Generation Pact did not in itself change the current situation that much … yet the EES has to a very important extent contributed to the fact that we consider the issue of ageing as a problem. It's the ultimate merit of the EES to have engendered a small conceptual revolution. We know that the employment rate is more important than the unemployment rate, we know we have to pay attention to the discouraging effect financial incentives can have in social protection … the European frame of reference made us aware that the Belgian system of early retirement is not the Belgian model, but the Belgian problem.
>
> (Interview BE1)

In the same vein, one interviewee added that, because of participation in more paradigmatic discussions at European level, Belgium has learned to turn away from its preoccupation with overly specific, single-purpose measures:

> The EES has had its impact on the 'state of mind' of policy makers, in the sense that the Strategy has contributed to stimulating a more global and rational approach to labour market policies. Although the EES did not 'invent' concepts such as making work pay or flexibility, they are discussed within the European setting and thereby gradually infiltrate the heads of national policy makers … In Belgium, we were preoccupied with very targeted measures, in complete absence of a more general debate. Today, however, such a more global approach *does* exist, e.g. because one thinks of transitions during careers, activation and the overall design of social security … and that's not to be neglected.
>
> (Interview BE6)

Indirect 'leverage' effects

Besides this cognitive impact, the EES can affect domestic settings in another indirect way, namely by serving as a resource which can be used strategically by domestic actors (e.g. at times of negotiations between the social partners and the government, or between unions and employers' organizations) in order to ensure that some issue 'must' be discussed. It can thus put new issues on the table, or render existing policy options less viable. According to our interviewees, such indirect effectiveness of the EES has occurred at the level of 1) cooperation between different ministries (and departments within these ministries), particularly in the Netherlands; 2) the involvement of the social partners; 3) the interaction between federal and regional levels in Belgium, and 4) the involvement of Parliament in the Netherlands. Each of these will be discussed below.

First, our Dutch respondents claimed that, because of the preparation of the National Action Plans (now Reform Programmes), cooperation between and within specific ministries has improved (see Mailand, López-Santana, and Jacobsson and Johansson, this volume for similar findings in Spain, Poland, and Sweden). For instance, the various ministries (e.g. Social Affairs and Employment and Economic Affairs) as well as different departments within these ministries (International Affairs and Labour Market Policy) now work more closely together in order to establish a common view in the EU Employment Committee (EMCO) (Interviews NL9; NL10; NL11):

> Through OMC one can claim a stronger interest on the part of the Ministry (Social Affairs and Employment) to look around and seek out what other countries do … EES has created new channels for interaction … in the Netherlands different departments/ministries now work more together to have a common view in the EMCO.
>
> (Interview NL9; NL10)

Moreover, the interviewed Dutch civil servants welcomed the EES, since it gave them stronger arguments to achieve national goals (Interview NL7). Even the recommendations coming from the Commission were often welcomed, since they could help to legitimate government decisions presented to the Parliament (Interviews NL6; NL9; NL10). In Belgium, on the contrary, there is no increased 'virtuous' coordination between ministries. At the federal level, there is no tradition of developing policies across different policy domains. The EES does not seem to have brought about any significant modification here. Yet, there is a somewhat heightened cooperation between departments since the relaunch of the integrated Lisbon guidelines for growth and jobs in 2005. However, our interviewees only report cooperation between policy areas for the purpose of assembling information in drawing up the NRPs (Interviews BE2; BE3). At the administrative level, the barriers between various policy fields remain very high.

Second, in both Belgium and the Netherlands, the social partners seem to have 'discovered' the EES (Interviews BE9; NL6; NL11). Whereas the involvement of social partners in Belgium was considered to be high, the Dutch social partners see their role in these activities as too limited (Interview NL5), despite the Commission's pressure on national governments to involve the social partners in the preparation of the NAPs. More importantly, in both Belgium and the Netherlands, the social partners have learned to use the EES as a strategic instrument in public debate (Interview NL5). For instance, the Dutch social partners claimed that the Commission's requests to them for advice while preparing its recommendations for the Netherlands were seized upon as an opportunity to raise certain issues in the public debate. More far-reaching examples of strategic usage of European dossiers can be found in Belgium. Most interestingly, interviewees among the social partners (both individual unions and the National Labour Council) observe that European debates have helped as useful arguments in order to broaden the contours of negotiations.

> Within the 'Group of 10' [the group in which the Interprofessional Agreements are negotiated], European dossiers are continuously read between the lines. Figures provided at European level allow the Belgian position to be assessed vis-à-vis other Member States in a certain field … This implicit presence of Europe has meant that the inter-professional agreements are no longer conducted concerning social issues in the strictest sense of the word. Rather, the scope has broadened towards socio-economic issues. Wage setting is now no longer viewed merely within the framework of competitiveness, but also of education and training, innovation, research and development … The range of themes has thus enlarged considerably, and this is an evolution to which the European agenda has certainly contributed. For instance, this has demonstrated Belgium's poor performance in the field of life-long learning, and in that way provided the unions with an argument because there is a European target. In that way, we think of Europe unconsciously.
>
> (Interview BE9)

This broadened scope of negotiation is confirmed by the unions:

> When there is a debate on life-long learning (LLL) at European level, this helps as a sort of context to put this issue on the table. It creates a certain atmosphere in which the unions can convince others that this issue 'must' be discussed and agreed upon. The fact that Belgium, once it had adopted those benchmarks, did not achieve them helps to raise the issue again, and to point to the fact that the employers' organization cannot just refer to competitiveness without discussing LLL. The conclusion is thus that Europe infuses into domestic politics very slowly, very calmly … and helps to put certain issues on the table.
>
> (Interview BE10)

As the life-long learning example shows, benchmarks seem to significantly increase the 'usability' of European arguments in debates and negotiation settings. They allow comparison of one's own country and its performance to another (preferably similar) country, which gives such arguments their persuasive power.

> It's not difficult to tell that the EES does particularly well on those themes where benchmarks are mentioned. They are given priority over others in the debate – think of issues such as child care or the time span

> in which an unemployed person should receive guidance … Although we don't like all the benchmarks, some of them are really useful. Benchmarks can serve as an authoritative argument and over time we have learned to use them in that way whenever it serves our purposes. Referring to these benchmarks, we argued that more adult people should be in training, and that more childcare facilities should be put in place. Moreover, we used the EES target on activation to obtain more financial resources for guidance of the unemployed, and we succeeded in doing that at the federal and regional level, especially for youngsters.
>
> (Interview BE11)

Third, in Belgium, the EES seems to have generated increased cooperation between the various levels of government sharing competences in the field of employment policies. The necessity of drawing up an NAP in a multi-level setting such as Belgium has engendered something which could be termed as a 'domestic OMC process'. More specifically, the external pressure to reflect on employment policies according to a predefined framework seems to have legitimized the federal level's coordinating role (Interview BE3). Since it can now invoke 'Europe' as an authoritative argument, the federal government is now more able than before to convince the regions to compare their labour market performances. Moreover, this appears to have raised awareness among the regions of each other's actions in this field, not least because people who previously had no reason to meet now know one another.

> The EES redefined the dialogue between the regions and the federal level. They have no choice but to coordinate their viewpoints. Despite the disparate problems and limitations of each of their labour market settings, they need to put their noses in the same direction; one cannot draw a caricature of the other too much. The impact of that is not to be overstated as well, because in the end the minister does what he wants to do in the Council. The position Belgium takes is the result of an exercise of mutual understanding, a check whether we understand the things in the same way. To a certain extent, this leads to a common language concerning the priorities we should set in our reforms. From my years of experience within this administration, I know that was not the case before.
>
> (Interview BE6)

An unforeseen side effect of the EES in Belgium has thus been a more 'virtuous' coordination of labour market policies between the various levels of government. Whereas an overview of Belgian labour market policy had to a large extent been lost due to the regionalization of competences, the EES has engendered an integrative dynamic by obliging countries to report on their policies as a whole.

Fourth, in the Dutch case, we also see greater cooperation between the parliament and civil servants at both national and EU level. Dutch respondents reported that Parliament has become more aware of European issues over time, and increasingly asks for more information from the Minister about matters such as active ageing and dismissal law (Interview NL9; NL12). Thus, for instance:

> There are questions asked in the Parliament about the ways in which other countries organize social matters and what the Dutch should and could learn from these experiences.
>
> (Interview NL12)

At least in the Dutch case, the increase in looking abroad thus applies not only to the small 'elite' of civil servants or social partners involved in the EES, as often argued in the literature (see e.g. Büchs 2004, 2005), but also to other actors in the process, such as Members of Parliament. Such parliamentary interest, however, seems to be totally absent in the Belgian case.

The observed cooperation at the level of the Member States (which is more or less absent in the OECD), makes it reasonable to assume that the EES can disseminate ideas at various levels (of government, or among social partners) more effectively. However, the comparison of Belgium and the Netherlands above shows that the EES can be very differently absorbed in different national settings. Indeed, it is remarkable that in the Netherlands we observe improved coordination between ministries and greater interest of Parliament, whereas in Belgium the EES has affected comparisons between regions and has been used by the social partners. This country-specific effect should not be neglected, but nevertheless supports our general argument that the EES has indirect impacts through its strategic use as a political instrument by domestic actors.

Drawing on our own empirical work, we thus see that, because of its open, deliberative, and negotiated character, the EES serves as a 'creative resource' for domestic actors by providing them with platforms (both formal and informal), networks, and (limited) financial support. This is much less true for the centralized, expert-driven, and de-contextualized OECD JS, which starts from a more narrowly focused set of ideas and thus demands learning 'from' others (Hemerijck and Visser 2001: 39). The interview material presented above thus confirms the conceptual distinctions drawn earlier in this section concerning the differences between the two strategies (prescriptive vs declarative, de-contextualized vs contextualized, stable vs dynamic). Yet we do not claim that the EES is *the* actual driving force for policy change. Rather, we concur with the argument that the EES should be seen primarily as a catalyst or 'selective amplifier' (Visser 2004) in national welfare reform (cf. also Büchs 2004, 2005). The next section concludes by bringing the learning dimension back into the debate about the mechanisms through which international benchmarking procedures can affect domestic policy settings.

3 Policy learning at work? Theories of policy learning and the national operation of the EES compared

The convergence of policy objectives in four different EU Member States raised the question to what extent this results from a convergence of policy paradigms in these countries. Since instruments such as the EES and the OECD JS are now embedded in national reform processes, we probed into their capacities to enhance processes of policy learning. In this third and final section we therefore confront our empirical findings with theories of policy learning.

In a seminal paper on policy learning in European welfare states, Hemerijck and Visser (2001: 21–9) distinguish between two influential perspectives. On the one hand, theories of *social learning* describe the concept as 'a deliberate attempt to adjust the goals or techniques of policy in response to past experiences and new information' (Hall 1993: 58). It is thus characteristic of such processes to be triggered by failure, which consequently incites policy makers to consider new ideas. From a functionalist perspective, profound changes in the social and economic environment thus trigger reform of European welfare systems (Hemerijck 2005: 37). This would imply that the observed convergence is the mere result of similar challenges posed to disparate welfare and employment regimes (cf. the earlier discussion of Hay's model of input convergence). However, the merit of theories of social learning is that they draw attention to the role of *ideas* in policy reform. In that sense, 'responses to policy problems cannot be adequately explained by functional pressures on existent institutional structures and policy repertoires [i.e. *input convergence*]. Policy development is shaped by the flow of ideas at the interface between problems and policy responses' (Hemerijck 2005: 45). On the other hand, there is also a large literature concerning another channel through which learning can take place, namely *policy transfer*. By copying (or 'mimicking') successful examples from abroad, policy makers may extend the repertoire of potentially effective solutions to policy problems (Hemerijck and Visser 2001: 26). The supranational coordination efforts of the EU and OECD are seen as exemplary channels through which such policy mimicking could take place.

Whereas the process of social learning from failure is first and foremost *inward* looking, policy transfer is instead *outward* looking. Based on our own findings as well as on the expanding empirical literature about the functioning of these processes, we argue that both versions of policy learning need revision.

First, our empirical findings about unemployment protection reform call into question Peter Hall's argument about the sequential relationship between first, second, and third-order learning. Our findings rather point to a reverse sequence of learning: we observed that goals have shifted (third-order learning) *without* major adjustments in instruments (first-order learning) or reconfigurations of policy techniques (second-order learning). Although we cannot entirely disentangle the role of internal and external factors behind this development, we suggest that, in the agenda-setting phase, the different countries under investigation have been exposed to similar transnational pressures, whereas they have followed their own trajectories in their implementation. As famously described by Heclo (1974: 305), policy making is the result of both 'puzzling' and 'powering': it is exactly in this phase of 'puzzling', where problems are diagnosed and feasible solutions identified, that we can expect different countries to encounter similar policy alternatives in the supranational coordination process. In a context of multi-level governance, where policy making no longer takes place exclusively within national arenas, supranational coordination offers a dramatic expansion of reform concepts. This is exactly where paradigmatic convergence can occur, since countries – however disparate their legacies – face more similar choice sets than ever before. However, once problems have been identified and courses of action selected, their actual implementation is not only time consuming, but prone to resistance. As Hemerijck (2005: 45) observes, 'normative and cognitive orientations are not (socially) constructed in isolation, but in politically charged and institutionally nested policy arenas inhabited by multiple social actors each with their own preferences and interests'. In other words, in the phase of 'powering', institutional constraints entail a dramatic shrinkage in the repertoire of feasible policy options and scope for reform (Hemerijck and Visser 2001: 21). In that respect, it is not surprising that we have observed different countries heading for the same destination, but along different paths.

Second, 'policy mimicking' theories also need adjustment in view of the growing number of accounts of the functioning and success of the EES. Reviewing this literature, we conclude that such empirical evaluations – including our own – provide cautious yet confirmative evidence of these processes' cognitive impact. Thus, for example, in her study of the influence of European soft law on domestic employment policies and governance structures in three countries, López-Santana (2006: 488) argues that 'by framing certain labour market policies as "good," "bad" or "necessary" the supranational level has influenced early stages of the policy-making process, such as agenda setting and problem definition'. However, many studies also underline the importance of the recognition of these challenges by domestic actors (Pochet 2007: 4; Heidenreich and Bischoff 2008; Zeitlin 2005: 476–83). Heidenreich and Bischoff's analysis of the EES in Germany and France puts this into perspective by adding that usually only a small administrative and political elite of actors is involved. However, within this highly professionalized 'EES-elite', they describe the 'cognitive impact in the perception, the conceptualization and the way of looking for solutions' as 'considerable' (Heidenreich and Bischoff 2008: 521). Most important, they add that this impact did not occur through a direct transfer of concepts, but rather through an open process of 'irritation' in which European ideas are used in a rather uneven fashion. Heidenreich and Bischoff underline that the impact of supranational coordination should not be understood only in terms of copying successful examples from abroad. Together with the gradual maturing of these processes, their mechanisms and results become progressively accepted, thus giving rise to 'autonomous policy networks, above and beyond the nation state' (Hemerijck 2005: 12). In so doing, these processes create opportunities to plant 'European' seeds in fertile national grounds.

Notes

1 For inspiring discussions and helpful comments on earlier versions of this chapter, the authors (who contributed equally to this chapter) wish to thank Gert Verschraegen, Bart Vanhercke, Philippe Pochet, Milena Büchs and Giselda Curvers. A first draft of this chapter was presented at the Amsterdam School for Social Science Research in August 2007, where Anton Hemerijck, Jelle Visser, Jonathan Zeitlin, Gerben Korthouwer, Peter Sleegers and Nynke Wiekenkamp provided useful and much-appreciated remarks. The authors also wish to thank the participants in the stream on the Lisbon Strategy at the ESPAnet Conference, 20–22 September 2007 in Vienna. Last but not least, we thank the editors of this volume for their comments, as well as the Belgian Science Policy Office for providing financial support for carrying out the interviews.

2 The first section is based on empirical analysis conducted in the framework of a PhD dissertation reviewing reforms of sickness, disability, unemployment, and social assistance benefit schemes in the UK, the Netherlands, and Finland since 1980 (van Gerven 2008). In this dissertation we listed and analysed the legislative changes implemented to eligibility and entitlement conditions in these countries. This review was supplemented, for the purpose of this paper, with information for Belgium, which supported the trends found in the above-mentioned dissertation.

3 National labour market policies aiming at activating people are nevertheless rather fragmented: many instruments and schemes are used to pursue the same goal. Our perspective covers only some of these activation measures, namely those systems and changes that apply directly to unemployment benefit rules.

4 These activation programmes were initially compulsory only for the young and long-term unemployed. Finnish municipalities were obliged to find work for youngsters in 1987. This was followed by the British YTS (Youth Training Scheme) in 1988 and the Dutch JWG (Youth Work Guarantee) in 1991. In Belgium, since the cooperation agreement between federal government, communities, and regions in 2004, more preventive measures have been directed towaards the young. Later, such activation measures have been extended to a much wider group of unemployed. For instance, in the UK after the ending of the gateway period, most working-age claimants are now obliged to participate in activation measures. The same goes for the Netherlands (where, three months after the onset of unemployment, jobseekers must participate in individually tailored plans to assist them back to work), for Finland (where this obligation takes effect after 500 days on Labour Market Assistance through the new Society Guarantee in 2005), as well as for Belgium (after 15 months).

5 We do not define targeting as situations where social security is 'redirected from less needy to more needy recipients (cf. Bolderson and Mabbett 1996: 16). Instead, we adopt a broader perspective, similar to one used by van Oorschot (2002: 173), where targeting is seen as an allocation to any group, whether specific categories of citizens (unemployed workers, pensioners, families with children), the needy (sick or disabled people), or people whose resources fall below subsistence level (i.e. the poor).

6 During 2007, we conducted 20 interviews with 22 key policy makers in Belgium, and with 9 respondents in the Netherlands. For the Dutch case, we had access to additional interview transcripts of 10 key policy makers conducted in the framework of

a previous evaluation study (2001–2) addressing similar questions. The interviewees represented actors from national ministries (Social Affairs, Employment, Economic Affairs), social partners (trade unions and employers' organizations), and European institutions (European Commission, European Parliament, European Trade Union Confederation). In the interviews, we asked whether respondents considered ideas of employment policies (in particular activation) to come from the OECD or the EU, and why they thought so. We also inquired whether the respondents could explain the impact of the EES and on which level they see observed it (i.e. ideas, policies, or procedures). The 2007 interviews were conducted as part of a research project on the Europeanization of social policies in Belgium, the Netherlands, and France, with financial support from the Belgian Federal Science Policy Office (2006–9), which we gratefully acknowledge.

References

Armingeon, K. (2007) 'Active labour Market Policy, International Organizations and Domestic Politics', *Journal of European Public Policy*, 14: 905–32.

Bolderson, H. and Mabbett, D. (1996) 'Cost Containment in Complex Social Security Systems: The Limitation of Targeting', *International Social Security Review*, 49: 3–17.

Büchs, M. (2004) 'Asymmetries of Policy Learning? The European Employment Strategy and Its Role in Labour Market Policy Reform in Germany and the UK', paper presented at the ESPAnet Conference, Oxford, September.

Büchs, M. (2005) 'The European Employment Strategy – Effective and Democratic?', *Welt Trends*, 13: 41–54.

Casey, B. (2004) 'The OECD Jobs Strategy and the European Employment Strategy: Two Views on the Labour Market and the Welfare State', *European Journal of Industrial Relations,* 10: 329–52.

Esping-Andersen, G. (1990) *The Three Worlds of Welfare Capitalism*, Princeton, NJ: Princeton University Press.

—— (1999) *Social Foundations of Postindustrial Economies*, Oxford: Oxford University Press.

European Commission (2007) 'Communication from the Commission to the European Parliament, the Council, the European Social and Economic Committee and the Committee of the Regions', *Official Journal of the European Union*, Towards Common Principles of Flexicurity: More and Better Jobs through Flexibility and Security, Brussels: European Commission. Online. Available HTTP: http://ec.europa.eu/employment social/employment_strategy/pdf/flex_comm_en.pdf (accessed 14 April 2008).

European Council (2001) 'Council Decision of 19 January 2001 on Guidelines for Member States' Employment Policies for the Year 2001', *Official Journal of the European Union*, L 022: 18–26.

Hall, P. (1993) 'Policy Paradigms, Social Learning, and the State: The Case of Economic Policy-making in Britain', *Comparative Politics*, 25: 275–96.

Hatzopoulos, V. (2007) 'Why the OMC is Bad for You: A Letter to the EU', *European Law Journal*, 13: 309–42.

Hay, C. (2004) 'Common Trajectories, Variable Paces, Divergent Outcomes? Models of European Capitalism under Conditions of Complex Economic Interdependence', *Review of International Political Economy*, 11: 231–62.

Heclo, H. (1974) *Modern Social Policies in Britain and Sweden: From Relief to Income Maintenance*, New Haven, CT: Yale University Press.

Heidenreich, M. and Bischoff, G. (2008) 'The Open Method of Co-ordination: A Way to the Europeanization of Social and Employment Policies?', *Journal of Common Market Studies*, 46: 497–532.

Hemerijck, A. (2005) 'Linking welfare recalibration and social learning', paper presented at the RC 19 Annual Conference, Chicago, September.

Hemerijck, A. and Marx, I. (2006) 'Redirecting Continental Welfare in Belgium and the Netherlands', paper presented at the conference 'A Long Goodbye to Bismarck? The Politics of Welfare Reforms in Continental Europe', Harvard University, June.

Hemerijck, A. and Visser, J. (2001) 'Policy Learning in European Welfare States', unpublished manuscript.

Kuipers, S. (2006) *The Crisis Imperative. Crisis Rhetoric and Welfare State Reform in Belgium and the Netherlands in the Early 1990s*, Amsterdam: Amsterdam University Press.

López-Santana, M. (2006) 'The Domestic Implications of European Soft Law: Framing and Transmitting Change in Employment Policy', *Journal of European Public Policy*, 13: 481–99.

Noaksson, N. and K. Jacobsson (2003) 'The Production of Ideas and Expert Knowledge in OECD. The OECD Job Strategy in Contrast with the EU Employment Strategy', *Score Research Report*, 2003: 7.

Pierson, P. (1994) *Dismantling the Welfare State? Reagan, Thatcher, and the Politics of Retrenchment*, Cambridge: Cambridge University Press.

Pochet, P. (2007) 'Influence of European Integration on National Social Policy Reforms in Bismarckian Countries', paper presented at the CONNEX Workshop/ESPAnet Expert Seminar on the Europeanization of Reforms in Bismarckian Welfare Systems, Paris, March.

Rhodes, M. (2006) *The Future of Europe: Renewing the Project*, London: Institute for Public Policy Research.

Van Gerven, M. (2008) *The Broad Tracks of Path Dependent Benefit Reforms. A longitudinal study of social benefit reforms in three European countries, 1980–2006*, Studies in social security and health 100, Helsinki: Social Security Institution.

Van Oorschot, W. (2002) Targeting Welfare: On the Functions and Dysfunctions of Means-testing in Social Policy', in P. Townsend and D. Gorden (eds) *World Poverty: New Policies to Defeat an Old Enemy*, Bristol: The Policy Press.

Visser, J. (2004) 'The EES as Selective Amplifier for National Strategies of Reform', paper presented at COST A15 Final Conference, Nantes, May.

Visser, J. (2005) 'The OMC as a Selective Amplifier for National Strategies of Reform. What the Netherlands Want to Learn from Europe', in J. Zeitlin and P. Pochet (eds) *The Open Method of Coordination in Action. The European Employment Strategies and Social Inclusion Strategies*, Brussels: Peter Lang.

Zeitlin, J. (2005) 'Conclusion. The Open Method of Co-ordination in Action. Theoretical Promise, Empirical Realities, Reform Strategy', in J. Zeitlin and P. Pochet (eds) *The Open Method of Coordination in Action. The European Employment Strategies and Social Inclusion Strategies*, Brussels: Peter Lang.

Zijl, M., van der Meer, M., van Seters, J., Visser, J. and Keuzenkamp, H. (2002) *Dutch Experiences with the European Employment Strategy*, SEO report no. 611, Amsterdam: SEO.

4 The Open Method of Coordination and domestic social policy making in Belgium and France

Window dressing, one-way impact, or reciprocal influence?

Marie-Pierre Hamel and Bart Vanhercke[1]

The 'state of the art' of academic writing about the Open Method of Coordination (OMC) provides contrasting findings about the effectiveness of this soft mode of European governance. Although many initial writings were quite supportive of the OMC, praise for it has recently turned into scepticism. These sceptical views seem to be in sharp contrast with other evaluations which provide convincing evidence of different kinds of 'impact' of these OMCs.[2] This confusion about OMC effectiveness, which is discussed throughout this book (see for example the chapters by Heidenreich, Preunkert and Zirra, Van Gerven and Beckers, and Zeitlin), raises the question of how to define and measure the effectiveness of soft modes of governance. This is indeed a key question, since the many (opposed) interpretations of the OMC's impact at national level are largely due to the absence of an agreed analytical framework for such an assessment.[3]

Drawing on a rigorous comparison of the OMC in action in Belgium and France, our central claim is that this mode of governance is having real consequences, at least for the social inclusion policies of certain Member States, provided that one is willing to look beyond legislative changes alone, through a process of reciprocal influence between EU and domestic settings.

Section 1 briefly describes the analytical instruments we will use to analyse the OMC's impact. Section 2 provides empirical evidence on the practical operation of the OMC on Social Protection and Social Inclusion (hereafter OMC/SPSI) in Belgium and France. Section 3 summarizes our findings and concludes.

1 Theoretical lenses for studying mechanisms and effects of soft law

In this section we briefly explain what kind of *effects* we will be looking for. It has been argued that the use of the OMC 'toolbox', consisting of common objectives, National Action Plans (NAPs), indicators, targets, and peer reviews, has both procedural and substantive effects (Zeitlin 2005: 450).

OMC can, first of all, cause procedural shifts in governance and policy making. Member States' commitment to 1) write forward-looking National

Action Plans on Social Inclusion (NAP/Inclusion) and 2) coordinate their social inclusion policies and involve all levels of government, could indeed lead to increased horizontal and cross-sectoral policy integration (e.g. between and within administrations). One could also expect a stronger vertical coordination between national and subnational administrations (inter-ministerial and multi-level policy coordination). Third, the pressure from the OMC cycle regularly to assess performance in light of the Common Objectives and indicators could lead to improvements in national steering capacity. Fourth, Member States' commitment to involve all relevant bodies in the OMC/Inclusion could lead to increased or better-structured involvement of non-state actors in national policies (e.g. grass-roots organizations and people experiencing poverty).

But we can also expect substantive effects on national policies (Barbier 2005). The OMC involvement may lead to cognitive shifts, e.g. the incorporation of EU concepts and categories into domestic debates and discrediting of certain domestic approaches, thus modifying the political agenda. OMC can finally contribute to shifts in specific national policies, such as legislative proposals.

Different governance *mechanisms* can explain such procedural and substantive shifts. One is the *creative appropriation of the OMC* by domestic actors, also termed the 'leverage effect' (Erhel et al. 2005). One could indeed expect bounded rational actors to use the OMC to legitimize their own preferences, advance their agendas, criticize official positions, demand increased participation in governance etc. A second mechanism is *socialization and discursive diffusion*, i.e. incorporation of European categories and concepts into the domestic debate through involvement in the OMC. While using the OMC, the ideas, norms, and beliefs of the actors involved may be altered, and so they import and incorporate the orientations on which it is based. *Mutual learning* is another mechanism that can explain procedural changes and substantive shifts, through 'a combination of enhanced awareness of different approaches and performance standards elsewhere on the one hand, and reflexive self-assessment, including improvements on institutional capacity for information gathering and monitoring on the other' (Zeitlin 2005: 479). Finally, *external or peer pressures* and associated practices, such as recommendations and 'rankings', can help to explain 'national' changes.

We might further hypothesise that the OMC's impact is related to the degree to which domestic actors have or have not been able to influence the EU decision-making process in the first place (uploading) (Börzel 2003: 3). Indeed, in order to avoid policy misfits between the EU and domestic levels, Member States try to upload their preferences in European fora. In this way they reduce compliance problems and the associated adaptational costs (Caporaso et al. 2001: 7). By integrating this uploading dimension, we can verify whether successful uploading effectively reduces the domestic impact of EU initiatives such as the OMC.

2 Traces of Eve: the (in)effectiveness of the OMC in action

This section provides detailed empirical evidence concerning procedural and substantial effects which can plausibly be attributed to the OMC, and highlights the mechanisms through which they operate. We structure our results according to the five 'instruments' of the OMC toolbox (common objectives, NAPs, targets, indicators, and peer reviews), because analytically they shed light on the different sets of actors involved in, and thus the varying uses of, the OMC process. Our analysis is based primarily on more than 60 interviews with European, national, and subnational civil servants, politicians, and stakeholders (social partners and NGO representatives) working in the area of poverty and social exclusion. We corroborate their claims with as many written documents as possible.

2.1 Common objectives

The new 'Common Objectives for Social Protection and Social Inclusion' were endorsed by the Heads of State and Government in March 2006 (European Council 2006: 70). They provide general orientations for Member States' social policies, which should, among others, have 'a decisive impact on the eradication of poverty and social exclusion' (CEC 2005: 9).

Raising the poverty issue on the political agenda

According to most Belgian actors involved in the OMC process, Heads of States' commitment to eradicate poverty pushed the fight against it higher on the political agenda, and keeps it there. Thus the coordinator of the Brussels Region section of the NAP/Inclusion says that:

> If the OMC were to be abandoned at EU level, I am not sure why the regional governments would continue to invest as much in this policy area. Sometimes I feel the OMC is only bluff, but then again I believe it has mobilized our three or four governments to intensify the fight against poverty.
>
> (Interview B1)

Her Flemish counterpart confirms that 'Through a detour OMC leads to more attention to the fight against poverty: because there is attention for the subject, because we have to 'sell' what we do, because we have to explain our actions' (Interview B2). Similarly, in France, one actor explained: 'The OMC prevents a race to the bottom in an enlarged EU. With the OMC, we see a phenomenon of emulation, through which the poverty issue stays on the agenda' (Interview F12). Put differently: 'With OMC, we cannot rest on our laurels. It pushes us to innovate and make further progress' (Interview F14).

Turning principles of activation into effective activation in France

It seems important to underline the significant role France played in the initial decision to launch a social inclusion OMC at EU level. Under the French Presidency during the second half of 2000, the Nice European Council approved the objectives of combating social exclusion and confirmed the request to submit NAPs/Inclusion (covering a two-year period) by June 2001, as well as the need to define indicators and monitoring mechanisms (European Council 2000: 18). Some actors refer to the personal determination of Martine Aubry, the Socialist Minister of Labour and Social Affairs at that time, to explain the large French influence in creating the OMC. According to a former President of the Social Protection Committee (SPC), Aubry saw the definition of a European inclusion strategy as a way to legitimize the French national strategy in this field, especially the 1998 Law to Combat Exclusion.[4] As a result, 'there were debates, but the inspiration was French over all' (Interview EU1).

If France was so influential in uploading its priorities in the Common Objectives, did they still have any effect at the domestic level? It seems indeed that some issues which were rather far from the national political culture were 'downloaded' from the OMC/SPSI. The reason is not so hard to understand: even if French influence was large, the initial Common Objectives ultimately represented a European compromise, some of them clearly illustrating Member States' different visions of the poverty issue. The definition of the first Common Objectives was particularly conflictual. Ultimately, the 'first' Common Objective was to 'to facilitate participation in employment *and* access by all to the resources, rights, goods and services' (our emphasis). According to a former SPC Secretary, this was a 'completely illogical EU compromise' (Interview EU2), since it is obvious that these are really two distinct priorities.

Even though the priority given to 'active inclusion' was opposed by France at the time (Interview EU2), the Commission kept up the pressure on this issue from the first Joint Inclusion Report in 2001 onwards. How far, then, has the European focus on active inclusion influenced the French domestic setting? Formally speaking, active inclusion is not a new theme in France: consider, for example, the 'insertion contracts' attached to the Guaranteed Minimum Income (RMI) since 1988. However, those contracts include very broad possibilities for activation, including 'activities to improve daily life'. Moreover, contracts are not always signed or applied: in 2006, 88% of the overall recipients of the RMI did not receive any support (*intéressement*) aimed at 'activation' (Cazain et al. 2006: 1).

This somewhat changed with the Active Solidarity Income (RSA) created in 2007. This new and experimental benefit provides the possibility for returnees to work to keep some of the social benefits they receive for a while. The RSA was proposed by Martin Hirsch, the former President of Emmaüs France (one of the main NGOs in the field of social inclusion) and, since May

2007, High Commissioner for Active Solidarities Against Poverty in the Prime Minister's Cabinet. Most of the actors interviewed refer to the RSA as an example of European influence: 'With the RSA, we follow Europe' (Interview EU3). Clearly, the concern for active inclusion does not come solely from the European level. Nevertheless, when proposing the RSA, Hirsch refers explicitly to the European level, arguably to strengthen his initiative. Furthermore, his 'National Commitment to Poverty Eradication' (17 October 2007), specifies that 'The Commission has published a communication on active inclusion, a process in which the implementation of the RSA is written' (Haut Commissaire 2007). Note that this declaration also refers to the future French presidency of the European Union in the second half of 2008, which was expected to 'give an impulse to these efforts'. Surely, a long bridge has been crossed since France opposed, only a few years earlier, the OMC/SPSI's focus on active inclusion. It seems safe to say that the debates at European level put the activation issue higher on the French inclusion agenda, slowly creating a substantive policy shift.

In more general terms, several French actors see the OMC objectives as a framing tool for national discourse. As one actor explains:

> The OMC structures the national debates. It is a *battle of ideas.* Would we speak of activation policies or of flexicurity without the OMC? The influence is massive and hidden. Some actors breathe another air and that affects the national policy.
>
> (Interview EU5)

A French civil servant in the European Commission confirms that: 'Without almost ever saying it, France is getting closer to the European process. France is bathed in the OMC, but almost nobody speaks about it' (Interview EU7).

Child poverty: agenda setting and new windows of opportunity

A more concrete example of a substantive policy shift through the OMC/SPSI is the arrival of 'child poverty' in the political arena in Belgium and France. Although the issue is not formally inscribed in the OMCs 'Common Objectives', it has acquired a similar status since the European Council asked the Member States 'to take necessary measures to rapidly and significantly reduce child poverty' (European Council 2006: 72). As a consequence, the Social Protection Committee asked its Indicators Sub-Group to establish a Task Force on Child Poverty and Child Well-Being, which produced its first report at the beginning of 2008 (SPC 2008). Moreover, the Commission invited Member States to tackle child poverty as a priority issue in their 2006–8 National Reports on Strategies for Social Protection and Social Inclusion (hereafter National Strategic Reports or NSR). The 'vast majority of Member States' followed suit (CEC 2007: 8, 170).

But is this an effect of the OMC in the case of Belgium? The 2007 Joint Report highlights that the third policy priority in the Belgian NSR 2006–8 is 'to tackle child poverty by breaking the poverty cycle' (CEC 2007: 170). According to Morissens et al. (2007: 5), 'the choice of child poverty as one of the policy priorities in the Belgian NAP/Inclusion illustrates the growing influence of Europe and the Open Method of Coordination on the Belgian social inclusion agenda.' Prior to the appearance of child poverty in the 2006–8 NSR, child poverty was not explicitly on the political agenda, to the point that children living in poverty were almost invisible in the Belgian social inclusion discourse (ibid). The European advisor to the Minister for Social Integration explains:

> Child poverty is now one of our three priorities in fighting poverty. If a message is repeated long enough in the right places … it will end up on the agenda anyway. The fact that this issue is now in our NAP proves that the OMC is used to set national policy agendas.
>
> (Interview B4)

Some Belgian domestic actors very quickly saw the advantages of the new focus. Thus, the federal Social Integration administration proposed to set targets for combating child poverty, requiring follow-up measures in different policy areas and at different levels of government. Clearly, this strengthens the demand for coordination by the federal level. Also, the Flemish Network 'will use the European focus on child poverty to demand thorough measures. This is a sensitive issue: after all, children cannot be blamed for being poor, so this provides us with many opportunities' (Interview B3). At the same time, it is acknowledged that there are a number of blind spots in knowledge about this issue (e.g. teenage pregnancies, children's experience of poverty, and the situation of migrant children), especially because the search for indicators only started after it was decided to select child poverty as a priority in the NAP/Inclusion (Morissens et al. 2007: 7, 23). In sum 'child poverty' has been catapulted from the OMC into the Belgian political arena through external pressure, and some of the key actors revised their attitude towards it surprisingly quickly.

A similar, yet less explicit, substantive shift occurred in France. Indeed, the 2006–8 French NSR, unlike the Belgian one, does not explicitly refer to 'child poverty' (CEC 2007: 249). Even if the French NSR does not mention this issue it is seen by several national actors as an 'importation' distant from the national culture (Interview F12). Just as in Belgium, some actors confirm that now that they are confronted with this European theme, they end up 'using it' at the national level. Certain actors judge that the emotional dimension related to the children can help to fight poverty in general, and they want to use this category to expand policies to other categories (the elderly, the young, the disabled etc.), so that they will eventually cover the majority of the excluded (Interview F2).

This perception of social inclusion actors is confirmed by the 2006 annual report of IGAS (Inspection Générale des Affaires Sociales), one of France's three inter-ministerial inspectorates-general. The IGAS report concludes that child poverty is now a preoccupation at the French domestic level because of European concerns. At the same time, the report deplores that no coherent and specific national policy was developed to effectively eradicate child poverty (IGAS 2006: 331). The child poverty rate (15.5%) is higher than the average in France, thus requiring targeted actions (Haut Commissaire, 2007). In conclusion: this EU concept has penetrated the Belgian and French domestic arenas and may lead to shifts in specific policies in the medium term.

2.2 National Strategic Reports

Following the streamlining of the OMC/SPSI in 2006, Member States are now charged with translating the common objectives into NSRs for each of its three strands (Social Inclusion, Pensions, and Health and Long-Term Care). Since the Common Objectives on poverty and social exclusion require Member States to ensure 'that social inclusion policies are well-coordinated and involve all … relevant actors, including people experiencing poverty' (CEC 2005: 6), the Commission has put a lot of pressure on Member States to involve a wide variety of actors in the preparation of the inclusion section of the NSR.

Involvement of non-state actors: reinforcement of initially different positions between Belgium and France

At the start of the Social Inclusion OMC in 2000, Belgium was rather confident about the way it organized stakeholder involvement in its social inclusion policies. Many considered Belgium a 'model' in this respect, which could be a source of inspiration for other Member States (Interviews BE2, BE3, BE4). Thus, the Resource Centre for the Fight against Poverty, Precariousness, and Social Exclusion was established in 1999 in order to ensure a permanent dialogue between representatives of the associations of the poor, the social partners, the (local) public agencies, and the health insurance organizations. One would think that, under such circumstances, with a large apparent fit between EU and domestic policies, a 'soft' mode of governance could hardly have any significant procedural impact at the national level.

The opposite is the case. To start with, as one can read from the evaluation of the first Belgian NAP/Inclusion, it seems that the Belgian 'model' of stakeholder involvement looked much better on paper than in practice: 'Grassroots organisations have not participated in its design and have been barely informed of its existence two weeks before its submission to the European Commission' (Nicaise et al. 2003: 29). Hence the Commission judged, in its first Joint Report on Social Inclusion, that 'The involvement of stakeholders … was limited due to time constraints' (CEC 2001: 87). In response, Belgium set up an 'Actions' and an 'Indicators' Task Force for the preparation and follow-up of the second NAP/Inclusion. Both the national and subnational (regional) level are represented, as are stakeholders of local administrations, representatives of both sides of industry (through the National Labour Council), academics, and associations of the poor.

This somewhat improved their effective involvement, but not drastically: for the second NAP/Inclusion 'the consultation with other stakeholders (including associations representing the poor) has been fairly extensive', but 'time was lacking for the other stakeholders to review and debate the preliminary draft of the NAP 2003–5' (Groenez and Nicaise 2004: 2–3). The Commission highlighted the fact that the Belgian government admitted that mobilization had only been partly successful and there was still much to do (CEC 2006a: 22). This second cold shower resulting from external (Commission) pressure, combined with the acknowledgment (through mutual learning) that perhaps Belgium was not the best pupil in the class after all, led to real procedural shifts; i.e. increased stakeholder involvement in the elaboration of the NAP/Inclusion at the beginning of 2005.

In sum, involvement of stakeholders in the preparation of the NAP/Inclusion matured step by step, and Belgian authorities learned that their 'participatory model' (which they uploaded with considerable success to the EU level) could (and still can) be further improved. The fact that they did actually adapt their ways of doing things is no coincidence. The coordinator of the Belgian NAP/Inclusion explains that:

> The sector of organizations where the poor take the floor use the reference to participation in the NAP/Inclusion to underline the fourth Nice Objective about the mobilization of the actors over and over again. They may not read the NAP, but they will use it to obtain subsidies if they can. 'Mobilization' works as leverage, a powerful argument.
>
> (Interview B5)

In other words, whereas the design and follow-up of the first Belgian NAP/Inclusion had to some extent been 'disconnected from "mainstream" policy-making and evaluation fora' (Nicaise et al. 2003: 26), it now seems that the social inclusion OMC now has a strong 'ownership' (Morissens and Nicaise 2007: 4). This is so despite the fact that NAP/Inclusion continues to coexist with the biannual reports on the evolution of poverty in Belgium, which are produced, since 2001, by the aforementioned Resource Centre for the Fight against Poverty, Precariousness and Social Exclusion.

Finally, it seems important to underline that the procedural shifts described here are becoming institutionalized at different policy levels, and are affecting stakeholder involvement in domestic social inclusion policies beyond the preparation of the NAP/Inclusion. First, there are strong indications that the 'Indicators' and 'Actions' Task Forces are increasingly integrated into pre-existing national coordination mechanisms, such as the Inter-Ministerial Conference (IMC) for Social Integration, which was set up to achieve greater coherence in social inclusion policies.[5] Second, procedural changes are taking place in Wallonia:

> The Walloon Combat Poverty Forum drew inspiration from its Flemish counterparts, which have been structurally involved in the NAP/Inclusion for a long time, and is now being invited to participate in the meetings. It seems that the Combat Poverty Forum will soon be entitled to structural funding as well. In this way the OMC provide stakeholders with a place in policymaking they never obtained before.
>
> (Interview B5)

In France too, there is a long-standing tradition of contacts between NGOs and government in the field of social inclusion. NGOs have been involved in structured political action since the mid-1980s, notably through the action of a group called ALERTE that played an important role in the preparation and adoption of the 1998 Law to Combat Exclusion. The involvement of NGOs in the NAP/Inclusion exercise runs mainly through the National Council for the Fight Against Poverty (CNLE). The process is the following: the unit responsible for writing the NAPs/Inclusion in the 'social' ministry, the General Directorate for Social Action (DGAS),[6] sends a first draft to the CNLE, which gives its opinion. DGAS then sends a 'final' draft to the CNLE for discussion.

The question then is: did the OMC, and the NAP/Inclusion exercise more specifically, influence the links between the NGOs and the state? According to some actors, since consultation was already effective before the OMC was launched, the latter did not really influence the involvement of non-state actors (Interview F12). Moreover, NGOs are often less involved in the NAP/Inclusion consultations than in the national policy process. One of the major problems with the NAP/Inclusion is that it is not seen as a strategic exercise. The French NAP/Inclusion presents policies that are already in place or have already been decided at the national level. Besides the NAP/Inclusion, other more strategic national plans on inclusion are published regularly in France (1998, 2003, 2004, 2007). As one of member of the CNLE comments on the 2004 Social Cohesion Plan (Sénat 2004): 'There was this important political step, while we were talking about the NAP, an administrative, imposed exercise where we put in boxes actions that are already done. It was frustrating' (Interview F13).

To improve things, some would like the French NAP/Inclusion to become a political exercise that could be presented to the Parliament (Interview F12). Many French, as well as Belgian, actors interviewed also suggest that the pre-existing national social exclusion plans and the NAP/Inclusion should be combined into a single plan, or at least their respective roles should be clarified.

Cross-sectoral coordination effects

The requirement for Member States to draft a NAP/Inclusion is particularly challenging in a country such as Belgium, where some of the key competencies, including the implementation of social assistance, are exercised by the subnational level (Regions and Communities). One consequence of writing OMC reports together is that existing differences in subnational policy making are brought into the spotlight.

Thus, cross-sectoral policy integration varies widely between the Regions. In Flanders, the annual Flemish Action Plan for Poverty Reduction (VAP), adopted by the regional government for the first time in 2001, coordinates the initiatives in some 10 different policy areas. The Walloon Region has created, within its Ministry and under the direct authority of the Minister-President, an Interdepartmental Directorate for Social Integration (DIIS), which coordinates the implementation of social inclusion policies. In Brussels, the Observatory for Health and Social Affairs produces yearly reports on poverty and social exclusion and provides technical assistance to initiatives of the regional government, but there are only limited cross-sectoral coordination efforts.

There is some evidence that the preparation of the NAPs/Inclusion has led to increased efforts to coordinate and streamline policy initiatives across sectors within each of the latter two regions. Brussels and Wallonia recently announced that they would start elaborating strategic poverty plans, which would probably not have happened without the EU. The coordinator of the Brussels Region part of the NAP/Inclusion confirms that:

> The new law of July 2006 announces a Brussels 'Action Plan against Poverty', which will probably be produced in 2008 for the first time. That is where you see an influence of the NAP. We decided to kill two birds with one stone: we will elaborate a real Plan for our own purpose, and it will also be the Brussels contribution to the NAP. In that way, the work we did for the NAP since 2003 ultimately affected the Brussels Region: both the political and administrative level have been mobilized to do something much more structured, much more coherent, rather than continue to superpose measures.
>
> (Interview B1)

In France, the fight against poverty and social exclusion is, since the 1998 Law to Combat Exclusion, formally 'a priority of all the public policies of the nation', based on inter-ministerial cooperation and partnership. A specific institution was created to implement this collaboration, namely the Inter-Ministerial Committee to Combat Social Exclusion (CILE). However, the members of the CILE met for the first time in July 2004, and a second meeting took place only in May 2006 (in preparation for the NAP/Inclusion 2006–8) (DGAS 2006). Another central actor in the coordination of social inclusion policies is the DGAS. Following national and European requirements, it submits drafts of the NSR to involved actors (mainly CILE and CNLE).

According to some of the people in charge, the preparation of the NAPs/Inclusion has enhanced the cooperation between administrations foreseen by the 1998 Law, but this is still very limited. Even the recent streamlining of the pension, exclusion, and healthcare OMCs (2006), which are now presented in the same NSR, has so far not led to real coordination between administrations. As one administrative actor told us that exchanges between those OMCs 'would be interesting, but nobody is really in charge of coordinating the exercises and there is no real dialogue between the ministries in charge. Without a real political will, this coordination could hardly happen' (Interview F4).

In sum, there is no convincing evidence that the horizontal collaboration aimed for by the 1998 exclusion law has been significantly improved by the NAP/Inclusion exercise, and it remains very limited in any case. Since the French NAP/Inclusion is seen by most involved actors as a mere reporting exercise, and not as a strategic document, it seems to be hard to create momentum around it.

Does this mean that the NAP/Inclusion will have no impact at all on horizontal policy integration in France? This may be too hasty a conclusion. Indeed, it seems that the cross-fertilization between the NAP exercise and France's new budgetary framework (Loi organique relative aux lois de finances, LOLF) may have a major impact on enhancing the horizontal cooperation aimed for by the OMC.

The LOLF is a new architecture of the French state budget and is often termed 'revolutionary'. Within the LOLF, in order to address a number of cross-cutting issues (such as road safety, delinquency prevention, and fight against global warming), 11 so-called Cross-Cutting Policy Documents (*Documents de politique transversale*, DPT) were created. One of these DPT presents all the financial resources of all the ministries that take part in the fight against poverty and social exclusion strategy in one single document. This 'Social Inclusion Cross-cutting Policy Document' (Social Inclusion DPT) was created by the aforementioned CILE in 2004 and has been published yearly since 2006. The DGAS is in charge of its management. The Social Inclusion DPT of 2006 underlines that its creation is part of this cross-functional approach which, although initiated along with the law of 29 July 1998, was enhanced and extended with the introduction of the NAP/Inclusion in 2003. Furthermore, in order to achieve consistency, the scope of the Social Inclusion DPT is the same as that of the NAP/Inclusion. The same goes for the internal structure of the DPT, which is based on the three common objectives of the NAP/Inclusion (Ministère de l'emploi, de la cohésion sociale et du logement 2005: 7–8).

For some within DGAS 'affirming and enhancing the inter-ministerial character of the fight against exclusion policy and linking the DPT to the NAP/Inclusion are ways to further enhance the legitimacy of the fight against poverty and social exclusion' (Interview F4). Moreover, as explained by one of the French OMC experts, with ongoing work on 'indicators', with the importance given to the 'goals', and with the organization of policies by programmes, there is an interpenetration of the management models between the French and European practices. The LOLF and the DPT are good examples of such cross-fertilization (Legros 2006).

In sum, it seems that the OMC, linked to a new national financial instrument, is creating new leverage in France, which may create important procedural effects, i.e. increased cooperation between different administrative units (horizontal and cross-sectoral policy integration). In Belgium, increased cross-sectoral coordination can be seen in Wallonia and (especially) Brussels, mainly because the differences from pre-existing coordination practices in Flanders were made explicit by jointly writing the NAP/Inclusion.

Vertical coordination in decentralized Member States

The new Common Objectives require Member States to ensure 'that social inclusion policies are well-coordinated' (CEC 2005: 6). The initial Common Objectives (agreed in 2000) stipulated that Member States need to 'mobilize the public authorities at national, regional and local level, according to their respective areas of competence' (European Council 2000: 9). In practice, the need to jointly prepare NAPs/Inclusion can be the main vector for this coordination (Zeitlin 2005: 459).

The latest episode of decentralization of social policies in France was approved in 2003 and implemented in 2005. At that moment, most of the responsibilities in the social field were transferred to the departments. After this last episode of decentralization, the national level had to construct a new role for itself, and created instances and tools such as the Departmental Commissions for Social Cohesion (set up in 2006) with a view to coordinating a wide range of actors at the local level (Prefect, state representatives, NGOs, family funds, etc). The Territorial Charters for Social Cohesion are another example: created in 2004, under the authority of the prefects, they aim to support a joint regional social cohesion strategy.

Despite these efforts, the Departmental Commissions are not effective, since many of the actors they were supposed to involve do not participate in them, whereas the Territorial Charters do not seem to be operational for the moment, due to a lack of enthusiasm on the part of the prefects and local actors (Interview F4). These difficulties in organizing vertical coordination of social inclusion policies in France are not hard to understand: since the (recent) decentralization, the departments simply want to control their own policies, and distrust any attempt by central government to impose its will on them.

But how does all this link up with the NAPs/Inclusion? As one interviewee stated 'French actors were trying to understand and implement decentralization of social inclusion policies at the time of the second NAP/Inclusion in 2003, so the NAP was perhaps seen as an inconvenience at the time' (Interview EU2). Interestingly, however, it seems that national civil servants saw the NAP exercise not merely as a distraction, but also as an opportunity to get a grip on the aforementioned Departmental Commissions and Territorial Charters by involving them in the preparation of the NAP/Inclusion. For example, with regard to the Territorial Charters for Social Cohesion, the idea was to pick an objective of the NAP/Inclusion that fitted with the local preoccupations, and to ask the local actors to propose actions to illustrate this objective. Those local examples, as well as proposals for future actions, would then be joined together into 'regional NAPs'. The Departmental Commissions for Social Cohesion are being defined by the national administration, as bodies which should 'provide Prefects with a tool for coordinating and ensuring a departmental coherence of the policies on social inclusion defined by the state and by the European bodies (NAPs)' (DGAS 2006: 7).

In other words, the DGAS was inspired by the OMC to define and implement its newly acquired role vis-à-vis the regional and departmental level. One actor puts it like this:

> We have integrated the OMC well and it suits us well. For us, the OMC has exclusive, or almost exclusive, influence on the governance process. It inspires us. It works with the new role that we have been trying to define for ourselves since the decentralisation process ... Nevertheless, political will would really help us to apply new forms of governance inspired by the OMC at the national level.
>
> (Interview F4)

A working group of the CNLE, issuing a report on 'Piloting and Articulation of the Fight Against Exclusion Policies Defined at the European, National and Local level', confirms the OMC as a source of inspiration in terms of governance when it proposes, among others, that a national OMC should be developed to create policy convergence (CNLE 2006: 28). This said, the fact that the national administration tried to seize the OMC (NAP/Inclusion) to reinforce its own position domestically does not mean that it was successful; so far, 'The departments are often opposed to the national interventions, invoking the "subsidiarity principle"' (Interview F4). On the other hand, it is not in the culture of the national level to collaborate with the 'lower' levels in the decision-making process. France has a long unitary state history, with a strong top-down management tradition. As one actor puts it, 'In France, the NAPs remain national exercises. For the local level, it is a "Parisian exercise"' (Interview F8).

> In Belgium, by contrast, the evolution from a unitary into a federal State has been the result of a gradual process initiated in 1970. The radical 1993 reform put in place, besides the federal level, both the Communities[7] and the Regions,[8] which became responsible for crucial social inclusion policies such as housing and employment policies, thereby further hollowing out the centre (Hooghe 2004).

How, in such a complex institutional setting, is the input in the preparation of the NAP/Inclusion organized? In its evaluation of the social inclusion and pensions OMCs, the European Commission noted that

> Several countries (Belgium, Finland, France, Germany, Ireland) stress that they took advantage of pre-existing coordination and consultation arrangements to prepare their NAPs, in some cases developing them further. For instance, Belgium uses federated structures but has added actions and indicator task forces to prepare and follow up the NAP.
>
> (CEC 2006a: 21–2)

Note that those 'Actions' and 'Indicators' Task Forces are prepared and presided over by federal civil servants, from the federal Social Integration and Social Security administrations, respectively. Furthermore, as regards evaluation, a specific online monitoring instrument for the NAP/Inclusion has been created by the federal Social Integration administration. As a federal civil servant explains:

> The federal administration has proposed the three priorities for the last NAP, which were inspired by the EU level. We have more or less steered the decision making in this direction, prepared the meetings in this sense. There have been discussions about why other priorities (for example debt) were not taken into consideration, but in the end everyone accepted our proposal.
>
> (Interview B5)

Finally, the federal administration is also in charge of the biannual conference during which the NAP/Inclusion is discussed with a wide variety of actors, and which increasingly takes the form of an 'internal Belgian peer review'. This new role for the federal administration has not gone unnoticed by most of the actors:

> The Federal Social Integration Administration keeps track of the implementation records, coordinates the NAP. The federal level has thereby regained a better overview over the poverty policies of the Regions and the Communities. You could speak of a 'light steering effect' or a 'more active coordination' than in the past. The Regions have changing moods about this situation. Sometimes they see it as a burden, sometimes they want to be part of it as well.
>
> (Interview B4)

With regard to the targets which were prepared for the third NAP/Inclusion, the federal administration interpreted its role very broadly:

> At the political level, Belgium has always been in favour of those targets, but we did not manage to develop them for our own NAP. So the administration had to take responsibility for it, and move faster than political decision making. Until recently we just waited, but now we were forced to write our own proposal, based on the work of the Indicators

> Taskforce. We set up an internal benchmarking, so that each region would perform well on at least one of the targets. The day before the final inter-cabinet meeting we sent our proposal to the cabinet. It was agreed without discussion, and integrated into the NAP – we are not even sure they know what they agreed to.
>
> (Interview B5)

In sum, in both countries, the European level is used to try to increase the coordinating role of the national government, through the NAP/Inclusion, in a context of decentralization. Europe inspires the national level that is trying to find a new governance model, and provides justifications for its 'new' potential role vis-à-vis the local or regional levels. In Belgium the effects are already tangible: the OMC/SPSI stimulates Regions, Communities and central government to exchange experiences. The Communities and Regions also seem to have delegated some authority to the federal level for coordination and follow-up of the OMC. Thus, even in the absence of a single, overarching cooperation system with regard to EU social policies, it seems that the OMC keeps the federal level at the centre, even in a policy area that has been regionalized to a very large degree. This finding confirms the general conclusions of Beyers and Bursens (2006: 1073), that because of European integration the Belgian central government remains an influential actor even with respect to issues outside its competences. And it confirms their finding that extensive regional capabilities coincide with a high (rather than low) level of cooperative behaviour within Belgium (ibid.: 1074).

Improving steering capacity in Belgium

A procedural effect of participation in the NAP exercise results from the fact that social inclusion policies are continuously being monitored, both by the EU and at the national level. A monitoring instrument for the NAP/Inclusion was set up by the federal Social Integration administration. Even though far from perfect, this monitoring seems to create at least some external pressure on those involved in policy making:

> The European process is our anchor point, sometimes we can say 'we have to do this', for example with regard to the requirement to set targets. The rhythm is important as well. We have to follow: writing a plan, evaluation, monitoring, writing a new plan. And being questioned about why some things were not realized. The continuity of this exercise cannot be underestimated, the OMC certainly keeps us focused, and it shortens the policy cycle, even though politics is never a straight line.
>
> (Interview B4)

A senior civil servant of the federal Social Integration administration claims that:

> So far, the existing instruments and institutions like the Resource Centre issue recommendations, but rarely verify what happens to them in policy terms. Let alone that the government itself would reflect upon what it realized as compared to the promises it made. This new policy phase, of monitoring and evaluation, has now been created in Belgian social policy making through the OMC and the NAP, also because it is a continuous process. We can now say: of all the measures that have been announced in the NAP 2001/2003, 80% have been put into place, and 20% have not.
>
> (Interview B5)

In other words, certain actors have successfully revised the institutional setting so as to advance a 'spirit of evaluation' in Belgian social inclusion policy making (Morissens and Nicaise 2007: 17). Even though technical and other obstacles still impede a thorough evaluation of the implementation of many measures, at least at the cognitive level the OMC has helped to create a U-turn in this respect.

2.3 Indicators: building statistical capacity through EU-SILC

According to Frank Vandenbroucke, one of the political architects of the Social Inclusion OMC, indicators constitute no less than 'the actual litmus test for the political readiness to engage in open coordination. Anyone who paid lip service to this method, should put their words into action when it comes to the development of indicators' (Vandenbroucke 2001: 3). In December 2001, the Laeken European Council adopted a battery of 18 commonly agreed and defined indicators for social exclusion, which was revised with the streamlining process in 2006 (CEC 2006b). Despite their different starting positions, involvement in the OMC had similar, and important, effects in Belgium and France.

At the end of the 1990s, Belgium's official statistical capacity with regard to poverty and social exclusion faced real challenges. The National Statistical Institute (NIS) possessed hardly any know-how in this area, and was completely dependent on two universities (Liège and Antwerp) to provide statistical information which the latter collected through the annual Panel Survey on Belgian Households (PSBH). These universities made these Belgian national panel data available to Eurostat, which then adapted them for integration into the European Community Household Panel Study (ECHP). The relationship between the Belgian National Statistical Institute and Eurostat was rather tense: for almost five years the NIS contested the validity of the Belgian ECHP data. This led to considerable confusion and sharp national debates: depending on the source used, Belgium performed between 'very well' and 'on average' as compared to other countries. Even more important, there was no agreement about the long-term evolution of the poverty situation: according to Eurostat calculations, poverty decreased over time, while the Belgian panel data indicated the contrary. In sum, Belgium faced a double challenge: weak official statistical capacity and contested poverty and social exclusion indicators.

During the second half of 2001, the situation changed in important ways, since the Action Programme on Social Inclusion boosted discussions on the SILC dataset, which has replaced the ECHP survey. At that moment, the technical problems facing social statistical capacity in Belgium arrived at the political level. Indeed, reaching an agreement on commonly defined indicators for social inclusion was one of the top priorities of the 2001 Belgian EU Presidency,[9] and thus it was inconceivable that the country would be unable to participate in the new statistical tool designed to provide the data on which they would be based. Vandenbroucke, then Belgian Minister for Social Affairs, therefore instructed his cabinet to resolve this situation as soon as possible, so as to ensure that Belgium would a) not be the only Member State with missing values for social inclusion indicators in the 2001 Spring Report, b) be able to participate from the very beginning, in the gentlemen's agreement between six Member States,[10] as well as Norway, that would pre-launch EU-SILC as from 2003 (Marlier et al. 2007), and c) be able to use (uncontested) Laeken indicators in the 2003 National Action Plan, since it had been pushing other Member States to do just that.

As a result of further negotiations between Eurostat and the Belgian authorities, a compromise was reached in November 2002, following which the Belgian ECHP data were released.[11] The national statistical institute thereafter decided to boost its own statistical capacity so that it could organize the collection of social data itself.

In sum, commitment to the OMC/SPSI had a major impact on statistical capacity building in Belgium. And this is not the end of the indicators story. Take, for example, the increase of the minimum income for elderly people, 'GRAPA' in French, since December 2006. The former Belgian Minister for Pensions, Bruno Tobback, explains that: 'Sometimes the OMC can be usefully applied in the national debate. For example, we legitimized the increase of the GRAPA by pointing out that the benefit levels were below the European risk of poverty line' (Interview B6). According to the deputy head of cabinet of the Belgian Ministry for Social Integration, the European risk-of-poverty norm acquired a broader mobilizing character:

> It has become widely accepted. It is a substantive argument in budgetary negotiations ... In order to determine whether people are entitled to free legal assistance, the European risk-of-poverty norm is also the relevant criterion now. References to European norms, and EU-SILC calculations, have become frequent in policy discussions and documents.
>
> (Interview B4)

Arguably, at the time of the agreement on the Laeken indicators, France started from a very different position. National statistical capacity in the social field was already well developed. As one (non-French!) indicators experts told us: 'France is one of the European countries which has the most valuable statistical system' (Interview EU4).

Even so, it would be wrong to assume that French involvement in the development of European indicators has been without effect. According to the former Director of the Division of Research, Studies, Assessment and Statistics (DREES), the definition of the (revised) Laeken indicators has further enhanced France's national steering capacity. 'The weight of European requirements gives us a means of pressure to develop statistical data. It also explains that some social indicators are more and more taken into account at the national level' (Interview F6). More concretely, the European level is used at the national level to try to push the harmonization of domestic indicators. In France, there is a lack of coherence between the indicators used in different settings and institutions. Different indicators of poverty and social exclusion are used or proposed by the NAP/Inclusion, the DPT, the Social Cohesion Plan, and by local authorities. The National Monitoring Centre for Poverty and Social Exclusion (ONPES), an organization set up in 1998 by the exclusion law, proposed in its 2005–6 Annual Report to start using, at the national level, 11 'harmonized' indicators based on the Laeken set (ONPES 2006: 51–5). Since then, CILE has asked CNLE to decide, together with ONPES and other concerned institutions, on a list of common indicators (CILE 2006: 15). So far, this has not been done.

Consider, finally, the influence of OMC on the French debate about the evolution of an important indicator, i.e. the monetary poverty indicator threshold. In France, the official poverty rate is 50% of the median income, while it is 60% at the European level (Eurostat). For a number of years now, France has officially refused to align its poverty rate with the European one, but this is changing. The use of the Laeken indicators in the domestic context, as proposed by ONPES, implies the use of the 60% rather than the 50% threshold. While CNLE still has to give its opinion on this issue, CILE has already decided to change the presentation of the poverty rate in the future NAP/Inclusion: it will align the poverty threshold with the EU norm (CILE 2006: 15). For the moment, we note that the National Institute for Statistic and Economic Studies (INSEE) presents both thresholds in its publications.

In sum, the statistical effort inspired by the social inclusion OMC enhanced both Belgium's and France's statistical capacity, even if they started from very different initial positions.

2.4 Targets: creative appropriation in Belgium, trickling down in France

Targets are the 'quantification' of the Common Objectives. In the first round of NAPs/Inclusion, submitted in 2001, only a minority of the then 15 Member States included outcome targets. This changed after the strong political impetus for an enhanced role for targets in the next round of NAPs/Inclusion from the March 2002 Barcelona European Council (European Council 2002). Yet, there were exceptions. Indeed, it came as some surprise to most *European* partners that Belgium did not integrate *any* quantified targets in its 2003 NAP/Inclusion (CEC 2004: 40). After all, Belgium was one of the most outspoken supporters, and arguably among the architects, of the Barcelona European Council Conclusions on this issue. And yet, the reason is actually quite simple: despite the lip service paid to the importance of precise targets, no political agreement could be reached on the targets, which has everything to with the operation of the principle of subsidiarity within the Belgian context.

Indeed, the design of most policy areas is complicated in Belgium by the fact that, even in areas with subnational competencies, framework rule making often remains federal (Hooghe 2004). For an agreement on almost any quantified target in the area of social policy, unanimous agreement is needed between five different governments which are on equal footing, since the federal government has no superiority over the subnational levels.

Thus, for some it came as a considerable surprise that in the most recent NAP/Inclusion (2006–8), Belgium *did* in fact propose a wide set of quantitative targets, for each of the policy priorities. This is in fact the first time that Belgium has formally committed itself to explicit targets in this area. Even more crucially, these targets also cover some of the most 'difficult' policy areas in view of the internal sharing of competencies described above. Thus, Belgian targets address housing and education, both of which are mainly subnational (Regional) competencies, but with important federal involvement. It is important to note that the NAP/Inclusion sets overall 'Belgian' targets, and not subnational ones. The importance of 'Belgian' targets being applied to subnational competencies cannot be overestimated: it is widely acknowledged that pursuing these national targets is only possible through increased coordination of regional policies, which is not self-evident, given the institutional context.

According to the President of the Flemish Network, which plays an increasing role in the preparation of the NAP/Inclusion,[12] this is exactly where OMC provides added value: 'the Network has insisted on finding agreement on targets in policy areas with shared competencies, since it is in those policy areas that deadlocks arise because of lack of coordination' (Interview B3). Some of the key actors involved in the Social Inclusion OMC are already seeing some impact of the precise targets that were agreed. Thus, the national coordinator of the Belgian NAP/Inclusion claims that

> With regard to social housing the National Action Plan clearly highlights that the numbers need to increase. After the European Commission's recommendations to Belgium in the Joint Report, social housing became an issue of discussion in Flanders. The Minister for Housing was questioned by the media, the sector, the Flemish Parliament: what will you do to increase social housing as you announced in the Plan?
>
> (Interview B5)

But Belgium was not the only Member State that was reluctant to set targets. In fact, national quantitative targets were never officially adopted in the French NAP/Inclusion. The 2003–5 NAP presented some (minimal) targets, but they were abandoned in the 2006–8 NAP (PNAI 2003: 117). A working group of the CNLE actually rejected, in 2005, the idea of national quantitative objectives in the field of poverty and social exclusion, referring mainly to practical difficulties (data for monetary poverty indicators are, for example, known only two and a half years later) (IGAS 2006: 312). To explain the absence of national targets in France, some of the actors interviewed also argue that it is hard to 'influence' a poverty rate or a child poverty rate. The interpretation of those indicators is also seen as problematic. A deterioration in the poverty rate can be a consequence of the inefficiency of public policies, or linked to the need for more resources (Interview F6). 'It is better to analyse and to disaggregate the indicators to understand the causes instead of fixing those targets. What is the point of having targets if we don't know how to affect them?' (Interview F6).

Another explanation for this opposition to the creation of quantitative targets is linked to the decentralization process. The difficult and unclear relationships between the national and local level certainly explain why it is hard to create those targets. According the annual report of the IGAS, national targets that would be fed by local indicators would be a way to attenuate the tensions between both levels. However, that would suppose a 'real' consultation process, which is far from the French tradition. Moreover, with common targets, common local indicators should also be developed. But until now, those indicators have not been defined, and so there are no information systems that provide comparable data at the local level (IGAS 2006: 322–4).

Nevertheless, the governance by 'targets' promoted by the European level is beginning to be introduced in France. The NAP/Inclusion 2006–8 explained that, in 2006, the CILE decided to fix some targets and indicators to evaluate progress in the fight against poverty and social exclusion. The CILE justifies this by referring to the Lisbon Strategy (CILE 2006: 14). Work on those targets was supposed to begin at the end of 2006 (CEC 2006b: 17), but this has not yet produced concrete results. However, in his National Commitment to Poverty Eradication, Hirsch proposes a quantified objective: diminishing poverty by one-third in five years. 'This is a good example of a completely new culture in France that largely comes from the European level' (Interview F8).

In sum, target setting is a new feature of social inclusion policy making in Belgium and France, which has been introduced, albeit at a slower pace in the latter country, through the OMC. In Belgium setting targets in well-chosen policy areas is becoming an additional strategic argument to obtain better coordination of those policies between vertical levels of government.

2.5 Peer reviews: limited learning from others, but internal spill-overs and a 'mirror-effect'

Peer reviews are supposed to be central to the OMC learning process. They are mutual learning processes based on the systematic evaluation of good practices and assessment of selected policies or institutional arrangements presented in the NAPs/Inclusion of the Member States.

By participating in peer reviews, actors should eventually learn from other countries' 'good practices'. This mechanism can inspire procedural and even substantive national shifts. However, it appears that the peer reviews are mainly considered, at least in France, as an exercise for civil servants and experts. Some of the French actors interviewed think that peer reviews could be useful, but that a good diffusion of their 'results' is lacking (Interview F12).

> The academics and the specialists who work in Brussels know about the peer reviews, but the administrative and elected actors are not often familiar with it. And even if they know about the exercise, they don't know where to get the results.
>
> (Interview F15)

And yet the peer review exercise had an unintended consequence. The French field of fight against poverty is often described as extremely intricate, involving many actors with a complex division of competences, and sectoral, specialized and fragmented policies (Palier 2005: 307). To facilitate cross-national comparison as part of a peer review exercise, the DGAS prepared a document presenting the national fight-against-exclusion policy field (DGAS 2006). Some actors told us that it was the occasion, for the first time, to identify all the actors in the national arena, their roles, and their policy responsibilities. In other words, the need to present the national system to others, which is necessary for any comparison, leads to what we call a 'mirror effect': exposing the national field to others gives a clearer vision of one's own practices.

Even though the perceived impact of the peer reviews is very low, a more systematic comparison with other countries is cited by most of the actors as one of the most important contributions of the European exercise: 'With Europe, it is more in the national culture to look for what the neighbours are doing' (Interview EU15). There is an increased awareness of policies, practices, and performances in other countries, by non-state as well as by governmental actors. Thus one French NGO activist organized a cross-channel study trip through the European Federation of National Organizations Working with the Homeless (FEANTSA) to investigate the domestic applicability of an 'opposable right to housing' introduced by the Homeless Scotland Act of 2003 (Interview F13). Such comparisons, through socialization and learning, may contribute to cognitive and eventually policy shifts. Yet, as one actor puts it, 'comparison is used more in a political way by actors that want to legitimate national actions (leverage). Comparison is less used to really learn about the way to change the national policies' (Interview EU5).

Belgian actors generally confirm the views of their French counterparts. At the same time, peer review as interpreted in Belgium provides a striking example of institutional change: the European way of doing seems to have spilled over in Belgium to create an internal learning process between different levels of decision making.

Thus, the national coordinators of the Belgian NAP/Inclusion see an increase in interregional exchanges, and refer to 'a kind of OMC within Belgium', which is complemented by increased informal contacts between regional and federal civil servants (Interview B5). Furthermore, 'There are a number of examples of conscious learning from each other, between the regions' (Interview B2). The Director of the President of the Flemish Network of Associations where the Poor Take the Floor confirms that 'discussing each other's policies, between regions, is a new feature in Belgian social policy making' (Interview B3). The Deputy Head of Cabinet of the Ministry for Social Integration provides insight about the actual mechanisms of the 'internal learning process':

> The Flemish see what the Walloons write in their Plan, and wonder why they could not do something similar. In principle this could also happen without the OMC, but the number of places where there is a wider view on the whole country and where exchange of ideas are possible, are becoming scarce. It is important that we hold on to them, certainly now that the process is clearly deepening: first all energy went to writing the process details, now it is clearer who the actors are, they require certain legitimacy. As a consequence, there is more room for substantial discussions now, we can be a bit sharper towards each other, now that we know each other and know what to expect. We do not have to evaluate each other, but still we can tell each other what we find good, and what we like less. We can do so, because people feel safer now, we have learned to trust each other.
>
> (Interview B4)

In conclusion, while mutual learning from other Member States is often quoted as an important *potential* added value of OMC, learning about one's *own* practices (the mirror effect) is an established practice within the OMC in both countries, and participation in the NAP exercise creates a cognitive shift towards internal peer review, at least in Belgium.

3 Summary and conclusions

The debate on the OMC is characterized by a lack of agreement about the analytical instruments to assess properly its effectiveness. Our detailed analysis of the effects of the Social Inclusion OMC[13] in Belgium and France confirms this: if the yardstick is 'regulatory change' (e.g. changes in legislation), then our research confirms the findings of the more 'critical' branch of OMC literature (Citi and Rhodes 2007): its impact is extremely limited. But if we look beyond regulatory changes to measure the effectiveness of OMC, then labelling this process 'cheap talk' seems extremely misleading.

We have identified two sets of effects which can be attributed to the Social Inclusion OMC. First, and probably least surprising, it has caused procedural changes in social inclusion policies in Belgium and France. We distinguish four categories. First, 'rationalization of policies': involvement in the social inclusion OMC boosted (Belgium) or strengthened (France) statistical capacity in both countries. This OMC also played a crucial role in launching a culture of monitoring and evaluation of social inclusion policies in Belgium; it helped to increase the coherence of national poverty indicators and reinforced domestic actors and policies in France. Second, 'vertical coordination': participation in the OMC is strengthening cooperation between (autonomous) Regions in Belgium, and has increased the coordination role of the federal level (e.g. through the setting of national targets for regional competencies). This increased vertical coordination has created a spill-over effect, namely prudent yet significant intra-regional policy learning (between Wallonia, Flanders, and Brussels). Third, 'actor involvement': participation in this OMC has led to further strengthening and institutionalization of NGO involvement in Belgian social inclusion policies (especially in Wallonia). We did not find a similar effect in France. Fourth, 'horizontal coordination': we observed increased cross-sectoral coordination in two of the Belgian Regions (Wallonia and Brussels), and a large potential (which has not yet materialized) for cross-sectoral coordination in France through the Social Inclusion Cross-cutting Policy Documents (DPTs). The latter produce cross-fertilization between the new architecture of the French state budget (LOLF) and the inclusion section of the NSR.

Our empirical analysis provides equally strong evidence for substantive shifts in social inclusion policies, in both Belgium and France. We distinguish 'political' and 'cognitive' shifts. First, participation in the OMC raised the profile of the poverty issue on the political agenda in Belgium and France, and it has also increased the focus on activation in French social inclusion policies. It provided bargaining arguments in budgetary negotiations in both countries, but most clearly in Belgium (e.g. legitimation for a significant increase in minimum income for the elderly). 'Cognitive shifts' are more difficult to trace. Yet we found compelling evidence that the social inclusion OMC pushed child poverty as a new issue onto the policy agendas in Belgium and France, despite rather strong initial resistance in both countries. Furthermore, participation in this OMC convinced domestic social inclusion policy makers of the utility of adopting 'targets', explicitly in Belgium, and largely covertly in France. The social inclusion OMC also serves as inspiration for the French national administration to redefine its new (coordinating) role in the context of decentralisation.

By far the most powerful mechanism through which the OMC works is 'leverage': actors creatively appropriate the different instruments of the OMC toolbox to legitimize their own preferences. This is true for the common objectives (e.g. use of the child poverty issue, in Belgium and France, to legitimize actions aimed at other target groups); the NAP/Inclusion (e.g. to demand increased NGO participation in Belgium), targets (as a means of increasing the coordination capacity of the federal government in Belgium); indicators (e.g. to show that national performance is not so good after all, in both countries studied); and peer reviews (as a means of pointing out deficiencies in policies in comparison to other Member States). Even though peer review is being taken up by actors in both Belgium and France, it is clearly the instrument in the OMC toolbox that is being least exploited in this respect.

A second mechanism through which OMC affects French and Belgian policies is 'learning': the empirical section gave examples of mirror effects, for example French actors 'discovering' the complete mosaic of domestic actors, their roles and responsibilities, through peer review. Similarly, Belgian policy makers learned that specific aspects of the child poverty *problematique* had been overlooked. Most unexpectedly, learning (e.g. with regard to cross-policy coordination or NGO involvement) is taking place now *between* Regions in Belgium, as a consequence of the regular European reporting obligations, which contributed to unprecedented trust building between actors.

A third mechanism is 'external pressure', which is in general not felt as 'soft' at all. Actors perceive strong EU pressure to take child poverty on board as a priority issue, to start monitoring social exclusion policies, to involve a wide variety of actors, to set ambitious and quantified national targets etc.

Do these findings allow us to draw conclusions about the 'conditions' for OMC effectiveness? First, our analysis underlines the importance of viewing OMC effectiveness as reciprocal influence (as opposed to one-way impact). Consider, for example the 'impact' of the social inclusion OMC on Belgian statistical capacity building, which is in large part the result of the successful uploading, by Belgium, of the Laeken indicators during the country's 2001 EU Presidency. The same goes for the OMC's 'impact' on France's new focus on active inclusion, which can be understood by looking at the key role the country played in 2000 in defining the Common Objectives. In other words, it seems that the 'impact' of the OMC depends, at least to some degree, on the involvement of national stakeholders in EU-level decision making in the first place.

This brings us to a second conclusion: our analysis demonstrates that the OMC's domestic influence is largely independent of the actual *success* of Member States' initial uploading efforts. Consider, for example, the strengthening of NGO involvement in Belgium as a consequence of OMC, despite the fact that there was already a large fit between EU-level requirements and Belgian practices. This casts further doubts on the usefulness of the fit/misfit paradigm to explain domestic adaptational pressures as a result of EU soft law initiatives. There are some obvious explanations: 1) actors may simply misjudge the extent to which they create a misfit (and thus adaptational pressure) by uploading their preferences to the EU level (e.g. Belgium discovering it was not such a good pupil in the class with regard to actor involvement); 2) during the time between uploading and downloading of EU policies a new situation (e.g. decentralization in France) may have arisen; 3) uploading is never perfect (e.g. even though France had a dominant role in writing the common objectives, it still had to accept a compromise which included 'active inclusion'); 4) however small the misfit, domestic actors can and do use it as a lever to force domestic changes (e.g. child poverty: first catapulted to, but then creatively seized by the domestic arenas).

A third conclusion is that the domestic effects of OMC are by no means predetermined by the institutional setting. On the one hand, *different* institutional settings lead to *similar* effects: consider, for example the significant effects the OMC had on statistical capacity building in Belgium *and* France, in spite of these countries' totally different starting positions. On the other hand, several examples have been highlighted where *similar* institutional settings resulted in significantly *different* effects. Thus, in the context of devolution of social inclusion policies in France and Belgium, national and subnational policy makers have reacted very differently to the social inclusion OMC (an increased national coordination role in Belgium, and rejection, for now, of this 'Parisian' role in France). Another example: strong NGO involvement in Belgium *and* France in the pre-OMC era, resulting in increased involvement through the OMC in Belgium and little change to the status quo in France.

Fourth: even though none of the Belgian or French actors we interviewed said the OMC was shaking domestic social policy making, Belgian actors perceive it as an increasingly important, and useful, tool in domestic policy making. French actors do so too, but to a lesser extent. Reference to the OMC is very common in domestic social inclusion policies, both in Belgium (Flemish Action Plan, national social inclusion targets, planning documents of local Public Centres for Social Welfare etc.) and, to a somewhat lesser extent, in France (National Commitment to Poverty Eradication, LOLF, DPT). In such circumstances, it seems very likely that feedback mechanisms between the domestic and EU level will further ensure the continuation of this OMC, not only as a 'paper tiger' but as an operational tool (in spite of its prematurely announced death by some academics). But there seems to be one important condition for this. If French civil servants, NGO representatives, and politicians are generally less supportive of the OMC this seems to be strongly related to the position of this process in the social inclusion policy arena. Even though in both countries the NAP/Inclusion is to a large extent a summary of decisions that have already been taken, the way these documents are elaborated differs significantly. The most important difference is that in Belgium these reports are coordinated at the political level ('cabinet'), while it is a largely administrative effort in France. Similarly, meetings of the Social Protection Committee are being prepared at administrative level in France, but typically involve political representatives in Belgium. Further strengthening of political involvement in the OMC seems a crucial precondition for its effectiveness, and its continuation.

With this caveat, our empirical analysis of the operation of the social inclusion OMC has shown that it is certainly more than window dressing. Through mechanisms such as leverage, policy learning, and external pressure, the OMC triggers significant procedural and substantive effects, at least in some Member States. These effects are the result of processes of reciprocal influence between the EU and the domestic setting, which are rather different, and more significant in impact, than could be expected from a 'hard law' perspective. The OMC has clearly grown more teeth than some had expected. Or had perhaps wished.

Notes

1 The authors are grateful to Martin Heidenreich, Jonathan Zeitlin, Josée Goris, Mieke Beckers, Anton Hemerijck, Gerben Korthouwer, Sandra Kröger, Florence Larocque, Eric Marlier, David Natali, Marc van der Meer, Jelle Visser, and Nynke Wiekenkamp for their stimulating comments on earlier versions of this chapter. The research for this chapter benefited from funding by the Belgian Science Policy Office (Society and Future Research Programme) and the Shifts in Governance Programme of the Dutch Science Foundation (NWO). The usual disclaimer applies.
2 See, for example Zeitlin and Pochet (2005), CEC (2006a), and the other evaluations cited by Zeitlin (this volume).
3 See Citi and Rhodes (2007) for an attempt to provide such an analytical framework.
4 Law no 98–657 of 29 July 1998.
5 The Inter-Ministerial Conference for Social Integration is entrusted with the design and monitoring of coordinated government policies at all levels of government (federal, community and regional). It is supposed to meet at least twice a year.
6 Within the DGAS, the 'Bureau des politiques de prévention, d'insertion et de l'accès aux droits' is responsible for preparing the NSR.
7 Flemish, French, and German.
8 Flanders, Wallonia, and Brussels.
9 The Belgian Presidency commissioned an in-depth methodological research project for this specific purpose (Atkinson et al. 2002).
10 Belgium, Denmark, Greece, Ireland, Luxembourg, and Austria.
11 As a result of the recalculations made by Eurostat, the Belgian at-risk-of-poverty rate decreased by no less than 2%.
12 Namely through the 'Task Force Actions' in which different stakeholders and experts are represented and which prepares the NAP/Inclusion, together with the 'Task Force Indicators'.
13 Or, to be more precise: the social inclusion strand of the streamlined OMC/SPSI.

References

Atkinson, T., Cantillon, B., Marlier, E. and Nolan, B. (2002) *Social Indicators: The EU and Social Inclusion*, Oxford: Oxford University Press.

Barbier, J.C. (2005) 'Research on "Open Methods of Coordination" and National Social Policies: What Sociological Theories and Methods?', in T. Bredgaard and F. Larsen (eds) *Employment Policy from Different Angles*, Copenhagen: DJOF Publishing, pp. 47–74.

Beyers, J. and Bursens, P. (2006) 'The European Rescue of the Federal State: How Europeanization Shapes the Belgian State', *West European Politics*, 29: 1057–78.

Börzel, T.A. (2003) 'Shaping and Taking EU Policies: Member State Responses to Europeanization', *Queen's Papers on Europeanization* 2/2003. Online. Available HTTP: www.qub.ac.uk/schools/SchoolofPoliticsInternationalStudiesandPhilosophy/FileStore/EuropeanisationFiles/Filetoupload,38412,en.pdf (accessed 10 September 2008).

Caporaso J., Cowles, M.G. and Risse, T. (2001) 'Europeanization and Domestic Change: Introduction', in J. Caporaso, M.G. Cowles and T. Risse (eds) *Transforming Europe*, Ithaca: Cornell University Press, pp. 1–20.

Cazain, S., Donné, S., Hennion, M. and Nauze-Fichet, E. (2006) *Le nombre d'allocataires du RMI au 31 mars 2006*, Etudes et Résultats 495. Online. Available HTTP: www.sante.gouv.fr/drees/etude-resultat/er495/er495.pdf (accessed 10 September 2008).

CEC (2001) *European Commission, Joint Report on Social Inclusion 2001*, Luxembourg: Office for Official Publications of the European Communities.

—— (2004) *Joint Report on Social Inclusion 2004, Statistical Annex*, Luxembourg: Office for Official Publications of the European Communities.

—— (2005) *Communication from the Commission to the Council, the European Parliament, the European Economic and Social Committee and the Committee of the Regions – Working Together, Working Better – A New Framework for the Open Coordination of Social Protection and Inclusion Policies in the European Union*, COM 2005, 0706.

—— (2006a) *Commission Staff Working Document. Evaluation of the Open Method of Coordination for Social Protection and Social Inclusion. A Synthesis of Replies by Member States and Other Actors to an Evaluation Questionnaire on the Open Method of Coordination in the Fields of Social Inclusion and Sustainable Pensions*, Brussels, SEC (2006), 345.

—— (2006b) *Portfolio of Overarching Indicators and Streamlined Social Inclusion, Pensions, and Health Portfolios*, Brussels, 7 June 2006.

—— (2007) *Joint Report on Social Protection and Social Inclusion 2007, Social Inclusion, Pension, Health Care and Long Term Care*, Luxembourg: Office for Official Publications of the European Communities.

CILE (2006) *Dossier de Presse*. Online. Available HTTP: www.cnle.gouv.fr/IMG/pdf/dossier_de_presse_CILE_120506.pdf (accessed 11 September 2008)

Citi, M. and Rhodes, M. (2007) 'New Modes of Governance in the European Union: A Critical Survey and Analysis', in K.E. Jorgensen, M. Pollack, and B. Rosamond (eds) *Handbook of European Union Politics*, London: Sage, pp. 463–82.

CNLE (2006) Rapport du groupe de travail: 'Pilotage et articulation des politiques de lutte contre les exclusions définies aux niveaux européen, national et local', Présidents: Bernard Lacharme et Véronique Fayet, Texte du 16 février.

DGAS (2006) 'Politiques d'inclusion sociale–France-2006: Coordination et Partenariat', internal document.

Erhel, C., Mandin, L. and Palier, B. (2005) 'The Leverage Effect. The Open Method of Coordination in France', in J. Zeitlin and P. Pochet with L. Magnusson (eds) *The Open Method of Coordination in Action. The European Employment and Social Inclusion Strategies*, Brussels: Peter Lang, 217–47.

European Council (2000) *Fight Against Poverty and Social Exclusion, Definition of Appropriate Objectives. Annex: Objectives in the Fight Against Poverty and Social Exclusion, Introductory Note*, Document no. 14110/00 soc 470, November 2000.

—— (2002) *Presidency Conclusions – Barcelona European Council 15–16*, March 2002, Document SN 100/1/02 REV1.

—— (2006) *Brussels European Council 23–24 March 2006*, Presidency Conclusions, Brussels, 7775/1/06 Rev 1.

Groenez, S. and Nicaise, I. (2004) *Evaluation of the Implementation of the Belgian NAP Inclusion 2003–05*, Leuven: Hoger Instituut voor de Arbeid.

Haut Commissaire (2007) *Engagement national. Réduire d'un tiers la pauvreté en France en cinq ans: un engagement partagé*, Haut Commissaire aux solidarités actives contre la pauvreté. Online. Available HTTP : www.premier-ministre.gouv.fr/IMG/pdf/Engagement_national_contre_la_pauvrete.pdf (accessed 10 September 2008).

Hooghe, L. (2004) 'Belgium: Hollowing the Center', in U. Amoretti and N. Bermeo (eds) *Federalism and Territorial Cleavages*, Baltimore, MD: Johns Hopkins University Press, pp. 55–92.

IGAS (2006) *La dimension européenne des politiques sociales – Rapport annuel 2006*, Paris: La documentation française.

Legros, M. (2006) *France. Trends, Recent Developments, Active Inclusion and Minimum Resources. First Semester Report 2006*, Peer Review and Assessment in Social Inclusion. Online. Available HTTP: http://ec.europa.eu/employment_social/spsi/docs/social_inclusion/experts_reports/france_2006_fr.pdf (accessed 10 September 2008).

Marlier, E., Atkinson, A.B., Cantillon, B. and Nolan, B. (2007) *The EU and Social Inclusion. Facing the Challenges*, Bristol: The Policy Press.

Ministère de l'emploi, de la cohésion sociale et du logement (2005) *Inclusion sociale: Document de politique transversale. Projet de loi de finances pour 2006*, Paris: Imprimerie nationale.

—— (2006) 'La Participation des personnes et la lutte contre l'exclusion', Journée du 18/09/2006, Co-organisée par la DGAS et l'ENSP, internal document.

Morissens, A. and Nicaise, I. (2007b) *Assessment of the Social Inclusion Strand of the Belgian National Strategy Report on Social Protection and Social Inclusion*, Leuven: Hoger Instituut voor de Arbeid (KULeuven).

Morissens, A., Nicaise, I. and Ory, G. (2007) 'Belgium, Tackling Child Poverty and Promoting the Social Inclusion of Children, a Study of National Policies, HIVA KU. Leuven', *Peer Review and Assessment in Social Inclusion*. Online. Available HTTP: http://ec.europa.eu/employment_social/social_inclusion/docs/experts_reports/belgium_1_2007_en.pdf (accessed 10 September 2008).

Nicaise, I., Groenez, S., Vleminckx, K., Demeuse, M. and Berghman, J. (2003) *The Belgian National Action Plan for Social Inclusion 2001–2003: a Preliminary Evaluation. Report of the Non-Governmental Experts*, Leuven: Hoger Instituut voor de Arbeid.

ONPES (2006) *Le Rapport de l'Observatoire national de la pauvreté et de l'exclusion sociale*, Paris : La Documentation française.

Palier, B. (2005) *Gouverner la sécurité sociale*, Paris : PUF.

PNAI (2003) *France, Plan national d'action pour l'inclusion sociale 2003–05, Annexe 1-B, Indicateurs de suivi et d'évaluation du PNAI 2003–05*. Online. Available HTTP: http://ec.europa.eu/employment_social/news/2001/jun/annex_fr1.pdf (accessed 10 September 2008).

Sénat (2004) *Projet de Loi de programmation pour la cohésion sociale*, Session extraordinaire de 2003–4, N°44. Online. Available HTTP : www.senat.fr/leg/pjl03–445.html (accessed 10 September 2008).

SPC (2008) *Child Poverty and Well-being in the EU. Current Status and Way Forward, Report from the Social Protection Committee*, Luxembourg: Office for Official Publications of the European Communities.

Vandenbroucke, F. (2001) 'Open Coordination on Pensions and the Future of Europe's Social Model', closing Speech at the Conference 'Towards a New Architecture for Social Protection?', Leuven, October. Online. Available HTTP: http://oud.frankvandenbroucke.be/html/soc/frame47.htm (accessed 10 September 2008).

Zeitlin, J. (2005) 'The Open Method of Coordination in Action. Theoretical Promise, Empirical Realities, Reform Strategy', in J. Zeitlin and P. Pochet with L. Magnusson (eds) *The Open Method of Coordination in Action. The European Employment and Social Inclusion Strategies*, Brussels: Peter Lang, pp. 447–503.

Zeitlin J. and Pochet P. with Magnusson, L. (eds) (2005) *The Open Method of Coordination in Action. The European Employment and Social Inclusion Strategies*, Brussels: Peter Lang.

5 Joining the European Employment Strategy

Europeanization of labour market policy in the Baltic states

Kerstin Jacobsson and Charlotte West

> Together with our Baltic brothers and sisters we helped dismantle the former Soviet Union and, as a result, regained our independence after five decades of Soviet occupation. But we understand that in order to remain independent, we must participate actively in European and trans-Atlantic structures of like-minded democratic nations. That's why we've made a choice with a very clear goal – to anchor ourselves where we belong, in Europe.[1]
>
> (Mart Laar, Estonian Prime Minister 1992–94, 1999–2002)

Introduction

In March 1990, Lithuania became the first republic to break away from the Soviet Union. One by one, the Soviet republics, as well as other states behind the Iron Curtain, declared their independence. As the Soviet Union dissolved, the countries of Eastern and Central Europe (CEEC) turned westward. Over the following decade, these states increasingly joined Western organizations, such as NATO and the EU. The culmination was two successive waves of EU enlargement, increasing the number of EU Member States from 15 to 27. The CEEC all share a legacy of centrally planned economies and non-democratic political systems. The path to EU membership was far more demanding for these countries – and hence institutional change was also more far reaching – than during previous rounds of enlargement. Furthermore, the speed of adjustment was rapid. The period between the dissolution of the Soviet Union and accession to the EU took little more than a decade.

Among the new Member States are the Baltics: Estonia, Latvia, and Lithuania. These were the only states among the other CEEC that were fully integrated into the Soviet Union. Besides the economic and political transition experienced by all the CEEC, the Baltic states had to either heavily transform – or even create – their entire state apparatus, including governmental, legislative, and administrative bodies. These circumstances left the Baltic states with the paramount challenge of meeting the political, economic, and administrative requirements laid down by the Copenhagen Criteria, but also with a potentially greater openness to external influence in terms of policy, administrative structures, and organizational practices. In this chapter, we will look at the EU's influence on labour market and employment policy in the Baltics.

The EU exerts its influence on national public administrations through a variety of channels. The most prominent is perhaps the nearly 100,000 pages of the *acquis communautaire*. Member States must also have the ability and resources to transpose, implement, and monitor the entire body of EU legislation. Throughout accession, the European Commission stressed the need for all areas of public administrations to be ready for full membership after May 2004, and the EU was an active player in national administrative reform. Another channel of influence is the Structural Funds, which provide financial resources aimed at reducing regional economic and social disparities within the EU.

However, not all mechanisms of EU influence are as obvious or as direct as hard law and the financial incentives of the Structural Funds. The *acquis* includes both hard legislation and soft rules and guidelines, which are often accompanied by monitoring and assessment mechanisms. In this study, we examine labour market and employment policy, where coordination is achieved primarily through soft law. How have the Baltic states responded to the EU's political ambitions and governance activities in this field? We study Europeanization by looking at changes in 1) organizational structures and 2) policy-making procedures and practices. In conclusion, we discuss the relative importance of different Europeanization mechanisms in this field, as well as in the post-socialist context more generally. Examining the impact of the EU on public administrations and policy-making practices is particularly interesting in the case of the Baltic states, since the entire employment policy field in these countries was created after 1989.

The study is based on official policy documents and interviews with some 60 national experts, including ministry officials, staff at local and national implementing agencies, social partners, foreign policy advisors, and domestic researchers. We also interviewed the country desk officers for Lithuania and Estonia at DG Employment in the European Commission. The interviews in Latvia were conducted in June 2003 and June 2004; the interviews in Lithuania in March and April 2004 and June 2005; and the interviews in Estonia in May 2004 and May 2005.[2]

1 Europeanization of labour market and employment policy

While there is a well-established body of literature on the Europeanization of the 15 'old' Member States (e.g. Knill and Lehmkuhl 1999; Radaelli 2003; Cowles et al. 2001), attention has recently turned to the new accession countries. For example, Grabbe identifies five mechanisms of Europeanization in Eastern Europe: *models*, *money*, *benchmarking* and *monitoring*, *advice* and *twinning*, and *gate-keeping* (Grabbe 2003: 312). These mechanisms have played a part in interactions between the EU and the old Member States, but they seem to have been even more important in the last two enlargements. In particular, power asymmetry has been a significant mediating factor between the EU and the CEEC during accession. Membership conditionality, in combination with the CEECs' strong motivation to become members, has led to power asymmetry. Comparative studies have consequently found more homogeneous outcomes of Europeanization in the new members than in the EU-15 (Schimmelfennig and Sedelmeier 2005; Grabbe 2003). These studies suggest two possible explanations for more uniform outcomes in the CEEC: 1) strong accession conditionality; and 2) the double burden of political and economic transformation, which reduced institutional inertia and increased openness to external influences.

Thus, the effects of Europeanization on the CEEC are likely to be much greater across all policy sectors, even in areas with 'soft' EU influence. In the case of the European Employment Strategy (EES), conditionality is likely to have affected employment policy adjustment in the Baltics, since the strategy was institutionalized long before their accession. In addition, they had little input into the development of the strategy. The special relationship with the EU resulting from membership conditionality, coupled with the fact that employment is a very new policy field, provides a solid basis for studying Europeanization of labour market policy in the new Member States.

Although the EES has a constitutional basis through the Employment Chapter of the Amsterdam Treaty, the common EU objectives are a form of soft law. This type of soft governance (Jacobsson 2004a, 2004b) gives considerable leeway for national policy makers to make their own decisions about how to adapt policy-making structures, procedures, and policies to EU demands. However, although there is no legal penalty to ensure implementation of EU objectives, the 'hardness' of the strategy increases when we consider its close connection to the European Social Fund (ESF), which provides strong economic incentive for developing policies in line with EU objectives (Hartwig 2007). This is even more apparent in the new Member States, which are more dependent on EU resources to achieve national goals.

For the new Member States, employment and social policy were covered by Chapter 13 of the *acquis communautaire*. This includes areas where there is binding legislation, such as health and safety at work, labour law, and equal treatment of men and women. However, employment falls under the 'soft *acquis*', where no formal legal compliance is required but where there is nonetheless strong pressure to meet EU standards. Progress on meeting the obligations of Chapter 13 was monitored by the European Commission in its *Regular Reports*. Moreover, great emphasis during accession was placed on the new Member States' ability to manage and absorb the Structural Funds. Special PHARE programmes prepared the public administration for the ESF prior to accession. Other PHARE programmes included projects to foster the development of internet technology, capacity building and preparation for implementation of the EES upon accession, and bipartite social dialogue. Collaborative twinning projects were also undertaken to help build up administrative capacity (Svensson 2007; Tulmets 2005).

The Europeanization mechanisms identified by Grabbe (2003) are all present in the EES. The *gate-keeping mechanism* was present through the conditionality criteria. *Financial incentives* are present through the coupling of the EES and the ESF. *Models* of public administration, such as management by objectives, have been diffused through twinning projects. Models of 'appropriate policy' are also established by the common policy objectives and employment policy guidelines, although we see the EES as a loose script rather than a precise model (Jacobsson and West 2007). The aim is convergence of goals, not means, and national policy actors interpret and translate ideas and norms about employment policy. Another important aspect of the EES as a model is the partnership principle, which calls for the involvement of trade unions and employer organizations as well as all relevant ministries, implementing authorities, local and regional authorities. *Monitoring* was present in the *Regular Reports* and continues to be important in the EES, which builds on a system of reporting (the production of National Action Plans and since 2005, National Reform Programmes). Moreover, the EES has institutionalized arenas for discussion and reflection on policy options and outcomes, such as the Employment Committee, as well as peer review and bilateral exchanges to promote mutual learning. It also includes organized scrutiny in the form of evaluations, comparisons, and benchmarking (Jacobsson 2004b). While all five mechanisms have been at work in preparing the Baltic states for the EES, we will argue that the soft mechanisms have gained their effectiveness by being effectively coupled with hard mechanisms, most notably the ESF.

Employment and economic background of the Baltic states

Prior to 1991, the Baltics were economic satellites of Moscow, subject to Soviet central planning. All three economies were dominated by an industrial-agricultural mix and were dependent on trade with other Eastern bloc countries. Immediately after independence, economic output fell dramatically and all three countries experienced domestic crises. Governments operated in survival mode, focusing on meeting basic housing, heating, and health needs. High levels of poverty were seen as an unfortunate but unavoidable outcome of transition, and were expected to normalize as economic growth resumed. (Aidukaite 2003; Vanags 2005).

Over the 1990s, economic growth eventually resumed and unemployment rates started to decline, although the benefits of economic growth failed to materialize for large segments of the population. In 1999, all three countries were once again hit by the Russian crisis, with spiking unemployment rates. By the time of membership, in 2004, however, unemployment had fallen in all three countries, to rates of less than 11%. Overall employment rates in 2004 were just slightly below the EU average of 63.3 (Eurostat 2004).

In 2004, the Baltics were the poorest countries to enter the EU, with the lowest GDP per capita in relation to the EU average. However, despite higher unemployment rates and lower levels of economic development, they have also experienced significantly higher economic growth. Cumulative GDP more than doubled in all three countries between 1996 and 2003. By EU accession, the Baltics were the fastest-growing economies in the EU (CEC 2005).

In terms of political transition, the Baltics have been characterized by high levels of instability, frequent government turnover, and a fractured political spectrum. Until 2003, the majority of governments in all three countries had been composed of centre-right parties. In 2001, Lithuania distinguished itself somewhat with the election of a coalition led by the restyled Social Democrats under Brazauskas. In terms of ideology, there has been popular and political reluctance to allow the state to play a large role in social policy provision, the predominant view being that individuals should be able to solve their own problems (Aidukaite 2003; civil servant and expert interviews). Nevertheless, there are differences in the three countries' social systems. Estonia has taken a very liberal approach to social welfare. It was the quickest of the three countries to dismantle the old system, choosing an Anglo-Saxon-inspired social model, with low, flat-rate universal benefits (Leppik 2003: 144). In contrast, Lithuania adopted contribution-based social insurance, considering the Scandinavian approach 'too socialist' (interview, former Minister of Social Affairs, 2004). Similarly, Latvia selected contribution-financed social insurance, inspired by Germany (Leppik 2003).

Labour market challenges in the Baltics are not unlike those that must be addressed in other EU countries. Like the rest of the EU, the Baltics face an ageing population combined with low birth rates. In addition, the Baltic populations have fallen, due to emigration of Russian minorities, as well as 'brain drain' to Western Europe. However, despite many similar problems, the Baltics also face unique labour market challenges that can be attributed to their Soviet heritage. A particular problem for Latvian and Estonian policy makers is a significant Russian minority, which has higher unemployment rates than ethnic Balts, due to concentration in former industrial areas. About one-third of the Estonian population is composed of ethnic minorities, and almost 40% of the population of Latvia.[3]

Unemployment benefits, in particular, are also extremely low. This not only discourages individuals from registering at public employment offices, but also contributes to the persistence of a shadow economy. In turn, this decreases state revenues. Finally, although the Baltics have well-educated labour forces, workers' skills are often outdated. This means a mismatch between labour supply and labour demand, which is exacerbated by a weak vocational education system.

2 The organization of labour market policy in the Baltics

Baltic labour market institutions were created in less than a decade. In contrast to most other post-socialist countries, labour market policy was an entirely new field at the beginning of the 1990s. While some Soviet-era institutions functioned as a social security system, they cannot be seen in the same light as Western European welfare states. Unemployment insurance, for instance, was unknown, since unemployment did not officially exist, and the state guaranteed all citizens a job (Aidukaite 2003: 409; see also Mailand, this volume).

When the Baltic social security systems were built, employment policy was often placed under large social ministries, responsible for everything from welfare to health. Health and pensions have generally received priority, while employment policy has often been the last item on the social 'to do' list. However, labour market policy received more attention after 2000, as EU membership came into sight and social disparities remained, despite economic growth. Since 2004, employment policy has also received a boost, thanks to the prospect of the extra funding through the ESF.

The Lithuanian Ministry of Social Security and Labour, the Latvian Ministry of Welfare, and the Estonian Ministry of Social Affairs and their respective labour market boards are the bodies responsible for administration and implementation of employment policy in the three countries. Labour market policy governance in the Baltics is characterized by centralized decision making with weak regions and municipalities, which has implications for the EES, such as poor implementation and lack of follow-up. In addition, there is a strict division between policy formulation and implementation, which may have implications for the relevance and effectiveness of measures.

National responses to the EES must also be looked at together with the ESF, as this offers Member States significant economic incentive for human resource development. For the 2004–6 programming period, the ESF funding was close to €3.6bn. In the new Member States, an average of 30% of ESF resources should finance the reintegration of the unemployed in the labour market as well as the development and modernization of labour market institutions (CEC 2005b: 111). This indicates how the EU puts pressure on Member States for reform. Furthermore, it shows that 'money talks'. National actors at all levels of government are also well aware of the opportunities provided by the ESF.

Between 2004 and 2006, Lithuania received €163.8m, Estonia €76.1m, and Latvia €132.7m in Community support, according to each country's Single Programming Document for 2004–6. The countries were required to provide an additional 20–25% in co-financing. While these numbers are quite small in absolute terms, these funds have been essential for the development of both policy priorities as well as the reform of labour market institutions, as chronic under-financing has been cited in our interviews and national policy documents as one of the major obstacles, especially in Estonia, but also in Latvia and Lithuania.

In particular, the ESF has been important for the financing of active labour market policy. Take Estonia as an example. Active labour market expenditures in Estonia were approximately 0.08% of GPD in 2003, which was the lowest among the new Member States as well as the EU-15. According to the Estonian NAP 2004, spending on active labour market policy (ALMP) should have increased by 42.2% by 2005, of which approximately half is ESF funding. The PRAXIS think-tank estimated that spending on active labour market policy spending would increase to 0.18% of GDP with the help of the Structural Funds (interview, 2004).

In all three countries, the ministries of finance were the designated managing authorities for structural funds. The social ministries are in general responsible for the administration of the social fund, with other line ministries responsible at the measure level. Departments responsible solely for the administration of the ESF have been created within the Ministry of Social Security and Labour in Lithuania, the Ministry of Social Affairs in Estonia, and the Ministry of Welfare in Latvia. The ESF departments in the intermediary bodies work closely with the departments responsible for drafting the National Action Plans (NAPs) for employment.

3 Building state capacities for implementation

A number of new agencies were created to implement the structural funds. Some were originally established to manage PHARE pre-accession support, but have since been assigned a new role. In Lithuania, for example, a single implementing agency under two different ministries has been created. The Human Resources Development Programs Foundation, which used to manage PHARE, administers applications and project evaluations for both the Ministry of Social Security and Labour and the Ministry of Education and Science. To handle this task, the agency more than doubled its staff in 2005, growing to more than 70 people. It was also necessary to develop sufficient administrative competence to become an accredited implementing agency. An interviewed representative explained, 'it means the new structure was set up, and now we have new departments, including administration and implementation, financial control, financial administration of projects, evaluation and assessment, and quality assurance' (Lithuanian HRD Foundation, interview 2005). Another example is Innove, an Estonian foundation for life-long learning. Innove is the spin-off of an organization managing PHARE. The agency is now responsible for the Da Vinci programme, Euroguidance, and its main task is to implement the structural funds. Innove's chairman described the long and tiresome preparation:

> There was quite a bit of bureaucracy that had to be prepared, through this we had to enhance our capacity in three ways: 1) to have the right staff … this is not easy because nobody has the previous experience so it means you have to find capable people and then train them; 2) then we had to prepare the administration system so there were handbooks and guidelines; 3) we also had to develop our supporting structures … Our internal procedures have to be quite detailed.
>
> (Interview, 2004).

The development of administrative capacity at the central level has largely been successful in all three countries. Staff training has included the attainment of language skills, training in monitoring and control methods and IT, in part through EU pre-accession assistance. However, one of the major problems has been 'spreading that capacity out into all of the little villages and all of the local centres and labour exchanges' (Interview, DG Employment, 2004).

Policy planning and evaluation is an area where the EU impact is clear. After independence, the Baltics did not have necessary systems in place to monitor and evaluate public policy. Decisions were based on political priorities, with little focus on implementation, and little attention was paid to following up the effects of proposed plans and policies. This lack of administrative capacity was cited repeatedly throughout the Commission's *Regular Reports*. Specifically noted in the case of employment policy was a lack of a policy evaluation culture.

In some instances, this seems to have resulted in a weaker bargaining position for the Baltics in relation to the EU, because they did not have the statistics and research to strengthen their own positions. A Latvian interviewee explained:

> To be honest I think that the Latvian administration never had the capacity, expertise ... and statistic(s) to find the best arguments and say 'No, this does not work for our labour market. We need another priority.' It is a problem that we cannot protect our interest, because of lack of expertise, knowledge, lack of human resources and lack of time.
>
> (Interview, Latvian mission to the EU, 2004)

The EU impact is clear also in the introduction of more knowledge-based policy making, such as the establishment of policy analysis units in Estonia and external evaluation of the Latvian vocational training system. There is increased transparency in response to evaluation, increased use of indicators and strategic planning documents (e.g. in Estonia on lifelong learning), and more uniform and coordinated strategies (Interview, Praxis, Estonia 2004). The establishment of regular reporting and monitoring has also been important in civil servants' day-to-day work.

Moreover, the EU has helped to modernize the public employment services, which have been troubled in all three countries. For example, in Latvia, the State Employment Agency has had difficulty with effective labour market service delivery as well with data management and collection (Latvian JAP 2003). The Estonian Labour Market Board has faced similar issues. After a 2003 review of Board economic activities, the Estonian State Audit Office (2004) found that 'the accounting ... is characterized by disorganisation – both the Accounting Act and other requirements applicable to financial accounting were violated en masse'. The Audit Office discovered the accounting in some local offices was still done according to cash-accrued principles, even though the national Accounting Act stipulates the accrual method. Furthermore, some offices had not yet computerized their records (Interview, Tallinn Labour Exchange, 2005). In Estonia, the EU's influence is clear in the adoption of a new labour market concept in May 2004 that reorients both policy and financing towards active labour market policy and introduces individualized case management and a new information distribution mechanism. This is important in Estonia, since there has been less public expectation that the state should be responsible for labour market policy than in, for instance, Lithuania (Interview, Swedish expert, 2004). 'The general conception was that there are enough job vacancies, everyone should be able to fill the vacancies or get the job without any mediation … So it was more like one has to survive on one's own' (Interview, Estonian Labour Market Board, 2004).

4 Pre- and post-accession participation in the EES

The new Member States began preparing to join the EES in 1999, and by 2002 all countries acceding in May 2004 had submitted a Joint Assessment Paper (JAP) on employment policy. Based on an in-depth employment policy background review done in each country, the JAP provided a general overview of economic developments and labour market trends, identifying the country's main employment priorities and measures that should be taken. The Commission then monitored the implementation of the JAP priorities annually.

Even before accession, the three Baltics started to prepare for the EES by producing voluntary National Employment Action Plans (NEAPs), similar to the NAPs. Since 2004, they have participated fully in the EES. The production of the action plans requires coordination between policy actors in order to produce coherent national plans. Has political coordination actually improved? What is the role of the NAPs in 'real' policy making: are they just reports for Brussels or do they play a strategic role in national policy making?

In Lithuania, national coordination for EES participation began in November 2000 with the JAP, which was drafted by an inter-ministerial working group. The government and the EU Commission approved the final JAP in January 2002. The social partners were only involved in the final stage of the preparation of the JAP, although the final draft was approved by the Tripartite Council (Interview, 2004). While the JAP contained a broad overview of national employment policies, it was also a trial run for national policy makers. According to many interviewees, the process was refined with subsequent NEAPs, which have consistently become more detailed. The transition from the JAP and NEAPs to the first real NAP in November 2004 meant that national actors took more ownership of the document:

> To be honest, when we were preparing the JAP we were candidate countries. We had to work a lot to conform to the requirements of the EU. It was an orientation to be in line with EU policy. The situation is changing now because we will see it more as a national policy document.
>
> (Interview, Ministry of Social Security and Labour, Lithuania, 2004)

The Ministry of Social Security and Labour oversaw the 2004 NAP. Five individuals within the Labour Market Division wrote the document, with some input from other departments. The ministry set the agenda, coordinated and monitored the activities for various working groups, negotiated and reached agreement with all relevant stakeholders and partners on the final draft of the NAP. Finally, it presented the NAP to the European Commission after government approval. The national parliament, the Seimas, was not involved, although it was informed after government adoption.

Preparation for the EES in Latvia officially began in 2003 with the JAP. However, Latvia followed the EES very closely prior to accession and drafted annual practice NEAPs from 2000, although this was not an EU requirement. Content-wise, the Latvian NEAPs were short-term and overly concerned with following procedural requirements. By and large, these documents were a compilation of measures intended to fulfil perceived EU expectations and were thus reactive, rather than forward-looking documents relevant for policy making. Olofsson and West (2004) have characterized the NAP process in Latvia as 'passive adoption' of EU rules rather than 'active translation' into the national context.

Yet the NAP process received a facelift when Latvia formally joined the EES in 2004. The Ministry of Economy, which also monitored NAP implementation, coordinated the process. The NAP steering group consisted of representatives of the Ministry of Welfare, the Ministry of Education and Science, the Ministry of Agriculture, the Ministry of Regional Development and Local Governments, and the State Employment Agency. The Ministry of Finance was not formally included in the working group, participating only 'if necessary' (Latvian NAP 2004). The most important employment policy issues were also reviewed by the National Tripartite Cooperation Council, which includes representatives from the Cabinet of Ministers as well as employer and trade union representatives. The NAP was adopted by the Cabinet of Ministers. The 2004 NAP was the first employment action plan to be approved by the Latvian parliament.

Like Latvia, Estonia also produced four annual NEAPs, but these documents initially lacked precise quantitative targets and it appeared that the 'objectives set out by the EES guidelines are taken over by Estonia as benchmarks and future goals' (Eamets and Kallaste 2002: 13). Väli (2004: 236) noted that at the time that Estonia had no single document outlining national employment policy. She also emphasized that most strategic goals have been set in EU-related documents. In her interpretation, employment policy is seen as an EU – rather than a national – policy field. She concluded that the NAP was a concern of the administration but lacked political support, which also decreased the motivation of the social partners to actively participate (2004: 256). This view is supported by our interviews: 'My view is that in many cases our government considers these as reports for the Commission. They are not … real attempts to change policy at home' (Estonian Trade Union Confederation representative, 2005). As an academic expert observes:

> they are very carefully following these guidelines from Brussels … I think it is true that they are following very much the last documents produced by the EU, sometimes word for word. I mean they are taking over these targets and objectives so sometimes I get the feeling that they are not producing this paper for Estonia but for Brussels.
>
> (Interview, Estonia, 2005)

The Estonian JAP was submitted to the Commission in 2001. There was a formal working group for inter-ministerial coordination, but its role was negligible. Interviews confirm that the input given by the relevant ministries was limited to their areas of competence, rather than a comprehensive review of employment policy. In Estonia, the NAP is drafted by the Ministry of Social Affairs. The first NAP as a full member (2004) was actually drafted during summer by one individual (Interview, 2005). Consultation of social partners and other actors was only formal. In Estonia, there has been considerably more interest in the broader Lisbon process than the EES. Consequently, the process improved significantly with the first national reform programme in 2005, with a steering committee including representatives from Education, Finance, Economy, Interior Affairs, and as well as social partners and local authorities. The initial meeting was primarily informative, but there had been an improvement in the coordination procedures from NAP 2004 (Interview, Ministry of Social Affairs 2005). The national parliament was not involved with the preparation of the NAPs. However, in 2005 the national reform programme was approved by the Riigikogu's EU Affairs Committee.

An important aspect of the formulation of employment policy, in general, and participation in the EES, in particular, are inter-ministerial relationships:

> This is THE issue. How to have closer relations between ministries inside the same country, because it is not the problem of just one ministry. Many people should deal with this. So to some extent this European Employment Strategy helps a lot because when everybody hears this, and they are obliged to go deeper.
>
> (Interview, Lithuania Mission to the EU, 2004)

Because of the small size of the Baltic public administrations, coordination to a large extent still depends on informal connections.

One of the major problems for coordination in Latvia was that the members of the working group did not include any high-ranking staff (Interview, Ministry of Economy, 2004). The absence of higher-ranking officials in the NAP drafting process decreased the overall importance of the NAP in the national policy cycle. The attitude of ministries was that coordination was 'only formal'. However, some improvements were made when the Ministry of Welfare took over the task (Interview, Ministry of Economy, 2004). An interviewed official at the Ministry of Welfare had a similar view: in contrast to the pre-accession

NEAPs, the 2004 NAP 'differs very much. The previous ones were very formal documents ... there were no strategic solutions, just a description of what was going on' (Interview, Ministry of Welfare, Latvia, 2004). But even if this official thought the 2004 NAP would be taken more seriously, he still thought that coordination was insufficient and that the civil servants at the Ministry of Economy in particular were not serious enough about the NAP.

One problem in all three countries has been the coordination of the NAPs with national budget cycles. The resources allocated for employment measures have consequently not been determined by the action plans (Väli 2004: 237). For example, the Estonian NEAP 2001 reported expenditures on labour market measures for 1995–99, but did not provide much information on the planned budget for labour market policy for the following year. Eamets and Kallaste (2002) point out that there was 'problematic coordination between the setting of labour policy measures and the state budget appropriations'. This is partially because the NEAPs were prepared prior to the state budget, and it was therefore impossible to estimate what finances would be allocated to labour market policy. This, however, changed with the NAP 2004, as the NAP was drafted at the same time as the 2005 state budget. Furthermore, the NAP 2004 was quite specific in terms of national funds allocated to labour market policy, particularly in connection to the ESF where co-financing from the EU was available. Many of these allocations were decided during negotiations for the National Development Plan 2004–6. However, in some instances, ESF funds were the only budgetary figures available.

The situation has been similar in Latvia. One problem has been that the Ministry of Finance was only included in the steering group 'if necessary' (Latvian NAP 2004). The fact that the Ministry of Finance did not participate in the NAP working group, while it was in charge of the money, has been seen as a problem by the other ministries involved. As expressed at the Ministry of Welfare: 'We don't feel the support from Ministry of Finance' (Interview, 2004). An employers' representative likewise expressed in an interview that the Ministry of Economy has 'developed different new good ideas and documents about the economic development but it has always stopped at the Finance Ministry' (Interview, 2004). An interviewed official at the Ministry of Finance, in turn, did not understand the criticism: 'we do not draft measures that support employment. We give money. This is the basic involvement. That is why the Ministry of Finance has not participated very actively in the discussions. This is not our competence' (Interview, 2004). Yet, the importance of the NAP diminishes if there is a decoupling between labour market policies and financial planning.

Policy actors in all three countries have said the EES provides a good policy framework, and the experience of drafting NAPs has helped foster a common approach to employment policy. It has provided an incentive for the ministries to come together, 'The EU approach has helped us see the issues in an integrated perspective and the ministries to move in the same direction' (Interview, Ministry of Welfare, Latvia 2004).

While all interviewees in all three countries have stressed that the EES has been helpful in developing national employment policy, the national role and profile of the NAP itself has thus far been rather small. It has, by and large, been a bureaucratic exercise involving only civil servants directly responsible for drafting the report. One of the problems has been that the NAPs have been reactive rather than proactive documents. This was most evident with the pre-accession plans, which were characterized by imitation and attempts to indiscriminately follow EU guidelines rather than making independent analysis.[4] However, the plans became more precise during preparation for the EES, and clear changes took place with the first 'real' NAPs in 2004, according to most interviewees. The transition to Lisbon reform programmes in 2005 meant an additional facelift, especially in Estonia. Moreover, even if the action plans are not always operational, they are not without consequences:

> Of course they are kind of reporting documents for the Commission, but at the same time they still form a basis for all the other activities and programmes. It is usually required that if you want to develop some kind of project you must point out how it is connected to the priorities set out in the national policy and also in the JAP.
>
> (Interview, Ministry of Finance, Estonia, 2004)

It should also be emphasized that the problems mentioned – the NAPs as reports for Brussels with little policy relevance domestically and the isolated groups of civil servants working with EU topics – are not unique to the new Member States, but also been identified in the implementation of the EES in the EU-15 (Jacobsson and Vifell 2007). It even seems that the post-accession NAPs are actually better integrated into national policy in the Baltics than they were in the EU-15. This is also the view of the European Commission: '[the NAPs] receive a higher profile in many of the new Member States where they tend to be more forward-looking and play a central role in the policy cycle' (CEC 2005: 12). Pisani-Ferry and Sapir (2006) also conclude that the new Member States have more 'ownership' of the Lisbon process than do the EU-15.

However, one can also question the European Commission's ability to evaluate the reality behind the NAPs or NRPs. For instance, the Estonian NAP of 2004 was drafted over the summer by one individual who had just begun working at the ministry. The input by other ministries and the social partners was minimal, due to both the narrow time frame and the summer holidays. The Commission nonetheless gave Estonia almost nothing but positive feedback. Although there was a much wider involvement in the production of the NPR in 2005, it is still surprising that Pisani-Ferry and Sapir (2006) ranked Estonia number one of all the EU-25 on their 'ownership index' of the Lisbon process. It leaves us with the impression that Estonia is better at 'image management' than, for instance, Lithuania, which has had the reputation of being a 'laggard' (Granqvist and Wallin 2007), but which in our view took the production of NAPs more seriously than Estonia. This can also be compared to the experience in other post-socialist countries. A representative from the Hungarian foreign ministry, for instance, spoke at a conference about 'hiding' their first NAP from the EU Commission, due to its poor quality and the fact that it had been given such little attention (Author's observation, 2004).

The EU's reluctance to push Estonia and Latvia regarding the social and labour market situation of their Russian minorities is also worth commenting upon. This is a policy-relevant problem that seems to have been avoided in both the country-specific recommendations and the peer reviews exerted by other Member States in the Employment Committee. When minority issues have been brought up it has been about the Roma instead:

> for a long time we had to fight against the Commission recommendation that suggested that we deal with fighting the discrimination of Roma. But differently from other Central European states, we have very few Roma living in Estonia (approximately 2,000 people). But because it was assumed that the new Member States have problems with the Roma, Estonia does too.
> (Email communication, Ministry of Social Affairs, 2005)

5 The limits of social partnership in the Baltics

The EES advocates the involvement of all relevant actors, such as local authorities and social partners, in employment policy making. However, contrary to the situation in the 'old' Member States, local actors and social partners in the Baltics have shown little interest or ability to take advantage of the EES's opportunity structures.

EU accession has been important for decentralization, with all three countries adopting the European Charter of Local Self-Government (EE 1995, LV 1996, LT 1999). However, Lithuania is the only one of the three countries that has achieved a comprehensive reform of local government administration. In Estonia and Latvia, municipal districts are based roughly on Soviet units of administration, with a very large number of local governments in relation to the size of the countries. For Estonia and Latvia, the major problems at the local level are the small size of territorial units and insufficient funding to ensure the quality of social services. While the EU has been important at emphasizing the need to decentralize employment policy making, there are still several local challenges that make real impact difficult, such as local authorities' lack of time and necessary resources to participate actively in the EES. Local activism is non-existent, as most efforts are focused on day-to-day tasks.

In Latvia, the EU has been important for vertical coordination, which did not previously exist. According to a 2003 interview at the Latvian State Employment Service, participation of municipalities has increased since 2000. However, as put by a representative from the Union of Local and Regional

Governments: 'We were and are only observers of the NAP process. We do not have the money or resources to participate actively' (Interview, 2004).

There is little local awareness of the EES itself; employees at local public employment offices, for example, had not even heard of the EES, although they were familiar with the ESF. However, even if there is not necessarily local knowledge about the EES, the strategy is still integrated into day-to-day tasks, as it was considered in the national formulation of employment policy. Another important factor was the hiring and training of EURES (European Employment Services) consultants at many local public employment offices to help facilitate labour mobility. There have also been initiatives to increase local administrative capacity to prepare local agencies for ESF funding. Local authorities in Estonia and Latvia have even attempted to address their lack of administrative capacity by teaming up to apply for ESF projects.

As for the social partners, the EU has been instrumental for the establishment of formal tripartite bargaining structures (Eamets and Philips 2004; Väli 2004). Many interviewed experts cite social dialogue, along with gender mainstreaming, as two social areas that have received more attention, due to EU accession. There has also been funding from PHARE projects and bilateral assistance from individual Member States to develop social dialogue.

However, despite the establishment of institutional structures for tripartite dialogue and central consultation, Baltic social dialogue remains weak. Many employees see little value in joining a trade union, due to their low density, as well as to residual public scepticism lingering from the Soviet era. In the 2004 NAPs, trade union membership in the three countries was estimated at 12–14%. Unlike in Poland, where trade unions, such as the Solidarity Movement, played a key role in government reform throughout the 1980s – in particular in the area of workers' rights – Baltic trade unions have been extremely passive and have had little influence over policy.

Despite the low density of both employers' and employees' organizations, national tripartite councils exist in all three countries. While they are mainly for consultation and discussion rather than for policy making, the importance of these bodies has grown, not the least because of the EU's promotion of social dialogue. However, bipartite negotiations are weak, due to the social partners' lack of administrative capacity. The trade unions lack the ability to negotiate actively, due both to lack of resources and to the fact that they represent a minority of workers. Winterton and Strandberg (2004: 46, 56) report that under 20% of workers in Latvia and Lithuania are covered by collective agreements. In Estonia, such agreements are almost non-existent.

In Estonia, regional tripartite committees and bodies have also been established, including involvement of local employers' and employees' organizations at the regional employment councils (under the local Labour Market Boards). However, both employers and unions have had difficulties appointing members to attend meetings (Väli 2004).

Another question is the social partners' actual interest in participating in social dialogue. A Latvian Ministry of Welfare official said the state has done what it can to develop social partnership: 'From the state side, we created the legal framework … We have set the minimum requirements and now it is up to them to negotiate' (Interview, 2004). A German policy advisor felt the social partners did not really understand the point of social dialogue. The employers, for instance, tended to have a short-term perspective (Interview, 2004). Although there has been some success in promoting social dialogue at the enterprise level, attempts at sectoral social dialogue have failed, since neither unions nor employers' associations showed enough interest (Interview, employers representative, Latvia, 2004).

In terms of organizational capabilities, the employers are in general in a better position vis-à-vis the trade unions (except in certain sectors; for example, the trade unions are relatively well organized in the public sector) in terms of their ability to negotiate. Although they represent a relatively small share of companies, they have more financial resources. For example, according to the chairman of the Labour Relations Committee of the Confederation of Industrialists in Lithuania, 'our Confederation is considered to be one of the most powerful organizations in Lithuania, and lobbying is not at the last place in our activities. Rather often Parliament and Government do listen to what we say' (Interview, 2004). Similarly, in Latvia, the employers' representative felt that 'the priorities of the government coincide very much with our own' (Interview, employers' organization, Latvia, 2003).

In summary, the social partners' weak organizational capabilities are a factor constraining the development of social dialogue as well as active participation in the EES consultation process. The problem is not the lack of a legislative framework for social dialogue so much as the social partners' lack of administrative capacity. They have not used the EES as a bargaining chip vis-à-vis the national government, as social partner organizations have done in the EU-15. Nor have they shown much interest in being active players in the national EES process. However, there is increasing attention paid to the possibilities of ESF funding.

Europeanization of labour market policy making in the Baltics

The three Baltic states provide an interesting case to study the EES. First, they provide an opportunity to study the EES in a post-socialist context. Second, they are distinguished from the other new members from Eastern and Central Europe as the only former Soviet republics. This has meant that their transformation has been even greater than in former Communist countries, which at least had their own central administrations. The fact that the public administrations have been rebuilt completely explains the relatively great impact of the EU on labour market policy.

The EU impact on employment and labour market policy in the Baltics is most obvious at the level of national public administration. An entire policy field was created from scratch in a span of 15 years. This involved the formation of organizational structures, the establishment of working routines and procedures, and the build-up of expertise:

> Ten years ago, we didn't have anything like this. Actually, all administrative structures have been reformed. So we have a lot of new ministries. Everything has a history of 15 years – but not more.
>
> (Interview, Estonian desk officer, EU Commission, 2004)

Contrary to the situation in other post-socialist countries, Baltic labour market ministries were new organizations, and when new ministries were created after independence, labour market issues tended to be squeezed in between health and pensions. Gradually, labour market policy has gained more autonomy and attention – largely as a result of the EU. Compared to most 'old' Member States, there has not been domestic pressure, from either trade unions or the general public, for labour market policy developments.

As a consequence of EU influence, a number of new administrative bodies have been created. Some preceded the EES and were part of the general social policy reform in the new independent states, while others were more clearly a response to the EES. These include the creation of administrative departments for the ESF; the establishment of implementing agencies; the hiring and training of ESF specialists within labour market departments; efforts to strengthen the capacity of the labour market departments themselves; and the development of coordination mechanisms. However, with the exception of departments created to deal specifically with the Structural Funds, EU accession has increased the workload of ministries and agencies without an equivalent increase in the number of staff.

The impact of the EES is also visible in the introduction of more knowledge-based policy making, as well as in the use of more concrete indicators and targets. There is an increased emphasis on monitoring, evaluation, and implementation. Moreover, there have been efforts in all three countries towards modernizing the public employment services; an increased focus on active labour market policies; reform of vocational education and systems of life-long learning; as well as moves to decentralize at least some elements of employment policy making. (Mailand, in this volume, reports the same type of impact of the EES in Poland.)

The principle of social partnership has been implemented in terms of formal structures, although this does not always work in practice, due to weak administrative capacity as well as lack of interest of social partners. The model inherent in the EES, where social partners, and increasingly also regions and municipalities, are expected to play an important role in implementation, does not fit well with the situation in the Baltic states, due to weakness of the social partners and the lack of resources at the local level. The weakness and illegitimacy of the trade unions is a feature that the Baltics share with other post-socialist countries, but it seems even more pronounced here.

The small size of the Baltic administrations has facilitated policy coordination through personal contacts. However, administrative capacity has been a problem, such as problems with understaffing, staff retention, language barriers, lack of experience in the policy field, poor coordination, and the lack of administrative capacity to apply for the ESF. Yet, in preparation for membership, a large amount of money went, via PHARE, into increasing administrative capacity: staff training, study visits to other Member States, recruitment of new staff, and bilateral twinning projects. This has been important, due to the small amount of resources available nationally.

Another constraining factor is the centralized structure of Baltic policy making. Although the EES has helped increase inter-ministerial coordination, vertical coordination is still underdeveloped. There exists a division between policy making and implementation, with implementing agencies mainly seeing it as their role to report on the outcomes of projects and leaving the 'politics' up to the ministries. 'They identify the priorities, we do it', seems to be the general attitude. Moreover, the horizontal coordination between implementing agencies is almost non-existent. The participation of local actors in the EES is passive. Their role is largely limited to responding to documents after they have been written. With a lack of time, money, and qualified staff, municipalities have other priorities.

Still, many of the implementation problems in the Baltic states are the same as those shown in studies of the EU-15 (Jacobsson and Vifell 2007), at least if compared with the first five years of the EES: problems applying for the ESF, which is perceived to be very bureaucratic, as well as problems with absorbing the resources and fulfilling the additionality requirement; coordination problems between various policy actors; lack of coordination with national budget cycles; problems with statistics and policy evaluation with no effective monitoring of measures; underfunding of active labour market policy from national sources; passive social partners; and little or no parliamentary involvement. With some exceptions, such as the situation of the social partners, the problems are not qualitatively different, but differ rather in terms of magnitude.

Also, the Baltics are small states, with little bargaining power in relation to the EU. This partly explains the reactive attitude to whatever comes from Brussels, which is sometimes reflected in the NAPs. The states' eagerness to present themselves as 'good' candidates for EU membership has also fostered this attitude. With full membership, the governments have taken more ownership of their NAPs, while the pre-accession plans were more passive and reactive. In all three countries, the integration of the EES with the national Lisbon reform programmes has increased its profile, due to increased political will on the part of national governments. Rather than its just being a bureaucratic process, ministers and parliaments have assumed greater roles.

Besides these general factors, various political ideologies in the three states also explain how the EES is implemented. In Estonia, with a notably liberal ideology, the willingness to provide budgetary means for active labour market policy has been low, while Lithuania has taken a more active approach to social welfare and allocated more means to ALMP. However, the EU also helped to boost social policy in Lithuania. An interviewed official at the

Office of the Prime Minister wondered whether or not 'we have enough national capacity to [make additional reforms] without pressure from Brussels … and whether or not social policy can be reformed without additional external pressure' (Interview, 2004).

Even so, the strong pressure and conditionality in the hard areas and the heavy workload meant that the soft areas were given less priority in the accession period, by both the EU and the national governments. Interviews in all three countries confirm that employment policy had a low profile during accession, because there were no legal requirements or financial incentives involved. This is why access to the ESF has been a watershed. The economic incentive provided by the Structural Funds significantly increased interest in human resources development in the Baltics. Parallels can be drawn between the role of the ESF in the Baltics and its role in southern European states such as Spain and Greece (see López-Santana, this volume). A civil servant in the Estonian Labour Market Board stated that they meet whatever regulations they have to 'because we desperately need the money' (Interview, 2004). The ESF has also increased the interest of the ministries of finance.

'Money talks', as did membership conditionality. But other mechanisms of Europeanization have also been at work in the creation of a labour market policy field in the Baltic states. Examples include the transfer of policy models, advice, twinning, and ongoing monitoring by the Commission. In this sense, the EES as a coherent system of governance (Jacobsson 2004b), drawing on several governance mechanisms, is perhaps better illustrated in the Baltic states than anywhere else. However, our study has also shown that soft governance mechanisms, such as advice and monitoring, are most effective when systematically coupled with harder incentives. The prospect of full membership, and with it the opportunity of funding through the ESF, provided the Baltic states with the motivation to build up the institutional capacity necessary to implement the EES. It remains to be seen, however, whether governments will also allocate enough national funding to put priorities on paper into practice. Thus far, the spending on labour market programmes in the Baltic states remains the lowest in the EU (CEC 2006b). The Baltic case illustrates that it is hard to fulfil European objectives if domestic actors are not prepared to make active use of the European strategy in the national context.

Notes

1 www.vm.ee/eng/nato/kat_360/3164.html.

2 We gratefully acknowledge the collaboration of Ragnar Olofsson, who did the interviews in Latvia, and the support of the Foundation for Baltic and East European Studies, which funded the research programme 'Baltic Sea States in Transition' directed by Professor Bengt Jacobsson.

3 Unless otherwise noted, statistics are taken from the Statistical Office of Estonia (www.stat.ee/), the Central Statistical Bureau of Latvia (http://www.csb.lv/avidus.cfm), and Statistics Lithuania (www.std.lt/en/). EU statistics are taken from Eurostat (http://epp.eurostat.cec.eu.int).

4 Unlike the other two Baltic states, which drafted annual pre-accession plans, Lithuania developed a medium-term national document governing employment policy (Program for Increasing Employment for 2001–4). Through the three-year plan Lithuania showed a slightly more active and independent handling and a more active translation of EU rules and norms into national context prior to accession.

References

Aidukaite, J. (2003) 'From Universal System of Social Policy to Particularistic? The Case of the Baltic States', *Communist and Post-Communist Studies*, 36: 405–26.

Cowles, M.G., Caporaso, J. and Risse, T. (eds) (2001) *Transforming Europe*, Ithaca, NY, and London: Cornell University Press.

Eamets, R. and Kallaste, E. (2002) 'Overview of Social Dialogue and National Employment Action Plan in Estonia in the Context of European Employment Strategy', unpublished paper, University of Tartu.

Eamets, R. and Philips, K. (2004) 'EIRO Thematic Feature – Social Partner Involvement in the 2004 NAP', unpublished paper, University of Tartu.

Grabbe, H. (2003) 'Europeanization Goes East: Power and Uncertainty in the EU Accession Process', in K. Featherstone and C.M. Radaelli (eds) *The Politics of Europeanization*, Oxford: Oxford University Press, 303–27.

Granqvist, E. and Wallin, E. (forthcoming) 'Recreating Public Administrations in the Baltic States', chapter for B. Jacobsson (ed.) *The European Union and the Baltic States: Changing Forms of Governance*, London: Routledge.

Hartwig, I. (2007) 'European Employment Strategy and Structural Funds: Spill-overs Towards Communitarisation', in I. Linsenmann, C.O. Meyer and W. Wessels (eds) *Economic Government of the EU: A Balance Sheet of New Modes of Policy Coordination*, Basingstoke: Palgrave Macmillan, 119–40.

Jacobsson, K. (2004a) 'Soft Regulation and the Subtle Transformation of States: The Case of EU Employment Policy', *Journal of European Social Policy*, 14: 355–70.

—— (2004b) 'Between Deliberation and Discipline: Soft Governance in EU Employment Policy', in U. Mörth (ed.) *Soft Law in Governance and Regulation: An Interdisciplinary Analysis*, Cheltenham: Edward Elgar, 81–101.

Jacobsson, K. and Vifell, Å. (2007) 'New Governance Structures in Employment Policy Making: Loose Co-ordination in Action', in I. Linsenmann, C.O. Meyer and W. Wessels (eds) *Economic Government of the EU: A Balance Sheet of New Modes of Policy Coordination*, Basingstoke: Palgrave, Macmillan, 53–71.

Jacobsson, K. and West, C. (forthcoming) 'Europeanization of Labor Market Policy Making in the Baltic States', chapter for B. Jacobsson (ed.) *The EU and the Baltic States: Changing Forms of Governance*, London: Routledge.

Knill, C. and Lehmkuhl, D. (1999) *How Europe Matters: Different Mechanisms of Europeanization*, European Integration Online Papers 3. Online. Available HTTP: http://eiop.or.at/eiop/texte/1999–007a.htm (accessed 11 September 2008)

Leppik, L. (2003) 'Social Protection and EU Enlargement: The Case of Estonia', in V. Pettai and J. Zielonka (eds) *The Road to the European Union*, 2nd edn, Manchester: Manchester University Press, 140–62.

Nakrosis, V. (2003) 'Assessing Governmental Capabilities to Manage European Affairs: The Case of Lithuania', in V. Pettai and J. Zielonka (eds) *The Road to the European Union*, 2nd edn, Manchester: Manchester University Press, 104–39.

Olofsson, R. and West, C. (2004) 'The EES in the Baltic States – a Process-oriented Case Study on the Europeanisation of Employment Policy', paper presented at conference on 'Enlarging Social Europe: The Open Method of Coordination and the EU's New Member States', University of Madison, European Union Center, October.

Pisani-Ferry, J. and Sapir, A. (2006)'Last Exit to Lisbon', paper presented to the European Union's finance ministers, Brussels, March.

Radaelli, C.M. (2003) 'The Europeanization of Public Policy', in K. Featherstone and C.M. Radaelli (eds) *The Politics of Europeanization*, Oxford: Oxford University Press, 27–56.

Schimmelfennig, F. and Sedelmeier, U. (eds) (2005) *The Europeanization of Central and Eastern Europe*, Ithaca, NY and London: Cornell University Press.

Svensson, J. (forthcoming) 'Governance through Meditation: EU Twinning in Lithuania', in B. Jacobsson (ed.) *The EU and the Baltic States: Changing forms of Governance*, London: Routledge.

Tulmets, E. (2005) 'The Management of New Forms of Governance by Former Accession Countries: Institutional Twinning in Estonia and Hungary', *European Law Journal*, 11: 657–74.

Väli, M. (2004) 'Preparations towards Participation in the EES: Estonia's Progress in Involving Social Partners', in B. Galgóczi, C. Lafoucriere and L. Magnusson (eds) *The Enlargement of Social Europe. The Role of the Social Partners in the European Employment Strategy*, Brussels: ETUI, 211–62.

Vanags, A. (2005) *The Governance of Employment and Economic Development in the Baltic States*, OECD, Vilnius, Lithuania, March.

Vanagunas, S. (1997) 'Civil Service Reform in the Baltics', paper prepared for presentation before the conference on 'Civil Service Systems in Comparative Perspective', Indiana University, Bloomington, April.

Winterton, J. and Strandberg, T. (2004) 'European Social Dialogue: An Evaluation and Critical Assessment', in B. Galgóczi, C. Lafoucriere and L. Magnusson (eds) *The Enlargement of Social Europe. The Role of the Social Partners in the European Employment Strategy*, Brussels: ETUI, 21–75.

National and EU policy documents

CEC (Commission of the European Communities) (2003) *Progress in Implementing the Joint Assessment Papers on Employment Policies in Acceding Countries*, COM 663 final.

—— (2005) *Joint Employment Report 2004/2005.*

—— (2005b) *Report on Social Inclusion 2005: An Analysis of the National Action Plan on Social Inclusion (2004–2006) Submitted by the 10 New Member States.*

—— (2006) *Joint Employment Report 2005/2006 More and Better Jobs: Delivering the Priorities of the European Employment Strategy.*

—— (2006b) *Employment in Europe.*

Estonian State Audit Office (2004) *Economic Activities of the Labour Market Board and its Local Authorities in 2003*, Audit Report No. 2–5/04/87, Tallinn.

Government of the Republic of Lithuania (2001) *Programme of the Republic of Lithuania for Increasing Employment for 2001–2004*, 8 May.

Lithuanian Ministry of Social Security and Labour (2003) *Report on the Lithuanian Social Security System*, Vilnius.

Estonian National Development Plan for the Implementation of the Structural Funds: Single Programming Document 2004–2006 (2003).

Estonia's National Action Plan for Employment (2004), Tallinn.

Estonian National Development Plan for the Implementation of the Structural Funds: Single Programming Document 2004–2006 Programme Complement (2005).

Latvia Single Programming Document 2004–2006 (2003), Riga.

Latvia Programme Complement 2004–2006 (2004), Riga.

Latvia's National Action Plan for Employment (2004), Riga.

Lithuanian Single Programming Document Lithuania 2004–2006 (2003), Vilnius.

Lithuanian National Development Plan for the Implementation of the Structural Funds: Single Programming Document 2004–2006 Programme Complement (2003), Vilnius.

Republic of Lithuania National Action Plan for Employment (2004), Vilnius.

6 Soft Europeanization?

The differential influence of the European Employment Strategy in Belgium, Spain, and Sweden

Mariely López-Santana

Introduction

The European Union (EU) has relied heavily on the Open Method of Coordination (OMC) in tackling its labour market and social problems. The OMC leads us to question and expand current explanations about when, how, why and to what degree the EU affects Member States, insofar as this method is grounded in an alternative set of assumptions about how and why this supranational entity may influence domestic structures. Given the accelerating development of such non-binding rules internationally and our limited understanding of them, this chapter summarizes a set of key research findings regarding the influence of the European Employment Strategy (EES) on Belgium, Spain, and Sweden.[1] The propositions presented here serve as a basis for further testing in other Member States and other regimes (e.g. federal, supranational, international) governed by non-binding rules.

Before presenting the results, the following section develops a theoretical 'toolbox' to help researchers analyse the differential effects of soft law (i.e. non-binding rules) on domestic settings. This discussion of *internalization* (the dependent variable) provides a framework for conceptualizing the influence of these instruments on various domestic structures. Subsequent sections focus mainly on the differential influence of the EES and its *political internalization*.

1 Framing the dependent variable: internalization

Scholars evaluating the effects of Europeanization and other transnational legal processes face multiple questions about how to capture, measure, interpret, and theorize implementation (see Zeitlin, Hamel and Vanhercke, this volume). The questions include: 'What constitutes implementation? How do we recognize implementation when we see it? How can we establish to what degree regional and international mandates matter at the domestic level?' These questions are particularly difficult to answer in the case of soft law, since implementation of non-binding rules does not mirror processes of compliance with hard law.[2] Hence, it is important to recognize that answering the question 'How are labour market policies (LMPs) and institutions being affected by the EES at the domestic level?' is as complicated as developing a solid model for understanding cross-national differences and patterns.

Given these challenges, I argue that 'soft Europeanization' in the form of the EES has a variety of consequences at the national level which can include (but are not limited to) policy (re)formulation, learning about desirable and potential policies (Visser, this volume), policy changes, and intra-governmental coordination.[3] This approach moves away from the traditional category of compliance and focuses on *process* and *internalization* as it 'opens and unpacks the black box of policymaking' to capture various modes of transformations not necessarily linked to ratification and transposition (López-Santana 2006a). In this way, the effects of non-binding agreements such as the EES on domestic settings ought not to be conceptualized as a dichotomous (occurs/does not occur) dependent variable, but rather as a continuous variable ranging from 'no influence' to 'transformation' of domestic settings. Figure 6.1 illustrates this continuum.

In these scenarios, one possible outcome is a lack of change (Radaelli 2003: 37). In other words, internalization does not occur; thus, soft law has no influence on Member States. Second, soft law could lead to partial internalization. This means that these non-binding rules are absorbed by domestic settings. In this context, internalization occurs and domestic settings make *accommodations* to these non-binding rules – policies and procedures change (not institutions), but key domestic institutional structures and political behaviour are not truly modified. For instance, as a consequence of supranational recommendations a Member State could spend more on active labour market policy (ALMP); still, this shift does not mean that the prevalent model of LMP and the role of the government as a provider have changed in this country. Finally, when full internalization occurs, domestic settings are transformed (Radaelli 2003). *Transformation* is different from *accommodation* in that it entails paradigmatic change – the fundamental logic of domestic structures is transformed. Along the lines of the aforementioned example, transformation in LMP entails a change in the role of the government in supporting inactive and unemployed populations, in addition to a change in how recipients of welfare are viewed by the government (as either passive recipients of aid or active seekers of employment).

Up to this point, I have referred to the effect of the EES on 'domestic structures'; but what, exactly, are these domestic structures? To disentangle the questions posed in this book, it is useful to distinguish between *policy*, *politics*, and *polity*. The implementation process can simultaneously impact each of these.[4] First, the EES can alter domestic *policies* by leading policy

Figure 6.1 Potential outcomes

makers to (re)consider and (re)frame their views and preferences. This, in turn, can lead to formal changes in the content of public policies and/or laws. Consequently, this process can spark civil, partisan and/or governmental deliberations (*politics*), since formal and informal policy changes (especially those tied to the welfare state and to Left/Right cleavages) tend to be contested. Finally, the process of implementing the EES can impact the *polity* (institutional structures) and *governance* structures by affecting or altering the relationships and balances of power among different types of domestic actors, including levels of government.

In considering the internalization of soft law, we can further differentiate between tangible and intangible effects on *policies* and *politics.* Furthermore, to specify the notion of *polity*, I differentiate between different types of actors and settings where change can take place. To do this, I borrow from the literature on international law and compliance the notions of *political* and *legal internalization* (Koh 1997).

1 *Political internalization* occurs if political elites accept an international norm and adopt it as a matter of government policy (Koh 1997: 2657). Political internalization could thus be understood as a precursor of statutory changes.
2 *Legal internalization* occurs when an international norm is incorporated into the domestic legal system through executive action, judicial interpretation, legislative action, or some combination of the three (Koh 1997: 2657). Although the term suggests a non-strategic process of norm absorption, I argue that this phenomenon can involve strategic calculations by domestic actors to advance their policy preferences and goals. For example, national governments could 'legally internalize' non-binding instruments in an attempt to advance domestic partisan agendas.

As indicated above, my findings show that the effects of the EES are not limited to ministerial policy makers and parliaments. For this reason, it is crucial to assess the *governance* and the *polity* dimensions of the effect of the EES.[5] Thus the implementation of the EES could challenge domestic power balances and the nature of intra-governmental coordination by affecting collaborative dynamics and procedures. In order to conceptualize these potential developments, I include two supplementary dimensions of *internalization*.

3 *Governmental–societal internalization* occurs when governmental and non-governmental actors transform their relationships and/or routines in the process of complying with a reporting requirement and/or of implementing an international norm. This category captures possible transformations in the collaborative relations and coordinating procedures between governmental entities and 'civil society'.
4 *Intra-governmental internalization* concerns whether soft law disrupts or transforms existing relationships and routines between national and

> subnational levels of government within a Member State. It occurs when formal and informal relationships between national and subnational entities (e.g. federal and federated entities) within a Member State are affected or transformed in the process of complying with a reporting requirement and/or of implementing an international norm.[6]

To recap, the effect of the EES is captured by various analytical dimensions – *political*, *legal*, *intra-governmental*, and *governmental–societal internalization*. Moreover, for each one of these four types of internalization the effect verges from 'no change' to 'transformation'. The theoretical framework having been laid out, Section 2 presents the findings for the three cases. Section 3 will then examine the domestic factors that explain cross-national patterns of internalization (i.e. differential internalization).

2 Comparing and contrasting the internalization of the EES

My research used a comparative case study design to identify and explain general patterns, cross-national similarities and variations in the effects of the EES on Member States. From June of 2002 to December 2003, I conducted more than 60 in-depth interviews in the EU, and in Spain, Belgium, and Sweden. At the national and EU levels, I interviewed high-level civil servants, policy makers, officials of trade unions and employers' organizations, attachés from the national Permanent Representations, and academic experts. In addition, I interviewed civil servants and policy makers at subnational levels in Madrid and Brussels.

The case selection was not random, but inspired by the logic of a 'most different systems design'. This choice is grounded in the empirical findings of the literature on implementation of hard law measures, which argue that the 'fit between EU measures and domestic institutions matters' when explaining compliance with EU hard law. I took the former idea as a baseline, and chose three countries with different apparent levels of 'misfit' (high, medium, and low) and with different types of 'welfare regime' (Esping-Andersen 1990). Each of these countries represents one of these 'values' – one with high levels of misfit and a Southern welfare regime (Spain), one with medium levels of misfit and a Continental welfare regime (Belgium), and one with low levels of misfit and a Scandinavian welfare regime (Sweden).[7] This variation in institutional settings, in turn, allows me to avoid selection bias.[8]

In relation to the implementation of the EES, all Member States have observed their procedural obligations to the EU by actively complying with the reporting task.[9] More specifically, the national ministries responsible for LMPs have been particularly involved with this task and have included other important parties in the creation of National Action Plans (NAPs). These developments go beyond the procedural obligations of Member States and have had important consequences for domestic coordination and, ultimately, policy making. The following sections develop these ideas by focusing on the four different types of internalization.

2.1 Governmental–societal internalization

An important consequence of the reporting process was the creation of an 'organizational labour market regime' that resembles an 'epistemic community' (Haas 1992). More specifically, the task of reporting to the EU level has created new political networks and arenas for national ministries, trade unions and employers' organizations, as well as subnational entities, to coordinate their actions. In all three countries, interviewees recognized that since the introduction of the EES they have been able to hold frequent and common policy discussions with their national and supranational peers, and with other national actors who normally would not participate in their policy-making spaces. In addition, since the introduction of the EES, in all three countries trade unions and employers' organizations have actively shared information with each other and the government.[10] In this context, policy makers in all three countries claimed that the implementation of the EES has improved domestic patterns of coordination. For example, in Belgium 79% of the interviewees claimed that European soft law has improved internal coordination between subnational levels and national levels, and governmental and non-governmental entities, whereas in Sweden 57% of the subjects and in Spain 45% did so.[11]

In these new spaces, we find policy makers using the same type language (e.g. activation, inclusion, employment) to describe and diagnose a set of LMP problems and solutions. One manifestation of this influence is that policy makers have started to view 'employment' as part of a bigger 'jigsaw puzzle' connected to other policy areas, such as taxation, inclusion, and housing. By developing a better understanding of how one policy area relates to another (a 'unity vision', as one interviewee called it) they have been able to strategize better when formulating and drafting policy. These developments are significant, as underlined in other chapters, because they suggest that, in some respects, greater horizontal and vertical coordination improves the capacity of employment policy making (Jacobsson and Vifell 2007).

Even if the process has opened up many new collaborative spaces, national ministries have tended to remain in command of implementation, thus deciding which groups are included and excluded. In contrast with the arguments of Preunkert and Zirra (the German case) and Jacobsson and Johansson (social inclusion in Sweden) (this volume), when it comes to the implementation of the EES in the early 2000s most non-governmental organizations in Spain, Belgium, and Sweden were not particularly involved at the domestic level, with the exception of the social partners, mainly because national governments failed to involve them (van Gerven and Beckers, Hamel and Vanhercke, this volume). In some cases, as argued by Jacobsson and Vifell (2007), civil society organizations have pressured national governments to include them in consultative fora, but the latter have resisted because they saw it as an intrusion into their autonomy (according to the principle of subsidiarity). Nonetheless, once national ministries opened the door to some domestic actors, civil society organizations were able to claim their role and participate in the reporting and implementation processes. For instance, at the supranational level they have been consulted, given that the EU Commission has had regular contacts with a variety of civil society actors, including Belgian, Spanish, and Swedish social partners. These findings are theoretically significant because they challenge alternative explanations of Europeanization which highlight societal activism and opposition as important factors for understanding differential rates of compliance (Falkner et al. 2005: 21).[12] I argue that in the case of the EES the involvement of societal actors does not help us to understand differential patterns of internalization, because they have not played a central role in the process.

To frame these findings we must consider the issue of whether soft law promotes 'governance' (Rhodes 1996) or the inclusion of societal actors in tasks traditionally dominated by national governments. The regular presence of social partners, and subnational authorities (mainly in Spain and Belgium), supports the idea that soft law stimulates the creation of new governance structures. Similarly, the absence of national parliaments in this process suggests strengthening of governance structures.[13] In addition, it points at the arguments advanced by several scholars about the process of integration, and specifically OMC, leading to a weakening of national parliaments, better known as deparliamentarisation (Schmidt 1999; Duina and Oliver 2005). Yet, as Duina and Raunio (2007: 409) have argued, even if OMC has marginalized parliaments, it has strengthened the role of national ministries, thus entailing 'a move towards executive federalism and, with that, a channeling of authority towards the executive branch'.[14]

Furthermore, with reference to these trends in *governmental–societal internalization*, some might argue that soft law is a governance tool that is undemocratic in nature, as it is more difficult for societal groups to participate in their implementation, at least in the case of the EES. In this context, critics of soft law may evoke episodes in the history of European integration in which societal groups and citizens have been able to take advantage of hard law enforcement mechanisms (e.g. rights claiming, litigation) (Alter 2000; Caporaso and Jupille 2001; Cichowski 2006). Nonetheless, work by Börzel (2006: 147) shows that the transformative effects of judicial power on democracy through law enforcement might be overstated, as the 'EU's legal institutions only increase opportunities for participation for those individuals and groups who possess court access and sufficient resources to use it'. Thus, soft law as a governance instrument might be no less democratic than hard law, given that non-binding agreements can partially advance governmental–societal internalization and, consequently, the development of new governance structures within Member States (see Zeitlin, this volume).

2.2 Intra-governmental internalization

My findings show that the 'collaborative influence' of the EES was especially marked on intra-governmental relations (López-Santana 2008). National ministries have been able to put on the table domestic global (holistic) and integrated LMP plans for subnational entities to follow; whereas subnational entities have created their own plans within the framework of the NAPs and the EES. National governments have actively monitored the performance of subnational entities. In the same manner, subnational authorities have showcased their policies in reporting to the national level. In Spain, the Ministry of Labour and Social Affairs created a new inter-governmental arena where other ministries, as well as the subnational levels, met to discuss the EES (reporting and implementation). And the *Comunidades Autonómas* have been actively consulted by the national level in the process of creating the NAPs. In Belgium, the subnational authorities have actively bargained with the Ministry of Labour at the federal level. The federal level is obliged to do so because the Belgian regions and communities have competence over many aspects of LMPs. Thus, as van Gerven and Beckers, and Hamel and Vanhercke (this volume) also underline, the implementation of the OMC has had an important impact on intra-governmental relations in Belgium. In Sweden, the central association of municipalities has been actively involved in the process of creating the NAP, a rare occurrence in that country (López-Santana 2008). These developments are important, especially in decentralized and federal systems, because: 1) they allow national levels of government to draft inclusive policy plans on how to tackle common labour market problems across levels of government, and 2) they have helped to overcome collective action problems and coordination dilemmas caused by information gaps.

In Spain, by exchanging data, both national and subnational levels of government were able to detect policy duplications, allowing a more efficient use of financial resources. Along the same lines, subnational entities in Belgium have created Regional Action Plans, which provide a new source of information to the federal government about their policies. Interviewed policy makers believed that these plans gave the regions an opportunity to demonstrate their successes to the federal level. Conversely, they also provided the Belgian national level with an opportunity to monitor the regions. Based on these developments, I argue that the implementation of the EES has increased *de facto* coordination between national and subnational levels. Thus, all three Member States have experienced *intra-governmental internalization*, by adapting (accommodation) their domestic procedures and collaborative routines to implement the strategy. Yet, the legal character of intra-governmental relations has not been transformed because *de jure* institutions remain the same after the introduction of the EES.

In addition to promoting better national–subnational coordination, the EES guided the creation of 'bottom-up' programmes and subnational partnerships. In all three countries, subnational entities created regional and local employment programmes to implement the EES. Furthermore, EU soft standards opened new regional spaces for collaboration between subnational public and private actors (e.g. social pacts) and influenced the general content of regional employment policy. For instance, in Sweden the Regional

Association of Sörmland has been working on communicating and integrating the national employment programmes and the objectives of the Lisbon strategy at the regional and the municipal levels. In addition, several Swedish municipalities participated in a project to create 'Local Action Plans'. The same has been true in Spain (*Proyecto Pleyades* among others) and Belgium (Territorial Action Plans). Thus, the EES serves as an instrument spurring subnational levels to claim their place as important actors in local policy making and decision making.

Yet, such 'bottom-up' initiatives remain weak, since the process has filtered down to lower levels from the top and many local entities do not have much knowledge about the EES. For example, an EU policy maker said:

> Our assessment is that there is a lack of information. Employment policy is established at the national level and coordinated at the EU level, but jobs are created locally. So we do have the feeling that there is an insufficient involvement of local and regional actors in employment strategy. In terms of being informed on how policies are established, and how they are meant to be implemented at the national and EU level, there we feel that they are under informed. Although that depends very much on the Member State.
>
> (Interview, EU, December 2003).

Even if these 'bottom-up' initiatives have not been common across Member States, the data indicate that we should not underestimate these new spaces, as they have promoted collaboration, the creation of partnerships and networks, and the diffusion of innovations at the subnational levels.

In this context, a key finding is that the development of subnational partnerships was facilitated by the availability of European financial and technical resources.[15] We cannot understand the links between soft law and 'bottom-up' developments in EU Member States without taking account of the important role of the European Structural Fund (ESF) and the Commission in promoting subnational partnerships (Mailand, Jacobsson and West, this volume). Once these EU resources are granted, soft law guides the content of policy and partnerships at the subnational level. Therefore, the availability of regional resources serves as an incentive for subnational levels to implement policies along the lines of EU non-binding rules. In addition, the data indicate that the likelihood of soft law diffusion to lower levels increases when the links between the ESF resources are directly connected to the EES process (Hartwig 2007). This is probably because the national levels and the European level are working together to associate the ESF and the principles of the EES (and other soft methods). For instance, in Spain, interviewees at the Community of Madrid did not feel particularly empowered by the EES, but instead by the ESF. An explanation is that the Spanish national level and the EU did not do a good job of connecting these two processes (López-Santana 2007a). By contrast, in the case of Belgium, through the 'European Social Fund–National

Action Plan Assessment Cell' the federal level and the EU, in conjunction with the federated entities, have invested in resources and put effort into clarifying, connecting, and implementing the links between both processes.

These findings are consistent with claims about EU regional policy as the leading edge of multi-level governance and devolution (Marks 1993; Jones and Keating 1995; Conzelmann 1998). In addition, they indicate that soft European employment policy strengthens current trends towards devolution (i.e. the New Regionalism), which are characterized by the development of human capital at the subnational level (Keating 1998). Yet it does not entail a weakening of national governments, but rather an increased ability of subnational authorities to operate as key actors and exert influence in decision and policy making (i.e. multilevel governance).

2.3 Political and legal internalization

To fully capture the influence of the EES, it is important to explore the stages that precede parliamentary activities and statutory changes. Using this framework, I argue that EU non-binding rules have had important consequences on early stages of the policy-making process, particularly problem identification, agenda setting, and policy formulation. Reporting to the supranational level and implementing the EU strategy has had important unintended consequences on Member States, since these processes have shaped labour market and employment policies by establishing (and reinforcing) what problems domestic policy makers should attack to increase productivity and competitiveness. In addition, the EES softly enforces and reinforces the idea that a policy is good, bad, or necessary, which consequently restricts and limits the policy options and courses of action that domestic policy makers develop (López-Santana 2006a). For instance, when referring to the agenda-setting effect, Hamel and Vanhercke (this volume) argue that an important influence of the OMC on Social Inclusion in France and Belgium is the 'arrival' of new dimensions of the poverty issue (e.g. child poverty and youth integration) (see also van Gerven and Beckers, this volume). In Belgium, this innovation led to a demand for coordination by the federal level; this example, in addition, corroborates my findings on the effect of the EES on intra-governmental relations.

As underlined in other chapters of this book, I found that the implementation of the EES has had substantive consequences for the shape and the content of LMPs and institutions by placing ALMPs at the centre of the policy debate. For instance, all three Member States increased the share of ALMP spending after 1997. In the case of Sweden, the European emphasis on ALMPs has reinforced its current policy stance, with the exception of tax reform, gender exclusion, and LMP for migrants, which were influenced by the EES and other soft processes. In Spain and Belgium, policy makers became increasingly aware that they should further reform and change many dimensions of employment policy if they wanted to follow European trends (Mailand, this volume; López-Santana 2007a). Furthermore, they argued that even if the issue of activation had been on their agenda before 1997, the EES has significantly affected their policy preferences by intensifying the domestic priority accorded to the development and modernization of ALMPs; thus, it forces them to take further actions. For example, when asked about the main impact of the EES, an interviewee said:

> That we spend more money on ALMPs. Every year the relationship between active and passive labour policies changes, and we try to impose more and more active ones. Or, even that passive ones include a higher level of activity (and we see that year by year in the budgets), and normative changes (and that is where the EES is situated), and it has had its effect.
>
> (Interview, Spain 2003, my translation)

Within this context a common policy across all three Member States was the attempt to implement activation and preventative approaches through a 'new start'. A 'new start' refers to employability measures to (re)insert the short-term inactive population into the labour market. Specifically, national ministries in all three countries sought to modernize public employment services (PESs) by instructing these organizations to create individual reinsertion plans for the population within 6 to 12 months of unemployment. When asked about this approach, interviewees in all three countries referred to the EES as one of the main explanatory factors behind the domestic emphasis on a new start. For most interviewees, the idea of acting early to prevent long-term unemployment, promoted by the EES, represented an innovative policy approach, as it shifted the focus from this population to the short-term unemployed. The findings regarding the important links between activation and the OMC are certainly compatible with the evidence presented in later chapters.

This analysis allows us to advance certain propositions about the formative characteristics of soft law and their relationship to *legal internalization*. Researchers studying policy areas governed by soft law should not assume a direct relation between soft law and ratification, parliamentary activity, transposition or statutory changes, since this mechanism of change is rarely observed. A more fruitful way to capture the mechanism of legal internalization is to see soft law as *framing* policies and *inspiring* domestic actors to place issues higher on the agenda (López-Santana 2006a). As Heidenreich (this volume) argues, this could be an instrumental process in which domestic actors strategically download soft law (e.g. a 'blame Europe' strategy) to further their goals and agendas, even in cases where reforms are highly unpopular.

Although the EES has not been directly linked to radical legal changes in LMPs, since 1997 governments and social partners (especially in Belgium and Spain) have created programmes, legislation, and collective agreements that match the principles and objectives promoted by the European guidelines and recommendations.[16] For example, in Spain the government cited the EES to pass a radical royal decree to reform unemployment insurance systems, in part to further its neoliberal agenda.[17] In Belgium, the government incorporated legislation that was in line with the EU employment guidelines and recommendations. Yet, in Belgium, these latter initiatives were not ground breaking and most soft policies remained at the level of policy proposals and were not converted into legislation.

In these scenarios we must stress the 'domestic assent' and 'time' factors, as they are even more salient than in policy areas ruled by binding agreements. Once political internalization occurs, we would expect legal changes to occur, so long as key domestic actors agree with the policy. If this last condition is not met and the government passes a law to respond to soft law or to further its partisan agenda, for example through executive action, then these legal changes would be very unstable. Moreover, given that national governments are not obliged to implement the EES, unpopular reforms under non-binding agreements tend to be highly unstable. In this sense, a plausible argument is that unpopular reforms are more reversible under soft law than under hard law.

In this context, the 'temporal dimension' of reform is particularly salient, given that processes of change and implementation are especially lengthy. This is especially true if we assume that welfare institutions are notably 'sticky'. Presumably, legal internalization takes longer under soft law than under hard law, since the threat of being punished by a higher level is virtually absent. This means that domestic actors do not feel the urgency to change their current policies and, in the short run, do not substantially deviate from their original path of development. Thus, as actors reinterpret their current conditions, institutional changes under soft law are based on institutional adjustments (accommodation) and incremental change, rather than on radical ones (transformations) (Hall and Thelen 2006).

To recap, the absorption of soft law (vs transformation) has been common across types of internalization and across countries. The implementation of the EES has not led to *transformations*; rather, these norms have been absorbed at the domestic level in the three cases mainly by accommodation of routines to comply with procedural obligations. Second, an important unexpected finding of my research is the influence of the EES on the relationships between national governments, subnational levels, and social partners. The data show that the EU has been partially successful in promoting new governance structures within Member States. Third, with reference to *political internalization*, in Belgium the effect of the EES was especially salient since policy makers put great emphasis on 'activation'. In Spain, policy makers were also influenced by the EES, but to a lesser degree than in Belgium. Thus, we do not see as much movement toward *political internalization* in Spain as in Belgium, for reasons I will explain in the next section. Finally, in Sweden the strategy had a limited impact, as most national policies were in line with the EU guidelines. Nonetheless, this was not the case for tax reform, gender exclusion, and LMP for migrants.

3 Explaining differential internalization

The differential effects of the EES on Member States cannot be explained by a single factor, since the significance of the causal factors is not constant across types of internalization. Given space constraints, I limit the discussion here to theoretical propositions about *political internalization.*[18] The propositions here presented should be seen a set of hypotheses to be tested in other Member States and other policy areas governed by soft law.

3.1 Political internalization: ideational fit

Even if the data suggest that 'soft Europeanization' of labour market models is taking place, the case studies also show that political internalization of soft law has occurred in some states more than in others. Compared to Belgium, Spanish policy makers did not move as much towards political internalization because they were not as shaken by the EES at the ideational level. In Spain, many EES policies were already present, since the ESF had actively introduced them into national thinking during the pre-soft law period (also see Mailand, this volume). In the same vein, Swedish policy makers perceived that most of their policies were already ahead of the EU (for example, they claimed that they had actively 'uploaded' their policies to the supranational level); hence political internalization there was not as salient as in Belgium.[19] By contrast, the data show that, compared to Spain and Sweden, Belgian policy makers moved more towards political internalization than their peers because many policies were 'innovative' for this country, since Belgium has not received as much ESF funding as Spain. Therefore, compared to Spain, Belgium has moved further towards *political internalization.*

Based on these findings, I borrow the metaphor of the *degree of fit* from a strand of the Europeanization literature to explain the differential influence of soft law on political internalization (Cowles, Caporaso and Risse 2001; Héritier et al. 2001; Börzel and Risse 2003).[20] My propositions do not mirror the main theoretical claims of this literature; rather, they stem from the idea, underlined in this volume (Preunkert and Zirra), that the shape of domestic institutional settings (tangible and ideational ones) helps us to explain cross-national differences (relative comparisons, not absolute ones). In contrast to the literature on the degree of misfit, 'adaptational pressure' is not included as an important factor driving the process of Europeanization given that under non-binding rules there are no tangible EU pressures.

Furthermore, this literature has assumed that the levels of misfit in each Member State are equivalent across different dimensions (e.g. ideational, policy, institutional); hence, the distinctions between tangible and ideational dimensions of misfit have not been fully explored by scholars of hard law, who have tended to limit their analyses to policy and institutional misfits (Cowles, Caporaso and Risse 2001; Héritier et al. 2001; Börzel and Risse 2003). As indicated by recent critical work on Europeanization (Mastenbroek and Kaeding 2006), I propose that, in order to understand the differential effects of soft law on political internalization, researchers should also examine the degree to which domestic policy makers' beliefs and preferences fit specific EU soft rules (ideational fit). This is illustrated by the fact that a country can have high levels of congruence with EU rules on one dimension, while experiencing low levels of congruence on another. For instance, in relation to policy outputs (a dimension captured by the quantitative indicators of the EES), Spain has high levels of misfit in employment policy because, for example, it had high levels of unemployment. Therefore, EU employment policy did not fit the Spanish status quo. By contrast, in considering the degree to which EU labour market policy approaches are embedded among Spanish policy makers (ideational dimension), this country has medium to low levels of misfit, due to the active transfer of such European policy approaches through the ESF. In this case the discrepancies between the institutional and ideational dimensions are explained by the availability of regional resources in the pre-soft law era, which partly determines: 1) the degree to which European norms and policies are embedded in a Member State (i.e. the belief system underlying the status quo), and consequently 2) how far domestic actors internalize (politically) soft law.

With reference to low levels of ideational misfit, there are two scenarios: 1) states that receive extensive resources from the EU, leading policy makers to internalize EU ideas (e.g. Spain, Italy),[21] and 2) states whose institutions are fully in line with EU rules and whose level of ideational misfit is independent of the EU (e.g. Sweden, Denmark). In the first scenario, it is important to point out that countries with high levels of institutional misfit have received substantial resources from the EU; consequently, in the majority of these states, pre-soft law EU policies have been actively diffused and embedded into domestic settings. In these countries, it is very likely that policy makers will not politically internalize soft law as much as in countries with fewer resources, because domestic ideas already fit EU soft policies. Therefore, I hypothesize that countries with 'high to medium levels of institutional misfit' and 'low levels of *ideational* misfit' will move *less* toward political internalization than will countries with 'medium levels of *institutional* misfit', since soft law reinforces policy makers' preferences and the goals attached to the resources in the former. *In this way, by reinforcing a set of policy goals, soft law should increase the likelihood of legal internalization in countries that received EU resources in the pre-soft law era.* This explains, for example, why Spain has not politically internalized soft law as much as Belgium, but has legally internalized the EES (López-Santana 2007a).

Alternatively, countries with 'medium levels of *institutional* misfit' (e.g. Belgium, France) have received less aid from the EU because they have not needed it as much as less-developed countries (with high levels of institutional misfit). In these settings, EU soft law policies are not as ideationally embedded (i.e. domestic policy makers do not have the same level of awareness of them) (see Preunkert and Zirra, and Hamel and Vanhercke, this volume, for analyses of the French case). In countries with medium levels of institutional misfit, EU soft law should significantly influence the early stages of policy making, such as problem definition and agenda setting, since pre-soft law domestic policy makers have not been as exposed to EU policies and ideas. Thus, soft law should serve as a force pushing policy makers to accommodate, learn, and update their belief system and, consequently, attempt to change the status quo. For instance, this explains why Belgium has politically internalized the EES more than have Spain and Sweden.

Finally, I hypothesize that countries with 'low levels of *institutional* and *ideational* misfit' (e.g. Sweden, Denmark) will internalize soft law *less* than countries with 'medium and high levels of *ideational* misfit' because their institutions and policy approaches already fit EU soft rules. Along these lines, Mailand (this volume) argues that the EES has not had any great impact in countries where the employment policy was in compliance before 1997. From the policy makers' point of view, why should they change domestic institutions and policy approaches if these already fit EU standards and they are not obliged to do so? These countries have put considerable effort into 'uploading' their policy preferences to the EU level; thus, they should have low levels of ideational misfit, because they have already transferred their policies to the EU level.

Nonetheless, we should not assume that countries with low levels of misfit will not be affected by soft law. First, 'institutional or policy gaps' (i.e. policy areas or institutions with high to medium levels of misfit) can explain some of the changes that have taken place in Sweden, since it is highly unlikely that there is perfect fit across policy areas and institutions. Second, implementation of soft law has had a set of unintended consequences on Member States. For instance, as highlighted by Jacobsson and Johansson (this volume), when it comes to gender exclusion, LMP for migrants, and tax reform, policy makers in Sweden have politically internalized the message from the EU. Therefore, along the lines of recent arguments, I acknowledge that 'misfit/fit' is neither a necessary nor a sufficient condition for internalization to take place (Falkner et al. 2005; Mastenbroek and Kaeding 2006).

4 Conclusions

What are the implications of these findings for the likelihood of domestic changes and reforms? First, political internalization of the EES entails a convergence of European paths of development and LMP models and paradigms.[22] For instance, many Member State policy makers claimed that they increasingly use European LMP as a point of reference, especially when it comes to the modernization of the PES and the promotion of ALMPs. A quick look at labour market reforms in the last decade, for example, in Germany, France, Spain, Sweden, Italy, and Belgium, illustrates how Member States have adopted policies and have created institutions that are conspicuously in line with the supranational soft agenda.

The political internalization of soft law is also a significant phenomenon if we consider that policy implementation is not always dependent on the legislative branch, but on the executive (Duina and Raunio 2007), through ministerial rulings and bureaucratic mandates. If policy makers in the executive branch accept and understand the need to implement soft law, then they can adopt policies that reflect these non-binding rules. Political internalization, moreover, increases the likelihood of legal internalization because, once key ministerial policy makers internalize the rules promoted by soft law, they can shape parliamentary and executive activities. Finally, political internalization can also be significant for policy implementation (after legal internalization has taken place) because, once policy makers incorporate these soft frameworks into their belief systems, it is very likely that they will push for their implementation. Thus, policy makers will do their part to prevent laws from being 'lost in implementation'. For example, in policy areas simultaneously governed by binding and non-binding rules (such as gender equality policy), political internalization of soft law helps policy makers to understand why EU hard law and soft frameworks are important and necessary to achieve a set of common goals. Therefore, political internalization can increase the likelihood of successful compliance and implementation.

In contrast, the limitation of political internalization becomes evident when we consider scenarios where implementation is dependent on statutory changes. Even if political internalization is a necessary condition for legal internalization to take place (this is not necessarily true in non-consensual or dictatorial settings), it is not sufficient for the latter to occur. As Shelton (2000: 17) argues, 'once international regulations [are] perceived as necessary and action has been taken, compliance is expected and necessary, but not always sufficient, for the norm to become effective'. Since parliaments have been virtually absent in these scenarios, it could take considerable time for soft law to move from ministries to the legislature, and/or for political internalization to drive societal mobilization. Thus, under soft law, processes of domestic change could be lengthy and difficult, and at times even improbable. This is especially true if we take into account that Member States are not obliged to engage in statutory changes.

The findings presented here contribute to the literature on Europeanization by showing that 'adaptational pressure' is not a necessary condition for Europeanization to occur. This means that 'soft Europeanization' is not driven by coercion (and the threat of punishment), but by other types of cognitive mechanisms. This chapter also provides significant lessons about the ability of non-binding instruments (e.g. regional, international, federal) to serve as domestic change agents. An important conclusion is that soft law does not radically transform Member States. Rather, it is a slow process that inspires policy makers to make changes which, mixed with domestic politics, could lead to radical changes. These findings lead me to conclude that soft law is an efficient governance tool if the goal is for higher levels of government (in this case the EU) to diffuse a set of 'good' policies so that lower levels of government (in this case Member States) can follow similar policy prescriptions and paths of development (paradigm shift) without having to cede power to the former.

With reference to the ability of the EES (and other soft processes) to transform LMPs and employment policies, the aforementioned findings are not surprising, given that welfare institutions have been particularly 'sticky' and resistant to radical change (see, for example, Esping-Andersen 1999; Pierson 2001). This is the reason why we observe continuity and weak reforms of 'sticky' welfare institutions. In this context, the EES does not lead radical transformations, but it supports subtle accommodations. Taking this point into account, it is fair to say that welfare states might not be radically changing, but domestic procedures, policies, and institutions are subtly and slowly evolving.[23] These accommodations, in turn, can accumulate and can lead (in the long run) to far-reaching transformations.

In this context, the EES should be considered an external process or 'opportunity structure' that pushes domestic policy makers to update their belief system and to reform (or strengthen) their welfare policies, programmes, and institutions. For instance, ALMPs have been increasingly developed by Member States, but these actions do not entail the dismantling of social insurance systems (i.e. retrenchment) (Pierson 1994) since passive LMPs remain an essential part of policy in the vast majority of EU Member States (Swank 2006). Thus, I conclude that regional and international organizations play an important role in the process of 'recalibration' (Rhodes, Ferrera and Hemerijck 2000; Pierson 2001), since they have been promoting a set of 'good' policies for reconciling competitiveness with social protection in an era of increasing openness, mobility, and change.

Notes

1 The findings are drawn from my University of Michigan PhD thesis (López-Santana 2006b) presented at the Department of Political Science. This research was supported by the Max Weber Programme (European University Institute).

2 This research project focuses on *implementation* (Chayes and Chayes 1993), rather than on *compliance*. I conceptualize *compliance* as the extent to which institutional settings are compatible with a set of rules. Thus, a state can comply with international rules even if it does not make an effort to incorporate them into its domestic arrangements because the latter are already in line with the former. *Implementation*, on the other hand, entails conscious efforts to incorporate these rules. Implementation goes beyond compliance, given that a state can further incorporate a set of guidelines even if it already complies with a target, for example.

3 See Heidenreich (this volume).

4 My typology overlaps in objectives, but differs in conceptualization from those presented in other chapters in this volume, notably Preunkert and Zirra, Heidenreich, and Heidenreich and Zeitlin.

5 The EU has recognized that the non-binding nature of the EES represents an obstacle for the achievement of domestic reforms. Given that legal internalization of the EES has been weak, the EU has asked national governments to diffuse the strategy to subnational administrations and societal actors and to involve them in

the process of reporting. By so doing, the EU has sought not only to increase the likelihood of implementation, but also to promote good governance (openness and democracy).

6 On these two points, see Hamel and Vanhercke (this volume).

7 For more information about the effect of the OMC in Sweden, see Jacobsson and Johansson (this volume).

8 See Mastenbroek and Keading's (2006: 339) critique of the Europeanization literature.

9 We should differentiate between procedural obligations (reporting and participating in forums) and substantive obligations (implementing supranational mandates) (Brown Weiss and Jacobson 2000). In policy areas governed by soft law, Member States have procedural obligations toward the supranational level. Once a state agrees to form part of a soft regime, it must comply with its procedural obligations. Procedural obligations vary from regime to regime – some non-binding procedures involve more procedural obligations than other types of agreements (e.g. gentlemen's agreements) (Hillgenberg 1999). Under soft law, a state does not have substantive obligations toward higher levels of government.

10 Spanish trade unions were not very enthusiastic about their participation. In Belgium, trade unions were very happy with their involvement. In Sweden, the trade unions were, more or less, indifferent to the exercise, given the strong tradition of social concertation.

11 First, the interviews conducted at the EU level were not included in this analysis. The reasoning behind this choice is that EU policy makers do not participate in the process of policy making in Member States. Second, I did not test these data for statistical significance, because this is a small sample that was not randomly selected. The samples were chosen similarly across sites, as I mainly conducted interviews with subjects who have been involved in the implementation of the EES at the domestic level. Third, the goal of this analysis is to illustrate the trends discerned with the interviews, by showing aggregate descriptive figures.

12 Falkner et al. (2005: 303) emphasize that no real knowledge has been acquired about the '*direction* of the effect exerted by interest group involvement'. They point out that some authors have argued that interest groups might advance compliance by exerting pressure on governments. However, others have stressed the blocking power of these groups (Héritier et al. 2001).

13 See Jacobsson and Johansson (this volume).

14 Duina and Raunio (2007) also identify a series of mechanisms whereby OMC could strengthen the legislative and oversight capacities of national parliaments, though these have not yet been fully exploited.

15 This finding should not be surprising to students of federalism. For example, Peterson (1995: 13) argues that in the United States 'most national efforts to influence state governments come in the form of federal grants'. This literature points out that grant-in-aid of transfers to states and localities served as a way to 'buy' states' governments, and to move the United States from 'dual federalism' to a 'cooperative' model.

16 For more details, see López-Santana (2007b).

17 The 2002 Spanish reform of unemployment benefits, better known as '*el decretazo*', illustrates this argument. Following the failure of a process of negotiation between the social partners, the ruling government unilaterally passed the Royal Decree Law 5/2002. Aznar's government took advantage of its soft obligation to Europe to pass unpopular reforms. The law adopted 'urgent measures' to reform the unemployment benefit and protection systems, as well as to modernize the PESs. The reform introduced obligations and mechanisms for the unemployed to actively seek employment in the shortest amount of time possible. This law made direct references to the employment guidelines and the conclusions of the Barcelona European Council. The reform was not supported by the social partners and the general

public: in June 2002 the trade unions organized a general strike and on one day more than 620,000 people gathered in different parts of Spain to protest. Given the unemployment situation, a period of social unrest and lack of support, the government had no choice but to abolish this decree law and replace it by Law 45/2002 (López-Santana 2007a).

18 For more details on other three types of internalization, see López-Santana (2007b).

19 As Hamel and Vanhercke (this volume) show, this phenomenon is also applicable to France and the OMC on social inclusion.

20 Scholars working on Europeanization have identified 'the degree of (in)compatibility (fit) between European measures and domestic institutions as one important factor to predict the likelihood of implementation success of supranational binding rules. These authors focus on the 'goodness of fit' between EU and domestic institutions to explain why some countries experience greater adaptational pressures towards Europeanization than others. They argue that the greater the 'misfit' (incompatibility) between domestic institutions and European measures, the higher the likelihood of compliance failure, because a larger policy response is necessary to comply with EU mandates. Furthermore, they predict that when there is low misfit between domestic institutions and EU measures, we are likely to observe weak or no change because domestic institutions already match EU standards. Thus, 'business as usual' prevails in countries where domestic rights and obligations (i.e. legal or customary) are already in line with EU requirements (Bugdahn 2005). Based on these propositions, transformations are more likely to occur when a country has medium levels of misfit, because the degree of institutional misfit does not represent a major obstacle for compliance, but still there is enough space for improving the domestic situation.

21 Preunkert and Zirra reach similar conclusions in analysing the Italian case.

22 On the importance of paradigm changes, see Hall (1993) and van Gerven and Beckers (this volume).

23 These arguments follow the literature on institutional change, which argues that subtle evolution of domestic welfare policies occurs within long-lasting institutions; therefore, current processes of change are not radical in nature, but gradual and incremental. This model differs from the strong, punctuated equilibrium model, which is used – explicitly or implicitly – by much of the institutionalist literature (Streeck and Thelen 2005).

References

Alter, K.J. (2000) 'The European Union's Legal System and Domestic Policy: Spillover or Backlash?', *International Organization*, 54: 489–518.

Börzel, T.A. (2006) 'Participation through Law Enforcement: The Case of the European Union', *Comparative Political Studies*, 39: 128–52.

Börzel, T.A. and Risse, T. (2003) 'Conceptualizing the Domestic Impact of Europe', in F. Featherstone and C. Radaelli (eds) *The Politics of Europeanization*, Oxford: Oxford University Press.

Brown Weiss, E. and Jacobson, H.K. (2000) *Engaging Countries: Strengthening Compliance with International Environmental Accords*, Boston, MA: MIT Press.

Bugdahn, S. (2005) 'Of Europeanization and Domestication: The Implementation of the Environmental Information Directive in Ireland, Great Britain and Germany', *Journal of European Public Policy*, 12: 177–99.

Caporaso, J. and Jupille, J. (2001) 'The Europeanization of Gender Equality Policy and Domestic Structural Change', in M.G. Cowles, J. Caporaso and T. Risse (eds) *Transforming Europe*, Cornell, NY: Cornell University Press.

Chayes, A. and Chayes, A.H. (1993) 'On Compliance', *International Organization*, 47: 175–205.
Cichowski, R.A. (2006) *Litigation, Mobilization, and Governance: The European Court of Justice and Transnational Activism*, Cambridge: Cambridge University Press.
Conzelmann, Thomas (1998) 'Europeanisation of Regional Development Policies? Linking the Multi-Level Governance with Theories of Policy Learning and Policy Change', *European Integration Online Papers*, 2 (4).
Cowles, M.G., Caporaso, J. and Risse, T. (2001) *Transforming Europe: Europeanization and Domestic Change*, New York: Cornell University Press.
Duina, F. and Oliver, M. (2005) 'National Parliaments in the European Union: Are there Any Benefits to Integration?', *European Law Journal*, 11: 173–95.
Duina, F. and Raunio, T. (2007) 'The Open Method of Co-ordination and National Parliaments: Further Marginalization or New Opportunities?', *Journal of European Public Policy*, 14: 489–506.
Esping-Andersen, G. (1990) *The Three Worlds of Capitalism*, Princeton: Princeton University Press.
—— (1999) *Social Foundations of Postindustrial Economies*, Oxford: Oxford University Press.
Falkner, G., Treib, O., Hartlapp, M. and Leiber, S. (2005) *Complying with Europe: EU Harmonization and Soft Law in the Member States*, Cambridge: Cambridge University Press.
Featherstone, K. and Radaelli, C.M. (2003) *The Politics of Europeanization*, Oxford: Oxford University Press.
Haas, P.M. (1992) 'Introduction: Epistemic Communities and International Policy Coordination', *International Organization*, 46: 1–35.
Hall, P.A. (1993) 'Policy Paradigm, Social Learning and the State', *Comparative Politics*, 25: 275–96.
Hall, P.A. and Thelen, K. (2006) 'Varieties of Capitalism and Institutional Change', *Newsletter of the European Politics and Society of the American Political Association*, 5: 1–4.
Hartwig, I. (2007) 'Towards a Communitarisation? Spill-overs between Structural Funds and the European Employment Strategy', in I. Linsenmann, C.O. Meyer and W. Wessels (eds) *Economic Government of the EU. A Balance Sheet of New Modes of Policy Coordination*, Basingstoke: Palgrave Macmillan.
Héritier, A., Krewer, D., Knill, C., Lehmkuhl, D., Teutsch, M. and Douillet, A.M. (2001) *Differential Europe: The European Union Impact on National Policymaking*, Oxford: Rowman and Littlefield Publishers.
Hillgenberg, H. (1999) 'A Fresh Look at Soft Law', *European Journal of International Law*, 10: 499–515.
Jacobsson, K. and Vifell, Å. (2007) 'New Governance Structures in Employment Policy-Making? Loose Co-ordination in Action', in I. Linsenmann, C.O. Meyer and W. Wessels (eds) *Economic Government of the EU. A Balance Sheet of New Modes of Policy Coordination*, Basingstoke: Palgrave Macmillan.
Jones, B. and Keating, M. (1995) *The European Union and the Regions*, Oxford: Clarendon Press.
Keating, M. (1998) *The New Regionalism in Western Europe*, Cheltenham: Edward Elgar.
Koh, H.H. (1997) 'Why Do Nations Obey International Law?', *The Yale Law Journal*, 106: 2599–2659.

López-Santana, M. (2006a) 'Framing and Transmitting Change in Employment Policy: Domestic Implications of European Soft Law on Member States,' *Journal of European Public Policy*, 13: 481–99.

—— (2006b) 'Soft Europeanization? The Differential Influence of European Soft Law on Employment Policies, Processes, and Institutional Configurations in EU Member States', unpublished PhD thesis, University of Michigan.

—— (2006c) 'Having a "Say" Without Having to "Pay": The Differential Effect of the Open Method of Coordination in Member States', paper presented at the Governing Work and Welfare in an Enlarged Europe Conference, Madison.

—— (2007a) 'La "Internalización" de la Estrategia Europea de Empleo en España', *Revista Española de Derecho Europeo*, 21: 57–87.

—— (2007b) 'Soft Europeanisation: How the Pressure from Above Affects the Bottom Differently: The Belgian, Spanish, and Swedish Experiences', *Max Weber Programme, EUI Working Papers* (MWP 2007/10), Florence: European University Institute.

—— (2008) 'The Multilevel Governance of the European Employment Strategy', paper presented at the OMC within the Lisbon Strategy: Empirical Assessments and Theoretical Implications, Vienna.

Marks, Gary (1993) 'Structural Policy and Multilevel Governance in the EC', in Alan W. Cafruny and Glenda G. Rosenthal (eds) *The State of the European Community. The Maastricht Debates and Beyond,* Volume 2, Boulder, CO: Harlow Longman.

Mastenbroek, E. and Keading, M. (2006) 'Europeanization Beyond the Goodness of Fit: Domestic Politics in the Forefront', *Comparative European Politics*, 4: 331–54.

Peterson, P.E. (1995) *The Price of Federalism*, Washington, DC: Brookings Institution Press.

Pierson, P. (1994) *Dismantling the Welfare State? Reagan, Thatcher, and the Politics of Retrenchment*, Cambridge: Cambridge University Press.

—— (2001) *The New Politics of the Welfare State*, Oxford: Oxford University Press.

Radaelli, C.M. (2003) 'The Europeanization of Public Policy', in K. Featherstone and C. Radaelli (eds) *The Politics of Europeanization*, Oxford: Oxford University Press.

Rhodes, M., Ferrera, M. and Hemerijck, A. (2000) *The Future of Social Europe: Recasting Work and Welfare in the New Economy*, Lisbon: Ministério do Trabalho e da Solidariedade.

Rhodes, R.A.W. (1996) 'The New Governance: Governing without Government', *Political Studies*, 44: 652–67.

Schmidt, V.A. (1999) 'European "Federalism" and its Encroachments on National Institutions', *Publius*, 29: 19–44.

Shelton, D. (2000) *Commitment and Compliance. The Role of Non-binding Norms in the International Legal System*, Oxford: Oxford University Press

Streeck, W. and Thelen, K. (2005) *Beyond Continuity: Institutional Change in Advanced Political Economies*, Oxford: Oxford University Press.

Swank, D. (2006) 'Activating Change: International and Domestic Sources of Unemployment Policy Reform in the Capitalist Democracies, 1980–2002', paper presented at the Annual Meeting of the American Political Science Association, Philadelphia, August.

7 North, South, East, West

The implementation of the European Employment Strategy in Denmark, the UK, Spain, and Poland

Mikkel Mailand

Introduction

The European Employment Strategy (EES) was created in the mid-1990s. Its goal is to coordinate Member States' various attempts to address persistently high levels of unemployment and low employment rates. The main instruments used in the strategy form part of a cycle including Employment Guidelines, National Action Plans for Employment, and the EU's Joint Employment Report, which includes country-specific recommendations. Similar cycles exist in other policy areas and this mode of governance has been termed the 'Open Method of Coordination' (OMC). Despite revisions in 2003 and 2004, the basic principles of the EES remain the same.

The impact of this cycle and its accompanying peer-review processes on the employment policies of the Member States has been a matter of controversy for many years. An evaluation conducted by the European Commission in 2002 concluded that even though the main employment policy features in some countries were already in place prior to the Luxembourg summit, the EES had 1) strengthened national policy frameworks and focused attention on targets and deadlines; 2) started a process of convergence between Member States' employment policies towards increased activation and prevention of long-term unemployment for specific target groups; 3) supported the process of convergence; 4) ensured that policies had been maintained and reshaped in line with the strategy in countries where active labour market policies (ALMP) were already in place; 5) inspired employment policy reforms among some of the 'laggards'; 6) impacted policies other than ALMP; and 7) improved inter-ministerial coordination and the involvement of regional authorities, social partners, and NGOs (European Commission 2002: 11–13).

However, when examining the national reports behind the evaluation, it is difficult to point to more than a few specific examples of EES impact on national-level employment policy. This is especially true regarding the *content* of the policy (the employment policy programmes and economic resources spent on them). The evaluation as well as other studies (e.g. Jacobsson and Schmid 2001; Foden 1999; Langhoff-Ross 2001; Umbach 2003; López-Santana 2004) indicate that the impact on *policy processes* (e.g. coordination among governmental departments; consultation with social partners, NGOs, and regional governments; the use of evaluations and statistics etc.) has been more profound. More recent studies largely confirm this picture. Building on seven national case studies examining the impact of the EES and the EU's Social Inclusion Strategy, Zeitlin (2005) concludes that these strategies have contributed to shifts in national policy orientation and thinking (for instance, from reducing unemployment rates to increasing employment), as well as shifts in specific policy areas, most importantly in relation to gender equality. Zeitlin's study confirms that the impact on national policy procedures has been more profound. Further, Zeitlin finds great variation between Member States as well as between the two OMCs in terms of the extent to which the national parliaments, the social partners and the NGOs play a role in the process. According to this author, mutual learning has taken place between Member States, largely in terms of identifying common challenges and potentially successful approaches, rather than learning from cases of good practice.

These studies offer some insight into the impact of the EES on national employment policies. However, most of these studies are limited to the period before 2002 – that is, before the first revision of the strategy in 2003. Furthermore, it is difficult to compare findings across Member States, because the studies tend to focus on one or two countries at most and do not use a common methodology. Systematic comparisons of the impact in more than two Member States are rare.[1]

One consequence of the paucity of comparative impact studies is a lack of knowledge of what factors of the EES affect its impact. If such knowledge were available, it might help to explain the uneven influence of the EES. *Therefore, the aim of this chapter is to analyse the uneven impact of the EES across countries and discuss possible explanations for this variation.*

This chapter draws on findings from a systematic comparative study of the direct impact of the EES on employment policy in four Member States representing very different labour market models and welfare state traditions (Denmark, the UK, Spain, and Poland[2]), examining the extent to which the Member States' employment policies have been influenced by the EES. The four countries can be seen as maximum-variation cases in terms of welfare state and labour market regulation, providing the best opportunity to generalize the results to other countries in the EU (Preworski and Teune 1970: 39; Flyvbjerg 1991: 150).

This introduction is followed by a discussion of the theoretical and methodological literature on the impact of the EES. The third section summarizes the results of the four national case studies. The final section compares the cases and concludes.

1 Theoretical and methodological reflections on impact analyses of the EES

1.1 How can the EES influence national policies?

Supranational institutions can influence national-level policies in several ways.[3] Zeitlin has provided a useful overview of possible mechanisms for the impact of the EES and the OMC on social inclusion. Building on the work of, *inter alia*, Barbier (2005), Ehrel et al. (2005), Ferrera et al. (2002), Jacobsson (2002), Vifell (2004) and Visser (2005) – he distinguishes four mechanisms of influence (Zeitlin 2005: 31–8).

First, Member States may put *peer pressure* on one another to reach common targets and carry out mutually agreed commitments (e.g. Jacobsson 2002, 2005; Vifell 2004). This pressure works through recommendations as well as other forms of written communication coming from the EU, such as the Joint Employment Reports. Moreover, meetings of the EU Employment Committee can serve as a channel through which peer pressure is exerted. Peer pressure is not just a theoretical possibility; it is a component of how the strategy works, which is illustrated by the fact that Member States try to avoid or reformulate the recommendations in bilateral meetings, and especially try to avoid quantitative targets.

Second, *strategic use* of the EES by national and subnational actors is another important, deliberate mechanism. The EES may be used by national governments for external legitimation of unpopular measures or reforms. However, this mechanism also can also be used in inter-ministerial struggles as well as by non-state actors, for instance, social partners' attempts to legitimize their own positions or move the government or other non-state actors in certain directions. This use of the OMCs as a strategic resource has been referred to by Barbier (2005) and Ehrel et al. (2005) as the 'leverage effect'. Visser (2005) also analyses the OMCs in this light. He sees the OMC as a 'selective amplifier', through which actors can search for legitimacy or share blame for unpopular reforms. Whereas peer pressure could be seen as a 'top-down' mechanism working from the EU level to the national level, strategic use is best seen as a 'bottom-up' mechanism, where actors at the national level seize the elements at EU level they find useful.

Other mechanisms of influence of the EES and the OMC include socialization/discursive diffusion and learning. *Socialization and discursive diffusion* take place, for instance, when a common frame of reference for national employment policies is developed through the participation of high-level civil servants in EU committees, and through the adoption of a common vocabulary and reporting formats. In this environment, Member State representatives cannot simply advance positions on the basis of national interest alone, but must instead use reasoned arguments grounded in common objectives, guidelines, targets, and indicators.

Zeitlin distinguishes between indirect and direct forms of *mutual learning*. Indirect learning works through a combination of enhanced awareness of different approaches and performance standards used elsewhere, on the one hand, and 'reflexive self-assessment', including improvements in institutional capacity for information gathering and monitoring on the other. Direct learning, also termed 'policy transfer', occurs when policies are copied – or, more frequently, adapted – from foreign models abroad, based on evidence of what works and what does not.

Peer pressure and strategic use represent more *direct forms of impact* than learning, socialization, and discursive diffusion. Moreover, peer pressure and strategic use, unlike socialization and at least some forms of learning, are conscious, deliberate mechanisms. However, the term 'pressure' will be used instead of 'peer pressure', because the actors exercising the pressure include not only Member States (peers) but also the Commission.

Since the main concern of this chapter is opportunities to *deliberately and directly* steer and coordinate policies, the following analysis will focus mainly on peer pressure and strategic use, even though the more indirect forms may be equally important. As a consequence of this focus, what follows will only describe part of the overall impact of the EES on national-level policies (see below).

1.2 Methods

It has been rightly argued that impact analyses of the EES are very difficult, since the direction of causality is unclear. This is related to the fact that Member States in the European Council most likely will not approve guidelines that they believe they will not be able to fulfil in the short term. Moreover, the individual Member States tend to advocate inclusion of measures and policies in the EES that they themselves have already introduced. It may therefore appear in some areas that the EES has affected a particular Member State's employment policy, although this is not the case (Greve 2005: 15). However, regarding the first problem, what often happens – due to the pressure mechanism – is that guidelines and indicators are agreed upon even though they will highlight bad performance in some Member States. The second problem can be reduced substantially by paying attention to the timing of various actions and by analytically distinguishing between compliance (whether a national policy is in line with the EES – which might not have anything to do with the EES) and impact (whether the EES is a causal factor behind specific changes in national policies).

Furthermore, it has also been rightly argued that civil servants in some countries, where the legitimacy of EU intervention is weak, might tend to underestimate the impact of the EES (Zeitlin 2005; Jacobsson 2003). Nevertheless, civil servants have detailed information about political processes and are valuable sources of information. The tendency to underestimate the impact of the EES could be counteracted by triangulating information from such interviews with other sources.

The data sources for this chapter include: 1) EU documents; 2) government publications; 3) academic texts analysing the EES's impact on national employment policies; and 4) 68 semi-structured interviews[4] with civil servants and social partners at EU and national level,[5] members of the European Parliament, members of the Employment Task Force and High-Level Group on the Lisbon Strategy chaired by Wim Kok, and academic experts, conducted between May 2004 and April 2006. Where no other source is mentioned, the information in this chapter is drawn from these interviews.

The dependent variable in the study is national-level employment policies, even though a full analysis of the impact of the EES would have to include subnational levels as well. This leads to a systematic overestimation of the impact, since there is no guarantee that the policies and perceptions will reach 'the ground' in companies and the frontline of administrations. On the other hand, the focus on the two mechanisms of strategic use and pressure, together with the exclusion of mutual learning and socialization/discursive diffusion, leads to a systematic underestimation of the overall impact of the EES.

This chapter focuses mainly on the period from 1998, when the first National Actions Plans for employment (NAPs) were written, to the spring of 2006, when the last interviews were conducted. However, since the analyses pay special attention to the recommendations given to Member States, the main focus will be on the period during which they were issued – i.e. between 2000 and 2004.

2 The EES in the four corners of Europe

2.1 Denmark

It is difficult to find evidence of direct impact of the EES in Denmark, although the level of compliance predating the EES is high. Activation policies were developed in the 1970s, with a volume and content from the early and mid-1990s that was largely in line with what later became the EES. Spending on active measures has been among the highest in the EU and accounts now for 1.74% of the GDP, whereas passive measures account for 2.68% (OECD 2005). With employment rates above the 2010 target of the EES (for instance, an overall employment rate of 76%) and unemployment levels around 4%, increasing the labour market performance of Denmark has been like 'reforming the best pupil in the class' (Jacobsson 2003).

Nevertheless, Denmark, like all other Member States, has received EU recommendations on its employment policies from 2000 to 2004. All EU recommendations in the Danish case have been related to policy content, not to processes. There has been one recurring recommendation: to reduce the taxation of labour, whereas a recommendation on mainstreaming/gender segregation disappeared in 2003, and a new recommendation on encouraging more people to take up employment, especially immigrants, has been repeated in different versions since 2002. In 2003, a recommendation regarding active ageing was added, and in 2004 yet another on 'monitoring trends in vocational training in the light of recent increases in training fees'. According to interviewees, the most controversial recommendation has concerned active ageing, which directly asked the Danish government to discontinue its Voluntary Early Retirement Benefit Scheme. Because this scheme had previously proved to be very sensitive politically, and because the government believed that the Commission had no legal basis for interference in specific national policy programmes, the interviewees reported that it had asked the Commission to remove the part of the recommendation that directly referred to this scheme. The Commission complied with this request in the final version of the recommendations. But the 'cat was already out of the bag'. In April 2004, the influential newsletter of the Danish Employers Confederation (DA) – which, like the Danish media in general, very rarely refers to the EES – published an article mentioning the proposed recommendation. According to the interviewees, however, even though the proposal fit its own preferred direction for the development of active ageing and retirement policy, the DA refrained from following up the article with further pressure on the centre-Right government (which it generally supports) because of the issue's politically sensitive nature. In the end, changes to the scheme came only in 2006 and even not as a result of the EES. Hence, although both pressure and strategic use mechanisms were at work, this can hardly be seen as a case of effective impact.

Political action has been taken in areas related to other recommendations. However, the interviewees reported no connection between these actions and the recommendations. Looking beyond the recommendations to the activation indicators, it is nevertheless possible to find an area where the EES has had direct influence on the content of Danish employment policy. During the first years of the EES, there was a fundamental discrepancy between the Danish strategy, which focused on activating the long-term unemployed, and the EES, which prioritized initiatives to prevent jobless people from falling into long-term unemployment through guidelines demanding activation after 6 months (young people) or 12 months (adults). Denmark did not meet these goals, even though it had been one of the countries pushing for quantitative targets in connection with the strategy. On this point, Denmark has not received formal recommendations, but instead a so-called 'second-order recommendation' to give higher priority to prevention rather than remediation of long-term unemployment, and to fulfil the demand for activation after 6 or 12 months (see also Langhoff-Ross 2001).

This 'second-order recommendation' was considered of less a problem in itself than the fact that other Member States could see from the NAPs and elsewhere that Denmark had failed to fulfil one of the central employability targets. This was taken very seriously by the Danish government, especially by the former Prime Minister, Poul Nyrup Rasmussen. In spite of scepticism among civil servants about the preventive approach, because it was perceived as a heavy burden on the public employment service, the introduction of the 6 and 12-month limits agreed by the European Council in autumn 1997 became hard to avoid when the Prime Minister reported to the Danish Parliament's European Affairs Committee that the targets would be implemented in the third phase of the labour market reform (Christensen et al. 2004: 100). Some interviewees who confirmed this pointed out that the Prime Minister and the Minister of Labour – as well as some high-level civil servants and leaders of the regional public employment service – used the EES in their arguments for a more preventive approach, but reported that this affected mainly the timing of the policy shift. The preventive approach, they claimed, would have been introduced properly at a later stage, even without the pressure from, and the strategic use of, the EES. In sum, it seems that the pressure worked in this case.

Some commentators have further pointed to the remarkable level of compliance of the government's most recent (2005) overall programme with nine of the integrated guidelines (Ransby 2005). This indicates that even though the direct impact from the EES is limited, the Danish government is eager to ensure that there are no inconsistencies between what it agrees with other Member States at the EU level and its own political statements on the national scene. Most of these overlaps are of a very general nature or not part of the EES process, but the wordings are remarkably similar. However, the target that 85% of each youth cohort should have completed at least secondary education by 2010 may have its roots in the EES, and may thereby be a case of direct impact. This can be seen as a result of strategic use as well as of pressure.

Contrary to many other Member States, Denmark has received no recommendations regarding *policy processes*, such as consultation procedures with social partners, regional and local authorities, or other stakeholders. Nor did the interviewees point to any spill-over from the NAP process to the internal coordination of the public administration or its relations with external stakeholders, such as the social partners or NGOs. Strategic references to the EES in political and media debates are also very rare, according to the interviewees. The examples described above seem to be unique.

2.2 The United Kingdom

Similar to Denmark, there are only a few cases of direct EES impact in the UK. British employment policies show a general high level of prior compliance with the EES, but not so marked as in the Danish case. The origins of the UK's embrace of supply-side activation policies can be traced, to some extent, to the Conservative governments' (1979–97) response to the country's unemployment crisis during the 1980s. Activation policies focusing more on compulsion, an individual approach, and choice between different options, were introduced in the mid-1990s (Lindsay and Mailand 2004). However, despite the greater attention to activation policy, spending in this area is still among the lowest in the EU, with just 0.34% of the GDP devoted to active measures and 0.37% to passive measures (OECD 2005: 274).[6] With employment rates at 72% and unemployment at 5%, the UK in recent years has developed into one of the strongest performers in the EU.

As an indication of its slightly lower level of compliance as compared to Denmark, the UK has received a few more recommendations. These recommendations have been even more stable than the Danish ones. Four recommendations have been given every year from 2000 to 2004. Recommendations related to the gender pay gap and childcare facilities have been repeated in different versions since 2000. So has the recommendation regarding ALMP.

A third recommendation on training and life-long learning was added in 2001 and has been repeated each year since then. The fourth near-constant recommendation has concerned strengthening social partnership. It was not repeated in 2004, but was replaced by a new recommendation asking the UK to keep wage development below productivity growth.

One can point to several political initiatives in the areas covered by the recommendations. However, the interviewees had difficulty showing a single clear case of impact from the EES and the recommendations. Furthermore, it was the impression of the British interviewees that the EES is not a high priority area. However, one interviewee reported that the EES may have had an impact, but that it is very difficult to isolate this from the impact of recommendations from other international organizations such as the OECD. The interviewee added that the EES and the recommendations help to keep an issue on the agenda, even though the strategy did not put it there in the first place, as, for example, in the case of childcare and the ALMP recommendations.

A few interviewees also mentioned skills and life-long learning and the gender pay gap as areas where an impact from the EES could be seen, because the government has taken action in relation to them. However, these interviewees failed to specify a clear connection between the EES and these actions.

The UK has also received recommendations regarding *policy processes*, more specifically on developing social partnership. This recommendation was repeated from 2000 to 2003, but disappeared in 2004. According to the interviewees, the recommendation on social partnership has been the most controversial and it has been discussed bilaterally with the Commission several times and commented on in the NAPs every year. However, the interviewees could not clarify whether the recommendation was removed because the Commission saw more partnership developing in the UK (due to EES pressure or other reasons), or because the Commission had finally accepted the British government's argument that even though it has not developed the highly formalized and institutionalized structures for social dialogue known in continental Europe and Scandinavia, a variety of tri-, multi- and especially bipartite partnerships nevertheless exist at national, sectoral, regional, and workplace levels. Some of these partnerships have been developed since New Labour came into power – as with the Low Pay Commission, the Employment Task Force, National Training Organisations, and the Learning and Skills Councils. The latest NAPs also emphasize the role of the NGOs/voluntary sector in employment policy and in the partnerships connected with it. One of the civil servants interviewed further emphasized that the role of NGOs is much more extensive in British policy than in most other Member States, and that partnerships with these organizations in targeting marginalized people are much more relevant than collaboration with the social partners.

One interviewee confirmed that the EES has had an impact on the form and intensity of social partnerships in the UK. The establishment of Learning and Skills Councils was mentioned as a specific example. Another interviewee reported that the NAP process has helped in 'opening up channels of communications', not only for the social partners, but also for NGOs. This is confirmed by a European Trade Union Confederation survey focused on the two first NAPs from 1998 and 1999 (Foden 1999: 535; 2001: 66). But most interviewees saw no impact from the EES in this area, and reported little or no extension or intensification of social partnership during the present decade, although they admitted that the change of government in 1997 had opened more doors for social partner influence. Hence, the pressure mechanism seems not to have been fully effective in this case. Moreover, the EES has not been used strategically by the actors – the interviewees could hardly point to any cases where the actors referred to the EES in political and media debates.

2.3 Spain

Spain also took its first steps towards the development of an employment policy during the 1970s, but national policy in the late 1990s largely failed to comply with the EES. Spain has nevertheless experienced an impressive 8% growth since 1999 in its employment rate, which reached 61% in 2004. However, many of the new jobs are temporary ones. Unemployment has declined to 9%. Like the UK, Spain has relatively low levels of spending on active and passive labour market policy measures as a share of GDP: 0.77% on active measures and 1.22% on passive ones (OECD 2005: 272).

Not surprisingly, Spain has received more *recommendations* than Denmark and the UK. These have been related to: activation/prevention (including modernization of the PES); gender equality (including increasing the overall employment rate and improving childcare facilities); training, education, and life-long learning (including early school leaving); modernization of work organization (including increasing part-time contracts, decreasing fixed-term contracts, and balancing flexibility and security); and mobility (including coordination among the regional PES). Most of these recommendations have been repeated over several years.

Like other Member States, the Spanish government has been involved in bilateral discussions about the recommendations. The addition of the sentence 'increase the attractiveness of temporary agency work for workers' to one of the recommendations in 2004 caused some confusion and resistance among the government and the trade unions, according to the interviewees. Spanish trade unions, even more than in most European countries, have been opposed to temporary work agencies. The government was quite sceptical about this addition, because only around 1% of temporary agency work contracts were open ended and therefore a greater use of these would counteract the development of more permanent contracts. However, the government was not successful in getting this sentence removed. Another example of a controversial recommendation concerned part-time work. In this case, the government convinced the Commission to change the wording to clarify that the intention was to benefit women's employment.

There are more cases of direct impact in Spain than in the UK and Denmark, most of which concern areas addressed by the recommendations.[7] First, several interviewees mentioned that the preventive approach would not have been introduced without the existence of and pressure from the EES. At the same time, however, most interviewees acknowledged that active polices as such were introduced prior to the EES, while also observing that it was very difficult actually to implement the preventive approach or to make activation compulsory because of the very large number of unemployed people and the limited capacity of the PES.

Second, gender issues/equal opportunities were mentioned by the interviewees as areas where the EES has had an impact. In this case, however, the EES was most often seen as one of several forces, whereas it was identified as *the* most important factor for the development of the preventive approach. The interviewees see impact from the EES in the increased attention given to gender issues and in the inclusion of women in the target groups for job creation programmes, as well as in initiatives concerning childcare provision and the introduction of gender equality issues into collective agreements. But it is difficult to separate the EES's influence in this area from that of European gender equality directives and decisions of the Court of Justice.

Regarding impact on *policy processes*, the picture is more mixed. Interviewees' views on the EES's impact on policy processes tended to focus on inter-ministerial coordination, coordination between the ministries and the regions, and the degree of consultation with the social partners, whereas the potential developments of quantification and an evaluation culture were not mentioned. Most interviewees reported that the EES had no procedural impact on Spanish employment policy, but some argued that coordination between the ministries had improved.

Apart from showing more specific cases of direct impact, Spain differs also from the other two older Member States in terms of the salience of the EES in the media as well as political debates on employment policy. The debates often include references to the EES, and the various actors, especially the trade unions, have often used the EES strategically by referring to it in order to back up their arguments. Employment legislation – such as the 2003 Employment Policy Act – also refers to the EES, which is not the case in Denmark or the UK.

Finally, EES impact can also be seen in a way not mentioned by the interviewees, namely the *framing* of employment legislation. The Employment Policy Act of 2003, for example, makes direct reference to the EES and emphasizes that Spanish employment policy should be drawn up in accordance with it (Aragón et al. 2007). This could be a result both of pressure and of strategic use. In addition to committing the government to compliance with the EES, such references also facilitate strategic use of the strategy by other actors, who can then invoke this public commitment.

2.4 Poland

Employment policy has a shorter history in Poland than in the other three countries. The concept of 'unemployment' was first officially introduced in 1989 and the new, modernized model of the public employment service was established in 1991. The first programmes to counteract the newly recognized phenomenon of unemployment date from 1992 and 1995. These included elements such as job creation, economic growth stimulation through investment in housing, new rules for vocational education and training, etc. However, these programmes were mostly declarations of intent; the measures were poorly developed, and funding was lacking (Wolinska 2003).

Poland has the highest unemployment rate in Europe. Unemployment increased rapidly after the transition had begun and already exceeded 10% in the 1990s. It has since reached 20%, but declined slightly in 2004, to 18%. There are no comparable OECD figures for public spending on active measures in Poland; but the inflow from the European Social Funds has increased available financing for employment projects considerably in recent years. Public spending on passive measures has decreased in recent years and in 2004 represented 0.82% of the GDP (OECD 2005).

Poland joined the EU in 2004, but had been preparing to take part in the EES for much longer. The Polish government, like that of the other candidate countries, had participated in ongoing dialogues with the Commission since 1999 to ensure that it would be able to implement the employment title of the Amsterdam Treaty and would be ready to receive financial support from the European Social Fund (ESF). It was agreed as a first step that candidate countries and the Commission should analyse the key challenges for employment policies in a Joint Assessment Paper (JAP). This work started with some background studies and the Polish JAP was completed in early 2001.

In its feedback on the JAP in 2003, the Commission recognized the government's response to the ever-worsening employment situation. However, the Commission noted the following outstanding needs: to develop piecemeal tax initiatives into an in-depth review of the tax-benefit system to further reduce the tax wedge; to continue social assistance reforms to promote active job search; to ensure that PES is a key instrument for implementation of national employment policies and allocate sufficient resources for its operation; to develop a coherent framework for life-long learning and allocate sufficient resources for this task to the social partners; and to promote structural change at the enterprise level. Furthermore, the Commission expressed concern about the following: fewer than 1% of low-skilled adults participated in education and training; spending on active measures remained low; long-term unemployment was more than 10%; and the employment participation of older workers was low (European Commission 2003a; 2003b). Formal recommendations were issued in 2004 and included the following: to develop ALMP; to accelerate the establishment of the new public employment service with sufficient resources; to remove obstacles for part-time work to sustain job opportunities for women and older workers; and to invest more, and more effectively, in human capital and life-long learning (European Commission 2005).

Regarding the impact of the EES, the interviewed Polish civil servants involved in the drafting of the JAP pointed to two issues that have been introduced or that obtained a far more prominent place in national employment policies than they would have without pressure from the EES. One is the tax wedge, i.e. the difference between the employees' take-home pay and what it costs to employ them (including income tax and social security contributions). This is an issue the Commission had already introduced in 1999 in the initial discussions on the JAP. Because the revenue from these sources was – and still is – important for financing welfare programmes, it is very unlikely that any steps would have been taken in this area without pressure from other actors, such as the EU.

Another issue that has been influenced by pressure from the EES, according to the interviewees, is the financing of pensions. As early as the initial talks in 1999, the Commission pressed the Polish government to raise farmers' share of contributions to their pensions from the very low level of 5%. The government has considered following this advice, but it still remains to be seen whether it will actually do so. Until now, the reform has been delayed by strong opposition from the farmers' unions and parliamentary representatives.

It is difficult to confirm any specific impact of the EES regarding the other policy changes for which the Commission has been pushing. The pressure to increase on active measures dates back to initial discussions before the JAP was written, but actual spending on these measures decreased rather than increased in the late 1990s. However, spending is now increasing, thanks to support from the ESF (Giermanowska 2004). Both unemployment benefits and active measures are financed from the same fund, and when unemployment increases and the fund is not enlarged, less money remains for active measures. Gender equality was not addressed in the 2004 recommendations or in the feedback on the JAP, but was nevertheless mentioned by one of the interviewees as a case of impact. The relationship to the EES remains unclear.

With respect to policy *processes*, it seems that the JAP and other forms of communication with the Commission have had a slightly greater impact than on policy content. The interviewees reported at least three areas in which the JAP process has had an impact. The first is the *strengthening of inter-ministerial cooperation*. According to several interviewees, cooperation between the relevant ministries hardly existed prior to the JAP. The Commission emphasized this aspect in discussions on the JAP and checked whether coordination had taken place in connection with the different aspects of the JAP. A second impact of the EES on policy processes is the development of an *evaluation culture*. The first steps to set up measurable objectives were taken in connection with the formulation of the JAP process and the formulation of the National Strategy.

A third case of impact in relation to policy processes resulted from EES pressure concerning the Employment Act of 2004, more specifically the *restructuring of the public employment service*. The first JAP progress report from 2003 emphasized the need to secure public employment services as a key instrument for implementing national policies, and the second report commented on the government's planned actions in this direction, even before these were transferred into legislation. Several interviewees mentioned this area as a case of impact of the EES and the JAP processes.

Finally, as in Spain, the EES's impact can also be seen in a way not mentioned by the interviewees, namely the *framing* of employment legislation. This is evident in the very broad plans, such as the National Strategy and the Sectoral Operation Programme, which both follow the structure of the EES closely. Moreover, the wording in more specific pieces of legislation, such as the Employment Act of 2004, is clearly closer to the EES than in the other three countries. This can be seen as a strategic use of the EES by government departments, but may also be a result of pressure.

3 Comparative discussion and conclusions

The four national cases illustrate how pressure and strategic use have worked in the context of the EES. Through these mechanisms, the EES has influenced national employment policies in some cases. However, the relatively few cases of impact and their cross-national variation lead to the conclusion that *the EES has had a direct impact on the employment policies of Member States only to a limited extent and that this impact varies between them.* As summarized in Table 7.1, more evidence for this influence is found in Spain and, especially, Poland than in Denmark and the UK. This impact is spread across several issues. However, four of the cases are related to activation policy (activation, preventive approach) and there are two instances of improved inter-ministerial coordination, as well as two cases of introduction or improvement of statistics and evaluations.

Table 7.1 Cases of direct impact from the EES

	Denmark	*UK*	*Spain*	*Poland*
Content	Preventive approach Youth education	Activation policy?	Preventive approach Gender equality	Tax wedge Financing pensions Activation policy Gender equality?
Processes		Social partnership?	Inter-ministerial coordination? Statistics and evaluations Programme frameworks/wording	Inter-ministerial coordination Statistics and evaluations Reforming public employment service Programme frameworks/wording

Note: ? = impact debatable in this area

It is one thing to describe the operation of these mechanisms and how they have influenced national policies – it is another to locate which factors are decisive for impact/lack of impact. Without being able to directly confirm or reject hypotheses regarding these factors, they nevertheless support some hypotheses more than others. *Pre-existing compliance between the EES and national employment policy, national consensus on the main lines of employment policy, employment rates,* along with *economic and political dependence on the EU* are factors which help to explain the varied impact of the EES across Member States, as found in this study, whereas the results concerning *Euroscepticism are inconclusive.*

The EES, generally speaking, has had little impact in countries where employment policy *was already in compliance before 1997* with what later became the EES. Hence Denmark and, to some extent, the UK have been more difficult to influence. In these countries, pressure is reduced because the level of non-compliance is low and 'naming, shaming and blaming' is therefore difficult. Strategic use is reduced for the same reason.

A *high level of national agreement on the main issues of the employment policy* is also a barrier to EES impact. Domestic employment policy will be shielded from pressure and consensus will prohibit any (widespread) strategic use. In Denmark, where consensus on the main issues of the employment policy was obtained (at least in the 1990s), no incentive was left for the main actors to use the EES strategically in national-level political and media debates, from which it has largely been absent. In Spain, on the other hand, where no such consensus exists, the EES has been an important issue in employment policy debates, especially during the early years of the strategy. In Poland, references until recently have been rare but, according to several interviewees, this has been changing since the country joined the EU.

Euroscepticism also represents a barrier to the impact of the EES, because references to it under such circumstances may not be helpful. Denmark and the UK are countries with high levels of Euroscepticism, which has had this effect on EES impact. Hence, Euroscepticism has the same effect as consensus, in that it 'shields' domestic policy from external pressure. Furthermore, this makes strategic use less effective or even counterproductive. However, the geographical distribution of Euroscepticism is currently changing, which challenges this explanation. In addition, the fact that Euroscepticism is widespread in Poland, where references to the EES are increasing, according to the interviewees, challenges the explanation.

All Member States are, to a certain extent, politically and economically dependent on the EU, but some are much more dependent than others – or rather, this dependence affects their room for manoeuvre. Applicant and accession countries and the main recipients of European funds are especially dependent. Strong *economic dependence* is evident in both Spain and Poland. This dependence provides the EU institutions with potential power to sanction these countries by diminishing funding or postponing membership if they do not follow advice on how to comply with European regulations. In these countries, the ESF is – or has been – a major source of finance for their employment policies. Since the EES and the ESF are partly coordinated and administered by the same Directorate-General of the Commission (DG Employment and Social Affairs), failure to comply with EES recommendations may negatively influence the allocation of funds. This is yet another way in which the pressure mechanism works and is part of the reason why greater impact is found in these countries than in the two northern European countries. But the interviewees did not report incidents where explicit links between the EES and the ESF have been drawn in communications with the EU institutions. However, such pressure could still have been felt. Poland is – or was – furthermore, a representative case of strong *political dependence* on the EU. This dependence facilitated the EES's impact in the JAP process of 1999–2003, during which the Commission and the Polish government discussed how the country could improve its employment policy as part of its preparation for receiving financial support from the ESF and full participation in the EES. According to the interviewees, compliance with the EES and the ESF were explicitly linked in these discussions.

It is not possible to find a connection between the *goals and ideologies of the governments* and the level of impact from the EES, as in none the four Member States could these be said to be in direct conflict with the EES or, for that matter, more in line with the strategy than others. The general nature of the employment guidelines – and to some extent also the recommendations – leaves room for socialist, social-democratic, liberal as well as conservative government policies, even though the EES could be said to have had a social-democratic bias in its early days (Madsen 2003).

Yet, one conclusion is that, in spite of all efforts, *neither the revision in 2003, nor that in 2005, have increased the impact of the EES.* If anything, the impact has diminished since the early years of the EES, because the attention which the strategy received in its first years has not been sustained. This is so despite the efforts made by EU-level actors to increase the profile of the NAPs/NRPs by involving national parliaments and social partners in them more, and by appointing high-level civil servants or politicians as a hub for the Lisbon process in each Member State.

Moreover, the integration of the economic guidelines and national reports with those on employment in 2005 could potentially have facilitated the EES's impact by giving it a higher profile as part of the overall Lisbon Strategy, since economic policy has a higher status than employment policy in most Member States. With the exception of Spain, where the NRP in 2005 seemingly did receive more attention than did the EES, there were no signs that the integration of the economic and the employment guidelines meant that the national reports had attracted more attention. In the Spanish case, it may be that the NRP did receive more attention than did the later NAPs; but this was probably due more to a change of government than to the revision of the Lisbon process.

By focusing on the 2005 NRP, a general observation can be made about the way the EES works : the *impact of the EES – through national actors' strategic use of it – depends very much on timing.* The drafting of the 2005–8 NRP in the UK, Denmark, Poland, and partly even in Spain, was badly timed for various reasons. In Denmark, reports from the Welfare Commission and the Globalization Council received attention that potentially could have been given to the NRP; and these reports do not even mention the EES or the Lisbon process. In the UK, heated debates on pension reforms took place at the same time as the NRP was published. In Poland, a general election took place after the submission of the first draft of the NRP, which therefore had to be redrafted; hence, the new government could not – and would not – use it as a strategic document. Furthermore, the redrafted Polish NRP was delivered on the 26 December – not the best time to attract media attention! Only in Spain does the timing seem to have facilitated strategic use of the EES/Lisbon by the government. However, in other respects the timing was bad, because ongoing tripartite talks during the consultation process on the NRP meant that the government did not feel able to revise the draft in response to the comments of the social partners. Therefore, in general, national reports have to be timed perfectly vis-à-vis the domestic policy cycle in order to have a chance of exerting a larger-scale impact.

Notes

1 See Larsen et al. (2004) – an empirical study of the OMC effect in France, Spain, Sweden and the UK – and López-Santana (2004, 2006, this volume) – a study of EES impact in Sweden, Spain, and Belgium – for some of the few exceptions.

2 The fact that Poland has only been an EU member since 2004 makes this case different from the others. This complicates the comparison, even though the new Member States have been preparing for participation in the EES for some years. Nonetheless, we considered it important and valuable to include a new Member State in the study.

3 See Falkner et al. (2005) for an excellent discussion of the impact of EU directives on Member States.

4 A great majority (59) of these 68 interviews were face-to-face interviews – the rest were conducted by telephone or were based on questionnaires and followed by short telephone conversations.

5 The national-level civil servants were mostly of two types: Employment Committee (EMCO) representatives and civil servants involved in the drawing up of NAPs/NRP. The EMCO formulates opinions at the request of the Commission or the Council and prepares, *inter alia*, the employment guidelines. De facto, most discussions on the EES take place in EMCO and its sub-committees.

6 Some forms of labour market policies – for instance tax credits – do not show up in these statistics

7 Some areas of *EES impact* pointed to by the interviewees are the same as those found in the earlier studies of the impact of the EES in Spain (Gullién and Alvarez 2004; López-Santana 2004; Andersen and Mailand 2002).

References

Andersen, S.K. and Mailand, M. (2002) *The Role of Employers and Trade Unions in Multipartite Social Partnerships*, Copenhagen: The Copenhagen Centre.

Aragón, J., Rocha, F., Santana, A. and Torrents, J. (2007) 'The Commitment to Be Actively Available for Work and Employment in Spain', in A. Serrano Pascual and L. Magnusson (eds) *Reshaping Welfare States and Activation Regimes in Europe*, Brussels: Peter Lang.

Ardy, B. and Umbach, G. (2004) *Employment Policies in Germany and the United Kingdom: The Impact of Europeanisation*, London, Berlin: Anglo-German Foundation for the Study of Industrial Society.

Barbier, J.C. (2005) 'The European Employment Strategy: A Channel for Activating Social Protection?', in J. Zeitlin and P. Pochet with L. Magnusson (eds) *The Open Method of Coordination in Action: The European Employment and Social Inclusion Strategies*, Brussels: Peter Lang.

Christensen, P.M., Nørgaard, A.S. and Sidenius, N.C. (2004) 'Pisk og pæne ord – partsindflydelsen på politiske præmisser. Arbejdsmarkedsreformens tredje fase', in P.M. Christensen, A.S. Nørgaard and N.C. Sidenius (eds) *Hvem skriver lovene? Interesseorganisationer og politiske beslutninger*, Magtudredningen, Aarhus: Aarhus universitetsforlag.

Ehrel, C., Martin, L. and Palier, B. (2005) 'The Leverage Effect: The Open Method of Coordination in France', in J. Zeitlin and P. Pochet with L. Magnusson (eds) *The Open Method of Coordination in Action: The European Employment and Social Inclusion Strategies*, Brussels: Peter Lang.

European Commission (2002) 'Taking Stock of Five Years of the EES', Supporting COM (2002) 416 final, Brussels: European Commission.

—— (2003a) 'Progress on the Implementation of the Joint Assessment Papers on Employment Policies in Candidate Countries', COM (2003) 37 final.

—— (2003b) 'Supporting Document to the Communication Progress in the Implementation of the Joint Assessment Papers on the Employment Policies of the Candidate Countries', SEC (2003) 200.

—— (2005) 'Commission Staff Working Paper', Annex to the Joint Employment Report 2004/2005, SEC (2005) 67/2.

European Employment Task Force (2003) *Jobs, Jobs, Jobs – Creating More Employment in Europe*, Report from the Employment Taskforce chaired by Wim Kok, Brussels: European Employment Task force.

Falkner, G., Tarp, O., Hartlapp, M. and Lieber, S. (2005) *Complying with Europe – EU Harmonisation and Soft Law in the Member States*, Cambridge: Cambridge University Press.

Ferrera, M., Matsaganis, M. and Sacchi, S. (2002) *Rescued by Europe? Social and Labour Market Reforms in Italy from Maastricht to Berlusconi*, Amsterdam: Amsterdam University Press.

Flyvbjerg, B. (1991) *Rationalitet og magt. Det konkretes videnskab*, Bind 1, Århus: Akademisk Forlag.

Foden, D. (1999) *The Role of the Social Partners in the European Employment Strategy*, Transfer 4/99, Brussels: European Trade Union Institute.

—— (2001) 'Social Partnership and the European Strategy against Youth Unemployment', in A. Serrano Pascual (ed.) *Social and Civil Partnership in the Framework of European Employment Strategy for Young People*, Brussels: ETUI.

Giermanowska, E. (2004) 'Poland: The Specificity of Public Employment Service', *European Employment Observatory Review*, Spring 2004.

Greve, B. (2005) 'Har den europæiske beskæftigelsesstrategi indvirkning på nationalstaternes beskæftigelsespolitik?', *Økonomi and Politik*, 78: 14–22.

Guillén, A. and Alvarez, S. (2004) 'The EU's Impact on the Spanish Welfare State: The Role of Cognitive Europeanisation', *Journal of European Social Policy*, 14: 285–99.

High Level Group chaired by Wim Kok (2004) *Facing the Challenge – the Lisbon Strategy for Growth and Jobs*, Brussels: European Communities.

Jacobsson, K. (2002) 'Soft Regulation and the Subtle Transformation of States: The Case of EU Employment Policy', *SCORE Working Paper*, 2002–4.

—— (2003) 'Trying to Reform the "Best Pupils in Class"? The OMC in Sweden and Denmark', draft paper prepared for the workshop on the Open Method of Coordination, Florence, July.

Jacobssen, K. and Schmid, H. (2001) 'Real Integration or Just Formal Adaption? – On the Implementation of the National Action Plans for Employment', paper for presentation at the Conference of the European Sociological Association, Helsinki, August–September.

Langhoff-Ross, K. (2001) *Anderledes efter Amsterdam? – Et case-study af beskæftigelsespolitikken i Spanien og Danmark siden vedtagelsen*, Speciale, København: Institut for Statskundskab.

Larsen, T.P., Taylor-Gooby, P. and Kananen, J. (2004) 'European Policy Co-ordination and the OMC – An Empirical Study of the OMC's Effect in France, Spain, Sweden and the UK', article to ESPANET Conference, Oxford, September.

Lindsay, C. and Mailand, M. (2004) 'Different Routes, Common Directions? Activation Policies for Young People in Denmark and the UK', *International Journal of Social Welfare*, 13: 195–207.

López-Santana, M. (2004) 'How "Soft" Pressure above Affects the Bottom: Europeanization, Employment Policy and Policy (Re)formulation – The Spanish Case', unpublished paper, University of Michigan.

—— (2006) 'The Domestic Implications of European Soft Law: Framing and Transmitting Change in Employment Policy', *Journal of European Public Policy*, 13: 481–99.

Madsen, P.K. (2003) 'Fyrtøj eller Slæbejolle – dansk arbejdsmarkeds-og beskæftigelsespolitik og den europæiske beskæftigelsesstrategi', in L. Pedersen and P.M. Madsen (eds) *Drivkræfter bag arbejdsmarkedspolitikken*, København: Socialforskningsinstituttet.

Nedergaard, P. (2005) 'Mutual Learning Processes in the European Employment Strategy: Theoretical Approaches and Methodologies', in T. Bredgaard. and F. Larsen (eds) *Employment Policy from Different Angles*, Copenhagen: Jurist-og Økonomforbundets Forlag.

OECD (2005) *Employment Outlook*, Paris: OECD

Preworski, A. and Teune, H. (1970) *The Logic of Comparative Social Inquiry*, New York: Wiley.

Ransby, K. (2005) 'EU-mål tages alvorligt i Danmark', Arbejdsmarkedspolitisk Agenda, April.

Rhodes, M. (1997) 'Spain', in H. Compston (ed.) *The New Politics of Unemployment – Radical Policy Initiatives in Western Europe*, London: Routledge.

Umbach, G. (2003) *Employment Policies in Germany and the United Kingdom – The Impact of Europe*anisation, *Anglo-German Foundation for the Study of Industrial Society.*

Vifell, Å. (2004) 'Speaking with Forked Tongue – Swedish Employment Policy and European Guidelines: A Case of Europeanization Through Soft Co-ordination', paper presented at the 2004 Conference of Europeanists, Chicago, March.

Visser, J. (2005) 'The Open Method of Coordination at Selective Amplifier for National Reform Strategies: What the Netherlands Wants to Learn from Europe', in

J. Zeitlin and P. Pochet with L. Magnusson (eds) *The Open Method of Coordination in Action: The European Employment and Social Inclusion Strategies*, Brussels: Peter Lang.
Wolinska, I. (2003) *The National Action Plan for Employment in Poland*, Warsaw: The Labour Market Department, Ministry of the Economy, Labour and Social Policy.
Zeitlin, J. (2005) 'Introduction: The Open Method of Coordination in Question', in J. Zeitlin and P. Pochet with L. Magnusson (eds) *The Open Method of Coordination in Action: The European Employment and Social Inclusion Strategies*, Brussels: Peter Lang.

8 The micro-politics of the Open Method of Coordination

NGOs and the social inclusion process in Sweden

Kerstin Jacobsson and Håkan Johansson

Introduction[1]

The Open Method of Coordination (OMC) challenges national political settings in various ways. The Swedish welfare state is characterized by principles of universalism and a strong connection between welfare and work. Comparative research has demonstrated that the European Employment Strategy (EES) fits very well with this social-democratic welfare regime (Jacobsson 2005; López-Santana 2006). But the translation of the OMC on social inclusion into the Swedish policy context has encountered various barriers and met, at least initially, with less enthusiasm. In Sweden, policy makers tend to view the EU's social inclusion policy as selective, thereby deviating from the universalistic principles of the Swedish welfare state. Some social NGOs have expressed similar concerns, while others have approached the OMC on social inclusion (OMC/Inclusion) as a new opportunity structure, i.e. as a means of establishing contacts with national policy makers and possibly challenging the position of other privileged actors.

Much current work on OMC processes tends to look at the policy level and ask questions about learning, yet fails to study policy and politics in conjunction. In order to understand the national reception of the OMC, this chapter takes seriously both the institutional context of implementation *and* the micro-politics of the OMC/Inclusion in Sweden, i.e. actor responses and inter-actor relationships. The chapter demonstrates that although the OMC/Inclusion has had limited direct influence on the policy content of national reforms, it has been an important catalyst in establishing new patterns of cooperation among social NGOs in the Swedish welfare state.

First, we show how the enactment of the OMC/Inclusion has contributed to new forms of institutionalized consultation and cooperation between ministries and social NGOs. Second, we show how this OMC has contributed to new patterns of cooperation and/or conflict among social NGOs. Third, we investigate which factors still hamper the successful implementation of the OMC in Sweden.

1 The OMC and domestic opportunity structures

A growing number of studies have been concerned with the outcomes and mechanisms of Europeanization (Grabbe 2003; Knill and Lehmkuhl 1999; Radaelli 2003; Cowles et al. 2001; Schimmelfennig and Sedelmeier 2005). Often this Europeanization literature has a top-down perspective, focusing on the processes by which EU rules and norms are incorporated into domestic policy making. This presupposes that distinct European practices, institutions, policies, or discourses are first developed at the EU level, which, in turn, creates pressure for reform or change in structures, processes, and policies at the domestic level. The adaptation pressure varies according to the type of EU rule in question, as well as the degree to which it fits with pre-existing policies and policy-making practices in the Member States.

While it makes sense to adopt a top-down perspective on Europeanization, it is also important to acknowledge that domestic actors are never just passive receivers and implementers of European rules and norms. These are always mediated and interpreted in local contexts – it is never a case of direct transfer. Rather, we see active translation whereby rules and norms are interpreted and adapted in ways appropriate to the domestic context: 'changes … are neither purely an adjustment to pressure and demands emanating from the EU nor solely the result of conscious national strategies or of historical legacies and administrative traditions' (Jacobsson et al 2004: 115). The translation element is even more evident in the case of the OMC, which builds on soft regulation, is explicitly supposed to be translated into national policy according to existing structures and traditions, and is procedural rather than substantive in nature. In other words, political support for the reform process must be mobilized domestically.

Consequently, OMC processes must be studied in context, whereby domestic factors, such as political ideologies and policy paradigms, state traditions and administrative legacies, state capacities and resources, actor constellations and social interests, can mediate national responses to Europeanization as well as affecting what types of policies may be implemented (Cowles et al 2001; Jacobsson and West 2007). In this chapter, we will conceptualize the domestic context as a *social field*, looking at three components, namely 1) the existing policy paradigm, 2) institutionalized patterns of cooperation, and 3) actor constellations (and thus power relationships).

To study the implementation of the OMC/Inclusion in a specific domestic context, an analytical framework is required that allows the institutional context and active responses to Europeanization pressures to be studied jointly. EU-level processes may imply both opportunities and constraints for domestic actors, who may also work proactively to change them. Our analytical framework must allow a double focus on institutional context and opportunity structures *and* actor incentives and activities (cf. Fligstein 2001). In our view, the OMC is likely to exert an impact mainly by changing domestic opportunity structures and by allowing or encouraging various types of actor relationships and dynamics nationally and subnationally (see also Jacobsson 2005; Jacobsson and Vifell 2007). The OMC:

- may function to shift resources and alter the power balance between different players;
- may empower actors by providing them with an opportunity for voice and participation in public policy making;
- may foster new alliances between actors and strengthen them as pressure groups;
- may foster new practices of cooperation, coordination, and networking;
- may provide fuel in national debates and 'ammunition' for certain interests in their arguments for policy change and help legitimize domestic reform (Radaelli 2003);
- may 'infuse' the national policy debate with new knowledge and ideas, such as policy concepts, causal beliefs, links between policy areas, and thereby change the ways actors conceive of problems and solutions, a discursive or cognitive type of impact (Jacobsson 2004), that, again, may empower certain interests at the expense of others;
- may provide policy actors with a new arsenal of instruments.

Thus far, we know relatively little about the actor-related processes around the OMC/Inclusion. What kinds of resources are embedded in the OMC process for the different actors involved? The dynamics that arise among actors, for instance among various voluntary organizations, are underplayed in analyses of the OMC. Civil society is not homogenous, neither in its interests nor in its responses to the OMC. Few studies have focused on relationships of cooperation and/or competition among NGOs or on relationships between government actors and NGOs (but on the participation of civil society in the OMC process in Germany, see Friedrich 2006, Kröger 2006; on Britain see Armstrong 2005, 2006).

2 The OMC/Inclusion in the Swedish welfare state

The Swedish context in which the OMC/Inclusion is to be implemented can be understood as a *social field*, with institutionalized ideas about appropriate policy, institutionalized rules of the game and patterns of cooperation, and a set of actor relationships.

In terms of policy paradigm, the Swedish welfare state is characterized by a strong connection between welfare and work, and also by the principle of universalism. The EU's focus on social exclusion, and in particular the development of specific programmes to combat social exclusion (the EU's anti-poverty programmes and more recently the OMC/Inclusion), has met with some scepticism among Swedish social policy analysts (Axelsson 2005; Halleröd 2003) as well as policy makers. For instance, Axelsson (2005) has argued that EU social policy is doubly selective: social rights are granted to individuals in their position as workers and based on supranational legislation, while selective programmes are developed for special groups on the basis of identified needs rather than citizenship rights and obtained through political coordination rather than legislation. EU social inclusion policy is seen to be formulated in a selective manner, with specific policies for special groups classified as needy, which is seen as a (potential) deviation from the universalistic principles of the Swedish welfare state. The Swedish welfare state has relatively little means-tested social policy, the exception being social assistance proper. Instead of constructing special programmes for certain vulnerable groups, the aim is to include everybody in the general welfare policy system (Halleröd 2003: 5). As the Swedish Strategy Report of 2006 put it, 'Universal welfare is the foundation for social protection and social inclusion' (Ministry of Health and Social Affairs 2006: 7).

Swedish scepticism about selective policies is based on the conviction both that such policies are not very effective in alleviating poverty and that they tend to stigmatize the recipients. In contrast, universal welfare is considered not only more effective but also as a way of securing support for the welfare state among broader strata of the population, since everyone gains from the welfare state, not just certain groups. However, this self-image tends to deny patterns of social exclusion and marginalization that actually exist in the Swedish welfare state. For instance, for groups who lack a stable and permanent position in the labour market, the Swedish welfare state tends to be less universal and generous. Since they do not qualify for unemployment benefit, they are directed instead to the selective social assistance system. Hence, in times of rising unemployment levels (like the 1990s) the selective character of the Swedish welfare state tends to increase. Regarding social services, there are signs that it has become more difficult to get access to public services and these are increasingly directed at those considered the most in need.

If we look at institutionalized patterns of cooperation, it is notable that while the Swedish welfare state rests securely on a corporatist tradition, in the sense that policy reforms include consensus building between the government and the social partners (organizations of employers and employees), this has been much less true in relation to NGOs, citizen groups, and voluntary organizations. When making social policy, the Swedish welfare state has rarely included organizations representing poor, marginalized or excluded groups. Social partners, along with a few large social NGOs, have been selected to represent the wider society in discussions with national ministries. One obvious reason is that poverty has not been a high-profile issue in Sweden. Although social redistribution and economic equality are important political aims, fighting poverty has not been identified as a separate issue requiring a specific arsenal of anti-poverty measures. Swedish social policy rests, rather, upon the assumption that poverty is a residual problem, best combated through active employment-promotion policies combined with an encompassing system of social benefits.

The OMC/Inclusion was a novelty in the Swedish policy context, and new forms of cooperation needed to be established. The Ministry for Health and

Social Affairs has, from the start, been responsible for the production of the National Action Plan (NAP) on social inclusion. Other ministries are consulted, as well as state agencies, such as the National Board of Health and Welfare. Trade unions and employers' associations are consulted through the regular social partner consultation, which meets at the Ministry for Social Affairs about every second month. However, since the start of the OMC/Inclusion, social partners have given priority to the action plan on employment. For social NGOs, the OMC/Inclusion has been an important resource and catalyst for establishing new patterns of cooperation.

The social partners, used to having a privileged access to policy making, tend to emphasize that, in contrast to NGOs, they are *partners*, able to assume responsibility for implementation, and not just 'a participant'. The trade unions also tend to question the NGOs' representativeness, arguing that they represent only themselves, while the trade unions, besides having a density of about 85%, have internal democratic structures for representation. Trade unions tend to see themselves as representative of all relevant interests – at least so far as labour market policy is concerned. The NGOs, for their part, argue that the trade unions fail to represent people outside – and sometimes far from – the labour market, such as the long-term ill, immigrants, the disabled, or the homeless. Arguably, by requiring the participation of NGOs, the OMC/Inclusion has challenged existing actor relationships and structures of consultation. Not only has the OMC/Inclusion challenged Swedish self-understanding by making poverty and social exclusion a political issue, it has also challenged institutionalized patterns of consultation.

3 Mobilization of new actor constellations

The following sections will analyse how the OMC/Inclusion has functioned as a catalyst for mobilizing new forms of cooperation among social NGOs in Sweden. The mobilization efforts among social NGOs started before the formal OMC process was established nationally. Swedish experiences with the social inclusion strategy illustrate what has commonly been referred to as the 'boomerang effect' of NGO transnational activities (Keck and Sikkink 1998). This refers to the fact that NGOs may reach beyond national governments and political structures, seek support through their affiliation or membership in transnational networks or organizations, and then – like a boomerang – bring this support back to the national context.

Contrary to what might be expected, representatives of Swedish social NGOs began exploring what opportunities the OMC process would provide and how they could best take advantage of them nationally, before the government itself. They were members of EU networks and fora, such as the European Anti-Poverty Network, the European Disability Forum and the Euro-Diaconia, which followed the development of the OMC/Inclusion closely in Brussels. One person from the Swedish national cooperative had a central position in an EU body, as a representative in the advisory European

Economic and Social Committee. Individuals knowledgeable about the development of the OMC process at the EU level provided other social NGOs with information and experience on the content and implications of the process. This enabled NGO representatives to clarify their strategies, develop their capacities, and direct their efforts to mobilize partners at an early stage. Consequently, initiatives were taken to form a national network on social exclusion, called the 'Network Against Social Exclusion' (Network). The OMC was clearly a catalyst for the mobilization of this network.

This development is interesting in relation to changes in the existing social field. First, the Network consists of social NGOs and voluntary organizations, representing marginal citizens with limited resources for full participation in society. It has gathered organizations belonging to the Swedish movement of people with disabilities, religious organizations and communities, user organizations, client organizations, social economy organizations, immigrant organizations, and ethnic associations. The blue- and white-collar union confederations were invited to participate in the Network, but both declined. Some of these organizations provide services, while others express a voice. Several organizations are large, in terms of members and resources, and have a central position in Swedish social policy. Others are small, with few members and limited resources. In our view, the Network constitutes an innovation in relation to the existing social field, since it is the first national network gathering a majority of social NGOs working in the field of social welfare and social exclusion. It has established itself as a collective actor for a spectrum of national organizations that previously worked individually or with different agendas.

Second, despite lacking substantial economic resources, the Network brings together top spokespersons (general secretaries, chairpersons, or senior advisers) from a large number of social NGOs. This has given it a fairly high status among social NGOs. Choosing the network model, top spokespersons do not have to comply with formal or long-term obligations; instead, they use the Network as a general framework for interaction and communication. This proved to be an important strategy in mobilizing the Network, yet also difficult to handle. Members have pointed to its weak legitimacy, since it is not a 'democratic' organization with formal standards and clear membership rules.

Third, what significantly distinguishes this Network from other forms of associations, alliances, and coalitions of social NGOs, is the role EU policies play in it. In a short time, these NGOs successfully mobilized a Network prioritizing the fourth objective of the OMC/Inclusion, i.e. 'mobilizing all relevant bodies'. Hence, from an opportunity-structure perspective, the OMC was a significant factor in building new alliances between actors and strengthening them as pressure groups. However, not only was the OMC process of great significance for establishing the Network, it is also the first group using EU policies to put pressure on the national government. Since its inception in 2000, the Network has had a threefold aim: 1) to explore the possibilities of the OMC/Inclusion; 2) to form a network capable of speaking to the Swedish government with one voice; and 3) to become the single recognized actor for cooperating with the government in drafting the NAPs on social inclusion.

This means that the OMC/Inclusion constitutes the 'common discourse', 'common framing of claims' and 'conception of problems' which the Network needs to hold itself together. However, the Network has remained largely unnoticed in the public sphere. Most likely this is due to its network character, the diversity of organizations participating, and the fact that the Network mainly works with EU-related issues, which tend to have a low profile in Sweden. Moreover, the Network has faced some internal difficulties in developing a detailed programme that goes beyond the OMC. Although internal working groups have tried to come up with some more detailed aims and objectives, this remains a largely unresolved issue in the Network.

The policy positions of the Network are probably best expressed by the points that it has delivered to the government in relation to the NAPs and Strategy reports; a contribution from the Network is always annexed to the official report. In general, the Network presents its vision as a society based on solidarity and social justice, combined with strong universal welfare policies. It focuses on the most vulnerable sections of Swedish society (poor, socially excluded, homeless, drug addicts, immigrants, etc.) and claims that these have a right to a decent standard of living, equal treatment, access to welfare services such as care, education and housing, on equal terms, based on their needs. The Network's demands can be grouped into three themes. First, it demands of the Swedish government that it take a more holistic perspective on issues of social exclusion, and has identified the NAP as a device to encourage more coordinated public efforts (for instance, between ministries, but also in relation to the social partners). Second, the Network demands of the government that it include users and citizens in vulnerable positions more directly in the decision-making process. Third, it demands of the government that it develop partnership agreements with the social NGO sector in order to clarify resources and agendas.

The Network tends to avoid domestic policy issues, as its members have different views and this would cause too much disturbance. Even when Network members have similar opinions on certain issues, these have rarely been clarified in greater detail. As expressed by one member: 'if we get too much into details, the Network will fall apart' (Interview, 2004). The Network's internal 'policy programme' also relates to the special role of social NGOs in the Swedish welfare state. Despite the ambition of social NGOs to make their voice heard in debates and to influence public policy, they do not want to be reduced to being executors or instruments of public policy. They are strongly in favour of universal welfare state arrangements, and they are extremely cautious not to take over what they consider the responsibility of the welfare state. This is always a delicate balance and, according to our interviews, a matter of constant internal debate in the Network.

4 Contestation over consultation

The Network has engaged in several strategic activities in relation to the NAP/Inclusion. The following section analyses these activities, which had already started in late 2000. At this stage, it was apparent that officials from the Ministry of Health and Social Affairs did not know much about the OMC process, nor did they show any great interest. Although social NGOs invited representatives from the Ministry to discuss the EU initiatives, these invitations were turned down. The first years of the OMC/Inclusion gave the Network limited opportunities to influence the process, and can mainly be characterized as a contentious period.

The Swedish government defined the NAP as a state-of-the-art document that would not describe future actions or welfare reform (Jacobsson 2005; Johansson 2007). Only a few people at the Ministry were involved in drafting the NAP, which meant that the Swedish government kept it under very tight control and circumvented social NGO demands for inclusion in policy making. The Ministry considered it necessary to inform the Network only before and after the NAP, expressing clearly that it could not expect to influence the NAP. In the Ministry's view, the NAPs, as responses to EU processes, necessarily have a different status from domestic action plans, since the latter are preceded by a much more thorough preparation and are passed the 'ordinary way', i.e. preceded by public investigations and followed up by government bills which provide funding. Although the Network and other external actors would be invited to submit their comments in the NAP work, they would not be allowed to see and to comment on drafts of the report. This remains the government position: policies are not made in the OMC process, NAPs or Strategy Reports. In an interview, the former minister emphasized that his mandate came from the Swedish citizens, not from the EU. He also said that the importance of the NAPs 'should not be exaggerated. They were compilations of what we already did in this field' (Interview, 2007).

Initially, government officials also questioned the contacts between national social NGOs and European networks. They questioned whether the Network represented EU bodies – such as the European Anti-Poverty Network or similar – or marginalized groups in Sweden. According to Ministry officials, it was not possible to have a dual representation. In principle, government officials had a point. Some umbrella networks operating in Brussels are more or less completely funded by the European Commission. For the Commission, having close contacts with social NGOs can be an important tool to influence other EU institutions, and – indirectly – exercise pressure on reluctant governments to reach agreement (Bauer 2002). By referring to civil society, the Commission seeks to legitimize its own proposals.

Throughout the OMC process, the government's position has challenged the Network, and from 2001 to 2003 the Network developed several alternative strategies for involvement in discussing, drafting, and implementing the NAPs. The Network wanted to be a full partner in the formulation of the

NAP, arguing that this kind of partnership was an explicit objective of the OMC/Inclusion. The Network established different task forces to decide which issues to bring forward and how best to influence the OMC process. It argued that the government presented an inadequate picture of the Swedish welfare state by failing to describe domestic social policy from the perspective of social NGOs and voluntary organizations, and thereby implying that it was produced only by the state and public policy actors. To demonstrate both its criticism and its willingness to be a partner, the Network produced a 20-page alternative action plan, discussing its view of the EU objectives, which was delivered to the Ministry of Health and Social Affairs in April 2001. By presenting an alternative plan, the Network substantiated its claim that the Swedish government did not fulfil the common EU objectives to which it had officially agreed.

In a comment on the NAP of 2003, the Network stated its support for the OMC and argued that a clearer framework for consultation was needed to actively engage authorities and voluntary organizations both in the shaping and in the implementation of the action plan, and at both local and national levels. It also pleaded for a user and bottom-up perspective and for cross-sectoral coordination and a holistic policy overview. To further challenge the attitude of the national government, several of the NGOs in the Network integrated the NAP into their own activities, e.g. developing informational material based on it.

Throughout these years the Network did not involve itself in other activities. Its main goal was to gain recognition in relation to the OMC/Inclusion and to influence the NAP. The tension between the government and the Network hence centred on the scope and ambition of the OMC process: whether to understand it as one of limited importance for national policy making or as one involving local, national, and supranational actors. The Network, for its part, believed that the process was and should be out of the hands of national governments, as they had signed the Amsterdam Treaty and taken part in developing the Lisbon and Nice conclusions. The Network also used its contacts and affiliations with EU networks to push the OMC process beyond the complete control of the Swedish government. Members of the Network have since commented upon this period of its activities as somewhat naive, in terms of its aspirations to actually become a partner with the government in completing the NAP (authors' interviews).

5 Towards a new consultative framework

Previous patterns of (non-)consultation between the Network and the government changed a couple of years after the OMC/Inclusion started (in autumn 2003), when the government decided to initiate a forum for information exchange and consultations with user organizations, i.e. a 'user committee on social and welfare issues'. The committee's main aim was to highlight the perspective of poor and socially excluded people and to strengthen user involvement and influence in outlining and implementing the NAPs on poverty and social exclusion. Various factors influenced the committee's establishment. First, interviews indicate that the initiative for the committee came from the Network and was picked up by ministry officials. Second, changes in the government most certainly were also important. A new Minister was appointed in autumn 2003, with formal responsibility for social inclusion policies. This new Minister hence had more time for and interest in building new forms of consultation, above all with groups holding a marginalized or even socially excluded position in the society.

The committee has no formal decision-making power. The formal aims of the committee are to share knowledge, constitute a forum for discussions and analyses regarding the possibilities and challenges of extended user involvement, and bring together organizations in seminars and conferences, etc. (Ministry of Health and Social Affairs 2006). For the Minister, the committee constituted an environment where he could test ideas, initiate discussions, and get information from the NGO sector (Interview, 2007).

The establishment of the user committee represented substantial progress for the Network, since it gained access to a forum in which top politicians and public officials participated. The Minister chaired the committee, accompanied by his senior political adviser. The Director General of the National Board of Health and Welfare and higher officials from the Swedish association of local authorities also participated. The Network was offered the right to nominate representatives to the newly established committee. What previously had been a Network mainly involved in EU-related affairs and with ambitions to influence a single document now turned into a body with a highly privileged position in relation to domestic affairs. Hence, to be a member of the Network potentially meant to have direct contact with the government and the Minister of Social Affairs.

These new opportunities caused some tensions within the Network, above all concerning election procedures. Communication with members of the Network reveals that some individuals claimed a dual role, representing the Network, on the one hand, and their individual organization, on the other hand. The complex nomination and election procedure that followed demonstrates that the relationship between the committee and the Network is ambiguous, and obviously involves disagreements over substantial resources. In this procedure, Network members had the opportunity to nominate delegates, but only on condition that they met certain criteria, such as having the capacity and strength to express the voice of users and their organizations to the Ministry in a critical and constructive manner; experience of working in organizations with the socially and economically vulnerable (at grass-roots level); and ability to contribute to the committee's role in strengthening user involvement in the completion of the NAP. Members also had to represent 'excluded women' and 'excluded immigrants' and, on top of that, the Ministry required an equal gender profile (Minutes Network meeting 28 August 2003). Finally, the Network decided that the committee should include representatives from church organizations; disability organizations; social economy organizations; immigrant organizations; organizations for homeless people; and the client movement umbrella organization. However, despite lengthy discussions and ambitions to reach an agreement, the Network could not come up with 10 delegates. Instead, it selected 11 representatives, which was later accepted by the Ministry.

Since the committee started, it has met four times a year (up to June 2007). In contrast to the Network, the committee discusses 'domestic issues', and for instance arranged a series of seminars: two seminars in 2005 on homelessness and on the encounter between people and power; two seminars in 2006 on homelessness and social enterprises. Interviews with members of the committee and the Network state that they are generally pleased with it and with the role of the Minister, who showed personal interest in issues of user involvement. They even described the committee as a possible model for how to implement the NAP locally, i.e. to build local partnerships between public agencies and citizens' organizations. Equally important, they state that the committee probably would not have been set up, had it not been for the OMC process.

However, members of the committee also expressed some unresolved ambiguities. Instead of ending the Network's arguments and struggles with the Ministry over influence and participation, these now initially took place within the committee itself. While the forum was formally presented as one for consultation and information exchange, Network members said that they had limited influence on the agenda. In the first year, the delegation held meetings concentrating on topics of interest to the Minister. While the government invited external experts to meetings, NGOs were not allowed to invite their own. The agenda was distributed only a few days in advance, restricting the Network's preparation, and the Minister tended to leave the meetings early.

The government's behaviour draws attention to the disadvantaged role of social NGOs in the making of public policy. Some members of the committee even called it a 'hostage situation', in which they functioned mainly as 'experts' on the user perspective, answering questions from the Minister when asked. From its point of view, the government needed the committee in order to fulfil EU objectives. Other members of the committee believed that these problems merely resulted from it having been recently established and not yet having found its procedure or form. They expressed a pragmatic approach, arguing that social NGOs had to accept some difficulties when working closely with public authorities, as a necessity for gaining additional influence. Moreover, some Network members criticized it for focusing only on establishing contacts with the government, and for failing to develop an agenda for further action. However, communications with members of the Network indicate that some of the unresolved ambiguities tended to be worked out. They show that recent meetings, hearings, and seminars have resulted in new working methods, and greater opportunities for NGOs to present their views and opinions.

In our view, the introduction of the user committee represents an institutionalization of participation and cooperation between the government and social NGOs. The OMC process has been a catalyst for this and provided social NGOs with a point of access to the Ministry, previously mainly a privilege of social partners. One can also observe a division of labour between the Network and the committee, as the government discusses domestic issues with the user committee, while consulting the Network regarding the NAP/Inclusion. Each forum possesses resources of different kinds for NGOs to exploit and to fight over internally. The Strategy Report on Social Protection and Social Inclusion (completed in summer 2006) confirmed this division: the Network was presented as the actor participating in the drafting of the Report, and only the Network presented its claims in an annex (Ministry of Health and Social Affairs 2006).

6 Cooperation and competition among social NGOs

The development of the OMC/Inclusion has demonstrated that the process contains resources for social NGOs to exploit. These include access to arenas for cooperation and dialogue between social NGOs and to institutionalized patterns of consultation between NGOs and the government. However, these resources have given rise not only to new patterns of cooperation, but also to competition and struggles between NGOs. The social NGO sector is not homogenous, neither in its interests nor in its responses to the OMC.

Analysing the OMC process from a political opportunity-structure perspective, it is apparent that it has proved a challenge for social NGOs to cooperate and 'speak with one voice'. In the Swedish case, the government expected a unified social NGO sector which it could consult from time to time. For the government, this was highly convenient, as it did not have to deal with a variety of organizations in terms of analysing multiple views and opinions. In that respect, the formation of the Network made it easier for the government to 'fulfil' the objective of mobilizing all relevant actors. The situation has been somewhat more ambiguous for the Network. It has continuously aimed to be as all encompassing as possible. Fewer participating organizations would mean that the Network no longer could claim to be the single actor, which the government could expect to represent 'all' relevant organizations working in the field.

Until now, the Network has generally succeeded in its ambitions, as few organizations have left it. However, acting as a unified actor has proved difficult. Some members have argued for a more radical and claim-making position in relation to the government, expressing the view that social NGOs have the role of criticizing public policy. Others have expressed a more consensus-oriented opinion. Arguably, this is why the Network has aimed to remain an informal body, with no formal rights or obligations for members and operating on the basis of deliberation and dialogue as its main internal decision-making procedure. Together with the wide variety of participating organizations, the Network's ambition to form an actor 'speaking with one voice' stands in sharp contrast to the fragmented profile of the voluntary sector.

Nevertheless, participating in the OMC process means that social NGOs gain access to processes and discussions which constitute resources for them to explore and exploit in strengthening the position of their members (Marks and McAdam 1996). The OMC process provides them with possibilities for acquiring resources, knowledge, and contacts to be used in national as well as international contexts. We have shown how national social NGOs see both the OMC process and the Network as important resources in terms of the right to represent the NGO sector in consultations on the NAP inclusion, nominating delegates to the user committee, and constituting an important arena for knowledge sharing. Moreover, in interviews with members of the Network, they say that participation provides them with insight into EU policy and contacts with organizations with different backgrounds.

However, NGO actions in relation to EU policies require economic resources, linguistic skills, and knowledge about policies and policy making. Organizations that have a clear EU profile (and competence) tend to have a central position in the Network. They have contacts with European networks or organizations and can get hold of general information, for instance on the status of NAPs in other Member States. Interviews also illustrate that members of the Network experience barriers. Some find it difficult to understand the relevance of EU policies for the national policy context. Similarly, others say that it takes years to fully understand the complex and technical language of EU policies in general and the OMC process in particular. Difficulties in understanding the technical language of EU documents make it difficult for NGO activists to comprehend what consequences EU policies may have for their organization and their daily work.

Resources may give rise to internal competition and struggles. The Network has had difficulties in reaching an agreement about which organizations should represent it (and the social NGO sector) in the user committee, i.e. some organizations emphasized that they represented a special interest/group that could not be left out of discussions on poverty, social exclusion, and marginality. Observations at meetings further demonstrate that some organizations adopt a dual position in contacts with the Minister (and partly also in the Network), as representatives both of the Network and of their individual organizations. These mixed interest patterns illustrate how members of the Network have their own agendas, seeking to use the OMC/NAP for their organizations' own purposes. This could already be observed when the Network started, as some members aimed not only to influence social inclusion policy and establish consultation procedures with the Ministry of Health and Social Affairs, but also to influence employment and labour market policy and the related Ministries. Here the Network became a platform for the ambition to break the social partners' monopoly on employment issues. Hence, we cannot reduce the OMC process merely to dynamics between the government and NGOs; instead, it is obvious that social NGOs develop the OMC process for their own purposes.

7 Conclusions: new power resources for social NGOs

This chapter has studied the micro-politics of the OMC/Inclusion within the existing social field. We have seen how a new collective actor, a network of social NGOs, has used the OMC as a resource to challenge the existing structures of consultation as well as dominant problem perceptions, yet with rather limited results in terms of concrete policy impact. Here we will summarize the main findings.

7.1 Continuity and change in the policy paradigm

In policy terms, the OMC/Inclusion has meant little new. The Strategy Report itself is of very limited policy relevance. As in other countries, it is more of a report about measures taken than a forward-looking action plan (see Kröger 2006 on Germany and France), which in the Swedish case is the deliberate choice of the Ministry, and possibly also in line with the EU's intention in moving from a NAP to a Strategy Report integrating all social coordination processes. The NAPs have introduced neither new policy thinking nor many new concrete initiatives. Swedish governments have, rather, continuously emphasised the national style of combating social exclusion: a universal social security system and active labour market policy (the activation or 'primacy of work' principle).

It has been the firm belief of the Social Democratic governments (in office until autumn 2006) as well as that of many Swedish welfare policy experts that the universal welfare model is the best way to combat social exclusion (Halleröd 2003). However, this does *not* mean that Social Democratic governments have not taken the work against social exclusion seriously. Besides pursuing the universal welfare and work principles, specific groups have received special attention. Increased resources have been allocated to support people in vulnerable situations, such as drug abusers, mentally disabled persons, homeless people, people threatened with honour-related violence, and newly released prisoners. In the Social Democratic Strategy Report for 2006–8, three priority groups were identified: long-term unemployed, older people, and people of foreign background, who tend to have difficulties in labour market integration. The following policy priorities were established: 1) promote work and/or education and training for everyone, 2) increase integration, 3) ensure good housing and fight homelessness, 4) strengthen groups in particularly vulnerable situations (Ministry of Health and Social Affairs 2006).

The persistence of the universal welfare paradigm is striking. The non-socialist government that took office in 2006 also emphasizes this as the foundation for social protection and inclusion, but with some amendments. A coalition government of four non-socialist parties, headed by Reinfeldt, has taken over the traditional language of Social Democrats, such as the 'primacy of work principle' and 'full employment', while giving it its own interpretation. The new government has reinforced the 'welfare through work' policy line, by strengthening the incentives to work in unemployment insurance as well as in the tax system. It has also addressed a number of issues related to social exclusion, such as homelessness, violence against women, at-risk children, and drug addicts. The new government chose to submit its own Strategy Report in spring 2007, replacing the previous government's report, which had already been accepted by the EU. The non-socialist government also identified long-term unemployed, drug abusers, mentally ill persons, homeless people, and people under threat of domestic violence as special target groups. The Social Democratic opposition, in turn, has resisted the new government's interpretation of the 'primacy of work principle' and reductions in benefit levels and duration. Arguably, even if there is consensus about universal welfare as a principle, concrete formulation of social security programmes is a contested matter.

These changes in national policies are not dependent upon the OMC process. However, the change in government has implied some greater recognition of the process as such. Launching its updated Strategy Report, the conservative coalition government headed by Reinfeldt held a press conference. This was the first time a press conference had been held on the OMC/Inclusion, which the civil servant responsible for the Strategy Report interpreted as an attempt to increase its political profile (Interview, 2007). The Network also chose to rework completely its contribution in the annex. It changed its contribution to fit the policy positions of the new government, and now focused on access for all to work and to housing, stressing the special needs of the most marginalized groups. More concretely, it stressed access to rented accommodation, since the non-socialist local governments tend to convert public rented apartments to privately owned ones, which are only available to people who can afford to buy them. The Network also emphasized the role of the social economy in reintegrating the long-term unemployed in the labour market (Ministry of Health and Social Affairs 2006, annex 3).

7.2 A new collective actor in the social field

If we look at the politics rather than the policy side, we can see a number of interesting developments which illustrate how the OMC touches upon delicate principles in the Swedish welfare state. Although as has been observed in Germany and France (Friedrich 2006; Kröger 2006), the OMC process in Sweden is of primary interest mainly to a few bureaucrats within the national administrations; with a low degree of parliamentarization, it also attracts a lot of interest from NGOs. As a direct result of the OMC on social inclusion, a network of social NGOs was mobilized in 2000 and the OMC continues to provide a platform for the Network and legitimize its claims to participation in social policy making. The importance of the OMC process as a lever extends beyond its impact on the action plans. Armstrong (2005, 2006) has reported that in Britain the OMC/Inclusion has empowered social NGOs in relation to the government, and the NGOs there hope that the new working relations will spill over from the NAP on Social Inclusion to domestic policy making. This is precisely what we have seen in Sweden, where the production of the NAP, or Strategy Report, has meant an avenue for social NGOs to enter into dialogue with government officials.

Just as importantly, the OMC in Sweden has been a catalyst for changing the organizational landscape, by fostering new alliances and forms of cooperation among social NGOs. In this highly diverse and fragmented sector, the Network, mobilized in direct response to the OMC, has sought to gather together social organizations, to pursue common interests as far as possible, and to speak to the government with one voice. It remains to be seen whether this is the start of greater collaboration within the voluntary sector generally. The OMC has at least begun to unite a fragmented sector.

The Network's informal character has allowed a broad participation and helped legitimize its claim to represent 'all relevant interests'. However, the ambition to 'speak with one voice' in practice means seeking the lowest common denominator. The informality and diversity of interests and perspectives implies that the Network cannot align behind other than very general goals, hence it is unlikely to have much concrete policy impact. It is rather an 'investment' for the future in good working relations with the Minister and government.

As it has developed, the Network depends on the engagement of a few key persons, their contacts, and knowledge. One of the premises when establishing the Network was that the participants should have an open mandate from their organizations. Although this can be a strength, it can also be a disadvantage in that the OMC process may be weakly 'anchored' in its constituent organizations. This risks making the Network a 'fragile' actor and possibly weakens its capacity to take part in OMC implementation. The Network as such has no resources but is dependent on those of the participating organizations. However, we have shown that some groups involved in the Network try to use the platform to forward their own agendas. This is not surprising, since participating organizations have, above all, a domestic policy agenda.

7.3 New institutionalized patterns of cooperation and consultation

Sweden has had no tradition of involving NGOs and citizens' groups in public policy making, in stark contrast with the participation of social partners. It is fair to argue that the EU has broken the ground for institutionalized partnerships, including not only employer and employee interests but also social NGOs, first through the European Social Fund (ESF) and later through the OMC. The EU required the participation of social economy organizations in the ESF partnerships, and without that requirement it is doubtful whether social NGOs would have been included. For Swedish social NGOs, the EU has clearly functioned as a lever.

One of the founders of the Network realized early on the importance of trying to influence not only social inclusion policy but also employment and labour market policy, and of trying to break 'the monopoly of the social partners' in that field, as he put it (quoted in Jacobsson 2005). Thus, the Network tried to break into the long-institutionalized social partner consultation that takes place at the Ministry of Industry, Employment and Communications on a regular basis. However, it did not succeed in becoming a regular participant in the consultation at that ministry, but only in being invited on special occasions. Neither the Ministry nor the social partners recognize the social NGOs as legitimate regular partners in the dialogue on labour market policy.

In the social field, the NGOs have been more successful and a standing committee for user participation was established in 2003, alongside the regular consultation at the Ministry of Health and Social Affairs. While some social organizations represent strong and well-organized interests, which already had established channels of communication with the political sphere, sometimes through informal contacts and their own initiative, sometimes because they had been invited (e.g. the disability organizations in Sweden), the OMC process has empowered and given voice opportunities to less well-resourced social NGOs and networks, such as representatives of the homeless. The OMC helped to establish new forms of cooperation among social NGOs, which claim to represent the most marginalized groups in the Swedish welfare society.

However, here we encounter a delicate issue in the Swedish welfare state, which divides not only political parties but also the social NGOs. As we have observed, Social Democratic governments may be interested in inviting social NGOs to discussions on welfare issues. However, in principle Social Democratic governments tend to reject the involvement of the voluntary sector in the delivery of services, since this could conflict with the principles of universalism and equality. Non-socialist parties tend to be more positive about involving NGOs in service delivery. In 2007, two ministers from the government expressed the ambition to sign long-lasting agreements with the third sector on its engagement in social services (Sabuni and Hägglund 2007). Explicit role models mentioned were agreements in the UK, Denmark, Estonia, France etc., but without any reference to the EU. On 23 October 2008, such an agreement was signed between the government, idea-based organizations in the social field and the Swedish Association of Local Authorities and Regions.

Members of the Network had raised demands for a general agreement. Both as individual organizations and as a Network, they have taken initiatives to formalize the terms of cooperation with policy makers, not least municipalities, with regard to the division of labour between NGOs and public bodies. This is a way to make visible and to gain recognition for the work actually performed by voluntary organizations in the Swedish welfare state. A formal agreement can also be a way of preventing the state and the municipalities from leaving too much welfare responsibility to the voluntary sector, and thus abdicating public responsibility. Social NGOs are concerned to retain their independence in relation to the public authorities, and do not wish to be seen as executors of public policy. Their role in actually *implementing* policy objectives does not follow automatically from their engagement in the policy-making process. The role of NGOs in service delivery will remain a contested issue.

In conclusion, the OMC has served as a resource for social NGOs, which have sought to destabilize and renegotiate the institutionalized social field, by demanding voice and participation in policy making. This has been successful in the field of social policy, where no strong competitor exists, while in labour market policy, social partners still stand out as exclusive partners. In policy terms, the OMC/Inclusion is a marginal process in the Swedish welfare state, given the government's insistence that the NAP or Strategy Report should not be seen as a policy-making tool but as a report on policy made elsewhere. Policy makers believe that Sweden has little to learn from other EU countries when it comes to poverty and social exclusion. The importance of OMC/Inclusion lies in its side-effects on the NGO sector and its relationship to public policy making.

Note

1 Our research has been supported by the Swedish Research Council and the Swedish Council for Working Life and Social Research.

References

Armstrong, K. (2005) 'How Open Is the United Kingdom to the OMC Process on Social Inclusion?', in J. Zeitlin and P. Pochet with L. Magnusson (eds) *The Open Method of Co-ordination in Action: The European Employment and Social Inclusion Strategies*, Brussels: Peter Lang, pp. 287–310.

Armstrong, K. (2006) 'The "Europeanization" of Social Exclusion: British Adaptation to EU Co-ordination', *British Journal of Politics and International Relations*, 8: 79–100.

Axelsson, C. (2005) 'Social exkludering som policy i EU och Sverige', unpublished paper, Södertörn University.

Bauer, M. (2002) 'The Commission and the Poverty Programmes', *Journal of Common Market Studies*, 40: 381–400.

Cowles, M.G., Caporaso, J. and Risse, T. (eds) (2001) *Transforming Europe*, Ithaca, NY and London: Cornell University Press.

Fligstein, N. (2001) 'Social Skill and the Theory of Fields', *Sociological Theory*, 19: 105–25.

Friedrich, D. (2006) 'Policy Process, Governance and Democracy in the EU: The Case of the Open Method of Co-ordination on Social Inclusion', *Policy and Politics*, 34: 367–83.

Grabbe, H. (2003) 'Europeanisation Goes East: Power and Uncertainty in the EU Accession Process', in K. Featherstone and C.M. Radaelli (eds) *The Politics of Europeanization*, Oxford: Oxford University Press, pp. 303–27.

Halleröd, B. (2003) *The Fight against Poverty and Social Exclusion: Non-governmental Expert Report No 1b – 2003*, Sweden. Online. Available HTTP: http://ec.europa.eu/

employment_social/soc-prot/studies/sweden_1st_report_final_en.pdf (accessed 8 September 2008).

Jacobsson, B., Lægreid, P. and Pedersen, O.K. (eds) (2004) *Europeanization and Transnational States. Comparing Nordic Central Governments*, London: Routledge.

Jacobsson, K. (2004) 'Soft Regulation and the Subtle Transformation of States: The Case of EU Employment Policy', *Journal of European Social Policy*, 14: 355–70.

—— (2005) 'Trying to Reform the "Best Pupils" in the Class'? The Open Method of Coordination in Sweden and Denmark', in J. Zeitlin and P. Pochet with L. Magnusson (eds) *The Open Method of Coordination in Action: the European Employment and Social Inclusion Strategies*, Brussels: Peter Lang, pp. 107–36.

Jacobsson, K. and Vifell, Å. (2007) 'New Governance Structures in Employment Policy Making? Loose Co-ordination in Action', in I. Linsenmann, C.O. Meyer and W. Wessels (eds) *Economic Government of the EU. A Balance Sheet of New Modes of Policy Coordination*, Basingstoke: Palgrave Macmillan, pp. 53–71.

Jacobsson, K. and West, C. (forthcoming) 'Europeanization of Employment Policy Making in the Baltic States', chapter for B. Jacobsson (ed.) *The EU and the Baltic States: Changing Forms of Governance*, London: Routledge.

Johansson, H. (2007) 'Europeanization "from below": The OMC Process on Social Inclusion in the Swedish Welfare State', in B. Hvinden and H. Johansson, *Citizenship in Nordic Welfare States: Dynamics of Choice, Duties and Participation*, London: Routledge, pp. 125–38.

Keck, M. and Sikkink, K. (1998) *Activists Beyond Borders*, Ithaca, NY: Cornell University Press.

Knill, C. and Lehmkuhl, D. (1999) *How Europe Matters. Different Mechanisms of Europeanization*, European Integration Online Papers 3. Online. Available HTTP: http://eiop.or.at/eiop/pdf/1999–007.pdf (accessed 11 September 2008).

Kröger, S. (2006) *When Learning Hits Politics or: Social Policy Coordination Left to the Administrations and the NGOs?*, European Integration Online Papers 10. Online. Available HTTP: http://eiop.or.at/eiop/index.php/eiop/article/view/2006_003a/18 (accessed 11 September 2008)

López-Santana, M. (2006) 'Framing and Transmitting Change in Employment Policy: Domestic Implications of European Soft Law on Member States', *Journal of European Public Policy*, 13: 481–99.

Marks, G. and McAdam, D. (1996) 'Social Movements and the Changing Structure of Political Opportunities in the European Union', in G. Marks, F.W. Scharpf, P.C. Schmitter and W. Streeck (eds) *Governance in the European Union*, London: SAGE Publications.

Ministry of Health and Social Affairs (2006) *Sweden's Strategy Report for Social Protection and Social Inclusion 2006–2008*. Online. Available HTTP: http://ec.europa.eu/employment_social/social_inclusion/docs/2006/nap/sweden_en.pdf (accessed 11 September 2008).

Radaelli, C.M. (2003) 'The Europeanization of Public Policy', in K. Featherstone and C.M. Radaelli (eds) *The Politics of Europeanization*, Oxford: Oxford University Press, pp. 27–56.

Sabuni, N. and Hägglund, G. (2007) 'Satsning på ideella krafter löser landets vårdproblem', Dagens Nyheter, June.

Schimmelfennig, F. and Sedelmeier, U. (eds) (2005) *The Europeanisation of Central and Eastern Europe*, Ithaca, NY and London: Cornell University Press.

Smismans, S. (2003) 'European Civil Society. Shaped by Discourses and Institutional Interests', *European Law Journal*, 9: 473–95.

9 Europeanization of domestic employment and welfare regimes

The German, French, and Italian Experiences[1]

Jenny Preunkert and Sascha Zirra

Introduction

In Europe, Continental and Mediterranean welfare states in particular, currently face severe exogenous and endogenous challenges. Increasing global competition, demographic changes, and changing values render established welfare and employment policies ever less adequate to ensure jobs, prevent unemployment, and cover new social risks. Trapped between Member States' common need to confront these developments and their individual power claims, the European Union (EU) has relied on the institutionalization of instruments such as benchmarking, peer review, and exchange of best practices within the Open Method of Coordination (OMC) and the European Employment Strategy (EES). In recent years, Germany, France, and Italy have undertaken at least attempted extensive reforms, aiming at a more empowering and integrative employment and welfare regime. These reforms coincide in many aspects with the demands of the EES and OMC/Inclusion (cf. Radaelli 2003: 50) but differ considerably in extent and reform area (cf. Zeitlin and Pochet 2005, Serrano Pascual and Magnusson 2007). So how can we explain these similarities and differences? We argue that in order to answer this question we need a better understanding of the domestic processes of appropriation. Previous works have conceived the EES as a transnational learning process between European governments (Jacobsson and Vifell 2007) or examined the institutional effects of OMC processes (López-Santana 2006). We argue that while comparative scholars of national models tend to overemphasize institutional continuity (Streeck and Thelen 2005), many researchers on European integration tend to underestimate the stickiness of domestic institutions. We aim to avoid both pitfalls by introducing an intermediate level of organizations interacting within a domestic social field (cf. DiMaggio and Powell 1983, Fligstein 2001). Their actions thus refer to both domestic institutions and experiences from European learning fora (cf. Heidenreich and Bischoff 2008). The ideas, policy examples, and financial incentives of the OMC processes and supporting programmes provide an additional resource for such domestic practices (cf. Giddens 1984). The actors appropriating these resources have interpreted them according to the established institutional structure and their own preferences. We argue that the form and extent of domestic appropriation thus depends on two conditions: the respective design of the OMC process, and the ideas, interests, and strategic positions of the mediating actors in the domestic field. Hence in this chapter we seek to test two hypotheses:

1 the different design of OMC processes has significant effects on the course and outcomes of domestic reforms;
2 national institutions nonetheless guide domestic appropriation.

Institutional change is more likely to occur the more ready relevant actors are to reconsider existing paradigms (e.g. due to perceived policy failures), the better 'best practice examples' fit into the institutional environment, and the more important the position of the mediating actor within the domestic field. We test these hypotheses in the following sections against our empirical evidence on the domestic appropriation of the EES and the OMC/Inclusion in Germany, Italy, and France between 2000 and 2005. We find that the EES is more able to affect Member States' governmental bureaucracies, while the OMC/Inclusion tends more to influence civil society organizations. Because of cross-national differences in domestic institutions, in Germany these effects are felt predominantly on a cognitive level (1), in France adaptations of individual policy schemes predominate (2), whereas in Italy the main effects fall on governance (3).

1 Germany: A new paradigm of labour market policy and perpetuation of traditional welfare policy

For a long time, the German employment and welfare regimes were considered particularly difficult to reform. Even in 2003, Germany was regarded as a country unable to respond to economic challenges associated with increasingly globalized markets (Kitschelt and Streeck 2003: 28). While labour market policies (LMP) have aimed to protect existing jobs, the dominant goal of the welfare regime was to protect employees' living standards. In addition, poverty was considered to be a phenomenon that was defeated by a guaranteed minimum income (Buhr 2004). Since 2003, Germany has undertaken a series of far-reaching labour market and welfare reforms. Perceived failures in employment policy have opened up a 'window of opportunity' (Kingdon 1984), facilitating a paradigmatic change of LMP largely inspired by the EES. The EES guidelines and recommendations have been used as a new frame of reference guiding ongoing reform processes. In welfare policy, such OMC-driven reforms cannot yet be observed, but the European discourse on social inclusion has influenced debates among non-state actors.

In the following sections we demonstrate that the focal role of the Labour Ministry within both the EES and domestic reforms facilitated a paradigmatic change of LMP (1.1), while the OMC/Inclusion has been regarded as a marginal process within the federal government and local authorities.

However, NGOs have taken up OMC concepts and benchmarks and used them as a framework for international comparison (1.2).

1.1 The EES in Germany

From 2003 to 2005, the German labour market experienced a series of reforms, named after the president of the Commission set up in 2002, Peter Hartz. Initially, the recommendations of this body of scholars, social partners, politicians, and civil servants were regarded merely as a short-term reaction to the 'placement scandal' in the federal public employment service. Today, the Hartz Reforms are associated with a paradigmatic shift in LMP (cf. Kemmerling and Bruttel 2006). While in the past, German LMP has been geared to job security, the main goal of the reforms was to increase the quantity and quality of labour supply by 'making work pay', intensifying counselling, and training the unemployed. Three clusters of objectives can be distinguished in these reforms (Kemmerling and Bruttel 2006): 1) to directly increase labour supply, 2) to improve counselling by the public employment service (PES), and 3) to reform the unemployment benefit system by 'activating' 'inactive' social benefit recipients. How far these reforms are linked to the EES is widely discussed in Germany (cf. Schmid 2006, Büchs 2005). While Büchs (2005: 227–55) claims that the EES has been used as 'strategic reference' in a purely domestic debate, we argue that although there was a shared perception of the need for LMP reforms, many of these would not have taken the same path without the EES. At neither the national nor the European level was it necessary for the reforms to play out the way they did, which is instead the outcome of a fruitful interaction between pre-existing domestic institutional structure and European resources.

Both major reform projects – the JobAQTIV law in 2001 and the proposals of the Hartz Commission in 2002 – strongly referred to individual EES guidelines. Our interviewees broadly agreed that these reforms were due to a learning effect on the German Ministry of Labour fostered by the EES. Our findings indicated that these civil servants subsequently used the EES as a 'window of opportunity' opened by the 'placement scandal' to establish a reform agenda.

> This has, for example, focused certain processes within the federal agency … , it was said: There is an agreement within the EU, now we have to take this direction as well.
>
> (Interview D1)

These labour market reforms coincided with a period in which the competences for domestic, as well as European, labour market policy were located within a single subunit of the Federal Ministry of Labour. According to our interviews, this led to a strong influence of the EES on the domestic employment policy field. Needing orientation in a dynamic environment, these civil servants introduced EES guidelines to the domestic reform discourse. Thus, they actively used their strong position in the employment policy field to promote European policy goals.

> We, as policy advisors – what we in a German ministry are – also relay these new insights. We write reports, draft bills, propose something and, on the other hand, participate in shaping the process within the EU.
>
> (Interview D1)

The close informal and formal collaboration within the Ministry and with the social partners has spread paradigmatic change within the domestic field. Thus, the administration could easily refer to the guidelines as arguments to legitimate the announced reforms.

> They [the guidelines and recommendations] are an important intensifier. They help to advance the reform processes that pre-exist within a Member State.
>
> (Interview D3)

However, even paradigmatic change must respond to preceding mindsets. The European targets have always been interpreted in the light of domestic institutions. Hence, the pre-existing debate on jobseekers' responsibilities and the German system of vocational training provided a central hub for introducing the activation paradigm (cf. Ludwig-Mayerhofer 2005). Although, in the wake of this reorientation, current inequalities have become ever less accepted – for example, gender equality on the labour market is now widely discussed by the German public (Wrohlich 2005) – institutional inertia still impedes many individual policy measures introduced by the reforms (cf. Zirra and Preunkert 2009). First, the intended 'one-stop shop' for benefits and assistance to the long-term unemployed could not be fully implemented, due to resistance from the German regions (*Länder*) and municipalities, which are responsible for granting financial aid (Schmid 2006). Hence the people most in need still face the greatest obstacles in receiving help from the PES. Furthermore, new placement instruments, like Personal Service Agencies, and vouchers for private job placement agencies, have had few effects in terms of take-up rates and may even prolong the duration of unemployment (Mosley 2006). The creation of a subsidized low-wage sector has not yet produced the expected effects. While many 'mini- and midi-jobs' have been created, they do not function as a bridge to regular employment, as was originally intended. Quite the contrary, they have turned out to be poverty traps and often replace pre-existing regular jobs (Hohendanner 2007). While at the federal level the influence of the EES can be considered rather effective, the more peripheral actors are less committed to the new paradigm. Many policy measures that would need a collective agreement like 'job rotation' are not implemented because they do not fit the institutional environment, in this case the German career pattern (cf. Keller and Seifert 2002: 95). Moreover, as soon as the guidelines of the EES interfere with the competences of the federal states, the *Länder* fear for their constitutionally guaranteed cultural and political sovereignty. This refers to education as well as to the organizational reform of the PES proposed by Hartz IV. In short, despite these reforms, the institutionally structured segmentation of the labour market persists in Germany, as in both other countries (cf. Zirra and Preunkert 2009).

1.2 The OMC/Inclusion in Germany

The impact of the EES in Germany is not reflected in comparable results from the OMC/Inclusion. Until at least 2005 there were only individual learning processes within the Ministry of Social Affairs. However, our findings suggest that the OMC/Inclusion has shaped the discourse among social NGOs. Within the Ministry of Social Affairs, the Department for European Affairs prepared the meetings of the Social Protection Committee (SPC), while the Department for Economic and Financial Affairs of Welfare and Social Exclusion coordinated the drafting of the NAPs. The civil servants in charge used the results of the benchmarking process for their own work, for instance, the poverty and wealth reports referred to the objectives and definitions of the OMC/Inclusion, since this report was coordinated and drafted by the same department as were the NAPs. But, according to representatives of both the administration and the social NGOs, these definitions in the first part of this report had to be considered as a formal exercise without political meaning. Public debate on the report was focused on the analysis in the second part, which was submitted by other departments. Thus, the OMC/Inclusion could lead to individual learning processes, but these had little influence on the domestic situation more generally.

If we want to understand why the OMC/Inclusion had such limited influence on debates and government reforms, we must consider the domestic configuration of the process in Germany. The Ministry of Social Affairs interpreted the general and broad objectives of the OMC/Inclusion as a European approach to fighting poverty. As the majority of the government were still convinced that the German social assistance system protects its citizens from poverty, the political elite saw no need for a European coordination of welfare policies:[2]

> So Germany rejects the OMC … and if they [civil servants of the German government] must take part, they want to look good. …
>
> (Interview EU20a)

From this perspective, our interview partners in the Ministry of Social Affairs argued that a sufficient set of instruments and an adequate communication structure within the government to fight poverty already exists. Finally, the civil servants dealing with the OMC/Inclusion hardly had a chance to influence reform debates within the government. Conversely, the social policy experts within the government participated only indirectly in the processes.

> That means we [civil servants of the department] are not responsible for the content of the NAP … Now if one objective of the OMC/Inclusion deals with social assistance, I would tell the civil servants from the

> department in charge ... : You are technically responsible, and now tell me what you are doing on this issue. And then we write it down together.
>
> (Interview D22)

In addition, the federal government has only limited competences in the German system because, in many areas, the *Länder* and the municipalities decide their own policies. Consequently, the national civil servants in charge of the process could not push any new measures in these policy fields, while municipal administrations were only indirectly involved in the OMC/Inclusion through their umbrella organizations. The *Länder* participated in drafting the NAP through a working group, nominating a delegate to the SPC. However, a large number of *Länder*, as well as the municipal umbrella organizations, rejected the OMC/Inclusion because they feared that the European institutions might try to extend their competences through this process.

While the government defined social inclusion as integration into the labour market, and poverty as a problem successfully overcome through social benefits (Concialdi 2004), NGOs, as well as interested scholars, have long questioned these historical beliefs (Leisering 1993; Schäfer 1992). For them, poverty and social exclusion are crucial problems in Germany (Jacobs 2000). Their multidimensional analysis focuses not merely on the financial aspect of exclusion, but also on participation in cultural life, adequate housing, etc. This new paradigm of social inclusion has been induced by the objectives of the OMC/Inclusion and the preceding European debates and programmes on social exclusion in the 1980s and 1990s.

> The programmes of the EU ... have changed the national focus and added a European dimension in the discussion on poverty and social inclusion ... And secondly, there is an agenda setting [through the programme], so the topic of social inclusion is becoming popular [in the civil sector].
>
> (Interview D17)

Furthermore, the German welfare associations have got to know the approaches and the work of NGOs in other Member States through European debates and peer reviews of the Action Programme. They have introduced good practice examples in national debates as a framework for international comparisons and a benchmark for their own work. Finally, they have used the national projects of the programme and the national affiliate of the European Anti-Poverty Network to strengthen their domestic communication structures.

These effects of the OMC/Inclusion on civil society were possible because the NGOs have been willing to question the existing paradigm and have appreciated the resulting transnational exchange as an opportunity to learn from other countries. Furthermore, the national experts of the NGOs involved in the programme are also powerful actors in the debates among non-state actors. But at the same time, some limitations have become obvious. For example, whereas the national level is strongly involved in the programme, local NGOs are largely unaware of the programme and therefore cannot use it. In addition, NGOs had already exchanged ideas at the national level, prior to the OMC. Consequently, the OMC/Inclusion has helped to strengthen existing contacts, but new ones have hardly evolved within its framework.

1.3 Comparing the effects of the two processes in Germany

Both processes were introduced at a time when the government and the social partners were searching for a new approach to reintegrating jobseekers into the labour market. Thus, the EES has coincided with a general willingness of labour market experts to reconsider the prevailing paradigm and has provided an important stimulus for pending reform processes. Due to this window of opportunity, the Labour Ministry's agenda-setting strategy has been effective. Close coupling of European and national competences has had a strong domestic influence on the civil servants involved in European processes. Institutionalized industrial relations contributed to spreading paradigmatic change to all actors in the labour market policy field. However, this shift was preceded by smaller reforms and is still not completely successful. In particular, marginal actors in the field of labour market policy still defend the old policy. Furthermore, the successful implementation of many individual reforms has been constrained by the domestic institutional settings and institutional complementarities.

The OMC/Inclusion has significantly influenced the non-state sector by enabling social NGOs to exploit the Action Programme for their work at the national level. Wanting to overcome the prevailing paradigm of poverty, they have introduced the definitions and results of European debates into domestic discourse. Additionally, the projects of the Action Programme, as well as the national affiliate of the European Anti-Poverty Network, have strengthened collaboration among NGOs. However, the federal structure, in conjunction with the vague objectives of the OMC/Inclusion, has inhibited the successful appropriation of the process in German welfare policy. Although individual civil servants have learned from the benchmarking process, large parts of the Ministry of Social Affairs, the *Länder*, and the local authorities have rejected it for fear that the EU might gain more competences in the field. Hence, both domestic mindsets and power relations have, so far, hindered the influence of the OMC/Inclusion on national institutional design.

2 France: subsidizing atypical employment and state accountability for social cohesion

The French employment and welfare regimes are characterized by high protection of regular employment (Ughetto and Bouget 2002), an expansive social security system, and a fundamental role for the centralized state in economic and social modernization (Hall 1986). The strong statist bias of policy in the post-war period led to a central role for the public employment sector and social security provision. The state was viewed as responsible for reconciling the diverging and particularistic interests in economic and social life. As a result, it had to safeguard 'social cohesion' (cf. Bouget and Brovelli 2002). This regime coincided with a weak civil society, as well as with weak trade unions and a statist attitude among all relevant parties (Levy 2005: 113f). In addition, French governments have frequently reacted to public protest with concessions and expensive programmes, protectionist policies, and the withdrawal of previously announced liberalization measures.

The decline of standard employment is widely discussed in France. More than one-third of employees younger than 30 and many women are employed in atypical jobs (Estèbe 2005: 94). This inequality in the labour market incited a broad debate about 'social exclusion' and, more recently, 'precariousness' (Paugam 1996, 2000), among marginalized groups, particularly younger people and immigrants. In the following sections we demonstrate that, despite the EES's recommendations, the state has maintained its active role in creating employment and the administration has used the strategy to improve its labour market policy instruments (2.1). The civil servants in charge of the OMC/Inclusion have also used the results of the benchmarking process to improve their own capacities. However, the process has had little influence at the political level and only occasional effects on the work of the NGOs (2.2).

2.1 The EES in France

While a multiplicity of individual reforms has added up to a picture similar to that in Germany and Italy (cf. Barbier et al. 2006), there was no single outstanding reform project in France. The dominant reform discourse in France concerned the state's obligation to ensure employment and protect citizens from new social risks rather than obligations and individual training for jobseekers (cf. Levy 2005, Ughetto and Bouget 2002). This became particularly obvious in the Plan Cohésion Sociale of 2004, which focused strongly on providing and reforming subsidized jobs.[3] In France, employment is considered to be the most important component of social inclusion and the high in-work-poverty risk is seen as the main challenge for social cohesion (Estèbe 2005; Barbier and Fargion 2004).

> Today precariousness is often discussed. But the real problem of precariousness is background poverty. More and more people live in poverty despite having a job. The minimum wage only applies to full-time jobs, if one works 35 hours a week. But today we have problems with part-time jobs, with contracts to begin a job, CPE, all these contracts lead to the fact that people increasingly have to live in poverty.
>
> (Interview F8)

Most reforms therefore, combine these two aspects and aim to improve wages for low-skilled workers (cf. Barbier 2007). The most ambitious among these reforms was the Social Cohesion Plan drafted in 2004 under the aegis of the Minister for Employment, Labour, and Social Cohesion, Jean-Louis Borloo (cf. OECD 2005, 2007). Its aim was to combat social exclusion through a multi-dimensional approach addressing problems of unemployment, housing, and education. The employment pillar of this plan sought particularly to tackle the 'hard core' of unemployment, i.e. the almost 1.5 million people receiving guaranteed minimum income (RMI, *revenu minimum d'insertion*), and comprised two strands. The first involved a stronger sanctioning regime. It extended the possibilities introduced in 2000 by an agreement between the social partners on a catalogue of measures to reform public placement. This reform, enacted as the Plan d'aide au retour à l'emploi (PARE) was supposed to introduce a paradigm similar to the German 'support and responsibilities'. However, even after the renewed reform in 2004, these sanctions were still much weaker than in most other European countries (cf. Barbier and Fargion 2004). One reason for this was a strong perception of RMI as the absolute minimum social standard.

Much more attention, and money, was devoted to the second strand of the reforms. The programmes for labour market integration, introduced to avoid poverty traps of atypical employment, had gradually increased the number and variety of subsidized contracts. These schemes focused on providing perspectives for disadvantaged target groups, such as young people, migrants, and low-skilled workers (especially those who combined these risk factors). A majority of recent reforms, e.g. the Raffarin reforms of 2003, aimed at generalizing these integration supports. With the social cohesion plan of 2004, these schemes were streamlined and the number of programmes halved from 14 to 7. The most important insertion scheme is now the *revenue minimum d'activité* (RMA), which targets recipients of RMI and private employers.[4] In return, the employer has to offer further training to the beneficiary. In France, analysis of the EES's domestic influence has its own pitfalls (cf. Barbier 2004). The reason is that because of the negative image of the EU in France the EES cannot be used to legitimize a reform project.

> In France, nobody wants to admit that what is being done has to do with Europe … Thus it is somewhat harder to recognize what part of this comes from Brussels.
>
> (Interview F4)

Hence a direct link between the reforms and the EES cannot be established in any reform. But this does not mean that the EES had no influence on these reforms. The French administration instead uses the EES without emphasizing it publicly.

> One refers to the EES and transfers this to France. But one never says that the CNE or the CPE for adolescents was a recourse to the European employment guidelines.
>
> (Interview F11)

Because references to the EU are considered illegitimate in national reform discourse, learning experiences cannot be communicated in the domestic field. Moreover, administrative responsibilities are very fragmented. Since 2004 the Secrétariat Général des Affaires Européennes (SGAE) (which is part of the Prime Minister's office) has been responsible for drafting the NAP. The national Ministry of Employment, on the contrary, has both a low significance within the EES and a relatively low programmatic influence on domestic policy. A Committee for European Affairs (CDSEI), comprising social partners and the government, has been established. This has improved social dialogue on a formal level, but social partners were still not consulted either on domestic labour market reforms or the governmental part of the NAP. Instead, since 2000 the social partners have been invited to draft a separate annex to the NAP. They have refused to do so since 2003, for two reasons: first, they did not feel that this annex had any meaning for either the European or the domestic reform process, and second, they have increasingly feared that 'Europe' would become a means of reducing job security without counterbalancing this loss in any way. Since they had no institutionalized channel for influencing the position of the administration or the government, they have decided to withdraw from the EES more generally. Nevertheless, the Labour Ministry has strongly profited from the EES. This actor has used the exchange of 'best practices' – the 'ways of doing things' promoted by the EES – to create and improve individual labour market schemes. These schemes have often been reinterpreted and actively adapted to the pre-existing institutional environment. Accordingly, in France the everyday practice of labour market policy is seen as being completely in accord with the requirements of the EES.

> Yes, we do many things and all that we're doing on employment policy is in line with the guidelines of the EES ... So what we're basically doing every day corresponds always to a field which is addressed in the strategy.
> (Interview F1)

These adaptations, however, have mostly been limited to individual programmes for the improvement of labour market integration. Thus, instead of overarching reform projects, the EES in France has contributed to improving existing schemes and programmes as well as creating new schemes and programmes for various target groups.

2.2 The OMC/Inclusion in France

The French government is one of the biggest promoters of the OMC/Inclusion at the European level. For instance, the objectives of the process were shaped by the French presidency in 2001. Therefore, the process displays many features of the French model of social cohesion (Atkinson and Davoudi 2000: 429). Paradoxically, our findings suggest that the process has had only limited effects on the political level in the domestic field. Hence, we show in the following sections that the OMC/Inclusion has influenced the work of civil servants involved, but was hardly linked to the political debates within the French social cohesion policy field up to 2005.

The OMC/Inclusion is located in the Bureau of International and European Cooperation within the Direction générale de l'action sociale, an inter-ministerial department that coordinates the national fight against social exclusion. This bureau drafts the NAPs in cooperation with an inter-ministerial committee and it prepares the meetings of the SPC in the field of social exclusion without consulting other departments. The civil servants responsible for the OMC/Inclusion have started to use its instruments and the results of European discussions to improve their own work. One of the most prominent examples is the preparation of the new budget law. With the new budgetary legislation, public expenditure has to be evaluated against fixed objectives and indicators. The social cohesion indicators were developed by an inter-ministerial team, chaired by the head of the lead OMC/Inclusion department.

> So now each minister is obliged to present his actions and the budget he claims to the parliament and hereby they have to rely strongly on indicators and of course preliminary results. In this context the OMC and its indicators … have played an important role. It has helped us to select indicators at the national level.
>
> (Interview F17)

Building on experience with the OMC indicators, the team was able to develop national indicators very quickly. Furthermore, the social indicators served as a model for other policy areas. Later, the concept of the NAP/Inclusion 2003–5 was used as the basis of the first cross-cutting policy document (*Document de politique transversale*) for the social cohesion field. In addition to these effects, the civil servants reflected the domestic situation on the basis of the European debates and benchmarking processes.

> For example, the Commission suggests topics such as the situation of ethnic minorities and immigrants, but we are not used to making distinctions according to ethnic origin. But in the European context you cannot be opposed to this distinction since we have these problems with immigrants here in France. So … I think today we speak about ethnic problems in the context of social inclusion in a slightly different way than 10 years ago.
>
> (Interview F17)

Finally, the OMC/Inclusion has boosted inter-ministerial cooperation, at least at the administrative level. Inter-ministerial communication structures, which had only formally existed before, have been activated for the preparation of the NAPs.

The OMC/Inclusion has helped to improve the administration's capacities. However, until 2005, the process was implemented exclusively at the national administrative level. It was largely unknown or regarded as a meaningless set of instruments at the political level and within the local administrations. In addition, French NGOs were hardly involved in the process. Many of them did not know the OMC process; or if they did, regarded it as a merely governmental project, while smaller NGOs lacked the resources to participate in it.[5]

2.3 Comparing the effects of the two processes in France

The dominant reform discourse in France concerned social exclusion and in-work poverty. The government has been looking for more effective instruments to combat these problems. In this context, the administration has repeatedly used the OMC processes. However, due to public fears that the EU might threaten the French welfare state, the government avoided any reference to the EES. Although there have been many attempts to reform domestic employment policies, before the Presidency change of 2007, most of the successful initiatives improved existing instruments in line with the prevailing paradigm. A reflection on the goals and paradigms of domestic employment policy has hardly occurred in France. Mostly, there have been specific effects of adopting EES instruments: French policies have appropriated best practice examples that match the existing national paradigms and institutions. Domestic factors have hindered a further use of the EES, most importantly, the separation of competences for the EES and domestic employment policy within the state administration, and public resistance to European ideas.

The French government defined itself as an advocate of the social dimension of Europe and, therefore, has strongly supported the OMC/Inclusion at the European level (Palier 2004). At the domestic level, civil servants have exploited the OMC/Inclusion to strengthen their own capacities. They have appropriated the results of the European debates to rethink and strengthen their own approach. But the objective of mobilizing all relevant actors was not achieved. This was mainly due to the fact that local administrations and many French social NGOs had little or no contact with the process or considered it a purely governmental project.

3 Italy: greater flexibility on the labour market without strengthening social protection

The Mediterranean employment and welfare regime in Italy is characterized by an extremely rigid labour market with a familial-particularistic system of social protection (cf. Ferrera and Gualmini 2004). According to the Constitution, 'Italy is a democratic republic based on labour' (Constitution of the Italian Republic, article 1). This focus on labour united the two opposing movements of twentieth-century Italy: social Catholicism and the labour movement. As a consequence, this historical compromise led to strong segmentation of the labour market between well-organized, highly protected 'insiders' and precariously employed 'outsiders'. Furthermore, the fragile system of social insurance excluded the latter and left their protection to the family and the church (Ostner and Saraceno 1998). Thus, the Italian employment and welfare regime was confronted by strong exclusion of women, youth, and older people from the labour market, a low employment rate, and a high poverty rate.

In the following sections, we demonstrate that the EES and the OMC/Inclusion have mainly had effects on governance in both policy fields. While the EES contributed to increasing institutional capacities within the administration (1), the OMC/Inclusion has supported the creation of a more active civil society (2).

3.1 The EES in Italy

One of the first acts of the 2001–6 Berlusconi government was to publish a White Paper on labour market reforms. The authors of this paper developed a distinctive approach to flexicurity, complementing a flexible labour market with active LMP, without considering a reform of the welfare system (Biagi et al. 2002). The White Paper, like many other Italian texts, refers to the 'European challenge' of the EES in order to justify the need for reforms. In fact, many official documents refer to the Lisbon targets and Italy's bad performance in terms of employment rates. But we could not observe any use of precise guidelines in the domestic reform debate. Furthermore, many of the ambitious reforms attempted could not be accomplished, due to fierce opposition by relevant actors. For example, the intended general reduction of job security for the core labour force had to be postponed because of strong union and public resistance. Our findings indicate, rather, that two strategic incentives have dominated the domestic appropriation of the EES: a reference to the Lisbon targets in proposing labour market reforms in line with the policy of the Berlusconi government (cf. Cioccolo et al. 2004), and a strong financial dependence of regional LMP on the European Social Fund (ESF) (cf. Pirrone and Sestito 2006).

The first can be considered an outcome of the fragmented domestic organization of the EES in Italy. In Italian ministries, there is a clear division between policy makers close to the minister and a technical bureaucracy with a merely administrative role. In line with this tradition, Italy has been represented in EMCO by a top ministerial officer, whereas the NAP has been drafted at technical level. Additionally, in order to comply with the demands of the EES, a department for employment analysis was installed in the Ministry of Labour in 2000. This third, statistical pillar has strengthened an epistemic community of labour market experts, which was closely involved in European processes (cf. Graziano 2004). However, although we agree with Ferrera and Sacchi (2005) that the demand for evaluation within the EES has contributed to improving the potential steering capacity of the Italian ministry, our findings lead us to doubt this group's domestic influence. In our interviews these experts complained strongly that, so far, their conclusions have not been taken very seriously by social partners, policy makers, and the rest of the administration.

> I would say that this ministry to a large extent remains relatively weak in terms of economic and policy understanding … there are not many people capable of looking at the data … on the labour market in terms of employment, wages and so on. But most specifically in terms of what is going on with the policies.
>
> (Interview I5)

At least under the Berlusconi government from 2001–6, this group has been isolated within the ministry and loosely linked to both administrators and policy makers. Therefore, although reflection within this department on domestic labour market policy was initiated by the EES, we could not observe a paradigmatic change among policy makers and in the ministry as a whole.

In addition, as a result of the 2001 'devolution' reform, activation strategies now fall under the regions' legislative and organizational competences. But the regions often lack the resources to fulfil this mission.

> In practice, these training measures often work as unemployment benefits, rather than really training the people.
>
> (Interview I1)

Because of the small financial resources of the regions, 'the modernization of the Italian employment services and their future depended very much on intervention by the European Social Fund' (Interview I4).

> I have to say that the Employment Strategy was taken very seriously, predominantly at the local level. This is due to the fact that the structural funds have implemented all of our strategies. For us Italians, the European funds have always been a strong point of reference for the innovation of organizational models and steering concepts. The social funds have certain, clear rules and guidelines that have become guidelines for our regional policies as well.
>
> (Interview I3)

Our interviewees agreed that most of the actual reforms were due to European intervention and the financial incentives of the ESF. Therefore, in Italy the most important mechanism for EES-driven reforms has been the strategic incentives of the ESF in building regional and organizational capabilities, accompanied by a strategic use of the Lisbon targets to legitimize reform exigencies.

3.2 The OMC/Inclusion in Italy

The existing welfare regime has been discussed in the Left-orientated parts of society since the 1990s. Consequently, in 2000 the majority of the centre-Left parties adopted the law 328/2000 which was regarded as one of the most comprehensive welfare reforms in Italy (Ferrera and Sacchi 2005). According to the new law, a benchmarking process inspired by the OMC/Inclusion should be introduced at the national level. The regions' social policies should become comparable and assessable. However, two developments inhibited the successful implementation of this ambitious reform. In 2001 there was a constitutional reform which strengthened the regions' power in the social policy field. Thus, the proposed national benchmarking was no longer enforceable. In the same year, a new government was elected. This centre-Right government returned to the old model of Italian welfare. In 2003 the Berlusconi government published the White Paper on *Welfare: Proposals for a Dynamic and Solidary Society*. In this paper, the cabinet proposed the introduction of a multi-level monitoring system (encompassing the national, regional, and local levels) and adopted the OMC as a model for such a decentralized coordination system (Ministry of Labour and Social Affairs 2003: 29f, 37f). The OMC was regarded as a chance to support the capacities of the local levels without strengthening the national welfare state, even though this new governance approach has not been implemented so far. Thus, according to the White Paper, the OMC/Inclusion seems to have been very effective in the Italian welfare state. However, our analysis shows that the OMC was largely unknown among social policy experts and that its benchmarking processes and the peer reviews were not linked with the domestic debates until 2005. This contradiction between the official presentation and our findings can be resolved if we distinguish the OMC/Inclusion as an abstract model for reform plans and its actual implementation in the domestic field. On the one hand, the Berlusconi government used the process (understood as a decentralized governance approach) as an argument to legitimate its own reform plans. One the other hand, the same government rejected the OMC's objectives as interference with the sphere of the family and competences of the regions. It criticized the OMC's instruments as over-centralized and inappropriate for the Italian decentralized welfare regime.

> The minister Mr Maroni is a representative of the Lega Nord, thus of a party that is not much EU-oriented. So I think that the commitment to work together with the EU Commission is not so strong.
>
> (Interview I19)

In addition, the OMC/Inclusion was organized by individuals working outside both the government and the social policy field. Italy was represented in the SPC by an academic scientist and a member of the pension insurance institute, neither of whom was bound by government instructions. Until 2005, the NAPs were coordinated and drafted by five civil servants in the Ministry of Labour who had no competence in the field of social policy. Consequently, the key personnel of Italian welfare policy were only included in the process on the basis of individual contacts, if at all.

> And the NAP has always been more of a bureaucratic obligation than a real planning instrument for the government. NAP/Inclusion is a

> bureaucratic exercise of compiling data and facts in a way that makes Italy look good.
>
> (Interview I19)

Altogether, the process was only formally implemented by the Berlusconi government, without any link to domestic debates and reforms.

However, the Action Programme has had an influence on civil society. Since NGOs have been involved in European networks they have got into contact with their counterparts from other Member States and have learned from them. Thus, they were able to enhance their knowledge on how to combat social exclusion. For instance, some NGOs learned in a transnational project how to use indicators for their own work. Furthermore, the programme's national projects have strengthened the contacts between the NGOs and the local administrations. In particular, the national affiliate of the European Anti-Poverty Network has served as a platform where the different kinds of NGOs have come together and talked with each other.

> These days, they are closing the programme to hold 15 meetings in Italian cities in order to promote the strategy for fighting poverty. Hereby they involve more municipalities than the national government.
>
> (Interview I19)

In addition, some NGOs and local authorities have organized workshops and conferences within the Action Programme addressing the problem of social exclusion at a local level. Thus, NGOs have used the OMC/Inclusion to improve their own capacity and build up new communication channels in the domestic field. In this way, our results support the studies of de la Porte and Pochet (2005), who claim that the OMC/Inclusion might strengthen the non-governmental sector. However there is also some evidence of limitations. The success of the projects depends on the capacities of NGOs and local authorities. Small NGOs cannot often exploit programme opportunities, as they lack the necessary resources.

3.3 Comparing the effects of the two processes in Italy

Italian employment and welfare policy field is characterized by a high degree of fragmentation and political polarization. Domestic institutions have not only hindered reforms, but also restricted the influence of the EES and the OMC/Inclusion within the government. The EES predominantly had effects on the governance of Italian employment policy. These effects have relied on two strategic incentives: the ESF has obliged the regions to introduce activation policies, whereas the Lisbon objectives have endowed policy makers with ammunition to campaign for a more flexible labour market. In addition, the creation of an active epistemic community created the potential for a better steering capacity within the ministry. Alternative approaches have met considerable resistance within the government, the social partners, and the public.

The OMC/Inclusion had only marginal influence on national policy and the work of the government. There have been controversial debates and reform plans concerning the welfare state, but none of them has been successfully implemented. While the centre-Left government was voted out of office before it could implement its reform, social policy was not a priority for its centre-Right successor. The politicians in the coalition rejected the OMC/Inclusion as being centralized and inappropriate for the Italian familial-particularistic system, while the civil servants dealing with the process had, at best, contacts on an individual level with the key political personnel. Neither the experts within the government nor the local authorities participated in the OMC process. However, the NGOs have used the OMC/Inclusion to strengthen their own position in the domestic field. They have exploited the Action Programme and improved their organizational capacities through transnational learning processes and the creation of new local networks.

4 Conclusion

In our analysis, we have compared the effects and mechanisms of the domestic appropriation of the EES and the OMC/Inclusion in Germany, Italy, and France. We observed that the EES has led to a substantial policy change in Germany, shifting the paradigm from preventing unemployment towards supporting employability. The OMC/Inclusion has altered NGOs' perceptions in Germany, while domestic institutional settings and the distinctive design of the process have impeded its effective implementation within national welfare policy. In France, the EES and the OMC/Inclusion have mainly helped the administration to improve the instruments of state intervention. In Italy, the key actors have hardly used the benchmarking processes. But the ESF and the Action Programme have influenced regional labour market policies and the work of local authorities and NGOs to a considerable extent.

We demonstrated that the design of OMC processes influenced domestic appropriation. Relative to the OMC/Inclusion, the EES has had a greater influence on domestic debates and reforms. Both processes left domestic policy makers room for interpretation. While this space in the case of the EES has been used for cherry-picking preferred objectives, in the case of OMC/Inclusion it helped policy makers to block domestic implementation. The EES's main influence was on domestic governmental bureaucracy in Germany and France. The Action Programme and its projects have instead had a considerable influence on the work and beliefs of the NGOs in Germany and Italy. But, as our analyses of the OMC/Inclusion in France and the EES in Italy show, the design of an OMC process does not inevitably produce a particular outcome. Since French NGOs lacked the necessary knowledge and resources, they hardly made use of the Action Programme. Similarly in Italy, the national bureaucracy lacked the capacity to profit from the EES. Consequently,

ESF funding of regional labour market policy was the dominant influence. Thus the configuration of an OMC may have an influence on domestic institutions, but the crucial factors for its success were the ideas, interests, and capacities of domestic actors who mediated the OMC processes in the domestic field.

Our twofold comparison indicates a central implementation dilemma of both the EES and the OMC/Inclusion: the influence of both processes depends heavily on a responsive domestic institutional setting. This shows that paradigmatic change is more likely to occur if the dominant domestic discourse supports external pressures (e.g. in the case of German labour market policies). Even if there are no comprehensive reform projects, the EES and the OMC/Inclusion may contribute to improving existing policy instruments (e.g. in France). In addition, the ESF may encourage active labour market policies, and the Action Programme may strengthen civil society (e.g. in Italy).[6] Still, in all three countries the EES and the OMC/Inclusion have experienced strong resistance in fields where Member States face the greatest challenges (e.g. the inclusion of marginal groups in the labour market). Hence, despite remarkable progress in some areas, it is still uncertain whether both processes can achieve their long-term objectives.

Notes

1 The authors would like to thank Jonathan Zeitlin and Martin Heidenreich for very helpful comments on earlier versions of this article. We also thank the German Research Foundation, which provided the funds, our interviewees, who were extraordinarily cooperative, as well as Gunter Bechtle and Marianna Colacicco, who were a great help with the Italian interviews. This analysis is based on more than 100 interviews with representatives of the German, French, and Italian governments, regional governments, national and European social partners, national and European NGOs, the European Commission, and academic experts. The interviews were conducted between 2005 and 2006, therefore reflecting the situation from 2000 to 2005 (for Germany) and 2006 (for France and Italy) prior to the changes in governments. All interviews have been translated by the authors.

2 However, there are indicators that this position has changed since 2005. First, some of our interviewees stressed that the resistance to the OMC/Inclusion has declined over the years. Second, social exclusion has become a more broadly recognized and discussed problem in public and within the government. Finally, following the 2005 election, the Ministry of Social Affairs is part of the Ministry of Labour and Social Affairs, with a new head, who is regarded as being open to the European debates.

3 Although most recently this concept seems to be changing slightly, in line with the overall reform agenda of the Sarkozy presidency (cf. Reuter 2008).

4 In this programme the state grants RMI for another 6–36 months and the employer only pays €3.50 per hour. Critics fear that this could lead to unfair competition by employers avoiding the general minimum wage, and thus eventually to an expansion of the subsidized labour market (Barbier and Fargion 2004). Hence, it can be regarded either as a success or as a problem that the number of people employed on these contracts is growing continuously.

5 Hamel and Vanhercke (this volume) point out that in recent years the political elite has become more interested and involved in the process, while the participation of local authorities and NGOs has also improved.

6 This observation does not, however, imply a normative judgement. On the contrary, at different times and in different institutional environments, different mechanisms may be appropriate.

References

Atkinson, R. and Davoudi, S. (2000) 'The Concept of Social Exclusion in the European Union: Context, Development and Possibilities', *Journal of Common Market Studies*, 38: 427–48.

Barbier, J.-C. (2004) 'Research on "Open Methods of Coordination" and national Social Policies: What Sociological Theories and Methods?', paper for the RC 19 conference, Paris, September. Online. Available HTTP: www.cee-recherche.fr/fr/fiches_chercheurs/texte_pdf/barbier/BarbierRC19Paris.pdf (accessed 11 September 2008).

—— (2007) 'The French Activation Strategy in a Comparative Perspective', in A. Serrano Pascual and L. Magnusson (eds) *Reshaping Welfare States and Activation Regimes in Europe*, Brussels: Peter Lang, pp. 145–71.

Barbier, J.-C. and Fargion, V. (2004) 'Continental Inconsistencies on the Path to Activation. Consequences for Social Citizenship in Italy and France', *European Societies*, 6: 437–60.

Barbier, J.-C., Sylla N.S. and Edyoux, A. (2006) *Analyse comparative de l'activation de la protection sociale en France, Grande Bretagne, Allemange et Danemark, dans le cadre des lignes directices de la stratégie européenne pour l'emploi*, rapport de recherche pour la DARES, Ministère du travail.

Barbieri, G., Gennari, P. and Sestito, P. (2005) 'Do Public Employment Services Help People in Finding a Job? An Evaluation of the Italian Case', paper presented at the XXth National Conference of Labour Economics, Rome, September.

Biagi, M., Dell' Aringa, C., Forlani, N., Reboani, P. and Sacconi, M. (2002) 'White Paper on the Labour Market in Italy. Proposal for an Active Society and Quality Employment', in R. Blanpain (ed.) *White Paper on the Labour Market in Italy, The Quality of European Industrial Relations, and Changing Industrial Relations*, In Memoriam Marco Biagi, Bulletin of Comparative Labour Relations 44, The Hague, New York: Kluwer Law International, pp. 1–117.

Bouget, D. and Brovelli, G. (2002) 'Citizenship, Social Welfare System and Social Policies in France', *European Societies*, 4: 161–84.

Büchs, M. (2005) 'Dilemmas of Post-Regulatory European Social Policy Co-ordination: The European Employment Strategy in Germany and the United Kingdom', PhD thesis, Humboldt-University Berlin.

Buhr, P. (2004) *Armut und Armutsentwicklung in Deutschland. Status Quo und mögliche Folgen der Reformpolitik*, ZeS-Arbeitspapier, Bremen: Zentrum für Sozialpolitik.

Cioccolo, V., Furfaro, P. and Piras, P. (2004) 'La riforma Biagi: il lavoro atipico e flessibile', *Il Punto su …* , Informazione e pubblicità per il FSE dell'ISFOL.

Concialdi, P. (2004) 'Soziale Mindestsicherung und Sozialhilfe', in W. Neumann (ed.) *Welche Zukunft für den Sozialstaat? Reformpolitik in Frankreich und Deutschland*, Wiesbaden: VS Verlag für Sozialwissenschaften, pp. 155–80.

De la Porte, C. and Pochet, P. (2005) 'Participation in the Open Method of Co-ordination. The Cases of Employment and Social Inclusion', in J. Zeitlin and P. Pochet with L. Magnusson (eds) *The Open Method of Co-ordination in Action: The European Employment and Social Inclusion Strategies*, Brussels: Peter Lang, pp. 353–90.

DiMaggio, P. and Powell, W.W. (1983) 'The Iron Cage Revisited: Institutional Isomorphism and Collective Rationality in Organizational Fields', *American Sociological Review*, 48: 147–60.

Estèbe, P. (2005) 'Entstehung und Niedergang eines Sozialmodells', in A. Kimmel and H. Uterwedde (eds) *Länderbericht Frankreich 2005*, Bonn: Bundeszenrale für politische Bildung, pp. 87–100.

Ferrera, M. and Gualmini, E. (2004) *Rescued by Europe? Social and Labour Market Reforms in Italy from Maastricht to Berlusconi*, Amsterdam: University Press.

Ferrera, M. and Sacchi, S. (2005) 'The Open Method of Co-ordination and National Institutional Capabilities: The Italian Case', in J. Zeitlin and P. Pochet with L. Magnusson (eds) *The Open Method of Co-ordination in Action: The European Employment and Social Inclusion Strategies*, Brussels: Peter Lang, pp. 137–72.

Fligstein, N. (2001) 'Social Skill and the Theory of Fields', *Sociological Theory*, 19: 105–25.

Giddens, A. (1984) *The Constitution of Society*, Cambridge: Cambridge University Press.

Graziano, P. (2004) 'Europeanisation and Italian Unemployment Policy in the '90s: More Change than Continuity?', working Paper presented at the Final COST A15 conference 'Reforming Social Protection Systems in Europe: Co-ordination and Diversity', Nantes, France, May.

Hall, P. (1986) *Governing the Economy: The Politics of State Intervention in Britain and France*, New York: Oxford University Press.

Heidenreich, M. and Bischoff, G. (2008). 'The Open Method of Coordination. A Way to the Europeanization of Social and Employment Policies?', *Journal of Common Market Studies*, 46: 497–532.

Hohendanner, C. (2007) *Verdrängen Ein-Euro-Jobs sozialversicherungspflichtige Beschäftigung in den Betrieben?*, IAB Discussion Paper 8/2007. Online. Available HTTP: http://doku.iab.de/discussionpapers/2007/dp0807.pdf (accessed 11 September 2008).

Jacobs, H. (2000) 'Armut', in J. Allmendinger and W. Ludwig-Mayerhofer (eds) *Soziologie des Sozialstaats*, Munich: Juventa, pp. 237–68.

Jacobsson, K. and Vifell, Å. (2007) 'Deliberative Transnationalism? Analysing the Role of Committee Interaction in Soft Co-ordination', in I. Linsenmann, C.O. Meyer and W.T. Wessels (eds) *Economic Government of the EU. A Balance Sheet of New Modes of Policy Coordination,* New York: Palgrave Macmillan, pp. 163–86.

Keller, B. and Seifert, H. (2002) 'Flexicurity – Wie lassen sich Flexibilität und soziale Sicherheit vereinbaren?', *Mitteilungen aus der Arbeitsmarkt-und Berufsforschung*, 35: 90–106.

Kemmerling, A. and Bruttel, O. (2006) 'New Politics in German Labour Market Policy? The Implications of the Recent Hartz Reforms for the German Welfare State', *West European Politics*, 29: 90–112.

Kingdon, J.W. (1984) *Agenda, Alternatives and Public Policies*, New York: Harper Collins.

Kitschelt, H. and Streeck, W. (2003) 'From Stability to Stagnation: Germany at the Beginning of the Twenty-First Century', *West European Politics*, 26: 1–34.

Leisering, L. (1993) 'Zwischen Verdrängung und Dramatisierung. Zur Wissenssoziologie der Armut in der bundesrepublikanischen Gesellschaft', *Soziale Welt*, 44: 486–511.

Levy, J.D. (2005) 'Redeploying the State: Liberalization and Social Policy in France', in W. Streeck and K. Thelen (eds) *Beyond Continuity. Institutional Change in Advanced Political Economies*, Oxford: Oxford University Press.

López-Santana, M. (2006) 'The Domestic Implications of European Soft Law: Framing and Transmitting Change in Employment Policy', *Journal of European Public Policy*, 13: 4, 481–99.

Ludwig-Mayerhofer, W. (2005) 'Activating Germany', in T. Bredgaard and F. Larsen (eds) *Employment Policy from Different Angles*, Copenhagen: DJ/OF, pp. 95–114.

Ministry of Labour and Social Affairs (2003) *White Paper on Welfare State: Proposals for a Dynamic and Solidary Society*, Rome.

Mosley, H. (2006) 'Gemischte Zwischenbilanz', *WZB Mitteilungen*, 111: 31–33.

OECD (2005) *France – Economic Survey*, Paris.

—— (2007) *France – Economic Survey*, Paris.

Ostner, I. and Saraceno, C. (1998) 'Keine Arbeit, keine Kinder, keine Lösung? Italien und Deutschland in vergleichender Perspektive', in B. Cattero (ed.) *Modell Deutschland – Modell Europa, Probleme, Perspektiven*, Opladen: Leske und Budrich, pp. 183–205.

Palier, B. (2004) 'Social Protection Reforms in Europe: Strategies for a New Social Model', Canadian Policy Research Networks, *Social Architecture Papers*, Research Report F|37 Family Network.

Paugam, S. (1996) 'Poverty and Social Disqualification. A Comparative Analysis of Cumulative and Social Disadvantage in Europe', *Journal of European Social Policy*, 6: 287–303.

—— (2000) *Le salarie de la precarité. Les nouvelles formes de l'integration professionelle*, Paris: Presses Universitaires de France.

Pirrone, S. and Sestito, P. (2006) *Disoccupati in Italia. Tra Stato, Regioni e cacciatori di teste*, Bologna: il Mulino.

Radaelli, C.M. (2003) 'The Open Method of Coordination: A New Governance Architecture for the European Union?', *Sieps-Report*, 1/2003.

Reuter, E. (2008) 'The Interrelation between 'Activation' and Social Policy against Exclusion in Great Britain and France', paper presented at the International Conference 'Activation Policies on the Fringes of Society: A Challenge for European Welfare States', Nuremberg, May.

Schäfer, B. (1992) 'Zum öffentlichen Stellenwert von Armut im Sozialen Wandel der Bundesrepublik Deutschland', in S. Leibfried and W. Voges (eds) *Armut im Modernen Wohlfahrtsstaat*, Kölner Zeitschrift für Soziologie und Sozialpsychologie, Sonderheft: 104–23.

Schmid, G. (2006) 'Der Mensch denkt und die Institution lenkt: Zur Reformfähigkeit von Staat und Gesellschaft am Beispiel der deutschen Arbeitsmarktpolitik', *Politische Vierteljahresschrift*, 47: 367–79.

Serrano Pascual, A. and Magnusson, L. (eds) (2007) *Reshaping Welfare States and Activation Regimes in Europe*, Brussels: Peter Lang.

Streeck, W. and Thelen, K. (2005) 'Introduction: Institutional Change in Advanced Political Economies', in W. Streeck and K. Thelen (eds) *Beyond Continuity. Institutional Change in Advanced Political Economies*, Oxford: Oxford University Press, pp. 1–39.

Ughetto, P. and Bouget, D. (2002) 'France: The Impossibile New Social Compromise?', in J. Goul Andersen, J. Clasen, W. van Orschot and K. Halvorsen (eds) *Europe's New State of Welfare. Unemployment, Employment Policies and Citizenship*, Bristol: The Policy Press, pp. 91–105.

Vanhercke, B. and Hamel, M.-P. (this volume) 'The Open Method of Coordination and Domestic Social Policy Making in Belgium and France: Window Dressing, One-Way Impact, or Reciprocal Influence?'

Wrohlich, K. (2005) 'The Excess Demand for Subsidized Child Care in Germany', DIW Berlin und IZA, Discussion Paper, 1515.

Zeitlin, J. and Pochet, P. (eds) (2005) *The Open Method of Coordination in Action: The European Employment and Social Inclusion Strategies*, Brussels: Peter Lang.

Zirra, S. and Preunkert, J. (2009) 'Die Europäisierung nationaler Arbeitsmarktreformen: Die Auswirkungen der Europäischen Beschäftigungsstrategie in Deutschland, Frankreich und Italien', in H. Seifert and O. Struck (eds) *Arbeitsmarkt und Sozialpolitik. Kontroversen um Effizienz und soziale Sicherheit*,Wiesbaden: VS Verlag für Sozialwissenschaften, 287–314.

10 The Open Method of Coordination and reform of national social and employment policies

Influences, mechanisms, effects[1]

Jonathan Zeitlin

Introduction

Nine years after its annunciation at the March 2000 Lisbon Summit as a broadly applicable new governance instrument for the EU, the Open Method of Coordination (OMC) remains the subject of intense controversy among academics and policy practitioners alike. Much of this controversy revolves around normative questions concerning the OMC's democratic legitimacy and its implications for European integration (Zeitlin 2005a, 2005c). But the most widespread and persistent critique of the OMC remains its limited practical effectiveness and alleged lack of impact on policy reforms in Member States. Despite the explosion of research on the OMC in recent years,[2] much of the debate over its effectiveness continues to suffer from a serious empirical deficit, relying on a limited range of often outdated evidence onto which authors project their own theoretical and normative assumptions.[3] Thus many of the most critical assessments of the OMC are not based on original, first-hand research on the method in action (e.g. Radaelli 2003; Moravcsik 2005; Citi and Rhodes 2007; Hatzopolous 2007).[4] The 2004–5 mid-term review of the Lisbon Strategy, which reached harsh conclusions on the ineffectiveness of the OMC in promoting domestic reforms in EU Member States, was also a surprisingly non-evidence-based process. Thus the Report of the 2004 High Level Group chaired by Wim Kok did not systematically review the available evidence on the performance of OMC processes, such as the extensive mid-term review of the EES in 2002, or the report of the 2003 Employment Task Force (also chaired by Kok), both of which reached more positive assessments. Similarly, the European Commission's (2005) Lisbon New Start communication appears to have neglected both internal and external evidence on the successes and failures of different OMC processes, such as an independent evaluation of the eEurope programme and other information society initiatives, which concluded that the OMC in these areas 'cannot yet be said to be a success or failure', because it 'simply has not been fully implemented' (Tavistock Institute et al. 2005).

Empirical assessment of the OMC is extremely challenging, for a number of interrelated reasons. These include: the variety of distinct processes with different institutional characteristics subsumed under the OMC rubric; their relative newness, and the frequency of procedural changes to even the most highly institutionalized processes such as those for employment and social inclusion; and the horizontal and vertical complexity of OMC processes, which typically cut across sectoral policy domains and involve multiple levels of governance (European, national, subnational) in 27 Member States (15 before 2004). Most fundamental, however, are the methodological difficulties of assessing the causal impact of an iterative process based on collaboration between EU institutions and Member States, without legally binding sanctions. Thus, Member State representatives continuously participate in the definition of OMC objectives, guidelines, targets, and indicators, allowing 'uploading' of domestic concepts and preferences, which blurs the causal boundary between the national and European levels. OMC processes do not necessarily result in new legislation or justiciable obligations, rendering the concept of Member State 'compliance' problematic. Member States may often have political reasons for playing up or down OMC influences on domestic policy, from strategies of blame avoidance and credit claiming at home, to self-presentation as a 'good European' or a defender of the national interest in Brussels. Nor is it easy to isolate the influence of the OMC on national policy from those of other EU-level processes (such as the Stability and Growth Pact, European Court decisions, or the structural funds), other international organizations (such as the OECD, the World Bank, or the IMF), and domestic political changes (such as shifts in government). In each of these respects, the OMC encapsulates in extreme form the broader methodological problems involved in studying the impact of 'Europeanization' on domestic policy and politics.[5]

These difficulties are not merely theoretical. Researchers studying the same national and sectoral cases often disagree about the magnitude and significance of the OMC's influence. A noteworthy example is the impact of the European Employment Strategy (EES) in Germany, where some researchers see only 'surface integration' (Büchs and Friedrich 2005; Büchs and Hinrichs 2007), while others find deeper cognitive and practical influences on the design of key measures such as the Hartz labour market reform legislation, as well as on the strategies pursued by employers and other non-state actors (Preunkert and Zirra, this volume; Heidenreich and Bischoff 2008; Richardt 2004; Zolnhöfer and Ostheim 2005).

Thorny as these methodological problems are, they can be mitigated through a combination of research strategies:

- contextualized process tracing, in order to identify and assess the practical influence of the OMC (alongside other factors) on domestic actors, debates, procedures, and policies in specific contexts (national, sectoral, temporal);
- careful triangulation of documentary and interview evidence within and between studies, in order to multiply points of observation and offset sources of bias;[6]

- systematic comparison of research findings across countries, policy domains, and time periods, in order to identify and explain both general tendencies and dimensions of variation.

Yet many of the sources of controversy about the OMC's national influence are conceptual as well as empirical. Researchers disagree not only about the magnitude of the OMC's impact in different countries and policy fields, but also about what types of influence should count as significant, and through what causal mechanisms they might be generated. Thus, for example, Citi and Rhodes (2007) propose a comparative assessment of OMC processes in terms of their *ex ante* capacity for securing policy convergence across EU Member States. Analysts of the OMC as a new form of experimentalist governance argue instead that it is more properly assessed as a mechanism for promoting convergence of performance, through comparisons of experience in implementing alternative approaches to reaching common objectives in different national contexts (Zeitlin 2005a and 2005c; Sabel and Zeitlin 2008). Similarly, many critics of the OMC's capacity to promote cross-national learning consider the method a failure because peer review and exchange of good practices rarely result in direct transfer of identical policies and programmes from one country to another (Casey and Gold 2005; Kerber and Eckhardt 2007; Schludi 2003). Proponents of 'contextualized benchmarking' argue conversely, that successful borrowing from abroad typically requires extensive adaptation of foreign models and practices to fit local circumstances, while cross-national learning induced by such processes often takes an analogic rather than a directly mimetic form (Visser, van Gerven and Beckers, this volume; Hemerijck 2007; Zeitlin 2005a, 2003; Sabel 2004, 2005).

Many critics of the OMC take substantive policy change, especially as reflected in new legislation, as the main criterion for assessing its domestic influence (e.g. Moravcsik 2005; Kröger 2007; Citi and Rhodes 2007). Judged solely on this basis, as they insist, it is hard to show that the OMC has had a major impact outside of certain restricted cases, and even in those it is only one of several factors. But if we consider other types of impact, including not only procedural changes in governance and policy-making processes, but also cognitive and discursive shifts, along with changes in issue salience and political agendas, then we may identify deeper and more numerous influences, as the chapters in this volume demonstrate.

Hence, empirical evaluation of the impact of the OMC on national reforms can be advanced through the development of an appropriate conceptual framework. In the body of this chapter, I propose an analytical typology of influences, mechanisms, and effects for use in assessing the available evidence on the relationship between the OMC and the reform of national social and employment policies in EU Member States.[7] In focusing on mechanisms, my aim is to illuminate the causal and behavioural pathways through which the OMC can and has influence(d) the policy-making process in EU member states,[8] rather than to develop lower-level (individualistic) explanations of higher-level (collective) phenomena (Stinchcombe 1991; Hedström and Swedberg 1998), or to identify universal building blocks of recurrent causal patterns that can be combined to construct partial theories of aggregate outcomes applicable under different scope conditions (Tilly 2001; McAdam, Tarrow, and Tilly 2001; George and Bennett 2005).[9]

In deploying this analytical framework, I will draw not only on empirical material from the other chapters in the book, but also from the full range of available academic and policy literature on the operation of the EES and the OMCs in social protection and social inclusion, including several recent official evaluations.[10] To avoid duplication, I will concentrate on discussion of new evidence and refer readers to Zeitlin (2005b) for documentation of previously established claims. The analysis will focus primarily (but not exclusively) on the period prior to the restructuring of OMC processes in 2005–6, resulting from the Lisbon Strategy relaunch, the integration of the Employment and Broad Economic Policy Guidelines, and the streamlining of the OMCs on social inclusion, pensions, and health/long-term care into a unified process with both common and sector-specific objectives.[11]

Section 1 considers the major types of OMC influence on national social and employment policy reforms and examines the empirical evidence concerning their incidence. Section 2 analyses the main causal mechanisms and effects[12] through which the OMC has influenced domestic reforms in EU Member States, and assesses their relative importance. Section 3 concludes by asking whether OMC processes tend to reproduce pre-existing institutional configurations and regime pathways, or instead to promote hybridization and path-shifting reform of national social and employment policies.

1 Types of influence

Two major types of OMC influence on national reforms may be distinguished: its contribution to substantive policy change on the one hand, and to procedural shifts in governance and policy-making processes on the other.

1.1 Substantive policy change

Empirical studies of the EES and the OMCs in social protection/inclusion, such as those contained in this volume, provide evidence that these have contributed to three interrelated forms of substantive policy change: changes in national policy thinking (*cognitive shifts*); changes in national policy agendas (*political shifts*); and changes in specific national policies (*programmatic shifts*).

Undoubtedly the best-attested form of OMC influence on substantive policy change in EU Member States is *cognitive*. The chapters in this volume reinforce the findings of earlier academic studies and evaluation reports that the EES and the social OMCs have helped to reframe national policy thinking by incorporating EU concepts and categories into domestic debates;

exposing domestic actors to new policy approaches, often inspired by foreign examples; and questioning established domestic policy assumptions and programmes (Zeitlin 2005b: 450–7; Palier 2006; Guillén and Álvarez 2004; cf. also OPTEM 2007: 62–9; Eurévaì/Rambøll Management 2008: 22–6, 38–43). Thus, as the chapters by van Gerven and Beckers and by Hamel and Vanhercke document, the EES and the OMC/Inclusion have played a key role in diffusing into Belgian, Dutch, and French policy debates European concepts and orientations such as a comprehensive approach to fighting unemployment, raising the employment rate, making work pay, flexicurity, active ageing, sustainable social protection, child poverty, and active inclusion, while at the same time challenging deeply entrenched domestic commitments like the Belgian early retirement system. The chapters by López-Santana and Preunkert and Zirra similarly emphasize the ideational influence of these OMC processes on the policy orientations of both elite decision makers and non-state actors such as NGOs and social partners in Spain, Belgium, and Germany. These cognitive effects, as the chapters by Mailand and Jacobsson and West show, have been especially pronounced in the new Member States, such as Poland and the Baltic states, which had to fundamentally reconstruct their social and employment policies after the end of Communism and which had participated in the EES and the social OMCs for several years prior to joining the EU in 2004.[13]

A second well-attested form of OMC influence concerns *political shifts in national policy agendas.* Thus, as the chapters by López-Santana, Mailand, van Gerven and Beckers, Hamel and Vanhercke, Preunkert and Zirra, and Jacobsson and West variously demonstrate, the EES and the social OMCs have played an important part in Belgium, Denmark, France, Germany, the Netherlands, Spain, Sweden, Poland, and the Baltic states in placing new issues on the domestic political agenda, such as activation, prevention, life-long learning, gender mainstreaming, social exclusion, and child poverty, and/or increasing the salience of efforts to tackle long-recognized national problems like pension reform, early exit from the labour market, childcare provision, gender segregation, and the integration of immigrants.[14] National responses to the 2006 evaluation of the OMC/Inclusion, especially those from new Member States, emphasized its importance in reframing political agendas and focusing attention on the fight against poverty and social exclusion (European Commission 2006: 6–7). But such domestic political influences may themselves be affected by shifts in the EU's own policy agenda, such as the reduced emphasis on gender equality within the EES in recent years (Rubery et al. 2004; Fagan et al. 2005, 2006; O'Connor 2007).

The most elusive form of OMC influence, as noted earlier, concerns *changes in specific national policies and programmes.* Yet here too there is abundant evidence from academic studies, private interviews, evaluation reports, and official documents that OMC processes have contributed to social and employment policy shifts of varying degrees of intensity in many EU Member States. The best-documented cases regard the EES, whose influence previous research has traced on activation and unemployment prevention policies (France, Germany, Ireland, and the Netherlands); tax-benefit reforms (France, Germany); active ageing and life-long learning (France, Germany), reducing gender and ethnic segregation (Denmark, Sweden), and gender mainstreaming (most Member States).[15] The chapters in this volume provide further evidence of the EES's role in stimulating substantive changes in these policy areas, notably in Germany (activation, prevention, benefit reform, gender equality/mainstreaming), Belgium (activation, prevention, active ageing), Spain (activation, prevention, gender equality), and Poland (tax-benefit reform, pension finance), but also to a lesser extent in France (activation, tax-benefit reform), the Netherlands (prevention), Sweden (tax reform, gender segregation, integration of migrants), Denmark (prevention, early school leaving), and the Baltic states (activation, life-long learning).

Evidence about the influence of the social OMCs on national policy shifts remains more fragmentary, but here too recent academic research and evaluation reports have identified some significant examples. Thus, as Hamel and Vanhercke's interviews with French officials demonstrate, the introduction of the new Active Solidarity Income (*Revenue Sociale d'Activation*, or RSA), which allows social assistance recipients to add work earnings without losing their benefits, was strongly influenced by the EU's commitment to active inclusion, whose incorporation into the OMC/Inclusion France had earlier opposed. In Ireland, as a recent thesis argues, the emphasis on relative income poverty, integration of migrants, and comparisons with the experience of other European countries within the OMC on Social Inclusion as well as the EES have helped to inspire significant shifts in national policies on issues such as supporting the employment of lone mothers and combating anti-immigrant racism (Norris 2007: 115–19). In the Czech Republic, as another study reports, preparation of the country's first National Action Plan for Social Inclusion in 2004–6 facilitated the insertion not only of 'key words of the social inclusion strategy, but also its principles' in major pieces of social legislation, such as the Social Services Act and the Act on Assistance in Material Need, with direct consequences for the delegated competences of local authorities responsible for their implementation, even if the necessity for changes to these laws had long been debated (Sirovátka and Rákoczyová 2007: 24). National submissions to the 2005 evaluation attributed direct impacts to the OMC/Inclusion in a number of specific domains, such as indebtedness, lone parent, and childcare policies in the UK; tax credits in Slovenia; social assistance legislation in Slovakia; and the introduction of public assistance centres in Luxembourg (European Commission 2006: 6–7).

Even in the case of pensions, which is universally acknowledged to be more weakly institutionalized than the EES or the social inclusion process, there is evidence of the OMC's influence on national reforms. Thus both the European Association of Public Sector Pension Institutions (EAPSI) and the European Older People's Platform (AGE) report that the OMC has helped to enlarge the set of policy choices considered at national as well as European level by making the players more aware of the experience of reforms in other countries (European European Commission 2006: 10; AGE 2005: 4). Perhaps the best-known case is that of the French pension reform of 2003, where the Minister of Social Affairs led a preparatory 'European tour' of public officials and social partners to Germany, Finland, Sweden, and Spain, based on identification of good practices and bilateral contacts established through discussions in the EU Social Protection Committee (Natali 2007a: 17–18; European Commission 2006: 7). In Spain, officials similarly observe that the 'national discussion on pension reform benefited from its coinciding with the preparation of the first National Strategy Plans' in 2003, which were 'a valuable input for the administrative authorities to better approach the debate and compare the efforts made by other countries' (European Commission 2006: 7; Spanish evaluation report 2005; Guillén 2007: 129). Latvia likewise reported that the OMC 'has influenced the elaboration of legislation to promote progress to sufficient [i.e. adequate] pensions', one of the three core European objectives alongside financial sustainability and modernization of pension systems (Latvian evaluation report 2005). In Portugal, too, top officials explicitly cite the OMC's influence on a major pension and social security reform in 2006, which deliberately combined into a distinctive hybrid synthesis elements from the recent experience of other European countries (such as a sustainability adjustment factor related to contributions and life expectancy; a flexible age of retirement, with special provisions to those with long working careers; and indexing of benefits to the cost of living rather than the minimum wage) (Interview with Pedro Marques, Secretary of State for Social Security, 25 May 2007; da Paz Campos Lima and Naumann 2006; Portuguese evaluation report 2006; European Commission 2006: 7; Euréval/Rambøll 2008: 27). But as with the social inclusion examples cited above, more detailed research would be needed to verify the precise significance of the OMC's influence on these national reforms.

Even where more extensive evidence on domestic policy-making processes is available, disentangling the independent causal influence of the OMC presents formidable problems of interpretation. In some cases, the origins of changes in national policy thinking preceded OMC developments, even if they were also influenced by EU policy channels, as López-Santana for example argues with respect to Spain and the European Social Fund. Nor were the EU and the OMC the only external sources of new ideas about reform of social and employment policies. During the late 1990s, for example, the OECD Jobs Strategy offered a contrasting approach to labour market policy to that of the EES, although this was less influential than the latter in countries like Belgium and the Netherlands (Visser, van Gerven and Beckers, this volume).[16] In other cases, however, such as pension reform in Central and Eastern Europe, the impact of the World Bank and the IMF appears to have exceeded that of the EU, at least prior to formal accession (Orenstein 2008). More fundamentally still, as noted earlier, EU Member States themselves have frequently sought to shape the development of OMC processes by 'uploading' their domestic concepts and policy approaches, as in the cases of Sweden, Denmark, and the UK for the EES, France and Belgium for social inclusion, and Italy for pensions.[17] And even where the adoption of new policy concepts and messages within the OMC clearly preceded national developments, their multiplicity and ambiguity has often left broad scope for selective 'downloading' and 'translation' by domestic actors. For each of these reasons, as I have argued elsewhere, the relationship between OMC processes and Member State policies is better conceived as a two-way interaction than as a one-way causal impact (Zeitlin 2005b: 453–7).

1.2 Procedural shifts in governance and policy making

There is much broader agreement that the EES and the social OMCs have contributed significantly to procedural shifts in governance and policy-making arrangements. Five main forms of influence may be identified here: reinforced horizontal coordination and cross-sectoral integration between interdependent policy fields; improvements in national steering capacity; enhanced vertical coordination between levels of governance; increased involvement of non-state actors; and development of new horizontal and/or diagonal networks for participation of non-state and subnational actors in EU policy making processes.

In many countries, as previous research has shown, the obligation to draft National Action Plans (NAPs) for employment and social inclusion (more recently also National Lisbon Reform Programmes for Growth and Jobs) has strengthened *horizontal integration of interdependent policy fields* through the creation of new formal coordination bodies and inter-ministerial working groups (Zeitlin 2005b: 457–8; Meyer and Umbach 2007; Norris 2007: ch. 3). Similar developments have likewise been observed in new Member States such as Cyprus, Malta, Hungary, the Czech Republic, Poland, Slovakia, Lithuania, Latvia, and (to a lesser extent in employment) Estonia (European Commission 2006: 22–3; Mailand, Jacobsson and West, this volume). In Belgium, as Hamel and Vanhercke's chapter details, the preparation of the NAPs/Inclusion has given rise to new bodies for coordinating and rationalizing policy initiatives across sectors not only at the federal level, but also at the regional level, where first Flanders and then Brussels and Wallonia have created interdepartmental bodies to develop strategic action plans against poverty. Although the French Inter-Ministerial Committee to Combat Social Exclusion (CILE) has not so far played a similarly effective role, the annual production of a Transversal Policy Document (DPT) on Social Inclusion under the recent framework budgetary law (LOLF) has begun to exert a major impact in enhancing horizontal collaboration across policy sectors and administrative units in this field (Hamel and Vanhercke, Preunkert and Zirra, this volume).[18] Whereas NAPs have often been regarded more as reports to the EU than as genuinely operational planning documents, the OMC/Inclusion has been increasingly 'mainstreamed' into domestic policy making in countries such as Ireland, Portugal, Belgium, and France through linkages to National Anti-Poverty Strategies and budgetary planning processes (Norris 2007: ch. 3; Hamel and Vanhercke, this volume; for other examples, see European Commission 2006: 23–4). In a number of the new Member States, notably the Baltic states, the incorporation of the NAPs/Employment into the Lisbon National Reform Programmes since 2005 has reinforced their integration into domestic policy making. Conversely, in most of the EU15 (with the exception of Spain), the replacement of the NAPs/Employment by the Lisbon NRPs has instead reduced the salience and visibility of the EES in national policy debates (Jacobsson and West, Mailand, this volume; Zeitlin 2008; Euréval/Rambøll 2008: 31–6; OPTEM 2007: 42–4).

A second widespread procedural influence of the OMC on national social and employment policy making concerns *improvements in national steering and statistical capacities* (Zeitlin 2005b: 458). One side of this process involves the strengthening of national arrangements for data collection and analysis through the implementation of better and more Europeanized survey instruments, information systems, and statistical indicators. Thus, in Belgium, for example, the National Statistical Institute had to make a major investment in the development of internal capacity for the collection and analysis of data on poverty and social exclusion in order to participate in the initial round of the new EU Survey of Income and Living Conditions (EU-SILC) and apply in its first NAP/Inclusion the common European indicators agreed under the country's 2001 EU presidency. In France, where national statistical capacities in the social field were already better developed, the OMC/Inclusion and the common European indicators have spurred moves towards the harmonization of national indicators of poverty and social exclusion, which varied widely across different policy documents (Hamel and Vanhercke, this volume).[19] Another aspect of the OMC's influence on national steering capacity concerns the creation of new bodies and systems for monitoring and evaluating the implementation of social and employment policies. Among the best-documented cases is the impetus provided by the EES to the upgrading of institutional capabilities for data collection, monitoring, and evaluation of labour market policies in Italy (Ferrera and Sacchi 2005; Preunkert and Zirra, this volume). But joining the EES appears to have exerted a similar positive impact on new Member States such as Poland and the Baltic states, as the chapters by Mailand and Jacobsson and West observe. In social inclusion, too, the OMC has stimulated the development of national monitoring and evaluation capacities in many countries, especially in relation to local and regional tiers of governance (Hamel and Vanhercke, this volume; European Commission 2006: 14–15).

Enhanced vertical coordination more generally constitutes a third major procedural influence of the OMC. Both in employment and in social inclusion, OMC processes have resulted in the establishment of new formal and informal structures for closer coordination between national, regional, and in some cases local governments in countries such as Sweden, Spain, Belgium, France, Germany, Austria, and the UK (Zeitlin 2005b: 458–9; OPTEM 2007:

56; European Commission 2006: 24; Mailand, López-Santana, van Gerven and Beckers, Vanhercke and Hamel, Preunkert and Zirra, this volume). On the employment side, this process has been closely bound up with the reorganization of the Public Employment Services, based on various combinations of decentralization and management by objectives, to which the EES has given a powerful impetus in old and new Member States alike (Weishaupt 2008; Visser, Mailand, and Jacobsson and West, this volume). On the social inclusion side, the Action and Indicators Task Forces in Belgium and the Departmental Commissions and Territorial Charters in France offer striking examples of how the OMC has fostered more active coordination efforts between national and subnational authorities in both federal and unitary states. Not only has the OMC spurred moves towards the creation of Local and Regional Action Plans for social inclusion in a number of countries, as had already occurred in employment, but it increasingly serves as a cognitive and organizational template for reconceiving the governance of vertical relationships between national/federal governments and regional/local authorities in the context of widespread trends towards the decentralization of administrative and policy-making competences in these fields (Hamel and Vanhercke, Preunkert and Zirra, this volume; European Commission 2006; Zeitlin 2005b: 459–60, 467–8).

In terms of participation in and attitudes towards the OMC among local and regional authorities, wide cross-national variations can be observed which are influenced but by no means determined by differences in constitutional structures. Thus, for example, in federal states the Belgian Regions and Spanish Autonomous Communities have embraced the OMC in both employment and social inclusion as a planning and benchmarking framework for their own purposes, whereas the German Länder have regarded it more as a potential threat to their reserved competences. In unitary states, similarly, the Swedish associations of local, municipal, and county authorities seized on the EES as a means to gain a stronger voice within the country's historically centralized labour market policies, while their Danish counterparts appear instead to have considered themselves already well represented within national policy-making processes (Zeitlin 2005b: 466–8, 480–1; Jacobsson 2005; Kalavaris 2007: 48–51; López-Santana, Preunkert and Zirra, this volume).

A fourth major procedural influence of the OMC concerns *increased involvement of non-state actors in domestic social and employment policy making*. Thus, in many countries the EES and the social OMCs have led to the creation or reinforcement of consultative and participatory structures for the involvement of social partners and civil society organizations in policy formation, implementation, monitoring, and evaluation at national and (in some cases) subnational levels (Zeitlin 2005b: 460–5). This influence has been strongest in social inclusion, where 'mobilisation of all the relevant bodies' figures prominently among the EU's common objectives. Jacobsson and Johansson's chapter provides a detailed account of how the OMC/Inclusion in Sweden catalysed the formation of a national Network Against Social

Exclusion, which mobilized social NGOs and voluntary associations to demand an active voice in the preparation and implementation of the NAPs, resulting in the establishment of a new 'user committee on social and welfare issues' as an institutionalized channel for dialogue between civil society organizations and public officials. Similar developments can be observed not only in other old Member States like Belgium, Italy, Ireland, Portugal, Luxembourg, and the UK, but also in new ones such as Hungary, Cyprus, Malta, and Estonia (Hamel and Vanhercke, Preunkert and Zirra, this volume; Norris 2007: ch. 3; Armstrong 2005; European Commission 2006: 22; national evaluation reports 2005).

The picture in employment is more complex. Alacevich's (2004) comprehensive study of the EU15 found that in all but two countries (Italy and the UK) the EES had a reinforcing effect on national processes of social dialogue through the creation of new trilateral institutions or the revalorization of existing ones for the participation of unions and employers' organizations whose cooperation is needed for labour market and social welfare reforms subject to collective bargaining and/or shared governance. In a number of countries, like Spain and Greece, this participation was largely confined to ritualistic consultation or information exercises, and the social partners (especially unions) complained vocally about their lack of substantive influence on the content and evaluation of the NAPs. In others, such as Denmark and the Netherlands, both unions and employers' organizations remained suspicious of the potential threat to their bargaining autonomy and constitutional prerogatives posed by the European employment guidelines. But the trend over time was generally positive, towards deeper levels of involvement of the social partners and increased satisfaction with the participatory arrangements, despite some reversals linked to rightward shifts in the partisan composition of government, as in Austria and Portugal during the early 2000s (Alacevich 2004: chs. 4–7; Casey 2005; de la Porte and Pochet 2005; Zeitlin 2005b: 462–3). In the new Member States of Central and Eastern Europe, the EES has likewise simulated the reinforcement of tripartite bodies for the participation of the social partners. But more than in the old Member States, such arrangements have remained largely formal in most cases, reflecting the organizational weakness of unions and (to a lesser extent) employers' associations, as well as governments' reluctance to share policy-making authority with non-state actors (Jacobsson and West, this volume; Plomien 2008; Galgoczi et al. 2004; Palpant 2006; OPTEM 2007: 82–3).

As in the case of social inclusion, civil society actors such as the European Anti-Poverty Network (EAPN), the European Federation of National Organisations Working with the Homeless (FEANTSA), and associations representing the disabled have pressed for the right to participate in the EES at national as at European level. In a number of Member States such as Finland, Spain, Portugal, Ireland, Greece, Cyprus, Hungary, and Latvia, the NAPs/Employment have been opened up to involvement of social NGOs without great controversy, especially since 2003, when 'strengthening social cohesion' became one of the EES's three overarching goals. But in some countries with long-established corporatist traditions, like Belgium, Denmark, Sweden, and the Netherlands, such demands have met with stronger resistance to encroachment on the social partners' privileged position in employment policy (Alacevich 2004: 77–9, 82–3; Zeitlin 2005b: 465; de la Porte and Pochet 2005: 366–7; Jacobsson 2005: 117–19; OPTEM 2007: 38, 83–4; Kalavaris 2007; Jacobsson and Johansson, this volume). And even where social NGOs did succeed in joining the NAPs/Employment, they have found it difficult to sustain this role within the new Lisbon National Reform Programmes for Growth and Jobs, whose consultative arrangements are often dominated by Finance or Economics ministries with whom they had little previous contact (Zeitlin 2007, 2008; Begg and Marlier 2007: 12–14; EAPN 2007).[20]

A final procedural influence of the OMC is the development of new horizontal and/or diagonal networks for the involvement of non-state and subnational actors in EU policy coordination processes. Thus, European networks such as those belonging to the Platform of European Social NGOs (whose 41 members include EAPN, FEANTSA, AGE, SOLIDAR, the European Disability Forum, and ATD-Fourth World) and RETIS (the European Transnational Network for Social Inclusion, whose members include EUROCITIES and the Council of European Municipalities and Regions) are regularly consulted on the development of the OMC on Social Protection and Social Inclusion and to a lesser extent the EES, about which they regularly produce independent critical evaluation reports and position papers based on detailed information supplied by their national affiliates (available on their respective websites). All of these networks have received long-term financial support from the EU under successive Community Action Programmes against poverty and social exclusion (now subsumed under PROGRESS, the new Programme for Employment and Social Solidarity), and regularly organize European-wide conferences and roundtables in collaboration with the Commission. At the subnational level, both public authorities and civil society organizations have been engaged in a wide range of EU-funded Transnational Exchange Projects aimed at linking up local actors, including the preparation and comparison of territorial Action Plans for employment and social inclusion, as well as mutual learning, awareness raising, and follow-up activities for both processes (Zeitlin 2005b: 463–4, 466–8; de la Porte and Pochet 2005: 361–2, 366–7).[21]

As in the case of substantive policy change, however, assessing the procedural influence of the OMC poses challenging problems of interpretation. First, shifts in national governance and policy-making arrangements are also a response to ongoing transformations in public administration such as decentralization, agencification, and privatization, all of which create widespread perceived needs for increased coordination, both horizontally and vertically (see, for example, Sellers and Lidström 2007). Second, the durability of such shifts depend on the stability of OMC processes themselves, as can be observed from the advent of the Lisbon National Reform Programmes, which at least in the older Member States have disrupted previous improvements in employment policy governance and created new obstacles to the participation of social NGOs. Finally, as we shall see in greater detail below, the involvement of non-state and subnational actors in OMC processes depends not only on domestic institutional configurations (federal vs unitary constitutional structures; corporatist vs pluralist modes of interest intermediation), but also on their own strategies.

2 Mechanisms of influence

In analysing the causal pathways through which the OMC has exerted these substantive and procedural influences on national social and employment policy reforms, five main mechanisms may be distinguished: *external pressure; financial support; socialization and discursive diffusion; mutual learning; and creative appropriation by domestic actors.*[22]

2.1 External pressure

Discussions of the OMC's domestic impact in the European policy debate often focus on the effectiveness of external pressure on national governments, both vertically from the Commission and horizontally from other Member States in EU committees and the Council. Sometimes such pressure is presented as a form of friendly advice or helpful coaching (European Commission 2005), but more often as a form of soft sanctions through public 'naming, shaming, and faming' (Kok 2004). The core idea either way is that national governments will be induced to live up to their commitments and implement necessary but painful reforms in order to maintain their reputations and avoid embarrassment in the eyes of their peers and the wider public. There is evidence from the chapters in this volume, as well as from previous research, that such peer pressure is felt by those exposed to it, especially ministers and members of EU committees engaged in mutual surveillance of each others' national performance in meeting agreed objectives and targets, and that EU recommendations and negative rankings can sometimes contribute to domestic policy changes. Examples include the responses of the Danish and Dutch governments to their failure to reach the early activation targets associated with the preventative approach to fighting unemployment, and those of their French and Belgian counterparts to the recent priority given by the European Council to measures aimed at rapidly and significantly reducing child poverty (Mailand, Hamel and Vanhercke, this volume; for other examples, see Zeitlin 2005b: 477). But the effectiveness of such external pressures is highly dependent on domestic conditions, notably the perceived legitimacy, intellectual basis, and procedural fairness of EU objectives, guidelines, targets, recommendations, and rankings; the level of public support for the EU and sensitivity to European criticism; and the national visibility of OMC processes – all of which are often found lacking (Zeitlin 2005b:

477–8; OPTEM 2007: 75–6). Put another way, the effectiveness of external pressure through the OMC depends primarily on other causal mechanisms, notably socialization, mutual learning, and creative appropriation by domestic actors. Thus, recent official evaluations of the Integrated Guidelines for Growth and Jobs and the EES themselves conclude that 'the recommendations do not really exert pressure on governments but rather reinforce the legitimacy of reform promoters', except insofar as they also provide good critical arguments for non-state actors such as trade unions and NGOs (Euréval/Rambøll 2008: 3–4, 28–31, quotation at 31; OPTEM 2007: 75–6).[23]

2.2 Financial support

A second mechanism of influence, which has been largely neglected in previous discussions of the OMC, is financial support from the EU, especially through the Structural Funds.[24] Over the past decade, the objectives of the European Social Fund (ESF) in particular have become increasingly closely linked to those of the EES and the OMC/Inclusion. Both in old Member States like Italy, Ireland, and Portugal and in new ones like the Baltic states and the Czech Republic, the linkage between the OMC and the Structural Funds has contributed to reshaping national priorities in key policy areas such as activation and inclusion, while also redirecting EU finance from infrastructural to social and labour market projects. Even when domestic actors remain unaware of the OMC connection, Structural Fund projects have often served as a vehicle for diffusing related principles and practices. Thus, as López-Santana's chapter points out, the 'ideational misfit' of the EES was greater in Belgium than in Spain because of the latter's more extensive involvement with the ESF. Structural Fund projects (including pre-accession technical assistance and twinning projects in the new Member States) have helped not only to build administrative capacity for the implementation of social and employment policies, but also to extend the reach of procedural requirements associated with the OMC, such as gender mainstreaming and participation of non-state actors in local partnerships (Preunkert and Zirra, Jacobsson and West, López-Santana, this volume; Norris 2007: ch. 3; Sirovátka and Rákoczyová 2007: 77–9; Kilpatrick 2006; Trubek et al. 2006). As we have already seen, financial support from the Local Employment Development budget line of the EES, the Community Action Programme for Social Inclusion, and PROGRESS has likewise provided a major stimulus to the involvement of non-state and subnational actors in OMC processes at both national and European levels.

The effectiveness of this causal mechanism depends on several factors. One is the tightness of the linkage between OMC processes and European funding, which may vary over time with shifts in the EU's own priorities. Thus, NGOs have expressed concern that the obligation for Member States to earmark 60–75% of Structural and Cohesion Fund expenditure for the revised Lisbon Growth and Jobs priorities may lead to a reduction in support for social inclusion (EAPN 2008; Zeitlin 2008; Heidenreich, this volume).[25] Another is the relative size and importance of the Structural Funds in national budgets, which, as the chapters by Mailand, López-Santana, Jacobsson and West, and Preunkert and Zirra all emphasize, has been greatest in Southern Europe and the new Member States (along with Ireland). Finally, as Norris has shown in the cases of Portugal and Ireland, the impact of this mechanism also depends in no small measure on the creative use by domestic political actors of the discursive resources offered by OMC objectives, guidelines, and targets to push for support of innovative social and employment policies not previously covered by the Structural Funds (Norris 2007: 137–8).

2.3 Socialization and discursive diffusion

A third mechanism of OMC influence is socialization and discursive diffusion. As we have seen in earlier sections, one of the major effects of the OMC on national policy making has been the construction and diffusion of a shared cognitive and discursive frame of reference through the iterative use of EU concepts, categories, and metrics in formulating and reviewing Member States' plans for achieving common objectives. And there is also evidence that participation in OMC processes may lead to the internalization by national actors of common discursive conventions and behavioural norms through a process of mutual socialization and communicative interaction. Thus, as previous research by Jacobsson and Vifell (2007), Thedvall (2006), and others has demonstrated, to operate persuasively within EU committees, Member State representatives cannot simply invoke their national interests but must formulate reasoned arguments referring to the common objectives, guidelines, targets, and indicators of the EES and the social. And as Horváth (2007) has shown, following the 2004 enlargement, representatives of the new Member States on joint bodies like the Social Protection Committee have been consciously socialized by older hands into pre-existing norms of consensus seeking based on open discussion and information exchange. Such socialization and discursive diffusion mechanisms do not preclude sharp disagreements among the participants about the interpretation of shared European values or the most appropriate solutions to common problems[26] (and cannot therefore be fully considered as a form of 'cognitive harmonisation'), but they nonetheless function as a deliberative discipline on interest-based bargaining within OMC processes. And even where actors' outward adoption of European norms and concepts begins as strategic calculation or role playing, detailed case studies of OMC processes (including those in this volume) suggest that this can give way in time to deeper changes in their preferences and identities.[27] Such internalization of European discursive categories and behavioural norms undoubtedly runs deepest among members of OMC committees and other national officials in close touch with EU institutions. But there is also clear evidence, as a growing body of research illustrates, of the diffusion of these categories and norms outwards and downwards within Member

States to local authorities and non-state actors, often building on prior experience with related EU programmes such as Structural Fund and twinning projects (Zeitlin 2005b: 478–9, 482; Hamel and Vanhercke, van Gerven and Beckers, López-Santana, this volume; Norris 2007: ch. 3; Czech evaluation report 2005; Pasquier 2005; Guillén and Álvarez 2004; Vifell 2004).

2.4 Mutual learning

A fourth key mechanism of OMC influence is mutual learning. At the time of the EES five-year review in 2002, it was difficult to find extensive evidence of mutual learning in the national evaluation reports and interviews with participating actors (de la Porte and Pochet 2004: 73–4; Casey and Gold 2005; but cf. the conceptual critique of the 'naïve individualistic concept of learning' deployed by the latter in Nedergaard 2006a: 320). Six years later, the picture is radically different, as mutual learning is now among the most widely attested findings about the OMC's national influence emerging from official evaluation reports, academic surveys, and detailed case studies, including various chapters in this volume. Thus for example, in the Eurévål/Rambøll evaluation of the Integrated Guidelines for Growth and Jobs, 70% of interviewees reported some mutual learning, while in the OPTEM study of the EES, 'almost all respondents in all countries' paid tribute to its contribution to mutual learning, though interviewees from southern Europe and the new Member States were more forthcoming about their experiences in this regard than those from some old Member States such as France, Luxembourg, Germany, and Italy. In the mid-term evaluation of the social OMCs, similarly, 'many Member States' emphasized that 'mutual learning and policy exchange lies at the very heart of the OMC' (Eurévål/Rambøll 2008: 26–8; OPTEM 2007: 70–2; European Commission 2006: 27–31; Bischoff 2008; cf. also Nedergaard 2006b, based on a survey of OMC committee members).

But what kinds of mutual learning have occurred, and via which causal pathways? As previous research has shown, the OMC's strongest impact on cross-national learning has come through a series of indirect or higher-order effects, which may be termed *heuristic*, *capacity-building*, and *reflexive* or *maieutic*, respectively (Zeitlin 2005b: 470–2; Ferrera et al. 2002; Ferrera and Sacchi 2005). *Heuristically*, as we have already seen, both the EES and the social OMCs have contributed to increased awareness of policies, practices, and performance in other Member States; to the identification of common challenges and development of shared problem diagnoses; and to the identification of promising policy approaches, even if these remain subject to continuing controversy and debate. These processes have also stimulated policy learning from other EU Member States outside the formal framework of the OMC itself, involving not only government officials but also NGOs and other non-state actors. Beyond the French and Portuguese pension reforms discussed above, other examples of such autonomous cross-national policy learning include the Swedish government's new-found willingness to engage voluntary associations in social service delivery; Ireland's national pensions review; Estonia's disability policy reforms; and a French NGO study trip to investigate the domestic applicability of an 'opposable right to housing' introduced by new Scottish legislation (Jacobsson and Johansson, Hamel and Vanhercke, this volume; Irish and Estonian evaluation reports 2005).

In terms of *capacity building*, key learning effects associated with the OMC include the development of common European indicators and statistical bases such as EU-SILC; improvements in the quality and comparability of national statistics; and some elaboration of regionally disaggregated indicators and statistical data for both employment and social inclusion. The construction of these common indicators and data bases has resulted not only in the strengthening of national (and in some cases also subnational) statistical capabilities, but also in a European-wide debate, involving NGOs as well as administrators and academic experts, about how best to achieve comparability across Member States while respecting legitimate differences in domestic priorities and institutional practices.[28]

In *maieutic* or *reflexive* terms, the OMC processes in employment and social protection/inclusion have pushed Member States on the one hand to rethink established approaches and practices, as a consequence of their obligation to compare national progress towards common European objectives and targets with that of other countries; and on the other hand to re-evaluate the effectiveness of their own policies in reaching these goals. Hamel and Vanhercke's chapter demonstrates the power of the ensuing 'mirror effect' to trigger significant reforms in domestic policy-making arrangements, as in the case of Belgium, which discovered through the OMC/Inclusion that it was not actually the 'best pupil in the class' in terms of involving civil society actors.

As previous research has also shown, the OMC's effects remain weaker in terms of direct or first-order learning (Zeitlin 2005b: 472–6). There are still few examples of direct policy transfer from one country to another, since national reforms, as we saw in section 1. 1 above, typically draw analogical inspiration rather than detailed blueprints from the experience of other Member States, while selectively borrowing, adapting, and recombining elements of foreign programmes and practices to fit their own local contexts. Thus the same interviewees who praise the benefits of mutual learning are no less insistent that 'other countries' experiences cannot simply be transferred "exactly as they are" without taking the target country's specific situation and level of development into account' (OPTEM 2007: 70; cf. Euréval/Rambøll 2008: 27). But, as discussed earlier, this behaviour is a natural and appropriate response to the reflexive learning through 'contextualized benchmarking' which the OMC is designed to promote, in contrast to the 'one-size-fits-all' reform models pushed by 'expertocratic' bodies like the OECD, the IMF, and the World Bank.[29]

In terms of identifying what works and what doesn't work in specific policy areas such as labour market activation and reducing child poverty, there has been significant progress at EU level, mainly through the Mutual Learning

Programmes associated with the EES and the social OMCs, which have been upgraded significantly over the past five years (EMCO 2006; SPC 2007). But despite the growth of horizontal networking among non-state and subnational actors, there are still few examples of bottom-up learning from innovative local practices through the OMC, largely because of continuing limitations on participation in national social and employment policy making in many Member States (Zeitlin 2005b: 473–5). Yet the flow of creative ideas visible in the reports of European roundtables, networking conferences, transnational exchange projects, and 'shadow peer reviews' conducted by NGO federations provides abundant evidence of the OMC's incompletely tapped potential to stimulate such cross-national learning from below on focused themes such as combating homelessness or mainstreaming social inclusion (FEANTSA 2007; O'Kelly 2006; EAPN-EUROCITIES 2003).

Both EMCO and the SPC have conducted external evaluations and internal debates in recent years on how to improve mutual learning within the OMC. A number of core principles and procedural innovations have emerged from these deliberations, some of which have already been implemented. Thus, peer review/mutual surveillance of national plans and strategy reports within both committees now concentrates on key transversal themes such as flexicurity and active inclusion (selected each year in line with European priorities) in order to foster a more open and focused policy debate. Both groups are also committed to developing a more context- and process-oriented approach to peer review of both good and bad practices; stronger analytical frameworks for understanding the relationship between policies and outcomes; and better linkages between EU and national debates through improved dissemination of results, wider stakeholder participation, and development of transnational 'learning networks' (Bischoff 2008; SPC 2007; EMCO 2006).[30]

2.5 Creative appropriation by domestic actors

The strongest mechanism of OMC influence on national social and employment policies, as the chapters in this volume confirm, operates through creative appropriation by domestic actors (Zeitlin 2005b: 480–1). This 'leverage effect' (Barbier 2005; Ehrel et al. 2005) involves the strategic use of European concepts, objectives, guidelines, targets, indicators, performance comparisons, and recommendations by national and subnational actors as a resource for their own purposes. Here again, the OMC illustrates in extreme form a key finding of recent empirical research on Europeanization more generally: that there is 'no impact of Europe without usage by domestic actors' (Jacquot and Woll 2003, 2004; Palier, Surel et al. 2007).

Thus, Member State governments may use OMC processes as a 'selective amplifier' (Visser 2005) to legitimate and push through contested domestic reforms, as for example with the Hartz package in Germany or Berlusconi's 2003 labour market legislation in Italy (Preunkert and Zirra, this volume). In some cases, governments may even deliberately press for sensitive issues to be placed on the European agenda, in order to 'download' them subsequently into national reform debates, as in the case of Belgium's support for launching the OMC pensions process (Natali 2007: 11–12). But overly crude efforts to instrumentalize EU guidelines to advance controversial domestic agendas can also backfire, as with the Aznar government's invocation of the EES in support of its failed attempt to cut Spanish unemployment benefits by decree in 2002 (López-Santana, this volume).

But such creative appropriation is by no means confined to national governments or their core executives as unitary actors. As previous research has shown, employment and social affairs ministries and specialized agencies such as public employment services and gender equality/equal opportunity bodies have successfully used OMC objectives and commitments to enhance their policy influence and expand their budgets (Zeitlin 2005b: 480; Jacobsson and West, this volume). Non-state and subnational actors such as opposition parties, social partners, civil society organizations, and local/regional authorities can likewise exploit the leverage effect of the OMC to put pressure on governments and advance their own domestic agendas. No less importantly, non-state actors can also exploit the 'democratizing destabilization effect' (Sabel and Zeitlin 2008) of the OMC to hold governments accountable, demand increased participation rights, and criticize official proposals on the basis of richer comparative information about feasible alternatives and their relative performance than would otherwise have been available. Recent examples of both effects include parliamentary questions about the European employment agenda and the NAPs/Inclusion in the Netherlands and Belgium, and the critical invocation of OMC targets and cross-national performance comparisons by NGOs in Belgium, Sweden, and Ireland; by trade unions in Spain, Belgium, and the Netherlands; and by employers in Belgium, Denmark, and the Netherlands (Mailand, Jacobsson and Johansson, van Gerven and Beckers, Hamel and Vanhercke, this volume; Norris 2007: ch. 3; Zeitlin 2005b: 480–1).

Thus, OMC processes have not simply reinforced existing power arrangements and institutional arrangements, but have also empowered weaker actors within and beyond government. Both leverage and democratizing destabilization effects depend on domestic actors' creative appropriation of potential opportunities opened up by OMC processes. The OMC in this sense is not just an 'opportunity structure' (Jacobsson and Johansson, this volume), since the opportunities it generates are shaped by what actors make of them.[31] The extent of such opportunities, like the effectiveness of external pressure from EU institutions and other Member States, depends partly on the nature of domestic public attitudes towards the EU, as well as on the prominence and visibility of OMC processes in national policy making, and on the availability of EU financial and institutional support for independent initiatives by non-state and subnational actors. But the scope and significance of these opportunities also depend on domestic actors' own strategies and priorities. Thus weaker and less constitutionally entrenched actors tend to be more interested in new opportunities offered by the OMC for participation and voice in national policy making, as can be seen from the contrast between the attitudes of NGOs and social partners in most countries or between the Spanish autonomous communities and the German Länder, but not the Belgian regions, which have embraced the OMC despite their extensive constitutional powers. Although parliamentary bodies in some countries, like the Netherlands and Belgium, have begun to make use of the OMC's democratizing destabilization potential, others, like the UK House of Commons European Scrutiny Committee, remain more concerned about imagined threats to domestic sovereignty than about the possibility of holding governments accountable for their relative performance against European targets and indicators (López-Santana, van Gerven and Beckers, Hamel and Vanhercke, Jacobsson and Johansson, Preunkert and Zirra, this volume; Duina and Raunio 2007; UK House of Commons European Scrutiny Committee 2005; Zeitlin 2005b: 468–70, 480–1).

The strategic use of OMC processes by domestic actors for their own purposes may, at first blush, appear to follow a purely instrumental or rationalist logic of consequences (Mailand, this volume). But by embracing OMC concepts, categories, and metrics to advance their own goals, domestic actors at a minimum acknowledge and reinforce the discursive legitimacy of common European objectives and policy approaches. Over time, they may also subtly come to change their own preferences and even identities by linking themselves more closely with European goals, institutions, and partners (Zeitlin 2005b: 481–3). Hence, as Rosa Sanchez-Salgado has rightly observed in relation to the Europeanization of social NGOs, 'if there is no impact of Europe without usage by domestic actors', there are also 'no usages of Europe without an impact' (Sanchez-Salgado 2007a, 2007b).

3 Conclusion: following or altering domestic regime pathways?

As we have seen, the influence of OMC processes on national social and employment reforms depends partly on domestic institutional and political conditions, notably variations in popular/public attitudes towards the EU (integrationist/Eurosceptic); state and constitutional structures (unitary/federal/decentralized); forms of interest intermediation (corporatist/pluralist); and perceived levels of fit/misfit between European objectives, guidelines, and targets on the one hand and domestic policies and performance on the other. But OMC influence, as we have likewise seen, depends no less on its creative appropriation by domestic actors. Leverage and democratizing destabilization effects may empower weaker actors within and beyond government, not just reinforce existing power balances and institutional arrangements. Hence, as with EU legislation more generally, high levels of misfit are neither a necessary nor a sufficient condition for the OMC's domestic influence (Falkner et al. 2005; Mastenbroek and Kaeding 2006).

Nor does the OMC's domestic influence depend on Member States' prior success in 'uploading' national policies to the European level. Thus, as Hamel and Vanhercke's chapter shows, countries may misjudge their own relative performance standing, as with Belgium's discovery that it was not the 'best pupil in the class' in terms of arrangements for NGO involvement in social inclusion policy. Domestic situations may also change over time, giving unanticipated relevance to OMC processes, as with the decentralization of French social inclusion policies. Uploading in any case is never perfect, as can be seen from the fact that France had to accept 'active inclusion' despite being one of the prime movers behind the establishment of the OMC in this field. And domestic actors may be able to exploit even small misfits between European and national policies as a source of leverage and democratizing destabilization effects, as in the case of child poverty in France.

Although some European targets, such as the employment rate, are framed in uniform rather than relative terms, OMC processes nonetheless throw up adjustment challenges to all participating Member States, not only the worst performers or certain regime types (e.g. continental/conservative, southern/familial, central-east European/post-communist). Thus the EES has drawn attention to problems of gender segregation and immigrant integration in the Nordic states, while the OMC's multi-dimensional concept of social inclusion/exclusion, in which no country comes out top on all indicators, represents a frontal challenge to the self-image of the Swedish, Finnish, and German welfare regimes, all of which were convinced that they already had adequate domestic policies in place for fighting poverty (Mailand, Jacobsson and Johansson, Preunkert and Zirra, this volume; Saari and Kangas 2007; Marlier et al. 2007: 79–84; Zeitlin 2005b: 452–3). The OMC has likewise flagged social adequacy of pensions as a key problem for the British and Irish liberal regimes, while also highlighting the issue of low supplementary pensions for part-time women workers in the Netherlands, another EU employment paragon (Natali 2006: 19).

Cognitively, the EES and the OMC in social protection and social inclusion have helped to disseminate new European concepts and to challenge taken-for-granted assumptions in even the best-performing Member States. Politically, they have often empowered weaker actors by creating new opportunities for exploiting misfits between European and domestic policies and holding governments accountable for their relative performance in meeting agreed commitments. Procedurally, they have promoted new forms of coordination (horizontal, vertical, diagonal) among multiple types of actors (public, private, not-for-profit) and levels of governance (European, national, subnational). In policy terms, they have reinforced ongoing tendencies towards hybridization and path-shifting reforms, rather than reproducing pre-existing institutional configurations and regime pathways. Like the EU more generally, these OMC processes have thus contributed to bringing Member States closer together by eroding historic institutional differences between them, while at the same stimulating the continuous emergence of new forms of practical diversity through the creative adaptation of common European principles and policy approaches by domestic actors to suit their distinct circumstances.[32]

Notes

1 Earlier drafts of this paper were presented to conferences in Brussels and Bamberg. I am grateful to Martin Heidenreich and other conference participants, as well as to Sigrid Quack, for helpful comments and suggestions.

2 For a selective bibliography, see the University of Wisconsin-Madison's online Research Forum on the OMC, http://eucenter.wisc.edu/OMC/index.htm.

3 See for example Casey and Gold (2005), who present a highly critical account of the OMC's capacity to promote cross-national policy learning based exclusively on the first round of employment peer reviews conducted in 1999–2001; or Lodge (2007), whose critique of the OMC/Pensions for its lack of common indicators appeared after these had been agreed by the SPC.

4 A partial exception is Idema and Kelemen (2006), which draws on a small-scale study of the Social Inclusion OMC in the Netherlands.

5 For a comprehensive review of the Europeanization literature, see Graziano and Vink (2007).

6 Such biases are visible not only in interviews, but also in survey responses, where public officials and NGO representatives systematically disagree about the extent of the latter's participation in domestic OMC processes: see for example OPTEM (2007) on the EES and O'Kelly (2006) on social inclusion. These disagreements are not purely empirical, but also reflect different normative expectations on the part of the actors.

7 This typology overlaps in objectives, but differs in conceptualization from those proposed in other chapters of this book, notably Heidenreich, López-Santana, and Preunkert and Zirra, as well as by other researchers such as Serrano Pascual and Magnusson (2007).

8 In this regard, I have drawn inspiration from the literature on the effectiveness of international environmental regimes, which has been grappling for over a decade with analogous (though not entirely identical) issues: see Young (1999, 2001), and Underdal and Young (2004), especially the chapters by Underdal and Hovi.

9 This is not the place for an extended discussion of the recent social-scientific literature on explanation through mechanisms, whether in its reductionist or combinatorial variants, about which I remain sceptical on both theoretical and practical grounds. For useful overviews, see Hovi (2004); Mayntz (2004).

10 Important recent reviews of these OMC processes include the 2006 evaluation of the OMCs on social inclusion and pensions (European Commission 2006), a 2007 qualitative study of the EES based on interviews with national employment policy actors in 28 European countries (including Turkey) prepared for the Commission (OPTEM 2007), and a 2007 evaluation of the Integrated Guidelines for Growth and Jobs, based on 70 interviews with policy makers, experts, and stakeholders in 18 countries (Eureval/Rambøll 2008). Member State submissions to the social OMC evaluation have not been published, but are obtainable from DG EMPL; these will be cited hereafter by country name but not listed individually in the references. Submissions from seven European NGO networks are available on the Social Platform website, www.socialplatform.org/Page_Generale.asp?DocID = 12051.

11 For a critical analysis of these developments, see Zeitlin (2007, 2008).

12 By 'effects' I mean characteristic and recurrent intermediate outcomes produced by the various causal mechanisms analysed in section 2, which contribute in turn to the different types of OMC national influence identified in section 1. Thus, for example, as we shall see below, 'creative appropriation' of the OMC by domestic actors generates 'leverage' and 'democratizing destabilization' effects, which then influence substantive policy changes and procedural shifts in governance and policy-making arrangements in EU Member States.

13 On the greater propensity of recently acceded countries to 'accept or seek out ideas from other Member States', see OPTEM (2007: 71). For other studies of these

OMC processes in the new Member States, which often emphasize the imperfect fit between European policy concepts and local realities, see Sirovátka and Rákoczyova (2007); Palpant (2006); de la Rosa (2005); Schüttpelz (2005); Lendvai (2004).

14 For other examples of the EES's influence on national policy agendas, see OPTEM (2007: 35, 62–9); Eurėval/Rambøll (2008: 23, 25, 27, 31–2).

15 For a detailed discussion, see Zeitlin (2005b: 451–3).

16 Since 2000, the OECD Jobs Strategy and the EES have moved closer together, as the former has embraced flexicurity and social inclusion, while the latter has placed greater emphasis on making work pay (Watts 2006; Martin 2004; Weishaupt 2008).

17 On the latter two cases, see Hamel and Vanhercke (this volume) and Natali (2006: 34–5; 2007a); for a fuller discussion of national influences on all three OMC processes, see Zeitlin (2005b: 454–5).

18 This Transversal Policy Document was the subject of a Peer Review on 'Social Inclusion Cross-Cutting Policy Tools' in 2006 (synthesis report available at http://ec.europa.eu/employment_social/spsi/peer_review_en.htm).

19 For other examples of the positive influence of the OMC/Inclusion and the creation of EU-SILC on national data collection and indicator development, see European Commission (2006: 14–15).

20 In the pensions OMC, which is generally agreed to be the least open of the three processes (Pochet and Natali 2005), AGE nonetheless reports that, 'thanks to the open method', their affiliates in some of the new member states 'have been able to engage with governments, sometimes for the first time, on the situation of older people at risk of poverty and social exclusion'; other positive examples of NGO consultation in the preparation of National Strategy Reports on pensions include the Netherlands, Ireland, and Denmark (AGE 2005: 3, 11–12; European Commission 2006: 22).

21 For projects conducted within the Local Employment Development programme of the EES, see EMCO (2004); ECOTEC Research and Consulting (2006); http://ec.europa.eu/employment_social/local_employment/promotion_en.htm; for projects conducted within the Community Action Programme to Combat Social Exclusion (2002–6) and PROGRESS (2007–13), see Tavistock Institute et al. (2005); http://ec.europa.eu/employment_social/spsi/activities_en.htm.

22 For previous discussions and fuller references to the secondary literature, see Zeitlin (2005b: 476–83); Heidenreich and Bischoff (2008); Heidenreich (this volume).

23 Because external pressure from the EU can nonetheless provoke significant political embarrassment to national governments, it may engender perverse effects for the operation of OMC processes, such as bilateral negotiations aimed at obtaining the modification or withdrawal of critical recommendations, as in the cases of early retirement in Denmark and temporary agency work and part-time work for women in Spain. More significantly still, such domestic political concerns may spur Member States to resist indicators that might cast them in a bad light, such as Italy's attempt under Berlusconi to redefine 'quality in work' as any legal job; Poland and Slovakia's objections to relative at-risk-of-poverty rates; and most comical, of all, Sweden's complaint about the use of 'days lost in strikes' as a indicator of social dialogue because of the country's low level of industrial disputes (Mailand, this volume; Sacchi 2007: 86–7; Wóycicka and Grabowski 2007: 107; Slovak evaluation report 2005; Thedvall 2006: 110–12. For other examples, see Zeitlin 2005b: 478).

24 For exceptions, see Kilpatrick (2006: 133); Trubek et al. (2006: 82); Trubek and Trubek (2007: 545); Hartwig (2007).

25 An official analysis of ESF plans for 2007–13 shows, however, that more than one-eighth of the total budget will be spent on projects directly related to the EU's social inclusion objectives (European Commission 2008: 96–8).

26 Thus, for example, the Slovak evaluation report (2005) observes that 'the OMC has helped to create common shared views on the problem of social exclusion and inclusion', as well as on their possible causes, 'but not on their solution'.

27 For a theoretical analysis of the socializing role of international institutions, which distinguishes strategic calculation, role playing, and normative suasion as a continuum of mechanisms which may lead to different levels of internalization of community norms, see Checkel (2005); Zürn and Checkel (2005).

28 For detailed case studies of the conceptual challenges and practical work involved in creating common indicators for poverty, homelessness, and pensions, see Nivière (2005); Brousse (2005). See also the regular reports of the EMCO and SPC indicators groups, available on the DG EMPL website.

29 Both the OECD and the World Bank have moved a long way in recent years towards acknowledging the need for a more contextualized approach to national policy reforms: see, for example, OECD (2005); Rodrik (forthcoming).

30 The main issue which remains controversial is the participation of non-state actors in peer reviews, which is supported by the Commission and the leadership of the OMC committees, but opposed by some Member States.

31 In the second edition of his influential text on social movements, Sidney Tarrow emphasizes that external changes in political opportunities must be perceived by the actors concerned in order to serve as incentives to action, and should not therefore be interpreted as causally determinant structures (Tarrow 1998: 76–7, 221 n. 6).

32 For overviews of hybridization tendencies in European welfare and employment regimes, see Hemerijck (2007); Ferrera and Hemerijck (2003); Zeitlin (2003); and on the new post-Communist member states, Bakken (2008). For detailed comparative studies of hybridization in unemployment benefit and labour market activation policies, see van Gerven and Beckers, this volume; Weishaupt (2008); Serrano Pascual and Magnusson (2007). For a contrary view, see Preunkert and Zirra, this volume.

References

AGE (European Older People's Platform) (2005) *Response to the Questionnaire on the Evaluation of the Open Method of Coordination.* Online. Available HTTP: www.socialplatform.org/Page_Generale.asp?DocID = 12051 (accessed 8 September 2008).

Alacevich, F. (2004) *Promuovere il dialogo sociale. Le conseguenze dell'Europa sulla regolazione del lavoro*, Florence: Firenze University Press.

Armstrong, K.A. (2005) 'How Open is the United Kingdom to the OMC Process on Social Inclusion?', in J. Zeitlin, P. Pochet and L. Magnusson (eds) *The Open Method of Co-ordination in Action: The European Employment and Social Inclusion Strategies*, Brussels: Peter-Lang, pp. 287–310.

Bakken, P.G. (2008) 'National Welfare Systems in Central and Eastern Europe: A New "World" of Welfare?', unpublished MSc thesis, Department of Sociology, University of Wisconsin-Madison.

Barbier, J.-C. (2005) 'The European Employment Strategy: A Channel for Activating Social Protection?', in J. Zeitlin, P. Pochet and L. Magnusson (eds) *The Open Method of Co-ordination in Action: The European Employment and Social Inclusion Strategies*, Brussels: Peter-Lang, pp. 417–46.

Begg, I. and Marlier, E. (2007) 'Social Inclusion 2006: Second Semester Report', independent overview based on National Report of Independent Experts, Brussels: EU Network of Independent Experts on Social Inclusion, 1 May.

Bischoff, G. (2008) 'How to Improve Mutual Learning through OMC: Perspectives from the Trio Presidency', unpublished paper, Berlin: German Ministry of Labour and Social Affairs.

Brousse, C. (2005) 'Définir et compter les sans-abri en Europe: enjeux et controverses', *Genèses*, 58: 48–71.

Büchs, M. and Friedrich, D. (2005) 'Surface Integration. The National Action Plans for Employment and Social Inclusion in Germany', in J. Zeitlin, P. Pochet and L. Magnusson (eds) *The Open Method of Co-ordination in Action: The European Employment and Social Inclusion Strategies*, Brussels: Peter-Lang, pp. 249–86.

Büchs, M. and Hinrichs, K. (2007) 'Germany: Moving towards Europe but Putting National Autonomy First', in J. Kvist and J. Saari (eds) *The Europeanisation of Social Protection*, Bristol: The Policy Press, pp. 21–40.

Casey. B.H. (2005) 'Building Social Partnership? Strengths and Shortcomings of the European Employment Strategy', *Transfer*, 11: 45–63.

– and Gold, M. (2005) 'Peer Review of Labour Market Programmes in the European Union: What Can Countries Really Learn from One Another?', *Journal of European Public Policy*, 12: 23–43.

Checkel, J.T. (2005) 'International Institutions and Socialization in Europe: Introduction and Framework', *International Organization*, 59: 801–26.

Citi, M. and Rhodes, M. (2007) *New Modes of Governance in the EU: Common Objectives versus National Preferences*, EUROGOV Working Papers No. N-07-01. Online. Available HTTP: www.connex-network.org/eurogov/pdf/egp-newgov-N-07-01.pdf (accessed 8 September 2008).

da Paz Campos Lima, M. and Naumann, R. (2006) *Agreement Reached on Framework for Social Security Reform*, EIROnline. Online. Available HTTP: www.eurofound.europa.eu/eiro/2006/08/articles/pt0608019i.htm (accessed 8 September 2008).

de Búrca, G. and Scott, J. (eds) (2006) *Law and New Governance in the EU and the US*, Oxford: Hart.

de la Porte, C. and Pochet, P. (2004) 'The European Employment Strategy: Existing Research and Remaining Questions', *Journal of European Social Policy*, 14: 71–78.

—— and — (2005) 'Participation in the Open Method of Co-ordination: The Cases of Employment and Social Inclusion', in J. Zeitlin, P. Pochet and L. Magnusson (eds) *The Open Method of Co-ordination in Action: The European Employment and Social Inclusion Strategies*, Brussels: Peter-Lang, pp. 353–90.

De la Rosa, S. (2005) 'The Open Method of Coordination in the New Member States – the Perspectives for its Use as a Tool of Soft Law', *European Law Journal*, 11: 618–40.

Duina, F. and Raunio, T. (2007) 'The Open Method of Co-ordination and National Parliaments: Further Marginalisation or New Opportunities?', *Journal of European Public Policy*, 14: 589–606.

EAPN (2007) 'Making Lisbon Deliver for People Experiencing Poverty: EAPN Response to 2006 Implementation Reports on the National Reform Programs', Brussels, January.

—— (2008) 'Contribution to the European Commission Consultation on the Future of European Union Cohesion Policy', Brussels, January.

EAPN-EUROCITIES (2003) 'The EU Strategy for Social Inclusion: Making It Work at the Local Level', report of a conference held in Athens, February–March.

ECOTEC Research and Consulting (2006) 'Idele – Identification, Dissemination and Exchange of Good Practice in the Field of Local Employment Development and Promoting Better Governance: Executive Summary of Thematic Learning', report submitted to DG EMPL, December.

Ehrel, C., Mandin, L. and Palier, B. (2005) 'The Leverage Effect. The Open Method of Coordination in France', in J. Zeitlin, P. Pochet and L. Magnusson (eds) *The Open Method of Coordination in Action: The European Employment and Social Inclusion Strategies*, Brussels: Peter-Lang, pp. 217–48.

EMCO (2004) 'Local Employment Development: 2001–4', EMCO/14/220404/EN, Brussels, 22 April.

—— 'Reinforcing the Mutual Learning Programme', EMCO/23/131106/EN, Brussels, November 2006.

Euréval/Rambøll Management (2008) *Evaluation of the Integrated Guideline Package (IGP) for Growth and Jobs*, final report to the European Commission, ECFIN/R/3/2007/004-IGP. Online. Available HTTP: http://ec.europa.eu/economy_finance/multiannual_eval_prg/multiannual_eval12403_en.htm (accessed 8 September 2008).

European Commission (2005) 'Working Together for Growth and Jobs: A New Start for the Barroso in agreement with Vice-President Verheugen', COM (2005) 24, Brussels, February.

—— (2006) 'Evaluation of the Open Method of Coordination for Social Protection and Social Inclusion', SEC (2006) 345, Brussels, March.

—— (2008) 'Accompanying Document to the Joint Report on Social Protection and Social Inclusion', SEC (2008) 91, Brussels, January.

Fagan, C., Grimshaw, D. and Rubery, J. (2006) 'The Subordination of the Gender Equality Objective: The National Reform Programmes and "Making Work Pay" Policies', *Industrial Relations Journal*, 37: 571–92.

Fagan, C., Rubery, J., Grimshaw, D., Smith, M., Hebson, G. and Figueiredo, H. (2005) 'Gender Mainstreaming in the Enlarged European Union: Recent Developments in the European Employment Strategy and the Social Inclusion Process', *Industrial Relations Journal*, 36: 568–91.

Falkner, G., Treib, O., Hartlapp, M. and Leiber, S. (2005) *Complying with Europe: EU Harmonisation and Soft Law in the Member States*, Cambridge: Cambridge University Press.

FEANTSA (2007) 'Untapped Potential: Using the Full Potential of the OMC to Address Poverty in Europe', Brussels, October.

Ferrera, M. and Hemerijck, A. (2003), 'Recalibrating Europe's Welfare Regimes', in J. Zeitlin and D.M. Trubek (eds) *Governing Work and Welfare in a New Economy: European and American Experiments*, Oxford: Oxford University Press, pp. 88–128.

Ferrera, M., Matsaganis, M. and Sacchi, S. (2002) 'Open Co-ordination against Poverty: The New EU "Social Inclusion" Process', *Journal of European Social Policy*, 12: 223–39.

Ferrera, M. and Sacchi, S. (2005), 'The Open Method of Co-ordination and National Institutional Capabilities. The Italian Experience', in J. Zeitlin, P. Pochet and L. Magnusson (eds) *The Open Method of Co-ordination in Action: The European Employment and Social Inclusion Strategies*, Brussels: Peter-Lang, pp. 137–72.

Galgoczi, B., Lafoucrière, C. and Magnusson, L. (eds) (2004) *The Enlargement of Social Europe: The Role of the Social Partners in the European Employment Strategy*, Brussels: ETUI/SALTSA/CREER.

George, A.L. and Bennett, A. (2005) *Case Studies and Theory Development in the Social Sciences*, Cambridge, MA: MIT Press.

Graziano, P. and Vink, M.P. (eds) (2007) *Europeanization: New Research Agendas*, Houndmills: Palgrave Macmillan.

Guillén, A.M. (2007) 'Spain: Starting from Periphery, Becoming Centre', in J. Kvist and J. Saari (eds) *The Europeanisation of Social Protection*, Bristol: The Policy Press, pp. 117–36.

—— and Álvarez, S. (2004) 'The EU's Impact on the Spanish Welfare State: The Role of Cognitive Europeanization', *Journal of European Social Policy*, 14: 285–300.

Hartwig, I. (2007) 'European Employment Strategy and Structural Funds: Spill-overs towards Communitarisation?', in I. Linsenmann, C.O. Meyer and W.T. Wessels (eds) *Economic Government of the EU: A Balance Sheet of New Modes of Policy Coordination*, Houndmills: Palgrave Macmillan. pp. 119–40.

Hatzopolous, V. (2007) 'Why the Open Method of Coordination is Bad for You: A Letter to the EU', *European Law Journal*, 13: 309–42.

Hedström, P. and Swedberg, R. (eds) (1998) *Social Mechanisms: An Analytical Approach to Social Theory*, Cambridge: Cambridge University Press.

Heidenreich, M. and Bischoff, G. (2008) 'The Open Method of Coordination. A Way to the Europeanization of Social and Employment Policies?', *Journal of Common Market Studies*, 46: 497–532.

Hemerijck, A. (2007) 'From Retrenchment to Recalibration: How Welfare States', unpublished paper, The Hague: Netherlands Scientific Council for Government Policy.

Horváth, A. (2007) 'Committee Governance after the Enlargement of the EU: The Institutionalisation of Cooperation within the Social Protection Committee', *European Political Economy Review*, 6: 53–73.

Hovi, J. (2004) 'Causal Mechanisms and the Study of International Environmental Regimes', in A. Underdal and O. Young (eds) *Regime Consequences: Methodological Challenges and Research Strategies*, Dordrecht: Kluwer, pp. 71–86.

Idema, T. and Kelemen, R.D. (2006) 'New Modes of Governance, the Open Method of Co-ordination and Other Fashionable Red Herring', *Perspectives on European Politics and Society*, 7: 108–23.

Jacobsson, K. (2005) 'Trying to Reform the "Best Pupils in the Class"? The Open Method of Co-ordination in Sweden and Denmark', in J. Zeitlin, P. Pochet and L. Magnusson (eds) *The Open Method of Co-ordination in Action: The European Employment and Social Inclusion Strategies*, Brussels: Peter-Lang, pp. 107–36.

—— and Vifell, Å. (2007) 'Deliberative Transnationalism? Analysing the Role of Committee Interaction in Soft Co-ordination', in I. Linsenmann, C.O. Meyer and W.T. Wessels (eds) *Economic Government of the EU: A Balance Sheet of New Modes of Policy Coordination*, Houndmills: Palgrave Macmillan, pp. 163–86.

Jacquot, S. and Woll, C. (2003) *Usage of European Integration – Europeanisation from a Sociological Perspective*, European Integration online Papers 7. Online. Available HTTP: http://eiop.or.at/eiop/texte/2003–12a.htm (accessed 8 September 2008).

—— *Les usages de l'Europe. Acteurs et transformations européennes*, Paris: L'Harmattan.

Kalavaris, A.H. (2007) 'The Open Method of Coordination and Extended NGO Participation – Why Hasn't It Materialised? The Case of the European Employment Strategy and Danish NGOs', unpublished Masters' thesis, University of Aalborg.

Kerber, W. and Eckhardt, M. (2007) 'Policy Learning in Europe: The Open Method of Coordination and Laboratory Federalism', *Journal of European Public Policy*, 14: 227–47.

Kilpatrick, C. (2006) 'New EU Employment Governance and Constitutionalism', in G. de Búrca and J. Scott (eds) *Law and New Governance in the EU and the US*, Oxford: Hart, pp. 121–52.

Kok, W. (2004) *Facing the Challenge: The Lisbon Strategy for Growth and Employment. Report from the High Level Group Chaired by Wim Kok*, Brussels: European Commission, November.

Kröger, S. (2007) 'The End of Democracy as We Know It? The Legitimacy Deficits of Bureaucratic Social Policy Governance', *Journal of European Integration*, 29: 565–82.

Kvist, J. and Saari, J. (eds) *The Europeanisation of Social Protection*, Bristol: The Policy Press.

Lendvai, N. (2004) 'The Indigenisation of Social Policy in Post-Communist Europe and Its Implications for EU Social Policy after Enlargement', unpublished paper presented to the ESPAnet conference, Oxford, September.

Linsenmann, I., Meyer, C.O. and Wessels, W.T. (eds) (2007) *Economic Government of the EU: A Balance Sheet of New Modes of Policy Coordination*, Houndmills: Palgrave Macmillan.

Lodge, M. (2007) 'Comparing Non-Hierarchical Governance in Action: The Open Method of Co-ordination in Pensions and Information Society', *Journal of Common Market Studies*, 45: 343–65.

Marlier, E., Atkinson, A.B., Cantillon, B. and Nolan, B. (2007) *The EU and Social Inclusion: Facing the Challenges*, Bristol: The Policy Press.

Martin, J.P. (2004) 'Reflections on the OECD Jobs Strategy and the European Employment Strategy', presentation to EMCO, February.

Mastenbroek, E. and Kaeding, M. (2006) 'Europeanisation Beyond the Goodness of Fit: Domestic Politics in the Forefront', *Comparative European Politics*, 4: 331–54.

Mayntz, R. (2004) 'Mechanisms in the Analysis of Social Macro-Phenomena', *Philosophy of the Social Sciences*, 34: 237–59.

McAdam, D., Tarrow, S. and Tilly, C. (2001) *Dynamics of Contention*, Cambridge: Cambridge University Press.

Meyer, C.O. and Umbach, G. (2007) 'Europeanisation of National Economic Governance through Policy Co-ordination? Gains and Pains of a New Policy Instrument', in I. Linsenmann, C.O. Meyer and W.T. Wessels (eds) *Economic Government of the EU: A Balance Sheet of New Modes of Policy Coordination*, Houndmills: Palgrave Macmillan, pp. 91–118.

Moravcsik, A. (2005) 'The European Constitutional Compromise and the Neofunctionalist Legacy', *Journal of European Public Policy*, 12: 349–86.

Natali, D. (2006) *Le pensioni nell'Europa a 25: Il coordinamento delle strategie di riforma*, URGE Working Paper 2/2006. Online. Available HTTP: www.urge.it./files/papers/2_wpurge2_2006.pdf (accessed 8 September 2008).

—— (2007a) *Pensions OMC's Influence on National Reforms*, NEWGOV Deliverable 1/D47. Online. Available HTTP: http://eucenter.wisc.edu/OMC/New%20OMC%20links/natali-d-08f.pdf (accessed 8 September 2008).

—— (2007) 'Pensions OMC: Why Did It Emerge and How Does It Evolve?', unpublished paper presented to the 10th biennial conference of the European Union Studies Association, Montreal, May.

Nedergaard, P. (2006a) 'Policy Learning in the European Union: The Case of the European Employment Strategy', *Policy Studies*, 27: 311–23.

—— (2006b) 'Which Countries Learn from Which? A Comparative Analysis of the Direction of Mutual Learning Processes within the Open Method of Coordination Committees of the European Union and among the Nordic Countries', *Cooperation and Conflict*, 41: 422–42.

Nivière, D. (2005) 'Négocier une statistique européenne: le cas de la pauvreté', *Genèses*, 58: 28–47.

Norris, J. (2007) 'Searching for Synergy: Governance, Welfare, and Law in Two EU Member States', unpublished PhD thesis, Department of Sociology, University of Wisconsin-Madison.

O'Connor, J.S. 'The OMC and the European Employment Strategy: Broadening the Possibilities for Gender Equality?', unpublished paper presented to the ESPAnet conference, Vienna, September 2007.

OECD (2005) Modernizing Government: The Way Forward, Paris: OECD.

O'Kelly, K.P. (2006) *The Evaluation of Mainstreaming Social Inclusion in Europe*, Dublin: Combat Poverty Agency.

OPTEM (2007) 'Qualitative Study on the European Employment Strategy: Analysis of the Attitudes of the Main Actors in Employment Policy in 28 European Countries', unpublished report prepared for DG EMPL, European Commission, July.

Orenstein, M. (2008) 'Out-liberalizing the EU: Pension Privatization in Central and Eastern Europe', *Journal of European Public Policy*, 15: 899–917.

Palier, B. (2006) 'The Europeanisation of Welfare Reforms', unpublished paper presented to the Inequality Institute, Kennedy School of Government, Harvard University, June.

——, Surel, Y. et al. (2007) *L'Europe en action. L'europèanisation dans une perspective compare*, Paris: L'Harmattan.

Palpant, C. (2006) *European Employment Strategy: An Instrument of Convergence for the New Member States?*, Notre Europe Policy Paper 18. Online. Available HTTP: www.notre-europe.eu/uploads/tx_publication/Policypaper18-en.pdf (accessed 8 September 2008).

Pasquier, R. (2005) '"Cognitive Europeanization" and the Territorial Effects of Multilevel Policy Transfer: Local Development in French and Spanish Regions', *Regional and Federal Studies*, 15: 295–310.

Plomien, A. (2008) 'The European Employment Strategy and Polish Employment Policies: A Gender Equality Perspective', unpublished paper, London School of Economics and Political Science.

Pochet, P. and Natali, D. (2005) 'Reseaux européens relatifs aux pensions: la participation d'intérêts organisées au processus décisionnel de l'UE', *Revue belge de sécurité social*, 2: 307–38.

Radaelli, C. (2003) 'The Open Method of Coordination: A New Governance Architecture for the European Union?', Swedish Institute for European Policy Studies, Stockholm, Sieps Report no. 1, March.

Richardt, N. (2004) 'European Employment Strategy, Childcare, Welfare State Redesign: Germany and the United Kingdom Compared', unpublished paper presented to the Conference of Europeanists, Chicago, March.

Rodrik, D. (forthcoming) 'Goodbye Washington Consensus, Hello Washington Confusion', *Journal of Economic Literature.*

Rubery, J., Figueiredo, H., Smith, M., Grimshaw, M. and Fagan, C. (2004) 'The Ups and Downs of European Gender Equality Policy', *Industrial Relations Journal*, 35: 603–28.

Saari, J. and Kangas, O. (2007) 'Finland: Towards More Proactive Policies', in J. Kvist and J. Saari (eds) *The Europeanisation of Social Protection*, Bristol: The Policy Press, pp. 153–74.

Sabel, C.F. (2004) 'Beyond Principle-Agent Governance: Experimentalist Organizations, Learning and Accountability', in E. Engelen and M.S. Dhian Ho (eds) *De*

Staat de Democratie. Democratie Voorbij de Staat, Amsterdam: Amsterdam University Press, pp. 173–95.

—— (2005) 'A Real-Time Revolution in Routines', in C. Heckscher and P. Adler (eds) *The Firm as a Collaborative Community*, Oxford: Oxford University Press, pp. 106–56.

—— and Zeitlin, J. (2008) 'Learning from Difference: The New Architecture of Experimentalist Governance in the EU', *European Law Journal*, 14: 271–327.

Sacchi, S. (2007) 'Italy: Between Indifference, Exploitation, and the Construction of a National Interest', in J. Kvist and J. Saari (eds) *The Europeanisation of Social Protection*, Bristol: The Policy Press, pp. 77–98.

Sanchez-Salgado, R. (2007a) *Comment l'Europe construit la société civile*, Paris: Dalloz.

—— (2007) 'L'européanisation des associations de lutte contre l'exclusion', unpublished paper presented to the conference on 'Economie sociale et solidaire, territoire et politique: regards croisés', Sciences Po Bordeaux, November.

Schludi, M. (2003) 'Chances and Limitations of "Benchmarking" in the Reform of Welfare State Structures – The Case of Pension Policy", unpublished paper presented at the Amsterdam Institute for Advanced Labour Studies, May.

Schüttpelz, A. (2005) 'The Europeanisation of Employment Policy in the Czech Republic', unpublished paper presented to the ESPAnet conference, Fribourg, September.

Sellers, J. and Lidström, A. (2007) 'Decentralization, Local Government, and the Welfare State', *Governance*, 20: 609–32.

Serrano Pascual, A. and Magnusson, L. (2007) *Reshaping Welfare States and Activation Regimes in Europe*, Brussels: Peter Lang.

Sirovátka, T. and Rákoczyová, M. (2007) 'The Strategy of Social Inclusion in the Czech Republic', unpublished paper presented to the ESPAnet conference, Vienna, September.

SPC (2007) 'Proposals Generated from the Summary of Member States' Replies to the Follow-Up Questions on How to Enhance Mutual Learning with the OMC Social Protection and Social Inclusion', Brussels, June.

Stinchcombe, A.L. (1991) 'The Conditions of Fruitfulness of Theorizing about Mechanisms in the Social Sciences', *Philosophy of the Social Sciences*, 21: 367–88.

Tarrow, S. (1998) *Power in Movement: Social Movements and Contentious Politics*, 2nd edn, Ithaca, NY: Cornell University Press.

Tavistock Institute et al. (2005) 'The Analysis of Impacts of Benchmarking and the eEurope Actions in the Open Method of Co-ordination. How the Europe OMC Worked: Implications for the Co-ordination of Policy under i2010', final report prepared for DG Information Society by the Tavistock Institute, London, Net Effect Ltd, Helsinki, and Istituto per la Ricerca Sociale, Milan.

—— (2006) 'Evaluation of the EU Programme to Promote Member-State Co-operation to Combat Social Exclusion and Poverty', report to DG EMPL, December.

Thedvall, R. (2006) *Eurocrats at Work: Negotiating Transparency in Postnational Employment Policy*, Stockholm Studies in Social Anthropology 58, Stockholm: Almqvist & Wiksell International.

Tilly, C. (2001) 'Mechanisms in Political Processes', *Annual Review of Political Science*, 4: 21–41.

Trubek, D.M., Cottrell, P. and Nance, M. (2006) '"Soft Law", "Hard Law", and EU Integration', in G. de Búrca and J. Scott (eds) *Law and New Governance in the EU and the US*, Oxford: Hart, pp. 65–94.

Trubek, D.M. and Trubek, L. (2007) 'New Governance and Legal Regulation: Complementarity, Rivalry, and Transformation', *Columbia Journal of European Law*, 13: 539–64.

UK House of Commons European Scrutiny Committee (2005) 'Health Care and Long-Term Care', *Eleventh Report of Session 2004–05: Documents Considered by the Committee on 15 March*, HC 38-xi.

Underdal, A. and Young, O. (eds) (2004) *Regime Consequences: Methodological Challenges and Research Strategies*, Dordrecht: Kluwer.

Vifell, Å. (2004) 'Speaking with Forked Tongue: Swedish Employment Policy and European Guidelines: A Case of Europeanization through Soft-Co-ordination', unpublished paper presented to the 14th International Conference of Europeanists, Chicago, March.

Visser, J. (2005) 'The OMC as Selective Amplifier for National Strategies of Reform. What the Netherlands Want to Learn from Europe', in in J. Zeitlin and P. Pochet, with L. Magnusson (eds) *The Open Method of Co-ordination in Action: The European Employment and Social Inclusion Strategies*, Brussels: Peter-Lang, pp. 173-216.

Watts, A. (2006) *Assessing the Reassessment of the OECD Jobs Strategy: Eppur Si Muove?*, European Economic and Employment Policy Brief no. 2, Brussels: European Trade Union Institute.

Weishaupt, J.T. (2008) 'The Emergence of a New Labor Market Policy Paradigm? Analyzing Continuity and Change in an Integrating Europe', unpublished PhD thesis, Department of Political Science, University of Wisconsin-Madison.

Wóycicka, I. and Grabowski, M. (2007) 'Poland: Redefining Social Policies', in J. Kvist and J. Saari (eds) *The Europeanisation of Social Protection*, Bristol: The Policy Press, pp. 99–116.

Young, O. (ed.) (1999) *The Effectiveness of International Environmental Regimes: Causal Connections and Behavioral Mechanisms*, Cambridge, MA: MIT Press.

—— (2001) 'Inferences and Indices: Evaluating the Effectiveness of International Environmental Regimes', *Global Environmental Politics*, 1: 99–121.

Zeitlin, J. (2003) 'Introduction: Governing Work and Welfare in a New Economy: European and American Experiments', in J. Zeitlin and D.M. Trubek (eds) *Governing Work and Welfare in a New Economy: European and American Experiments*, Oxford: Oxford University Press, pp. 1–30.

—— (2005a) 'Introduction: The Open Method of Co-ordination in Question', in J. Zeitlin and P. Pochet, with L. Magnusson (eds) *The Open Method of Co-ordination in Action: The European Employment and Social Inclusion Strategies*, Brussels: Peter-Lang, pp. 19–33.

—— (2005b) 'Conclusion: The Open Method of Co-ordination in Action: Theoretical Promise, Empirical Realities, Reform Strategy', in in J. Zeitlin and P. Pochet, with L. Magnusson (eds) *The Open Method of Co-ordination in Action: The European Employment and Social Inclusion Strategies*, Brussels: Peter-Lang, pp. 447–503.

—— (2005c) 'Social Europe and Experimental Governance: Towards a New Constitutional Compromise?', in G. de Búrca (ed.) *EU Law and the Welfare State: In Search of Solidarity*, Oxford: Oxford University Press, pp. 213–41.

—— (2007) 'A Decade of Innovation in EU Governance: The European Employment Strategy, the Open Method of Coordination, and the Lisbon Strategy', in Portuguese Presidency of the EU (ed.) *Perspectives on Employment and Social Policy Coordination in the European Union*, Lisbon: Ministry of Labour and Social Solidarity, pp. 129–44.

—— (2008) 'The Open Method of Co-ordination and the Governance of the Lisbon Strategy', *Journal of Common Market Studies*, 46: 436–46.

Zeitlin, J. and Trubek, D.M. (eds) (2003) *Governing Work and Welfare in a New Economy: European and American Experiments*, Oxford: Oxford University Press.

Zolnhöfer, R. and Ostheim, T. (2005) 'Paving the Way for Employment? The Impact of the Luxembourg Process on German Labour Market Policies', *Journal of European Integration*, 27: 147–67.

Zürn, M. and Checkel, J.T. (2005) 'Getting Socialized to Build Bridges: Constructivism and Rationalism, Europe and the Nation-State', *International Organization*, 59: 1045–79.

Index